How to Become a Creative Church Leader

A MODEM Handbook

Edited by

John Nelson

CANTERBURY
PRESS
Norwich

© MODEM 2008

First published in 2008 by the Canterbury Press Norwich
(a publishing imprint of Hymns Ancient & Modern Limited,
a registered charity)
13–17 Long Lane, London EC1A 9PN

www.scm-canterburypress.co.uk

British Library Cataloguing in Publication data

A catalogue record for this book is available
from the British Library

ISBN 978-1-85311-813-5

Typeset by Regent Typesetting, London
Printed and bound in Great Britain by
William Clowes Ltd, Beccles, Suffolk

Contents

Part 4 Organization

Part 5 Vision and the Future

Part 6 Transforming people's lives

Part 7 Appendices

Introduction

JOHN NELSON

This is MODEM's fourth book. It is the successor to *Creative Church Leadership* (2004), and is published in response to many MODEM members' requests for a sequel. Somewhat to the (welcome) surprise of the publisher, the demand for *Creative Church Leadership* has exceeded expectations, selling especially well in the United States.

Readers of *Creative Church Leadership* were excited by the personal visions of what creative church leadership meant to each of its contributors. When, as Editor, I invited contributors to give their own vision the only term of reference I gave was a free rein to interpret what creative church leadership meant to them personally. Each did just this and succeeded in inspiring readers to want to be creative themselves in their own church leadership.

But these readers didn't know how to be or become one. The book didn't tell them. It did succeed in implanting the wish in its readers to want to be a creative church leader but didn't explain how to achieve this. They pleaded, in effect, for a training manual, a How to Book: – How to Be – How to Become book. They wanted a training manual and they wanted it to be authentic and authoritative, that is, written by contributors who were, or had been, recognized (preferably those who still were) successful practitioners of creative church leadership (or that aspect of it which they were invited to address).

I decided to take advantage of this invitation by the publisher to MODEM to produce a successor to *Creative Church Leadership*, to introduce two new dimensions into it – an ecumenical dimension and a local church dimension. In retrospect, *Creative Church Leadership* and its two predecessors – *Management and Ministry* (1996) and *Leading, Managing, Ministering* (1999) – had been too heavily Anglican and not specifically focused on the church at grass-roots level.

I determined to aim to get an ecumenical team of highly recommended contributors and to focus on the local church, whatever its denominational allegiance. (In the event, this approach has unearthed the (to me) unforeseen advantage of revealing different denominational approaches to many aspects of creative church leadership at local level through, for example, their different approaches to specific aspects – not only between clergy and laity but also between different denominations.

One preliminary key issue was whether or not to limit the number of topics to be addressed. One alternative was to limit them to selected priorities. The problem with this alternative was that one person's priority wasn't necessarily that of another. The other alternative – the one I chose – was to include a reasonably comprehensive list in the hope that every reader would find at least some relevant and as priorities to them.

To help me choose this list of topics to be addressed and then to recommend whom I should invite to address them, I invited Dr Peter Brierley, former Executive Director of Christian Research. Peter happily accepted my invitation and became my editorial advisor for these two vital tasks. Together, we brainstormed and produced a list of potential contributors either for a specific topic or more generally. (I was happy to agree to the same topic being addressed when this would result in clerical/lay or different denominational representatives.)

Not all those invited were able to accept my invitation. But from those who did, I have, I believe, gathered a valuable collection of very readable and very practical chapters from a genuinely ecumenical team of Christian contributors although not all orthodox. (I had to wait quite a while for some promised contributions, and be most patient – and persistent. I consoled myself with the belief that recommended quality was worth waiting for, and thankfully that was the outcome – they were all worth waiting for.)

Every one of them is able to write from personal successful experience, including two professors, whom many might judge to inhabit academic cloisters far removed from parish church life, but not these two – one, Leslie Francis, is an ordained minister who has been in charge of a small rural parish and the other, Jennifer Tann, is a church warden in her own parish church and, through her consultancy, has a first-hand working knowledge of parish church life. May I here record my grateful thanks to them all and also to those whom I approached to recommend them; as well as for the trust the MODEM national Leadership Committee showed in inviting me to act as Editor-designate for this book. Finally, my thanks to Christine Smith, Mary Matthews and their colleagues at Canterbury Press for their unfailing support and encouragement in bringing to fruition the earlier three and now this fourth book for MODEM as the Voice of Leadership, Management and Ministry.

In the process of reading through the contributions as I received them, I came to realize that this successor to *Creative Church Leadership* would be incomplete if it were to comprise only practical advice and help on the means of achieving being/becoming creative church leaders in the local church. To provide a complete and comprehensive guide, it had to provide a relevant and realistic awareness of what the church was for and how creative church leadership could and should have, as its operational focus, the aim not only of providing a vision (of the Kingdom of God) but also of changing people's lives, that is, a transformational role. Creative church leadership begs the question: For what purpose? Without an expression of what it is for, explaining how to be (and become) a creative church leader lacks any sense of meaning, aim or direction.

What, then, is the purpose of the church? Is it to achieve a worshipping and witnessing community expressing and sharing its belief in God? Or is it, rather, to change people's lives, a transformational role – a step beyond belief into experiencing God's presence as a reality? If it is, then the church's true purpose is to enable people to experience God's presence for themselves.

My final contributors, Alan Fraser Bell and Heather (his daughter) address this ultimate question and explain how we can do this. They are lay members of the Church of England, devout and committed Christians. The leadership and sayings of Jesus are discussed in their thought-provoking chapter. Alan and Heather have experienced God's presence and achieved a world-wide reputation for helping countless others to experience God's presence for themselves.

Maybe this is the only way to encourage churches to at least consider and envisage such a transformational role based on the belief that God acts frequently – daily, hourly, within the range of ordinary life. It is a belief which was natural to our forbears in a less materialistic age but which has since been lost. Today the religious phenomenon is too often seen as exceptional and the likelihood of an encounter with God to be remote.

It is possible to progress beyond belief in God, to actually experience God's presence in today's world as a reality. Might this be a new way forward for the church to find its true purpose? It seemed to me a question eminently worth pursuing in a book about creative church leadership.

Part 1

A Denominational Overview

1. How to be a creative church leader in your local Presbyterian church

D. BEN REES

Introduction

Every individual who is called to be a leader in the local church has a tremendous responsibility on their shoulders. They must function as an ambassador of Christ who, after all, is the central character of the scriptures, the example for all who follow as his disciples. Jesus is the inspiration for all: for the Pentecostal and Charismatic tradition, for the Protestant tradition, for the Orthodox tradition, and the Roman Catholic tradition. Each one of these traditions calls for different expectations of their leaders.

I belong to the Protestant tradition but within that tradition there are even more divisions, in particular between Anglicans and the Free Churches. In Britain, the Free Churches includes the Baptist, United Reformed, Presbyterian (particularly in Ireland, Scotland and also in Wales), the Independent and Wesleyan Methodist communions. Some historians have used terms such as 'Dissenters', 'Puritans', 'Nonconformists' to describe the Free Church in the past. It can be claimed that there has always been a distinctive emphasis on the sovereignty of God and, for example, on the authority of scriptures, the importance of expounding the gospel message through preaching, the preference for extemporary prayers over liturgical prayers and an involvement in the community within the particular distinctive tradition concerned. Worship in the Free Churches has always had the Bible as a central focus, with an opportunity for involvement by the congregation in hymn singing, and also opportunities are provided for gifted men and women to become lay leaders of the church as elders and deacons.

The minister's role

I am going to concentrate mainly on the role of a minister of religion within the Presbyterian Church of Wales. After receiving a theological

3

training, the ministerial student is ordained by the Association, of which there are three within the Presbyterian Church of Wales for this specific purpose. He or she is to become a minister serving a pastorate or to serve in other arenas such as becoming a missionary or a chaplain. This 'call' is primarily regarded as a call from God and thus the Ministry cannot be regarded as an appointment in the secular sense of the word and hence there are no 'conditions of employment' involved, as in major professions.

When a minister of religion is inducted into a pastorate, which can include one or two or perhaps five or six or even more churches, they have to promise to fulfil five demands as a leader:

1 To give their utmost in the task of preaching the Gospel of Jesus Christ in all its riches and purity to the people of their pastorate.
2 To minister regularly the two sacraments of Baptism and the Lord's Supper, with reverence and dignity.
3 To provide a comprehensive religious education programme and to make every provision within the available resources to sustain and encourage all members under that care to understand the Christian faith and its implications for them as members of the local church.
4 To visit the bereaved that belong to their pastorate as well as those who do not attend the Sunday service or services regularly.
5 To bear witness, in a creative way, to the gospel and its message, in word and deed, to those who are outside the fold of the chapel but live within the local community or the immediate district, who might be adherents of other chapels.

This is the official statement of the Presbyterian Church of Wales with all its expectations. In other words, the minister is expected to lead the spiritual life of the church, to preside at the worshipping services and to offer pastoral care to those both within and outside the pastorate; and to inspire the missionary outreach of the church to people of all ages. But, of course a minister has to work within a team. Usually, he/she is the only paid official of the chapel.

But within the Free Churches there are other leaders, men and women who have been elected by their congregation to assist the minister, and indeed when none is available to fulfil the obligations of a minister within the local Church. These individuals are called from within the family of Presbyterian elders, often referred to as members of the 'sêt fawr' on account of where they sit beneath the pulpit. But, within other Free Church denominations, they are known as 'deacons' or, in Wesleyan Methodism, 'stewards'. Generally, in the Presbyterian family, they are elected for life, though there are exceptions to this practice, with some being elected for a shorter period of five years, with a possibility of being re-elected if they remain eligible and so desire.

Elders have responsibility, as trustees, for the administration of the practical affairs of the chapel community, for inspiring fellow members and for providing a supportive role to the minister. Every month they meet when minister and elders discuss the life of the church, plan the future programme of the church and issues raised in correspondence. The financial report from the treasurer is always on the agenda.

Elders often delegate responsibilities to different societies within the chapel community. In the church which I have served for 39 years in south Liverpool we have a large number of organizations that need to be considered. Chapels vary greatly in size, the most successful having from 400 to 500 on the membership roll. The smallest can have only 50 members and less. A Baptist chapel in Welshpool called a minister in 2006 with only 27 members on its roll. Membership size has to be taken into consideration but it is true to say that a church of any size will do better if it has a number of organizations belonging to it, and especially if it gives opportunities for younger people to undertake active responsibilities.

The creative church leader should have the following five concerns in his or her ministry.

Inspire members of the congregation to be involved

This needs to be done with sensitivity. I always feel that the weekly prayer meeting is an excellent place for involving and inspiring young members to take part, by inviting them to be one of three people who will sustain the spirituality of the prayer meeting. I always provide those who are new to the task with a book of prayers and appropriate scripture readings and ask them to choose two hymns, a reading from the Old or New Testament, and then a selection of appropriate prayers. Most of the spiritual leaders, in my experience, have been inspired in this way. This was the way in which I was taught by my own minister, when I was a young grammar school lad. From this inspiration I was encouraged to take a whole service, which gave me joy in the service of my saviour.

This pattern can be repeated in other aspects of chapel life. I have always encouraged literary and cultural involvement, and have asked individuals, who have the talent, to take part in literary and cultural events. This can be so stimulating.

Organize projects for congregational involvement

Every congregation can stagnate without constant reminders of a project for the local community of believers. The project has to be carefully thought through and a team must be invited to consider it. The team should not be too large and membership should be changed from year to year. It is always good to have projects that entail raising money for a specific worthwhile project. Every five years, we consider a Christian Aid project, raising a few thousand pounds for a specific African or Asian cause. In the past, we have helped worthy causes in Bangladesh and parts of India, such as Gujarat. In 2007, we are concentrating on projects in Sierra Leone. This work will involve the appointment of a liaison officer who will be the chairman or the secretary of the project committee. The Sunday School will be asked to contribute and every effort will be made to communicate information about the country that we are going to help, our motives, and what we ourselves intend to do in local activities. Such a project will bring a great deal of fellowship to the members who become involved and will fulfil the injunctions of Jesus to help the poor.

At other times the project might involve organizing a festival that focuses on a certain individual, now, perhaps, largely forgotten. But, in their day and generation, they did a great deal of work for our church, or for our Welsh nation, or city, or they may have worked in another country, as a member of the Christian Church. Such a festival might be held over a weekend, entailing at least four or five events, perhaps an exhibition, or a tea party, a special lecture, a service, a Cymanfa Ganu (singing session) or perhaps the performing of a play or showing a film, with opportunities for hundreds of people to be involved in the preparation or in participating in the festival. Such events can add immensely to the enrichment of the life of the church and make members proud of their allegiance.

These projects are very appropriate as they relate not only to the local church but also to the local community. Money can be raised by organizing a local talent concert that involves children from local schools in particular, at Christmas time with carol services and other worthwhile popular occasions.

Bring clear elements of joy to church activities

I always find the young people are appreciative of activities which give them opportunities for fellowship and networking. We always have at least three events every year that bring fun into the event in the name of the local church.

For example, we arrange in the summer a sports day for our church and, if possible, involve other churches within our denomination. This has always been a joyous affair. Each year, we also arrange at least one bus trip to a seaside resort or to a town which has particular cultural sites or churches or places where we can learn as well as enjoy ourselves. We also arrange a weekend away from home for people in every age group, staying at a centre that caters for children and young people. We ask the staff at the residential centre to prepare a programme for the children and young people and then I, as minister, will prepare a Bible class for the parents involved. We travel in our cars, arriving early on a Friday evening, spending the whole of Saturday and Sunday morning in a family atmosphere. On the Sunday afternoon, we travel back to our homes, grateful for the happiness, joy and spiritual enrichment that we have enjoyed together while away from home. Such events provide excellent opportunities to come to know young people in a holiday atmosphere. The programme has to be well thought out so that everyone on the course feels involved.

Be patient in approach and outreach

It is not easy to be an active Christian church in the postmodern world, where there are so many competing institutions and choices for our people. In his book, *Three Mile an Hour God*, Kosuke Koyama, a theologian in Japan, compares the movement (or speed) of God with the slow, never-ending walk of a water buffalo cart rather than with a fast jet plane.

Martin Goldsmith explains our frustration:

> As twenty-first century Christians, we find it hard to continue steadfastly when God is not evidently at work. How would we have got on if we had been alive during the 400 years of divine silence between the prophet Malachi and the coming of John the Baptist? (Goldsmith, 2006, p. 120)

Goldsmith suggests that, if we had been been in that situation, we would have been restless. But as the epistle to the Hebrews rightly states, 'we must contribute to the joy of leadership not its drudgery' (Petersen, 2003, p. 2199).

So, we must not be discouraged by our contemporaries when they disappoint us by their apathy and their apparent forgetfulness. Preachers sometimes feel that the urgent message of salvation has fallen on deaf ears and spiritually hardened hearts: but we should remain patient and hopeful. The leaders should say with the author of Hebrews: 'Pray for us. We have no doubts about what we're doing or why, but it's hard going and we need your prayers' (Peterson, 2002, p. 2199).

Base basic principles on models in the New Testament

Such principles have been extremely important in our past and they need to remain so today. Christian leaders should be above reproach. To remind ourselves of our responsibilities we should read and reread the third chapter of the First Epistle of Timothy, in particular those verses as translated for our postmodern days by Eugene H. Peterson:

> If anyone wants to provide leadership in the church, good! But there are preconditions. A leader must be well-thought of, committed to his wife, cool and collected, accessible, and hospitable. He must know what he's talking about, not be over fond of wine, not pushy but gentle, not thin-skinned, not money-hungry. He must handle his own affairs well, attentive to his own children and having their respect. For if someone is unable to handle his own affairs how can he take care of God's church? He must not be a new believer, let the position go to his head and the Devil trip him up. Outsiders must think well of him, or else the Devil will figure out a way to lure him into his trap. (Peterson, 2002, p. 2164)

But then Paul tells Timothy that the same principles apply to everyone who is a servant of the Church:

> They must be reverent before the mystery of the faith, not using their position to try to run things. Let them prove themselves first. If they show they can do it, take them on.

This epistle offers us wise guidance and there should be no exceptions to these general rules. We all have to remember the honour that has to be bestowed upon us to do the will of God through his son Jesus Christ. We should not miss an opportunity to be a co-worker with Christ along with his committed disciples who will work with us. Then we shall hear the splendid commendation, 'Those who do this servant work will come to be highly respected, a real credit to this Jesus-faith' (Peterson, 2002, p. 2164).

This last phrase should be an inspiration. Yes, you who have committed yourself are a 'real credit to this Jesus-faith'. For we are all followers of Jesus, all of us, with a vocation to fulfil, a vocation to be supportive of church leaders, helping enthusiastically the individual who has been set apart to be a minister of the Church. The whole

Church of God is called to be active: to be a warm, friendly community, where people want to belong and be involved in at least one or two or more of its activities. The Westminster Confession underlines this paragraph by stating clearly that the task of the local church is to glorify God and enjoy him for ever. Therefore, it is very important to be involved in the Sunday School, or youth work, or the Women's Society or the Literary Society; to glorify the name of God, and to ensure that others outside the fold realize that we are determined to do our utmost to communicate and to share what we are doing with them. Christian churches of all traditions need to recognize each other and make more contact with each other rather than living separate lives. It is always good to share our concerns with other local churches and, for me, this is a sign of a creative church leader. Indeed it is a reflection of the teaching of Jesus himself that 'you have only one Master and you are all brothers' (Matthew 23.8) and 'by this all men will know that you are my disciples, if you love one another' (John 13.35) (NIV).

Concluding note

This chapter has been based on long personal experience, on insights gleaned from the long history of the Church, biblical principles and a vision that we, who are living in a new age, need to be relevant and able to adapt to the changes around us. We must also recognize, as creative leaders, where, exactly, we want to lead our people. This is a major challenge. I would like to lead my people in ways so that they come to regard themselves as disciples of Jesus: to love the Lord and his principles, and to serve him in the time at their disposal according to the talents and opportunities given to us all by God. The local church should be a central focus; and, since every member of the church should feel at home within its community, I would like to see the leaders delegating as much work as is acceptable to others. There are certain tasks that cannot be delegated easily, but most tasks can. The minister can delegate most of the projects and the committees to others, but his preaching, his pastoral duties, his teaching ministry should remain his own central responsibility. This is his calling. Congregations have always been generous to young leaders. They still are.

Christian leaders have derived their authority from their religious denomination and from the tradition of the Church and from biblical insights. Timothy was instructed by the early church to teach all he could. It remains good advice, as we see in Chapter 4 of the epistle:

Get the word out. Teach all these things. And don't let anyone put you down because you're young. Teach believers with your life: by word, by demeanour, by love, by faith, by integrity. Stay at your post reading Scripture, giving counsel, teaching. And that special gift of ministry you were given when the leaders of the church laid hands on you and prayed – keep that dusted off and in use. (Peterson, 2002, p. 2165)

This is the best advice possible for the creative church leader. Paul has not finished. He says to Timothy: 'Don't be diverted. Just keep at it.' In my experience he is right, for the reward is wonderful: 'Both you and those who hear you will experience salvation' (Peterson, 2002, p. 2165).

Every religion is concerned with salvation, so creative leadership will ultimately lead individuals to the salvation of their souls as the New Testament promises.

References

Beckett, F., *Rebuild: Small Groups Can Make a Difference*, Leicester: Crossways, 2001.

Goldsmith, Martin, *Get a Grip on Mission: The Challenge of a Changing World*, Leicester: Inter-Varsity Press, 2006.

Koyama, K., *Three Mile an Hour God*, London: SCM Press, 1979.

Laniak, Timothy S., *Shepherds after My Own Heart: Pastoral Traditions and Leadership in the Bible*, Leicester: Crossways, 2001.

Peterson, Eugene H., *The Message: The Bible in Contemporary Language*, Colorado Springs: NavPress, 2002.

Tiddall, D. J., *Skilful Shepherds: Explorations in Pastoral Theology*, Leicester: Apollos, 1997.

Tiplady, Richard (ed.), *One World or Many: The Impact of Globalisation on Mission*, Pasadena, California: William Carey Library, 2003.

Part 2

Personal Characteristics

Learning What Kind of Person You Are

2. Learning what kind of leader you are

All the world's a stage? Clowns, clowning and change leadership[1]

VAUGHAN ROBERTS

Introduction

This chapter sets out to explore one small instance of organizational change and how, by reflecting upon this experience through the lenses of clowns and performing arts as metaphors for change leadership, light can be shed on the nature of being a 'leader' within the Church. The example described might be regarded as a 'success' or a 'failure', but judging the outcome and the criteria for making such a judgement is a crucial part of clarifying our understanding of leadership as a whole.

The context for the change in question was Thornton Hall – a small church plant built within the parish of St Timothy,[2] in 1958. The account of how the local community bought the land on which to build and how the vicar at the time set up a table on the plot to collect people's gifts towards the project was a crucial part of that community's self-identity, as was the story of how people from the locality came together and built the hall. These community memories ran deep and any attempt to cast them aside was treated as a great slight on the past. The Sunday School cupboard was a case in point.

When I was interviewed for the post of curate in St Timothy's parish, to be based at Thornton, I was told that the Sunday School had been a large part of the life of the Hall in the past and the present, and the small congregation hoped that this might be revived. However, many of the resources for the Sunday School were from a bygone era and I felt the best thing to do was to discard them and completely restock for the future. One thing that symbolized this need to move on for me was a framed print of *Jesus the Good Shepherd* which looked as if it had come from an ancient children's Bible. It clearly hadn't been used by the Sunday School for years and did not appear to have been taken out of the cupboard since it was first given. However, when a group of us started to tidy out the cupboard this was seen as throwing away the past – especially in the case of the obscure and redundant picture.

It turned out to have been given by Captain Brown, a much beloved Church Army officer known affectionately as 'Cap'y Brown', and an enormous furore ensued when it was learnt that his unused and largely forgotten gift to Thornton Hall was to be discarded. No amount of protest that it was no longer suitable for today's Sunday School could sway some people from the view that this picture should not be thrown out. Nor were they persuaded by the opposite argument that this important community heirloom should have a more prominent place in the hall. People were adamant that it had always been in the Sunday School cupboard and that that was where it should remain. In the end, Cap'y Brown's picture stayed but its threatened removal seemed to serve a number of purposes. First, it enabled the community to retell the stories of that period of its life. Second, it illustrated to me how the most innocuous of things can have a symbolic importance to a community. Third, by compromising over the picture it was possible to replace a great deal of other Sunday School material that was no longer of use, and retention of the picture of Jesus the Good Shepherd seemed to be a small price to pay.

There is a surreal element to this story of a picture which had little practical value being kept in a cupboard, while organizational change happened in spite of it. This might seem absurd from a leadership perspective but these surreal and absurdist elements point to an important aspect of understanding leadership. The next section will reflect upon how notions of clowns, clowning and the apparently ridiculous can be helpful tools for discovering more about different kind of leadership.

Clowns and ordained ministry

First, let us turn to some specifics of clowning. Roly Bain is an Anglican priest who has also trained as a clown. That sentence and the notion that clowns can receive 'training' immediately suggests that there is a tradition to clowning. Just as Alasdair MacIntyre (MacIntyre, 1994) and Avery Dulles (Dulles, 1992) have portrayed philosophy and theology as 'crafts' the same could also be said of clowns and clowning. Anyone who has seen clowns perform will know that it is a craft which involves skill and competence. It is not a free-for-all in which anything goes. Furthermore, as Roly Bain points out, there isn't just one type of clown or one tradition of clowning. There are several different clown characters:

- **Jester** – the oldest of clowns who resided in the court of monarchs and was licensed to tell the truth and invert status.
- **Harlequin** – traditionally wears a diamond patterned costume, and developed into a pantomime character. This clown is driven by dreams and is characterized by moods swings, intelligence, wit and cunning. Bain describes him as 'a loveable rogue doomed to be frustrated' (Bain, 1993, p. 26).
- **Auguste** – While this clown is always accident prone, it is the naivety, simplicity and playfulness which are the hallmarks of Auguste. As the clown who is on the receiving end, he or she is the naive scapegoat who is vulnerable and most often ends up getting hurt.
- **Whiteface** – wears a conical hat, white makeup, a spangled suit, and is often seen with a collection of brass instruments. He is frequently arrogant and pompous.
- **Tramp** – the little person fighting against the odds.
- **Trickster** – callous joker.

Each of these characters has a history in circus, music hall, cinema and other forms of entertainment culture. Speaking out of his own experience, Bain comments that: 'Part of the clown's role and task is to hold up a mirror to everyone so that they can see themselves in him, and while we may be able to write a clown off if he is too fantastic or overblown, it's more difficult if he somehow looks rather like us or the person next door' (Bain, 1993, pp. 31–2). The sociologist Peter Berger makes a similar point in his discussion about comedy. He argues that comic episodes are interludes – 'literally, an inbetween playing or inbetween game, but inbetween *what*? Well, clearly, inbetween the serious, mundane activities of everyday life' (Berger, 1997, p. 13). To put it another way, just as clowns provide mirrors for individuals and society, so comedy more generally provides a similar sort of reflexive space. Particularly, in Berger's terms, as a means of 'debunking power' (Berger, 1997, p. 24) and challenging our 'taken-for-granted reality' (Berger, 1997, p. 41). This reference to power leads to a second point. If clowns and comedy have a structure to them, they can also be creative metaphors of disclosure within many different forms of human activity, including all forms of leadership.

Significantly, these notions of a clown holding up a mirror for others to see themselves and comedy as providing reflexive space can find parallels in writing about Christian priesthood and leadership. Cocksworth and Brown in their work on priestly ministry argue that it is part of the role of the priest to symbolize the ministry which belongs to the whole Church:

> It is a calling to *indicate* the identity of the Church by embodying the characteristics of the Church. It is a calling to live out the way of being to which the Church is called. The Church is called to be a holy priesthood. The presbyter is called to signify this priestly calling. In more sacramental language, the presbyter is a *sign* of the priestly life of the Church. (Cocksworth and Brown, 2002, pp. 24–5)

In other words, the presbyteral role is to hold up a mirror to the Church so that the whole body of Christ can appreciate its priestly ministry. Bill Countryman intimates a similar approach when he speaks of how priestly ministry is something which is essentially human and shared by all in the Church, by virtue of Christ's incarnation and high priesthood. He believes that: 'To be human means to be engaged in priestly discourse – the unveiling of secrets' (Countryman, 1999, p. 4) or, in Berger's term, challenging our 'taken-for-granted reality'. From these perspectives the generic roles of priest and clown in the carnival of the Church can be seen to be very similar. One of the challenges that Roly Bain sets for those who exercise leadership within the Body of Christ is: what kind of clown is God calling us to be? Within English culture there is a sense in which vicars are often caricatured as 'Augustes' – naive, simple, accident prone; while those in the clerical hierarchy are depicted as 'Whitefaces' – pompous and arrogant. Perhaps the success of a character like the Revd Geraldine Granger in BBC TV's *The Vicar of Dibley* was that she frequently appeared to be a 'Tramp' – just one person fighting against the odds. If nothing else, the metaphor of the clown illustrates that the priest-like task, shared by the whole Body of Christ, of holding up a mirror for the world is more complex and nuanced than might first appear, and the management perspectives of William Torbert and Dalmar Fisher bring yet a further angle to this subject.

Types of leadership

William Torbert has regularly used the clown image in his work on organizations (Torbert, 1987, 1991; and Fisher and Torbert, 1995). He often uses the metaphor to describe organizational change, but he and Dalmar Fisher have also combined this image with the developmental work of Piaget,[3] outlining six *progressive* stages of leadership and their characteristics, which can be summarized as follows:

Opportunist

Short-time horizon; focuses on concrete things; manipulative; deceptive; rejects feedback; externalizes blame; distrustful; fragile self-control; hostile humour; views luck as central; flouts power; stereotypes; views rules as loss of freedom; punishes according to 'eye-for-an-eye' ethic; treats what they can get away with as legal.

Diplomat

Observes protocol; avoids inner and outer conflict; works to group standard; speaks in clichés, platitudes; conforms; feels shame if violates norm; sin seen as hurting others; punishment seen as disapproval; seeks membership, status; face-saving essential; loyalty to immediate group, no 'distant' organization or principles; cooperative.

Technician

Interested in problem solving; seeks causes; critical of self and others; decisions are based on 'craft' logic; chooses efficiency over effectiveness; perfectionist; accepts feedback only from 'objective' craft masters; dogmatic; values decisions based on merit; sees contingencies, exceptions; wants to stand out, be unique; sense of obligation to wider, internally consistent moral order.

Achiever

Long-term goals; future is vivid, inspiring; welcomes behavioural feedback; effectiveness and results oriented; feels like initiator, not pawn; appreciates complexity, systems; seeks generalizable reasons for action; seeks mutuality, not hierarchy, in relationships; feels guilt if does not meet own standards; blind to own shadow, to the subjectivity behind objectivity; positive ethic: practical day-to-day improvements based on self-chosen (but not self-created) ethical system.

Strategist

Creative at conflict resolution; recognizes importance of principle, contract, theory, and judgement – not just rules, customs and exceptions – for making and maintaining good decisions; process oriented as well as goal oriented; aware of paradox and contradiction; relativistic, aware that what one sees depends upon one's worldview; high value on individuality, unique market niches, particular historical moments; enjoys playing a variety of roles; witty, existential humour (as contrasted to prefabricated jokes); aware of dark side, of profundity of evil, and tempted by its power.

Clown, Magician or Witch

Disintegration of ego-identity; seeks participation in historical/spiritual transformations; creator of mythical events that reframe situations; anchoring in inclusive present, seeing light and dark, order and mess; blends opposites, creating 'positive-sum' games; exercises own attention, researches interplay of intuition, thought, action and effects on outside world; treats time and events as symbolic, analogical, metaphorical (not merely linear, digital, literal).

Rather than a *typology* of clowns or leaders, Torbert and Fisher are describing a *process* of leadership development and, in the transition from the penultimate stage of Strategist to the final stage of Clown, they become positively mystical in their description of how leaders make that move. In the following passage, Fisher and Torbert stress the importance of an individual *and* collective, reflexive process which they call 'Action Inquiry':

> In transforming to this managerial style, the person must face and learn how to transform the entire dark side of the human condition as it manifests itself in the person and the person's surroundings. Unlike the Strategist, who may believe that he or she is on the side of good and can beat evil, the Clown recognizes that the polarization between good and evil – between victory and defeat, between the sacred and profane, between classes, races, and sexes, between I and Thou – is recreated at each moment by our relatively fixed and one-sided perspectives on the world. Evil emanates from the character of our own fallen, passive attention; it cannot be permanently defeated. Indeed, to fight against it as though it were only outside ourselves is to reinforce it. Action inquiry becomes, for the Magician/Witch/Clown, not so much a theory of managing as an ongoing jousting, at one and the same time, with one's attention and with the outside world. (Fisher & Torbert, 1995, pp. 177–8)

In other words, experience itself and the process of reflecting upon our experience are fundamental to the process of human sensemaking whether that sensemaking is organizational, theological or (as in the present case) both.[4] We now turn to see how these insights based on the metaphor of clowns and clowning might be applied to the specific experience at Thornton Hall and Cap'y Brown's picture of *Jesus the Good Shepherd*.

Clowns and performing leadership

Roly Bain's outline of the tradition of clowning plus William Torbert and Dalmar Fisher's stages of leadership culminating in the images of clown, magician or witch all suggest discreet characters or performances. For example, Harlequins have certain characteristics and ways of dressing which set them apart from Augustes; the approaches and skills that Diplomats bring to organizational problem solving will be different to those of Achievers. If we map some of these characters onto the experience of Thornton Hall and Cap'y Brown's picture, however, a different dynamic begins to emerge. Some might see the approach of letting the picture of *Jesus the Good Shepherd* stay in the Sunday School cupboard, while clearing out the many other outmoded resources as Harlequinesque – a strategy motivated by a dream and driven by a calculating mind; but others (particularly those who wished to keep the picture) might see this as the action of a Whiteface – that is, an arrogant and pompous decision riding roughshod over local feelings.

Alternatively, we might ask in terms of Fisher and Torbert's approach: is this decision to throw out the picture the action of an Opportunist who has a short-time horizon and is unable to appreciate the history and traditions of Thornton Hall; or a Diplomat who is avoiding outer conflict; or a Technician with an interest in problem solving; or an Achiever seeking mutuality in relationships; or a Strategist being creative at conflict resolution; or even a Clown who is seeing light and darkness, order and mess in this situation and aiming to blend conflicting views? The key point is that, when it comes to applying these metaphors to the outside world and our lived experience, the categories become less discrete and much more fluid. It is harder for those exercising leadership in the Church or any organization to say 'I am a Jester', 'I am a Tramp', 'I am a Strategist' or 'I am a Technician' because we use approaches and characteristics from across the range of clowning traditions and leadership types.

So how can we apply some of these insights to this experience? Roly Bain offers a typology of clowns which helps to open up our understanding of the priestly ministry shared by the whole Body of Christ. Fisher and Torbert describe a process of leadership development in which the clown represents the final stage of growth. I have argued that it is important not to apply either Bain's typology or Fisher and Torbert's process in too rigid a fashion because it is by maintaining the breadth of these metaphorical frameworks that greater insight into the nature of leadership and any individual leadership role can be discovered. Indeed, these approaches themselves fit within a broader narrative which sees management and leadership as a performing art, including the writing of appropriate scripts.

Someone who developed this in detail was Iain Mangham (Mangham, 1978, 1986; and Mangham and Overington, 1987). Mangham and Overington argue that: 'The management of organizations is a *performing art*, an important aspect of that is the shaping of direction and the marshalling of support through appropriate rhetoric' (1987, p. 164 – my emphasis). Such an understanding has been taken on more recently by Keith Grint in his work on leadership. Like Mangham, Grint does not explicitly draw upon the notion of clowning but he does argue that one of the key aspects of leadership is the performing arts: 'In this we can include the theatrical performances that leaders must engage in if they are to achieve the necessary mobilization of followers and it is also derived from the skills of rhetoric and the skills of negotiation' (Grint, 2000, p. 23). He returns to this theme in his conclusion: 'leadership is a performance, an inventive display, and we can summarize this by suggesting that successful leadership depends upon the extent to which leaders "perform" the words and deeds conventionally associated with leaders – but it also requires followers to believe in the performance' (p. 419). From this perspective, leadership involves the performance of scripts and the taking on of characters appropriate to each particular organizational context. In order to understand what scripts are being used and which characters are involved we have to engage in the kind of action enquiry described by Fisher and Torbert that attends to organizational 'jousting' and the character of leaders within such dynamics. As part of this process, we have noted that the role of comedy in providing a mirror for characters to see themselves in more clearly (Bain) and humour in challenging 'taken-for-granted reality' (Berger) remain crucial. Mangham and Overington also draw attention to the important role played by these factors when they contend: 'theatre provides a place for both tragedy and comedy: without the critical distance offered by the comedic, we should be caught in the toils of tragic imagery – condemned to endless stories of fruitless resistance to fate' (Mangham and Overington 1987, p. 42).[5]

Conclusion

Cap'y Brown's picture in the Sunday School cupboard at Thornton Hall is undoubtedly a very minor matter in the scheme of God's Kingdom but, nevertheless, from such small organizational experiences some key questions about the nature of the organization, leadership and change can arise. Speaking personally, this instance of organizational conflict raised questions about priestly identity and role which have remained with me and have helped shape my approach to leadership in other contexts. Within Roly Bain's typology of clowns the role of 'Jester' is one that appeals to me, but it is difficult to place that character comfortably within Fisher and Torbert's process of leadership development – can a Jester be an Opportunist, Diplomat, Technician, Achiever and Strategist? Or can a Jester only be a Clown? Since that seems like mere tautology, it is at such a point we start to discover the limits of this leadership metaphor and need to turn elsewhere. It is here that the wider perspective of leadership as a performing art can help shed light on Cap'y Brown's picture.

Grint argues that leadership is focused on coordinating the organizational relationships between: the *who*, the *what*, the *how* and the *why*. By this he means:

1 *Who are you?* Your organizational identity.
2 *What do you want to achieve?* Your organization's strategic vision.
3 *How will you achieve this?* Organizational tactics; and, vitally,
4 *Why should people want to embody the identity, pursue the strategic vision, and adopt the organizational tactics?*

In essence, Grint believes all of this comes down to persuasive communication, and he argues that the key element of persuasive communication 'is the world of performing arts, the theatre of rhetorical skill, of negotiating skills, and of inducing the audience to believe in the world you paint with words and props' (Grint, 2000, p. 28).

We can see all these factors at work in this example from Thornton Hall.

1 The picture of *Jesus the Good Shepherd* played a significant part in the organizational identity of the Hall.
2 Thornton Hall had a strategic vision for growing its Sunday School but, for some people at least, 2 was in conflict with 1.
3 By employing a tactic of keeping the picture and honouring 1 but discarding the other outdated resources it was possible to keep on track with 2.
4 The subsequent growth of the Sunday School provided certain practical results which enabled Thornton Hall to continue pursuing its strategic vision and also facilitated the introduction of further organizational change within the church plant.

In terms of leadership, this experience encouraged me to reflect further upon the nature of organizations and how metaphors can open up creative space within the whole process of being a leader assisting churches and congregations in their stories of organizational sensemaking (Roberts, 1999, 2002).

Notes

1. I am grateful to Professor David Sims of the Cass Business School for his comments on an earlier draft of this chapter.
2. Place names have been changed.
3. For further discussion of Piaget's developmental ideas in the context of faith see Fowler, 1981, and, within ordained ministry, Roberts, 1992.
4. For further discussion on the concept of 'sensemaking' see Weick 1979, 1995 and 2001.
5. For a useful discussion of humour in organizations see Fineman, Sims and Gabriel, 2005, pp. 213–24.

References

Bain, Roly (1993), *Fools Rush In: A Call to Christian Clowning*, London: Marshall Pickering.

Berger, Peter L. (1997), *Redeeming Laughter: The Comic Dimension of Human Experience*, New York and Berlin: Walter de Gruyter.

Cocksworth, Christopher and Rosalind Brown (2002), *Being a Priest Today: Exploring Priestly Identity*, Norwich: Canterbury Press.

Countryman, William (1999), *Living on the Border of the Holy: Renewing the Priesthood of All*, Harrisburg: Morehouse Publishing.

Dulles, Avery (1992), *The Craft of Theology: From Symbol to System*, Dublin: Gill & Macmillan; New York: Crossroad.

Fineman, Stephen, David Sims and Yiannis Gabriel (2005), *Organizing and Organizations*, 3rd edn, London and Thousand Oaks: Sage.

Fisher, Dalmar and William R. Torbert (1995), *Personal and Organizational Transformations: The True Challenge of Continual Quality Improvement*, London and New York: McGraw-Hill.

Fowler, James W. (1981), *Stages of Faith: The Psychology of Human Development and the Quest for Meaning*, San Francisco: Harper & Row.

Grint, Keith (2000), *The Arts of Leadership*, London and New York: Oxford University Press.

MacIntyre, Alasdair (1994), 'A Partial Response to My Critics', in John Horton and Susan Mendus (eds), *After MacIntyre: Critical Perspectives on the Work of Alasdair MacIntyre*, Cambridge: Polity Press, pp. 283–304.

Mangham, Iain (1978), *Interactions and Interventions in Organizations*, Chichester and New York: John Wiley.

Mangham, Iain (1986), *Power and Performance in Organizations*, Oxford and New York: Blackwell.

Mangham, Iain and Michael A. Overington (1987), *Organizations as Theatre: A Social Psychology of Dramatic Appearances*, Chichester and New York: John Wiley.

Roberts, Vaughan S. (1992), 'Reframing the UCCF Doctrinal Basis', *Theology* 95, 768, November/December 1992, pp. 432–46.

Roberts, Vaughan S. (1999), 'The Church as an Embodied Organization', in G. R. Evans and Martyn Percy (eds), *Managing the Church? Order and Organization in a Secular Age*, Sheffield: Sheffield Academic Press, pp. 153–73.

Roberts, Vaughan S. (2002), 'Water as an Implicit Metaphor for Organizational Change within the Church', *Implicit Religion* 5, 1, 2002, pp. 29–40.

Torbert, William R. (1987), *Managing the Corporate Dream: Restructuring for Long-Term Success*, Homewood, Illinois: Dow Jones-Irwin.

Torbert, William R. (1991), *The Power of Balance: Transforming Self, Society, and Scientific Inquiry*, Newbury Park and London: Sage.

Weick, Karl E. (1979) [1969], *The Social Psychology of Organizations*, 2nd edn, Reading, Massachusetts: Addison-Wesley Publishing.

Weick, Karl E. (1995), *Sensemaking in Organizations*, Thousand Oaks and London: Sage.

Weick, Karl E. (2001), *Making Sense of the Organization*, Oxford and Malden, Massachusetts: Blackwell Business.

3. Psychological type and leadership styles

How to discern which type of leader you are

LESLIE J. FRANCIS

Introduction

The aim of this chapter is to examine the insights of Jungian psychological type theory for understanding different approaches to leadership within the Church. Psychological type theory suggests that individuals differ one from another in four important ways (defined as introversion or extraversion, sensing or intuition, thinking or feeling, and perceiving or judging) and that these basic and deep-seated differences in psychological type shape basic responses to many areas of life, including leadership styles. Since the use of psychological type theory for this purpose is somewhat controversial, it may be wise to begin by anticipating two objections: one voiced by theologians and one voiced by psychologists.

Theologians are properly concerned by the uncritical use of psychological theories and methods for influencing the agenda of the Church. Indeed, Kenneth Leech (1996) edited a collection of essays warning fellow theologians to steer clear of psychological type theory. If psychological type theory is to be of benefit to the Church, two theological problems need addressing, one rooted in the doctrine of creation and the other rooted in the doctrine of salvation.

The first theological objection to psychological type theory is that the very notion of fixed patterns of psychological individual difference may underestimate the rich variety of human life and constrain individuals within artificial typologies. It is here that the doctrine of creation is so crucial. What I have come to style a 'theology of individual differences' rooted in the biblical doctrine of creation, celebrates rather than rejects the recognition of patterns in the divinely created order. According to Genesis 1.27:

God created humankind in God's image
in the image of God, God created them,
male and female God created them.

The key insight provided by this basis for the doctrine of creation is that God embraces patterned diversity and that such patterned diversity is reflected in the image of God. The notion that God embraces diversity is also clearly consistent with the Christian doctrine of the Holy Trinity. A doctrine of creation grounded in Genesis 1.27 is committed theologically to recognizing that both men and women are created equally in the image of God, that men and women are created with very visible and highly significant differences, and that individual differences created equally in the image of God (male and female) need to be accorded equal value and status. If such a theology of individual differences holds good for sex differences, then, by extension, such a theology should hold good also for other differences equally grounded in creation, that is to say in the individuality of the divine creator. Such differences may well include those of ethnicity and those of personality.

The second theological objection to psychological type theory is that the very notion of fixed patterns of psychological individual difference may underestimate the power of the Christian gospel to challenge people to repentance and to effect real change. It is here that the doctrine of salvation is so crucial. In this connection a distinction needs to be made between personality and character. Personality (the level with which psychological type theory is concerned) describes the deepest level of human difference, like sex and ethnicity. Few preachers would call, say, on men to repent and become women. Few preachers would call, say, on people of colour to repent and to become white. On this account, it would be a mistake to call, say, on introverts to repent and to become extraverts. The doctrine of salvation is concerned with the transformation of character, not the transformation of personality.

Psychologists are also properly concerned by the uncritical use of psychological type theories by other disciplines, including theology. The crucial point to note is that psychological type theory does not claim to provide a complete view of personality in the way in which some theories claim to do, like the three-dimensional model of personality proposed by Eysenck and Eysenck (1991), the Five Factor model proposed by Costa and McCrae (1985) or the sixteen personality factor model proposed by Cattell, Cattell and Cattell (1993). Psychological type theory simply sets out to describe four fundamental human differences which are as basic as being male or female, being born white or coloured, being born left handed or right handed (see Francis, 2005).

27

Having faced the difficulties, I can proceed to describe the theory and to draw out the implications for models of leadership within the Church.

Introversion or extraversion

Introversion and extraversion are described as the two psychological orientations. They are concerned with the sources of psychological energy. Introverts are energized by the inner world, while extraverts are energized by the outer world.

Individuals who prefer *introversion* like quiet for concentration. They want to be able to shut off the distractions of the outer world and turn inwards. They often experience trouble in remembering names and faces. They can work at one solitary project for a long time without interruption. When they are engaged in a task in the outer world they may become absorbed in the ideas behind that task. Introverts work best alone and may resent distractions and interruptions from other people. They dislike being interrupted by the telephone, tend to think things through before acting, and may spend so long in thought that they miss the opportunity to act.

Introverts prefer to learn by reading rather than by talking with others. They may also prefer to communicate with others in writing, rather than face-to-face or over the phone; this is particularly the case if they have something unpleasant to communicate. Introverts are oriented to the inner world. They focus on ideas, concepts and inner understanding. They are reflective, may consider deeply before acting, and they probe inwardly for stimulation.

Individuals who prefer *extraversion* like variety and action. They want to be able to shut off the distractions of the inner world and turn outward. They are good at remembering faces and names and enjoy meeting people and introducing people. They can become impatient with long, slow jobs. When they are working in the company of other people they may become more interested in how others are doing the job than in the job itself. Extraverts like to have other people around them in the working environment, and enjoy the stimulus of sudden interruptions and telephone calls. Extraverts like to act quickly and decisively, even when it is not totally appropriate to do so. Extraverts prefer to learn a task by talking it through with other people. They prefer to communicate with other people face-to-face or over the phone, rather than in writing. They often find that their own ideas become clarified through communicating them with others. Extraverts are oriented to the outer world. They focus on people and things. They prefer to learn by trial and error and they do so with confidence. They are active people, and they scan the outer environment for stimulation.

As a consequence of these fundamental psychological differences, introverts and extraverts model quite different leadership styles, but both are valid and have their place in the Church. The extravert prefers to lead from the front, while the introvert prefers to lead from within.

Sensing or intuition

Sensing and intuition are described as the two perceiving functions. They are concerned with the ways in which people gather information. Sensing types prefer to focus on the realities of a situation as perceived by the senses, while intuitive types prefer to focus on the possibilities of a situation, perceiving meanings and relationships.

Individuals who prefer *sensing* develop keen awareness of present experience. They have acute powers of observation, good memory for facts and details, the capacity for realism, and the ability to see the world as it is. They rely on experience rather than theory. They put their trust in what is known and in the conventional. Individuals with a preference for sensing are aware of the uniqueness of each individual event. They develop good techniques of observation and they recognize the practical way in which things work now. Sensing types like to develop an established way of doing things and gain enjoyment from exercising skills which they have already learnt. Repetitive work does not bore them. They are able to work steadily with a realistic idea of how long a task will take.

Sensing types usually reach their conclusion step by step, observing each piece of information carefully. They are not easily inspired to interpret the information in front of them and they may not trust inspiration when it comes. They are very careful about getting the facts right and are good at engaging with detail. Sensing types may fail to recognize complexity in some situations, and consequently oversimplify tasks. They are good at accepting the current reality as the given situation in which to work. They would much rather work with the present information than speculate about future possibilities. They clearly agree with the old proverb that the bird in the hand is worth two in the bush. Sensing types perceive clearly with the five senses. They attend to practical and factual details, and they are in touch with physical realities. They attend to the present moment and prefer to confine their attention to what is said and done. They observe the small details of everyday life and attend to step-by-step experience. They prefer to let the eyes tell the mind.

Individuals who prefer *intuition* develop insight into complexity. They have the ability to see abstract, symbolic and theoretical relationships, and the capacity to see future possibilities. They put their reliance on inspiration rather than on past experience. Their interest is in the new and untried. They trust their intuitive grasp of meanings and relationships. Individuals with a preference for intuition are aware of new challenges and possibilities. They see quickly beyond the information they have been given or the materials they have to hand to the possibilities and challenges which these offer. They are often discontented with the way things are and wish to improve them. They become bored quickly and dislike doing the same thing repeatedly. Intuitive types enjoy learning new skills. They work in bursts of energy, powered by enthusiasm, and then enjoy slack periods between activity. Intuitive types follow their inspirations and hunches. They may reach conclusions too quickly and misconstrue the information or get the facts wrong. They dislike taking too much time to secure precision.

Intuitive types may tend to imagine that things are more complex than they really are: they tend to over-complexify things. They are curious about why things are the way they are and may prefer to raise questions than to find answers. Intuitive types are always striving to gain an overview of the information around them. In terms of an old proverb, they may prefer to pay attention to the two birds in the bush rather than the one in the hand. Intuitive types perceive with memory and associations. They see patterns and meanings and assess possibilities. They are good at reading between the lines and projecting possibilities for the future. They prefer to go always for the big picture. They prefer to let the mind inform the eyes.

As a consequence of these fundamental psychological differences, sensers and intuitives model quite different leadership styles, but both are valid and have their place in the Church. The sensing type prefers to offer a cautious lead stamped with realism, while the intuitive type prefers to offer an inspirational lead stamped with vision.

Thinking or feeling

Thinking and feeling are described as the two judging functions. They are concerned with the ways in which people make decisions. Thinking types prefer to make decisions and judgements based on objective, impersonal logic, while feeling types prefer to make decisions and judgements based on subjective, personal values.

Individuals who prefer *thinking* develop clear powers of logical analysis. They develop the ability to weigh facts objectively and to predict consequences, both intended and unintended. They develop a stance of impartiality. They are characterized by a sense of fairness and justice. Individuals with a preference for thinking are good at putting things in logical order. They are able to put people in their place when they consider it necessary. They are able to take tough decisions and to reprimand others. They are also able to be firm and toughminded about themselves.

Thinking types need to be treated fairly and to see that other people are treated fairly as well. They are inclined to respond more to other people's ideas than to other people's feelings. They may inadvertently hurt other people's feelings without recognizing that they are doing so. Thinking types are able to anticipate and predict the logical outcomes of other people's choices. They can see the humour rather than the human pain in bad choices and wrong decisions taken by others. Thinking types prefer to look at life from the outside as a spectator. Thinking types are able to develop good powers of critical analysis. They use objective and impersonal criteria in reaching decisions. They follow logically the relationships between cause and effect. They develop characteristics of being firm-minded and prizing logical order. They may appear sceptical.

Individuals who prefer *feeling* develop a personal emphasis on values and standards. They appreciate what matters most to themselves and what matters most to other people. They develop an understanding of people, a wish to affiliate with people and a desire for harmony. They are characterized by their capacity for warmth, and by qualities of empathy and compassion. Individuals with a preference for feeling like harmony and will work hard to bring harmony about between other people. They dislike telling other people unpleasant things or reprimanding other people. They take into account other people's feelings.

Feeling types need to have their own feelings recognized as well. They need praise and affirmation. They are good at seeing the personal effects of choices on their own lives and on other people's lives as well. Feeling types are sympathetic individuals. They take a great interest in the people behind the job and respond to other people's values as much as to their ideas. They enjoy pleasing people. Feeling types look at life from the inside. They live life as committed participants and find it less easy to stand back and to form an objective view of what is taking place. Feeling types develop good skills at applying personal priorities. They are good at weighing human values and motives, both their own and other people's. They are characterized by qualities of empathy and sympathy. They prize harmony and trust.

As a consequence of these fundamental psychological differences, thinking types and feeling types model quite different leadership styles, but both are valid and have their place in the Church. The thinking type prefers to lead through objective strategies and decisive organization, while the feeling type prefers to lead through consensus, harmony, agreement and compromise.

Judging or perceiving

Judging and perceiving are described as the attitudes toward the outer world. Judging types use their preferred judging function (thinking or feeling) in the outer world to create an organized and disciplined environment, while perceiving types use their preferred perceiving function (sensing or intuition) in the outer world to permit a flexible and responsive environment.

Judging types schedule projects so that each step gets done on time. They like to get things finished and settled, and to know that the finished product is in place. They work best when they can plan their work in advance and follow that plan. Judging types use lists and agendas to structure their day and to plan their actions. They may dislike interruption from the plans they have made and are reluctant to leave the task in hand even when something more urgent arises.

Judging types tend to be satisfied once they reach a judgement or have made a decision, both about people and things. They dislike having to revise their decision and taking fresh information into account. They like to get on with a task as soon as possible once the essential things are at hand. As a consequence, judging types may decide to act too quickly. When individuals take a judging attitude toward the outer world, they are using the preferred *judging process*, thinking or feeling, outwardly. Their attitude to life is characterized by deciding and planning, organizing and scheduling, controlling and regulating. Their life is goal oriented. They want to move toward closure, even when the data are incomplete.

Perceiving types adapt well to changing situations. They make allowances for new information and for changes in the situation in which they are living or acting. They may have trouble making decisions, feeling that they have never quite got enough information on which to base their decision. Perceiving types may start too many projects and consequently have difficulty in finishing them. They may tend to postpone unpleasant tasks and to give their attention to more pleasant options. Perceiving types want to know all about a new task before they begin it, and may prefer to postpone something while they continue to explore the options.

When perceiving types use lists they do so not as a way of organizing the details of their day, but of seeing the possibilities in front of them. They may choose never to act on these possibilities. Perceiving types do not mind leaving things open for last-minute changes. They work best under pressure and get a lot accomplished at the last minute under the constraints of a deadline. When individuals take a perceiving attitude toward the outer world, they are using the preferred *perceiving process*, sensing or intuition, outwardly. They are taking in information, adapting and changing, curious and interested. They adopt an open-minded attitude toward life and resist closure to obtain more data.

As a consequence of these fundamental psychological differences, judging types and perceiving types model quite different leadership styles, but both are valid and have their place in the Church. Judging types prefer to run a tight ship and a well-planned organization, while perceiving types prefer to operate a flexible and responsive church which can adapt to last-minute eventualities.

Preferred leadership styles

Until recently little has been known about the psychological type preferences of church leaders in the UK. A pioneering study was reported by Francis, Payne and Jones (2001), drawing on information provided by 427 male Anglican clergy in Wales. As a group, these clergymen shared clear preferences for introversion, sensing, feeling and judging. On the basis of such findings, four conclusions can be drawn about the preferred leadership style modelled within the Church in Wales.

First, 59% of the clergy preferred introversion, compared with 42% who preferred extraversion. Introverts may bring many strengths to ministry, including the ability to work by themselves on tasks, to invest time in reading and in preparation, to welcome one-to-one encounters in counselling and in spiritual direction, to develop an inward life of prayer and spirituality. At the same time, introverts may be drained by many of the social expectations of ministry, working with large groups of people, remembering names, visiting strangers and assuming a high profile in the local congregation and the wider local community.

Second, 57% of the clergy preferred sensing, compared with 43% who preferred intuition. Sensers may bring many strengths to ministry, including a fine awareness of the environment in which they serve and of the church in which they lead worship, a concern for the detail within the services they conduct and for the facts on which judgements and choices are made. At the same time, sensers may find it more difficult to formulate a vision for their church's future, to welcome change and experimentation in liturgy, or to see new and imaginative solutions to old problems.

Third, 69% of the clergy preferred feeling, compared with 31% who preferred thinking. Feelers may bring many strengths to ministry, including the desire to affiliate with others, the gifts of empathy and sympathy, a commitment to harmony, a deep understanding of people and a respect for inter-personal values. At the same time, feelers may find it more difficult to take tough decisions which affect other people's lives, to chair troublesome meetings, to be assertive on points of truth and justice, and to put other people in their place.

Fourth, 68% of the clergy preferred judging, compared with 32% who preferred perceiving. Judgers may bring many strengths to ministry, including the ability to organize their own lives, to organize the life of their parishes, to arrange services and events well in advance, to keep on top of administration and to manage local affairs. At the same time, judgers may become too inflexible and restricted by their own strategies, plans and routines, too unwilling or unable to abandon their plans in order to respond to unexpected crises, emergencies or opportunities, too bound to the present structure to embrace new ideas and possibilities.

It is of course unwise to assume that all groups of clergy are like clergymen in the Church in Wales. It is for this reason that Francis, Craig, Whinney, Tilley and Slater (forthcoming) reported on a second study conducted among clergymen in the Church of England.

In three ways, these data reflected the same preferences as those found among male Anglican clergy in Wales: preferences for introversion over extraversion, for feeling over thinking, and for judging over perceiving. In one crucial way, however, the profiles of the two groups of clergymen differed. In Wales, 57% preferred sensing and 43% preferred intuition; in England, the balance was reversed, with 62% preferring intuition and 38% preferring sensing. The authors suggested that these differences in psychological type reflect a crucial difference in leadership styles between the two Churches and in the character of the two Churches. The Church in Wales tends to be more conservative than the Church of England and, therefore, a place in which leaders who prefer sensing may feel more comfortable. They suggested that clergymen who prefer intuition may become restless and impatient in the Church in Wales and cross the border to England, while clergymen who prefer sensing may become restless in the Church of England and cross the border into the Anglophone parts of Wales.

Conclusion

Psychological type theory provides a coherent account of how and why church leaders may differ in preferred leadership styles, one from another. The theory suggests that our preferred ways of leading emerge as an expression of who we are. The theory does not suggest that we cannot operate outside our psychological preferences, or, indeed, that we cannot become very competent in our less-preferred modes. For example, introverts can function as extraverts. There are, however, both theological and psychological implications for operating outside our preferred mode. Psychologically, habitual operation outside our preferred mode can be quite expensive in terms of energy resources. The introvert who functions habitually in extraverted mode is vulnerable to personal exhaustion and to psychological burnout. Theologically, habitual operation outside our preferred mode raises fundamental questions about our attitude toward and acceptance of the person we are created to be and intended to become.

Perhaps the Johannine Jesus who proclaimed that there are many rooms in his father's house (John 14.2) might also be challenging us to recognize that there is room for many styles of leadership within his Church.

References

Cattell, R. B., A. K. S. Cattell and H. E. P. Cattell (1993), *Sixteen Personality Factor Questionnaire: Fifth Edition (16PF5)*, Windsor: NFER-Nelson.

Costa, P. T., and R. R. McCrae (1985), *The Neo Personality Inventory*, Odessa, Florida: Psychological Assessment Resources.

Eysenck, H. J., and S. B. G. Eysenck (1991), *Manual of the Eysenck Personality Scales*, London: Hodder and Stoughton.

Francis, L. J. (2005), *Faith and Psychology. Personality, Religion and the Individual*, London: Darton, Longman and Todd.

Francis, L. J., C. L. Craig, M. Whinney, D. Tilley and P. Slater (forthcoming), *Psychological Profiling of Anglican Clergy in England Employing Jungian Typology to Interpret Diversity, Strengths, and Potential Weaknesses in Ministry*.

Francis, L. J., V. J. Payne and S. H. Jones (2001), 'Psychological Types of Male Anglican Clergy in Wales', *Journal of Psychological Type* 56, pp. 19–23.

Leech, K. (ed.) (1996), *Myers-Briggs: Some Critical Reflections*, Croydon: The Jubilee Group.

4. Knowing you're doing well

TERRY TENNENS

Introduction – let's dig a bit deeper

Knowing you are doing well is far more complex than first impressions suggest.

Church leaders may use measures such as:

- the number of people who attend Sunday worship
- the number of individuals who have come to new faith in Jesus Christ
- the number of infant or believers' baptisms that occur
- the size of the congregational membership
- the number of sacramental services that take place each week
- the size of the annual budget or church building complex
- the number of salaried and volunteer staff.

Church congregations can also have their own measures of success such as:

- the effectiveness of their leaders in corporate worship according to their Christian tradition: this can range from expositional preaching to manifesting the gifts of the Spirit or to a sacramental prestige or to the executive entrepreneur who expands the organization or to the bastion of preservation of all Church patterns
- if a pastor offers 24/7 pastoral care with frequent visitation and crisis interventions
- how well the church leader listens to their adherents, and takes on board the recommendations, whether these are preferred music styles, the colour of the rooms in church buildings, the range of ministries to different age groups in the congregation
- how effectively spiritual input is provided by the leader, measuring their ability as a biblical scholar and executive leader, fundraiser and evangelist, strong, but not too pushy.

Don't forget that the wider community also has expectations of the church leader:

- to undertake civic functions, such as the annual Christmas service for the community
- being available to preside at weddings, baptise their children and bury the dead, even if they may have never participated in the local church
- to be involved in schools, colleges, hospitals, older people's residential homes and the local government
- to be visible in the community, always being friendly, and speaking to everyone, but not interfering with secular institutions!

With such unrealistic expectations it is not surprising that recent reports[1] estimate that 25% or more of ordained ministers are leaving church leadership, through conflict, stress, ill-health and boredom. This is a serious problem for those responsible for the training and ongoing care of church leaders. Today, theological colleges and denominational resources invest in providing mentoring, counselling and professional development schemes for the church leader to be continually renewed and equipped. Good practice shows that every five years it is necessary to add extra learning to one's professional credibility for work by learning new skills.

Should you be a church leader reading this, how well do you think you are doing in the overall scheme of things? Using a fitness metaphor, do you feel in good shape? Do you compare favourably as a long-distance runner, or are you a sprinter by nature? Are there occasions to pause and recover? And how do you measure your performance? Dare we use the words performance, success and measure? Later on in this chapter I shall provide some tools to assist you in evaluating and taking some strategic decisions about the next phase of your church leadership.

This brings us to the question of 'power' and the church leader. View this as a matrix – person, organization, God, community, history, cross-cultural identities and values. With this in mind consider how well your organization receives spiritual leadership. Some churches and Christian organizations force its leaders into unhelpful patterns and moulds that are no longer life giving and can deny the Spirit of God. Just because a church leader excels in one organization does not automatically mean that they will be successful in all organizations.

I am cagey about using terms like 'successful church leadership' because it might imply different things to different people. Certainly Jesus was successful in his mission according to John's Gospel, waiting for the 'hour' to come. But from a civil and governmental perspective Jesus' contemporaries viewed him as a failed prophet. Therefore, knowing you are doing well depends on whose perspective it is viewed from. This is crucial if you are a people pleaser and gain credence by the congregation's satisfaction with you. Yet, there are seasons in ministerial leadership when sacrifice and unpopularity will be the experience because, like Moses, you may lead people into a new land, the promised land, and initial enthusiasm turns to complaint and criticism.

So, as leaders we need the bigger picture of God's perspective, the macro view as well as the local, congregation specific, micro view. This is important at a time when churches can be infected with instant consumerism, chat show style leadership and quick fix solutions that are no more than the morning mist that comes and goes. We must learn to hold onto the long view of the Kingdom of Christ.

It is important to be reminded that God calls us to be two things in church leadership.

First, to be *faithful to the calling* he has given to us. I am mindful throughout biblical history that no calling was identical. Isaiah's calling was different from Hosea's. Peter's calling was unique compared to Paul's. Although the functions may have been similar, the personality of each meant that they put their unique stamp upon the ministry God had called them to. Therefore, comparisons are usually futile. Instead, we are called to be faithful to the gospel of Jesus Christ. Please don't misread that faithfulness is maintenance, refusal to change the patterns. I mean faithfulness to the journey of following Jesus – this is the single most important criterion to know if one is doing well. Congregationally, faithfulness may be venturing into a fresh expression of mission to reach a group of people who are avoided. Faithfulness is staying the course even when you feel like waving the white flag of surrender. And it is about discipleship, the planned formation of learners of Christ.

Secondly, following faithfulness, we are *invoked into fruitfulness*. In the UK we have four seasons; in the same way, there are seasons in leadership and church life, of seedlings, to maturity, to decay and renewal. For some, this is governed by the liturgical year, for others, by a leading of the Spirit of Christ. Fruitfulness is multifaceted, it's growing outwardly and inwardly, taking up new opportunities and laying down some, going deeper or more generically. Consider the fruits of the Spirit, love, joy, peace, patience, goodness, faithfulness, gentleness and self-control. How are you excelling in these as a leader, as a church? Are you a liquorice allsorts church, where sameness is not the goal, but difference and unity as the family of God move into maturity? The ebb and flow of seasons and generations, as well as the influence of Church leaders, requires the long view.

Assessing our wellness by appraisals has mixed reviews among church leaders, either owing to the fact that governing bodies, like a diaconate or PCC, use them inappropriately or because the individual is insecure about reflection on their ministerial practice or plain arrogant that they know best! The following tools can be used for self-review or for wider evaluation, not only of church leaders but also of the wider leadership executive as well.

A self-analysis tool – what are my strengths, weaknesses, opportunities and threats?

Peter Drucker has left an enormous legacy in developing the science of leadership and management as an academic discipline for voluntary organizations and business. This Catholic Christian man's influence cannot be underestimated in bringing common sense and wisdom to the art of leadership. I commend his writings to you.

One of the familiar tools of analysis Drucker contributed is the SWOT analysis. This is a simple, yet effective model to learn from.

STRENGTHS	WEAKNESSES
Internal issues	
OPPORTUNITIES	THREATS
External factors	

Strengths

These are internal attributes. For example, as a leader to the church, strengths may include exemplary preaching or teaching, pastoral care, or community networking.

Weaknesses

These are negative factors that inhibit your contribution. For example, inflaming conflict rather than bringing resolution, or not being a good people person, or poor administration and coordination skills.

Opportunities

These are external environmental factors. For example, your skills as a community networker may mean that you quickly spot a need in the community and draw the church and others together to respond to it. Or as a pastoral carer you can develop strategies for meeting the needs in the wider community linking with Social Services.

Threats

These are external factors that can negatively impact your leadership. These factors may cause the church to have a poor reputation in the wider community, for example, because it doesn't deliver what it says it will do. Or it may be a change in the funding of local councils that will have a knock-on effect on your initiatives, such as the carer and toddler group. Also, a lack of ambassadorial skills within the church can inhibit a positive resolution.

If the SWOT analysis is used for self-assessment, try to be as clear and open as possible. You may wish to have a spouse or trusted Christian friend comment to confirm and reveal hidden strengths and weaknesses.

Evaluating competences – our comfortable and uncomfortable zones

It is natural that we always seek to operate within our 'comfort zone'. This is the operating environment of the leader, where he or she feels safe to excel using their skills and to apply leadership. Our human default mechanism always moves us to that which is comfortable, easier and secure.

However, if we are intent on being leaders who are growing and developing throughout our service, then we shall be confronted with experiencing new scenarios that demand we operate in a different setting. Cross-cultural missioners are familiar with this, laying aside a set of assumptions of one culture to embrace those of a different culture, its, honourable norms and values. I have a friend who returned to the UK after serving for 25 years in South Asia as a missionary and found it to be most uncomfortable to be back in a British culture that had changed unrecognizably.

My sense is that a healthy leader will operate well in their comfort zone-uncomfortable zone and excel if the ratio is 60/40 comfort/discomfort or at most 70/30.

Should that ratio be 90/10 comfort/discomfort, I fear the adaptable learning that occurs has minimal effect on the leader.

If the ratio were 40/60 comfort/discomfort, then it seems likely this rough ride of change may cause the leader to disengage through breakdown, exhaustion, ineffectiveness, resignation or dismissal.

In my last church there was a superb carer and toddler group. For me, as a young male minister without children, to walk into a room filled with 30 mothers and carers, who were not part of the church, filled me with fear and it was like leaping off a high diving board. However, the weekly routine of going along soon became a crucial part of my ministry and the discomfort turned to comfort.

Too much comfort can lead to boredom, poor performance and lack of awareness to spot the opportunities to engage and develop as a leader.

Comfort checklist

Area of church leadership	Comfort zone	Discomfort zone	Retain	Refresh	Action to be taken	Review date
Worship menu – Breadth and depth						
Preaching and teaching style						
Pastoral care						
Community service						

Area of church leadership	Comfort zone	Discomfort zone	Retain	Refresh	Action to be taken	Review date
Evangelistic initiatives						
Global mission						
Personal spiritual input						
Fresh theological learning						
Inter-personal style						

This sample checklist can be adapted to your own descriptions. The responses in the comfort/discomfort zones could be responded to using the following measurements:

Performance related
- Hot   = Really excel
- Warm = Good at
- Tepid = Do okay
- Cool   = Perform poorly
- Cold   = Danger, keep out!

Attitude related
1 = Really like
2 = Positive about
3 = Content to get on with
4 = Dislike
5 = Loathe

You may dislike pastoral care, but actually be really good at it. It's worth comparing your sheet with a trusted member of the leadership team or congregation who you can be transparent with, to give you an outsider's view.

Critical incident reports – learning through practice

Checklist

Public document QUESTION	RESPONSE
Date, place, persons involved and time?	
Define the problem	
Generate alternate solutions	
Evaluate and select an alternative	
The next steps to selecting the solution	
Personal reflection QUESTION	RESPONSE
How do I evaluate my performance?	• Peace-keeping • Achieve the target • Gain group participation • Motivate others to get involved • People leave feeling good to have been at the meeting
What did I do well?	
What did I feel uncomfortable about?	
Did I communicate clearly?	
How did I manage conflict?	
What methods of communication did I use?	• Spoken • OHP • Powerpoint • Small groups • Leadership team members (pcc / elders / deacons)
What improvements can I make handling these situations?	

The action-centred model

John Adair, the first professor of leadership studies in a UK university, developed the action model based on the following:

The task

What are we here for? What has been given to us to aim directly for?

The team

What means, resources and people are required to work toward achieving the task? What competencies, skills and character are necessary to build a team to be effective in the aims? Who has a desire or passion or enthusiasm to see the task achieved and can assist in making it happen?

The team's roles will include such things as project management, where their knowledge and expertise, their direct competencies, lie in those areas. Other team skills will be necessary, from spiritual support, through communications, to fund development and financial controls. The team leader has a responsibility to equip, encourage and task the specialist leaders to release their groups for effective work.

The individual

As team leader, how can I minister to the individual? Relational leadership is imperative in this model, one of sustenance as well as challenge. Jesus tells the story of the 99 sheep and the 1 that gets lost. The shepherd knows their sheep!

Can you articulate in a couple of minutes your function in the action-orientated leadership model?

The seven core values of a mission church

The Centre for Mission Accompaniment (CMA) <www.mission-accompaniment.co.uk> has developed one of the widest UK pilot projects for assessing how churches are engaged in mission and how their leadership impacts the local community. This action-learning project lasted over a decade and was undertaken in more than 75 churches from Catholic to Pentecostal churches. Each church had a **Mission Companion** alongside them for a period ranging from 18 months to five years to assist the church in mission.

Although this is nothing new, since mission enablers, missioners and consultants have been around for some time, the unique contribution of the CMA's methodology was the selection of a Mission Companion from a different Christian church than the church being accompanied. For this to occur, rapport between the host church and the Mission Companion was necessary, a clear working agreement and understanding of their respective roles and responsibilities, with regular reviews of their activities. Mission Companions' skills grow from their experience of the Church in different places, whether local churches, regional church bodies, mission agencies and national leadership of denominations. Also, rapport depended on the length of time during which they had worked together, from 18 months to 3 years, to assist sustainable mission practice.

Of course, mission accompaniment is nothing new. The worlds of sport, education and business have been using it for the last decade under different names:

- Coaches
- Mentors
- Facilitators

The role of Mission Companion has close links with those of spiritual adviser, of listener – both to God and the church, as well as the world; of coach in encouraging the church, describing what they hear the church is saying or not saying about its inner and outer life; of mentor in articulating God's vision for the community and having the discipline to develop action plans and to report on their implementation at regular meetings of the Mission Companion with coordination teams.

The seven cores values of CMA provide the methodology through which the Mission Companion and the church address areas of focus, attention and action – these provide a means of ensuring 360-degree leadership!

1 Focusing vision
2 Building local partnerships
3 Sharing faith and values
4 Nourishing daily living
5 Developing shared leadership
6 Becoming learning communities
7 Contributing to and participating in wider church networks

The power of focus

Peter Drucker use to be asked 'what are the qualities of a leader?'[2] His response was to dispel the idea that being a leader is enough – he declared that was misleadership! What matters is not the leader's charisma, rather the leader's mission. What is the mission of this church or organization? This is fundamental and one of the questions that is frequently overlooked by the church.

The leader among the people needs to affirm **concrete action goals** and that begins with a simple mission statement that everyone can remember, agree and commit to. What is usually omitted once the mission statement is agreed to by the congregation is the subsequent question: **what is my contribution to the goal?** Therefore, the task of the leader is to convert the church or organization's mission statement into specifics. The mission statement may be forever, but the goals can be short term or until the mission is accomplished.

Furthermore, the mission statement and strategic goals can end up looking like a series of good intentions. However, leaders must resist this at all costs and focus the thinking on the strengths and abilities of the church. For instance, you might have an elderly congregation and what they do well is welcome people, whether young or old, new to the church or familiar. Use that strength to fulfil one of the goals: for example, establishing an afternoon tea gathering for their peers or young parents.

Look outside the church to the needs of the community and ask the question, where can we with our limited means, that include money, people and competence, really make a difference? What can we really do well? What do we really believe in and are willing to invest ourselves in? Be specific.

Drucker says that mission statements need: 'opportunities, competence and commitment'.[3] All three need to be present otherwise the mission of the organization will fail. An example of a mission statement and strategic goals from International Justice Mission is appended at the end of this chapter.

Conclusion

As we have seen, there are means to enable church leaders to develop and improve. Ultimately 'knowing you are doing well' is a combination of character, attitude and spirituality.

Character

Leaders of the 00s are no longer the cheer leaders (if they ever were), or Chief Executive Officers or gurus of their churches. Robert Greenleaf developed a series of essays that only now are beginning to see their larger effect upon leaders of organizations, entitled *The Power of Servant Leadership*. Since the authority and status of church leaders' position in the world has diminished, for good or ill, now more than ever they have to earn the respect of and right to influence others. Integrity is critical in church leadership. What you see is what you get! No Watergates, Enrons or Swaggarts to undermine the importance of walking the talk. Our Lord himself is the pinnacle of servant leadership with the bucket and towel in John 13.

Let your character be transparent to those you influence – for it will either inhibit or empower the bonds of trustworthiness and so enable others to flourish.

Attitude

I well remember the translation of the New Testament word *mathetes* as a learner of Christ. This is a lifelong pilgrimage of following the Lord, correcting negative habits and acquiring new ones.

Attitude will also affect the health of your leadership role, from how you handle the people whom you dislike to how you operate outside your comfort zones and handle such things as money and power in the church.

Spirituality

You cannot divorce character from attitudes to spiritual life. The hymn in the New Testament letter to the Philippians (2.5) refreshes our character, attitude and spirituality when we are once more reminded of the emptying of Jesus (*kenosis*) and our call to empty ourselves of ego. That does not mean relinquishing leadership, but using power for the purpose of the Kingdom of God. Today's informality hides the use of power, which nevertheless is used.

Which brings us back to the pivotal issue of knowing you are doing well.

- Are you faithful in your calling to lead?
- Are you in the place God wants you?
- Are you submitted to God?
- Are you cooperating with the Spirit of God?

Each of these can be an assignment in its own right. However, I think more than ever Christian leaders need to recover the biblical imperative to **celebrate** the achievements, however insignificant or profound. Celebration is a practice Jesus encourages. Linked to this is the need to take ourselves less seriously, not less professionally! Therefore, bring the **fun** (not frivolity) back into church leadership, the fun of seeing the miracle-making God at work.

Explore

- Coaching, mentoring and mission accompaniment
- Spiritual direction and listening companions
- Professional development via tailored post-graduate studies
- Myers-Briggs and other self-awareness tests
- Develop a 1–3-year personal (spirituality) and professional (developmental) plan
- As a preacher, develop a group to develop the sermon with you – the range of issues from the text
- As a leader, gather professional leaders to explore means and methods from their professional disciplines to exchange and enhance the church's functioning

Notes

1. Beasley-Murray, 1995, pp. 1–2.
2. Drucker, 1990, p. 2.
3. Ibid., p. 3.

References and further reading

Beasley-Murray, P. (1995), *A Call to Excellence*, London: Hodder & Stoughton.
Beasley-Murray, P. (1998), *Power for God's Sake*, Carlisle: Paternoster.
Coate, M. A. (1990), *Clergy Stress: The Hidden Conflicts in Ministry*, London: SPCK.
Croft, S. (1999), *Ministry in Three Dimensions*, London: Darton, Longman & Todd.
Dawn, M., and E. H. Peterson (2000), *The Unnecessary Pastor*, Vancouver: Regent College.
De Bono, E. (2006), *Why So Stupid? How the Human Race Has Never Really Learned to Think*, London: Blacknall.
Dever, M. (2004), *Nine Marks of a Healthy Church*, Wheaton: Crossway.
Drucker, P. F. (1990), *Managing the Non-profit Organization*, Oxford: Butterworth-Heinemann.

Goleman, D. (1998), *Working with Emotional Intelligence*, London: Bloomsbury.

Goleman, D. (2002), *The New Leaders*, London: Little Brown.

Greanleaf, R. (1998), *The Power of Servant Leadership*, San Francisco: Berret Koehler.

Herrick, V., and I. Mann (1998), *Jesus Wept*, London: Darton, Longman & Todd.

Howard, S., and D. Wellbourn (2004), *The Spirit at Work Phenomenon*, London: Azure.

Johnson, S. (1998), *Who Moved My Cheese?*, London: Vermilion.

MacDonald, G. (1984), *Ordering Your Private World*, Godalming: Highland.

Macintosh, R. (2002), *The Rule of St Benedict: Nine Disciplines for Effective Leadership*, Cambridge: The Leadership Institute.

Maxwell, J. C. (2000), *Failing Forward*, Nashville: Thomas Nelson.

Parker, R. (1992), *Free to Fail*, London: Triangle/SPCK.

Peterson, E. H. (1992), *Under the Unpredictable Plant*, Michigan: Eerdmans.

Richardson, R. W. (1996), *Creating a Healthier Church*, Minneapolis: Fortress.

Riem, R. (2005), *The Soul in Leadership*, Cambridge: Grove.

Sanford, J. A. (1982), *Ministry Burnout*, London: Arthur James.

Tearfund (2003), *Church, Community and Change*, London: Tearfund.

Tennens, T. R. (2007), *Journey into Growth*, London: CTBI.

Appendix – International Justice Mission (IJM): Mission statement and strategic goals

Mission

IJM is a Christian agency, led by human rights professionals, that helps people overseas, suffering from injustice and oppression, who cannot rely on local authorities for relief. The agency documents and monitors conditions of abuse and oppression, educates the Church and public about the abuses, and mobilizes intervention on behalf of the victims.

Strategic goals

1 To become an agency to whom the vast network of overseas Christian ministries regularly refer cases of abuse and oppression from the communities where they serve.

2 To provide effective documentation and intervention services (directly or by referral to other entities) to the victims of abuse and oppression who live in the communities where overseas Christian ministries serve.

3 To develop the relationships and tools of communication through which the Holy Spirit might fundamentally change the level of spiritual conviction within the Christian Church, in America,

Europe and around the world, about the need and opportunity to be biblically engaged in seeking justice on behalf of those who suffer abuse and oppression in our world.

4 To develop the spiritual support necessary to pursue these goals with a level of excellence that sets a standard for Christian ministry.

5 To develop the financial base and organizational proficiency necessary to pursue these goals with a level of excellence that sets a standard for the human rights profession.

Communicating and Sharing
What's Happening to Everybody

5. Sharing what's happening/ 'Selling' the idea

Riding waves of liturgical change*

VAUGHAN ROBERTS

Introduction

Water has long been recognized as a metaphor for organizational change and can be used in a number of different ways. The social psychologist Kurt Lewin has described such change coming about in terms of the thawing and freezing of water (see Hatch, 1997); the management consultant and academic Gareth Morgan has written about the fluidity of organizational flux and transformation (Morgan, 1997); while Stephen Cummins, a professor of strategy, has illustrated his understanding of the strategic challenges of change with an image drawn from ancient Greece – that of the *kubernetes*, the person steering the ship through dangerous inshore currents (Cummings, 2002). My own interest in the different ways in which this metaphor can be employed has been explored in two papers (Roberts, 1997, 2002), and the latter concluded by suggesting the contrast between the apparent permanency of land and fluidity of the ocean might be a useful image for the life of the Church: 'The place where the stability of land and the fluidity of the sea meet is the beach or coastline. It could be that in using water as an organizational metaphor the Church is implicitly called to live on the edge of both change and constancy, embracing a dialectic of conflict and consensus' (Roberts, 2002, p. 39). This section aims to go on from such a *theoretical* background to water as a metaphor for organizational change, and explore how it might work out in the *practical* sphere of local church ministry. In particular, how the image of 'surfing' might help understand change processes and explain them to others.

The specific context for this study is that of liturgical change which weaves in another personal, longstanding interest. It was the focus of a paper written in my first post as an Anglican minister offering reflections on liturgical practice in a suburban environment (Roberts, 1989). That concluded with a call for churches to offer a broad range of worship and, with hindsight, reflects all the idealism of youth:

> There will be those who need a quiet reflective service, those who need a formal 'performance' style of worship, others who want to worship God in a much more informal setting. Those who form the 'fringe' of the body of Christ are as vital to its life as those who are at the eucharistic centre. The *Book of Common Prayer* and the *Alternative Service Book* can actually meet the needs for diversity and unity. (Roberts, 1989, p. 14)[1]

That vision of liturgical diversity within ecclesial unity ('conflict and consensus') continues to be a key theme in my own understanding of local ministry and will be an important element in these reflections upon my experience of bringing about liturgical change in two very different contexts. The first of these is a three-parish group in a rural setting called the Benefice of Hillside and the second is a more urban parish of St Edward's, Old Town.[2]

Since what follows is grounded in personal experience it might be helpful to state what this implies. First, I'm not arguing that the most important example of organizational change is liturgical. It is my hope that, if there are lessons to be learned here, they could be applicable to other areas of church life and not only worship. Second, this is not a blueprint for parish ministry. It is not *The 10 Commandments for Strategic Renewal of Your Church*. What this chapter describes is the way one person went about things with the resources available. This will vary according to circumstances and the aim is to present some reflections on practice which will be helpful to others. Third, this is an example of a Church of England vicar at work in a particular tradition and as such it comes with the organizational vocabulary and structure of that denomination. Nevertheless, it is my hope that ministers in other traditions may be able to use some of these ideas in their situations. This chapter seeks to keep management jargon to a minimum and comes in the form of two case studies and a conclusion. Each study begins with (1) an outline of the context for ministry; followed by (2) a review of the liturgical changes that took place; then (3) it will explore some of the processes and thinking which contributed to these waves of change; and, finally, (4) show some statistical outcomes. To give a sense of immediacy the contexts of both studies are written in the present tense.

Case study 1: The benefice of Hillside

1 Context

Hillside is a rural benefice of three parishes – St Andrew, St Botulph and St Catherine.

1 **St Andrew** is in a village with a population of around 500 that has a main road running through it linking a major seaport and regional centre to a small cathedral city. It has a Church of England voluntary aided primary school, a pub, a general store, a residential care home, a village hall and a parish church. Until two generations ago all property was owned by the local Dudwell estate and there are people in the village who can recall the vicar living in the large vicarage (now the care home) with a cook, maid and chauffeur. The previous Earl Dudwell had attended church regularly and held some of the key lay offices, but the present Earl is much less directly involved.
2 **St Botulph** is in a village with a population of around 250 people. A busy minor road passes by the village, taking local traffic and commuters to the major port, which is also a significant financial centre. The village has a pub, a village hall and a parish church. A generation ago it consisted mostly of working farms but these have gradually closed or amalgamated and it has largely become a settlement for commuters. The church has a lively Sunday School.
3 **St Catherine** is in another village of around 500 people, also with a main route running through it, linking the port with another sizeable town. Its school and shop have closed down. It has a bus stop but no bus service. There is a residential care home, luxury hotel and a sports club, all of which depend on people from outside for their survival. The parish church is one of the last local community organizations but it is some way out of the main village. The local population is a mixture of a few significant farming families and incomers.

2 Liturgical changes

In the mid-1990s the benefice had a monthly pattern of services consisting of:[3]

First Sunday
8.00 a.m. Said Holy Communion (*BCP*) at St C
9.30 a.m. Choral Communion (*ASB* Rite B) at St A
6.30 p.m. Sung Evensong (*BCP*) at St B

Second Sunday

9.30 a.m.   Holy Communion with hymns and Sunday School (*ASB* Rite B) at St B

6.30 p.m.   Choral Evensong (*BCP*) at St A

Third Sunday

8.00 a.m.   Said Holy Communion (*BCP*) at St B

9.30 a.m.   Choral Communion (*ASB* Rite B) at St A

6.30 p.m.   Sung Evensong (*BCP*) at St C

Fourth Sunday

8.00 a.m.   Holy Communion (*BCP*) at St A

9.30 a.m.   Holy Communion with hymns and Sunday School (*ASB* Rite B) at St B

11.00 a.m.   Service of the Word in the residential care home at St C

Fifth Sunday

9.30 a.m.   Benefice Communion Service at St A, St B and St C on a rotational basis (*ASB* Rite B)

All the services, including the 'Service of the Word' at the residential care home, used traditional language and met the needs of those who attended worship. However, five years later the pattern had moved to this – with changes underlined and in bold:[4]

First Sunday

8.00 a.m.   Said Holy Communion (*BCP*) at St C

9.30 a.m.   <u>**Choral Family Service (*CW* Service of the Word)**</u> at St A

Second Sunday

9.30 a.m.   Holy Communion with hymns and Sunday School <u>**(*CW* [1]: Modern)**</u> at St B

6.30 p.m.   Choral Evensong (*BCP*) at St A

Third Sunday

8.00 a.m.   Said Holy Communion (*BCP*) at St B

9.30 a.m.   Choral Eucharist <u>**(*CW* [1]: Modern)**</u> at St A

<u>**11.00**</u> a.m.   <u>**Family Communion (*CW* [1]: Modern) at St C**</u>

Fourth Sunday

8.00 a.m.   Holy Communion (*BCP*) at St A

9.30 a.m.   Holy Communion with hymns & Sunday School <u>**(*CW* [1]: Modern)**</u> at St B

11.00 a.m.   Service of the Word in the residential care home at St C

Fifth Sunday

9.30 a.m.   Benefice Communion Service at St A, St B and St C on a
rotational basis **(*CW* [1]: Modern)**

3 Waves of change

This liturgical change came about in two waves: *Wave 1: The
Introduction of the Junior Choir*; and *Wave 2: The Introduction of Common
Worship.*

Wave 1: The junior choir

The first of two elements in this wave was the arrival into the benefice
of someone willing to set up a choir for children which would help
lead worship in the churches. Frances was a music graduate and a
teacher who had been involved with church choirs for much of her
life. She did not feel able to run the existing adult choir at St Andrew's
but was willing to start a junior choir which would sing in all three
churches. She also had two children who would be involved. The
second element was the local Church of England Primary School, of
which the vicar is a governor. This had reasonably close links with the
benefice, especially St Andrew's, to which the school went for a
termly service. Not only were the school willing to send a flier home
with all the children inviting any who wished to become part of the
new junior choir, but they also provided the school hall as a venue for
that choir to practise on Wednesday afternoons, following school.

There were two other contributory factors to this wave. First, the
number of people attending St Catherine's was very small. The community in which it was situated was the same size as the village in
which St Andrew's was set, but church attendance was considerably
lower. Interestingly, St Botulph had the smallest local population but
the highest degree of churchgoing. As a result, St Catherine's was
open to changing their services if it would draw more people into the
worshipping life of the church, and there was very little resistance to
stopping their poorly attended monthly evensong and trying a
monthly Family Eucharist instead. St Andrew's was more ambivalent
about exchanging one of their fortnightly services of Choral
Communion for a non-Eucharistic Family Service, but there were
sufficient numbers on the Church Council who felt the potential gain
was sufficiently attractive to try it as an experiment for a year. This
was the overall wave on which this aspect of organizational change
surfed and it was supported by other developments which emerged
following the changes. For instance, both St Andrew's and St
Catherine's decided independently that it would be good to offer

drinks and biscuits after their Family Services, which helped the congregation to mix afterwards.

Wave 2: Common worship

As already noted, my personal vision for church worship is one which encourages diversity. Furthermore, I would also argue that worship is one of the main expressions of Christian discipleship. In Graham Hughes's book *Worship as Meaning* he captures something of the contemporary multiplicity of culture with the delightful image of people who 'seem free to bring any sandwiches they like to the picnic of meaning' (Hughes, 2003, p. 199). In such a context, it is a crucial part of the Church's mission to offer a breadth of liturgy which will embrace the formal and informal, Eucharistic and non-Eucharistic, all-age worship and the Book of Common Prayer. Another significant factor in this evolving situation, which does not appear to be commented upon very often, is that, within those who have been life-long Anglicans, there are increasingly two groups – those who have been brought up using the traditional language of the *BCP* and those who have been brought up using modern language from Series 3, the *ASB* and *Common Worship*. While it is good that people are exposed to new liturgical experience, it is also important to provide that which is familiar – both in traditional *and* modern language.

It is also worth noting that it's not the role of the vicar to provide only worship that he or she finds meaningful. We have to acknowledge that at any point in our ministry we shall be at a particular stage in our own life. Whether we are single or married, have children or do not have children, have work experience outside church or have been ordained for most of our working life – we are all passing through stages of life when certain things will mean more to us than at other times. It is right that such experience shapes and informs ministry, but equally clergy should remain open to the fact that many other people are having many other forms of experience – making 'sandwiches' with completely different fillings to use Graham Hughes's image – and these other realms must be acknowledged and honoured as well. Self-awareness and awareness of others is an important element in this process. As Julia Balogun and Veronica Hope Hailey have observed in their book on strategic change:

Individuals view organisations in fundamentally different ways. Without realising it, change agents often allow their personal philosophy to influence the change approach and interventions they choose. As a result, they may give limited consideration, if any, to the actual change context and its needs. Change agents should be driven by the needs of the organisation rather than by their own perceptions or prejudices of what has constituted 'good' change management in the past. It may also be easier for change agents to understand, and if necessary argue against, other people's prejudices or biases if they are armed with a degree of self-awareness. (Balogun and Hailey, 2004, p. 9)

As will be clear from the initial monthly pattern of worship in the Benefice of Hillside, there was not a great deal of diversity offered in the liturgical diet. All services used traditional language, either in the form of *BCP* or *ASB* Rite B. However, the breadth of worship being offered had broadened with the advent of the junior choir and the introduction of the 'Family Eucharist' and 'Family Service'. It is important to note that my aim was not the wholesale change of benefice liturgy. My vision of the Church is inclusive rather than exclusive and the objective was to widen the circle while at the same time keeping those who were already inside.

The opportunity to broaden the circle of worship presented itself through the replacement of the *ASB* with *Common Worship*. In particular, the resources provided by Praxis (www.praxisworship.org.uk) were especially helpful in explaining the changing context of worship and the more specific changes to worship. We introduced a series of seasonal booklets for the 9.30 a.m. services of Holy Communion at St Andrew and St Botulph, which were adapted following comments from the congregations. It is fair to say that not everyone was happy with these developments. One useful tip is not to be reticent about using encouraging statistics. The figures used in this paper were initially compiled to see what effect, if any, the junior choir was having on service attendance. If attendances have risen then it can be helpful to present that information as part of the report to the Annual Meeting, which allows those in favour of change to show their support and makes it harder for those who are resistant to these developments to press their case.[5]

4 Statistical changes

St Andrew

- April–March 1995/96

Sunday Total	Easter Day	Christmas Day	Harvest
877	80	120	80

- April–March 2001/02

Sunday Total	Easter Day	Christmas Day	Harvest
1789	120	252	120

St Botulph

- April–March 1995/96

Sunday Total	Easter Day	Christmas Day	Harvest
1398	42	108	40

- April–March 2001/02

Sunday Total	Easter Day	Christmas Day	Harvest
1532	49	128	68

St Catherine

- April–March 1995/96

Sunday Total	Easter Day	Christmas Day	Harvest
198	37	8	47

- April–March 2001/02

Sunday Total	Easter Day	Christmas Day	Harvest
580	14	120	69

Summary

These changes produced a significant effect on the numbers attending worship Sunday-by-Sunday, especially at St Andrew and St Catherine. The totals do not distinguish between adults and children or between communicants and non-communicants but they show a rise that was over twofold at St Andrew and nearly threefold at St Catherine. There were also significant rises in attendance at Christmas services for these two churches. Attendance at St Botulph was already the healthiest of the three and the church experienced less liturgical change, so there was less of a marked rise in their numbers.

Case study 2: The parish of St Edward, Old Town

1 Context

St Edward's is in the centre of Old Town which has a growing population, presently standing at around 25,000. This is served by four parish churches and a Local Ecumenical Partnership (LEP) who work as a town-wide team. There are five ministers, each of whom has responsibility for one centre of worship plus a role across the team. St Edward's has a well-established choral tradition and many people travel some distance to share in this type of worship. The parish itself is a mix of commercial building, council property and small, owner-occupier houses. In its analysis of the data from the 1991 census the diocesan statistical unit concluded that the level of deprivation in the parish itself meant that it was close to qualifying as an Urban Priority Area (UPA). There is little to suggest there has been a wholesale change in this situation since that time. Much of the contact with those residing in the parish comes through the occasional offices of baptisms, weddings and funerals rather than regular Sunday attendance. For the most part St Edward's liturgy is formal and traditional. The *BCP* is still widely used for Evensong, 8 a.m. Holy Communion and weekday services. The main exceptions are the weekly Choral Eucharist which is *Common Worship*: Order 1 – Traditional Language and the monthly Family Service, which is loosely based on *Common Worship*: Service of the Word.

2 Liturgical changes

In 2002/03, the pattern of worship at St Edward's was:

First Sunday
8.00 a.m.   Said Holy Communion (*BCP*)
10.00 a.m.   Family Service (*CW* Service of the Word)
11.00 a.m.   Choral Matins (*BCP*)
6.30 p.m.   Choral Eucharist (*CW*1: Traditional)

Second, Third, Fourth and Fifth Sundays
8.00 a.m.   Said Holy Communion (*BCP*)
10.30 a.m.   Choral Eucharist (*CW*1: Traditional)
6.30 p.m.   Choral Evensong (*BCP*)

In 2004/05 it had changed to:

First Sunday
8.00 a.m.   Said Holy Communion (*BCP*)
9.30 a.m.   Family Service (*CW* Service of the Word)
11.00 a.m.   Choral Matins (*BCP*)
6.30 p.m.   Choral Eucharist **(*CW* [1]: Modern)**

Second, Third, Fourth and Fifth Sundays
8.00 a.m.   Said Holy Communion (*BCP*)
10.30 a.m.   Choral Eucharist **(*CW* [1]: Modern)**
6.30 p.m.   Choral Evensong (*BCP*)

3 Waves of change

Wave 1: The family service

The monthly 'Family Service' at St Edward's was started by the Church Council's Ministry Sub-Committee and has a dedicated team of lay people who resource and lead the worship. It is attended by the St Edward's Guides and Brownies, the Sunday School and a training choir for the main boys' choir. As an existing wave within the church, it clearly had momentum and was seeking to serve a different congregation to the main Choral Eucharist. One potential way of bridging the gap between St Edward's and those local people who brought their children for baptism could be the Family Service. We now ask those parents whose children are baptized outside a main act of worship to come along to the next all-age service for their child to be welcomed into the family of the Church. Whether we see contemporary culture as increasingly secular or as increasingly spiritually diffuse, it is important to work harder to maintain the links which many parents still want to establish with the church when children are born or adopted. This change has had a significant impact on the shape and attendance at the Family Service. The unique thing about this change, in my experience, is that no one has ever complained! Those who are involved with the local church always appear to love the opportunity of welcoming those who have been baptized and those whose parents who come along seem to enjoy meeting other parents at a similar stage of life.

Another change which has helped to nurture this service is a renewed commitment to making the Family Service a regular fixture. Once again, this is not a particularly groundbreaking development but it is sometimes easy to miss the obvious. In a church where the main act of worship is the 10.30 a.m. Choral Eucharist, there were a number of occasions when it was justifiably felt that the monthly Family Service could be dropped and the Choral Eucharist reinstated. However, that sends out a potentially negative signal to those who come to the Family Service and make it even harder to build up a steady congregation. By making a commitment to that service come what may, it has helped to establish it more firmly in the regular pattern of worship at St Edward's.

A much more controversial wave of change was to move the start-time of the service forward by half an hour. This wave started from the general practice of having drinks and biscuits after mid-morning services but, because the 10.00 a.m. Family Service was followed by 11.00 a.m. Choral Matins, refreshments were often a hurried affair. The Ministry Sub-Committee wanted the Family Service congregation to have more time to get to know each other, so it suggested that the Family Service should move to 9.30 a.m. for a trial period and see whether the new time worked. As we shall see, the improved statistics for the Family Service in the 2004/05 period suggest that these three waves of changes have had a positive effect on attendances.

Wave 2: Easter Liturgy

When I arrived, the liturgical context at St Edward, Old Town, was very similar to that of the Benefice of Hillside, in that all the services used traditional language, either in the form of *BCP* or *Common Worship*: Order 1 (with the single exception of the monthly Family Service). Since, by that time, *Common Worship* had already been established there was not a convenient wave about to break on the local church from the wider ocean but there were a number of ripples which came together to form a swell. The first of these was the rather mundane but chaotic practice of welcoming people to the 10.30 a.m. Choral Eucharist. This involved handing people a service booklet, a sheet with lectionary readings and prayers, a hymn book and a notice sheet (and a further sheet with additional liturgy on certain special occasions). Numerous comments were made that this was immensely complicated not only for regulars but also especially for visitors and it would be helpful if something could be done in this respect.

The second element in this swell was that, prior to the change of vicar at St Edward's, there had also been a change in the director of music. For the first time in its history, the centuries-old and predominantly male choral tradition would be led by a woman. Gillian had come with a background in cathedral music and, during the period between vicars, she had introduced some significant liturgical changes, especially at Christmas and Easter, and these developments in worship incorporated the use of modern language. Special service leaflets had been printed up for these occasions and no comment was made about the move to modern language. Lent was a particularly complex time liturgically, which involved worshippers receiving five items on arrival at church. By introducing a new, weekly service leaflet in the style of those already produced for special occasions, however, it was possible to reduce the number of things given out on the door from five to two. Since this was generally agreed to be a help-ful development, it was a relatively straightforward step to continue using such a leaflet after Easter with the modern language version and thus provide a better liturgical balance. There were some critical comments but generally this change has been welcomed.

4 Statistical changes

	April–March 2002/03	April–March 2004/05
8 a.m. Holy Communion	962	1009
10.30 a.m. Eucharist	4644	5136
Choral Evensong	1753	2633
Family Service	620	1058
Harvest Eucharist	170	174
Christmas Eve/Day	1688	1662
Good Friday Services	124	261
Easter Day Services	574	612
Sunday Total	**12,109**	**14,343**

Summary

These changes in liturgy at St Edward's correspond to a significant change in the numbers attending worship Sunday-by-Sunday. The regular 10.30 a.m. Choral Eucharist and the Family Service show a healthy increase. The additional worshippers on Good Friday are in large part due to an additional All-Age Service, while the large rise in numbers attending *BCP* Choral Evensong is attributable to a series of guest speakers during Lent.

Conclusion: riding the waves of change

In this section I have outlined some of my experience of bringing about liturgical change in two different contexts of ministry – the benefice of Hillside and the parish of St Edward. My approach has been to look for already existing waves of change, take advantage of that momentum and then 'surf' on the breaker or the swell. As was stated at the outset, this is not presented as an off-the-peg blueprint for everyone to follow – in my experience such programmes are rarely *directly* transferable. Instead, my aim has been to show how an organizational metaphor can be followed through, not only to aid the process of organizational sensemaking but also to facilitate the process of change itself. However, readers will perceive these matters in different ways and one means of illustrating this is to ask individuals to plot the changes described here onto Balogum & Hailey's types of 'change path' (Balogum and Hailey, 2004, p. 20):

End result

	Transformation	Realignment
Incremental	**Evolution**	**Adaptation**
Big bang	**Revolution**	**Reconstruction**

Nature

For some people, the changes outlined in this chapter would be merely 'adaptive'; for others, they would be 'revolutionary'; and, for others, they would fall somewhere in between – 'evolutionary' or 'reconstructive'. This brings us back to a key point that Balogun and Hailey make a number of times, that self-awareness is a key component in the change process. They argue that the first aspect of a capability for managing change is:

> the ability of individuals within an organisation to manage change within themselves. Anyone who has lived through a personal crisis such as a bereavement or a divorce will understand that personal change can be an overwhelming experience. However, the more reflective the individual, the more they can expect to learn from the experience, and hopefully then be able to manage the process more effectively if it recurs. (Balogun and Hailey, 2004, p. 77)

Some will find making the practical connections with this chapter harder than others – perhaps your church is less liturgically structured than the ones I served? Alternatively, you may be aware that some of the resources which I have had to hand will not be available in your own setting. In many ways that does not matter because what this section argues is not that others should do as I have done but instead look for comparable opportunities in their own context – to use the image of sea and surf: find your own beach and your own board for surfing. But more than anything, as we undertake such organizational 'surfing', we need to know and understand ourselves. As Stephen Cummings, who has also used this image, has observed:

> It goes without saying that no surfer can make waves; he or she must work with what the gods give them. But a competitive surfer's skill is related to their ability to pick out from all the waves occurring in the environment at that time, the ones that suit their objectives and particular style, and then riding or promoting them for all they are worth. In organizations, too, it is a matter of identifying and connecting to those historical currents that one wants to repeat and build upon toward the future. (Cummings, 2002, p. 278)

Organizational change is an unavoidable element within the life of the Church in the twenty-first century and, as such, those who exercise leadership within the Body of Christ must learn how cope with it and how to help those they serve share in that learning process too.

Notes

* This chapter began as a presentation to the Coventry Diocese Continuing Ministerial Education (CME) leadership course.

1. In some ways, this could be seen as a liturgical precursor to Chris Anderson's more recent argument that endless *commercial* choice is creating unlimited *cultural* choice (Anderson, 2006).
2. Place names are fictitious.
3. *BCP* = 1662 *Book of Common Prayer*; *ASB* = 1980 *Alternative Service Book*.
4. *CW* = 2000 *Common Worship*; *CW* [1]: Modern = 2000 *Common Worship* Order 1: Modern Language.
5. It can also be worth publishing the report and statistics in the first issue of the parish magazine following the Annual Meeting, which will reach a wider audience than the relatively small number who attend.

References

Anderson, Chris (2006), *The Long Tail: How Endless Choice Is Creating Unlimited Demand*, London: Random House Business Books.

Balogun, Julia, and Veronica Hope Hailey (2004), *Exploring Strategic Change*, 2nd edn, Harlow and London: Prentice Hall.

Cummings, Stephen (2002), *Recreating Strategy*, London and Thousand Oaks: Sage.

Hatch, Mary Jo (1997), *Organization Theory: Modern, Symbolic and Postmodern Perspectives*, Oxford and New York: Oxford University Press.

Hughes, Graham (2003), *Worship as Meaning: A Liturgical Theology for Late Modernity*, Cambridge: Cambridge University Press.

Morgan, Gareth (1997), *Images of Organization*, London and Thousand Oaks: Sage.

Roberts, Vaughan S. (1989), 'Umberto Eco and the "Habit" of Family Communion', *Modern Churchman*, NS, 31, 2, pp. 10–15.

Roberts, Vaughan S. (1997), 'The Sea of Faith: After Dover Beach', *Modern Churchman*, NS, 38, 3, pp. 25–34.

Roberts, Vaughan S. (2002), 'Water as an Implicit Metaphor for Organizational Change within the Church', *Implicit Religion*, 5, 1, pp. 29–40.

Relating to the World of Work

6. Work as worship

TIM HARLE

Setting the scene

'The expectations imposed upon Christian businesspeople resemble how women were treated during the Victorian era in regard to sex. Godly women were supposed to do it but not to enjoy it.'[1] It is fair to say that the worlds of church and work have not always been comfortable bedfellows. Two authors, who have done more than many to encourage exploration across boundaries, share a common theme. Richard Higginson protests against the 'mutual marginalisation' of Christianity and business,[2] while Malcolm Grundy writes of the 'scandal of the separation of Church and Industry since the Reformation'.[3]

Against this background, it may be helpful to sketch out what this modest contribution seeks to achieve. First, it offers pointers to some key biblical and theological contributions. Secondly, it outlines a perspective on getting into the world of work. Thirdly, it suggests some possibilities for relating work to church(es), with a focus on local ecclesial communities. Lastly, it points to representative resources which can lead to a deeper understanding and engagement with the subject.

One further introductory point. The review presented here acknowledges a range of positions in terms of theology, ecclesiology, politics and economics. Casting the net beyond our familiar circles can be productive. As one group of Anglo-Catholics notes, 'we have found that on many issues we have more in common with the liberation thinkers in the Roman Church or with Mennonites or with the evangelical radicals from Sojourners – or with non-Christians – than we have with other Anglo-Catholics'.[4]

Theological grounding

A number of books offer distinctive contributions.[5] Here we can highlight a few key pointers.

71

Work in creation

The canon which Christians and Jews share opens with two key dramas. God created the heavens and the earth, saw everything he had made was very good, and rested from all the work that he had done (Genesis 1.1, 31, 2.2). Then, in the garden, the two companions find the language of paradise replaced by toil and sweat (Genesis 3.17, 19). Work is at the very heart of the divine mystery.

Workers in the Bible

We can only scratch the surface. Constructing the tabernacle required 'skill, intelligence and every kind of craft' (Exodus 35.31). Ezra-Nehemiah records examples of work, organization and leadership as the temple is rebuilt. Shepherds abound, from Ezekiel through the Psalms to the Gospels. The 12 disciples represent a diverse mix, from fisherman to tax collector. Paul was a tentmaker. The Gospels even make one reference to banking, in the parable of the talents (Matthew 25.27 and parallels).[6]

Incarnation

But it is a carpenter who stands at the crux of the Christian faith. As the Eastern tradition reminds us, earth is lifted to heaven and heaven is come down to earth. Surely this impels us to believe that nothing on earth is beyond the interest, the saving grace, of the God who creates, redeems and sustains us. And that includes work: works of service, home making, caring, paid employment.

Work as worship

A fine New Testament scholar of the twentieth century reminds us that 'much of what is generally meant by worship in ordinary Christian usage . . . is represented in the New Testament vocabulary by *leitourgia* and *latreia*, "service". The modern Christian application of terms such as "divine service" or "a service" may tend to obscure the fact that in its New Testament context the word "service" does literally mean the work of servants'.[7] Professor Moule goes on to point out that 'one of the regular Hebrew words for worship, *abodah*, is derived from the same root as the word for the suffering "servant"'.[8] At the very least, this suggests a link between work and worship.

Some other considerations

- **Meaning**. The thesis that the rise of capitalism was linked to the Protestant (especially Puritan) work ethic is associated with the names of Max Weber and R. H. Tawney.[9] There are different nuances today, but the basic thesis remains that people need to find dignity and meaning in their work.[10]
- **Relationships**. Many point to the power of the Holy Trinity as a paradigm of relationships, including those at work. Unfortunately, not all suggestions are helpful. One book suggests the Father as chairman of the board, Jesus as Chief Executive Officer and the Holy Spirit as legal counsel.[11] Another, on relational leadership,[12] somehow manages to make no discernible reference to the profound significance of the Holy Trinity in its 216 pages.
- *Opus dei*. The Benedictine tradition seems to have a particular resonance with the world of work. An abbot of Ampleforth can contribute to a conversation about doing business with Benedict.[13] The relevance of stability and the conversion of life are considered in the chapter on sustaining a process of change. For our current topic, a key focus is on *opus dei*, the work of God in the daily cycle of community life. Father Dermot Tredget OSB from Douai Abbey can ask whether the Rule of St Benedict provides an ethical framework for a contemporary theology of work, and broadly answer in the affirmative.[14]

Bringing spirit to work

As we have seen, the worlds of work and faith have often remained at a distance. In the middle of last century, the worker priest movement flourished briefly in France, and pioneers appeared in England, encouraged by the Sheffield Industrial Mission.[15] Today's mix of Ministers in Secular Employment, Self-Supporting or Non-Stipendiary Ministers, Licensed Lay Ministers, Readers and Lay Preachers represent a kaleidoscope of attempts to bridge the divide (often far removed from the shop floor origins of the pioneers).

In recent years, the business community has witnessed a growing trend of those who are no longer prepared to keep their work and spiritual lives apart. One early writer dedicates his book 'to those who have the courage to bring their whole selves to work'.[16] A movement, generally referred to as Spirit at (or in) Work, is growing.[17] Proponents tend to emphasize that 'spirituality' should not be confused with organized religion, though Douglas Hicks[18] has challenged this. He promotes a 'respectful pluralism'. Many Christians would welcome the opportunity to be more explicit about the contribution their faith makes. Observing the US scene, Laura Nash from Harvard Business School has spoken of a taboo being broken, resulting in an 'uneasy détente' between business leaders and the churches over the place of faith at work.[19]

We can do no more than point to the excellent introduction provided by Sue Howard and David Welbourn in their *Spirit at Work Phenomenon* (see Further Reading). Asking, What is Spirituality?, they reach the thoroughly postmodern conclusion that 'our outlook is made up of a mishmash of ideas' and unpicking our inheritance 'is a personal task which no one else can complete for us' (p. 42). Their central theme is 'that personal transformation is the gateway to leading organizational transformation' (p. 166). Here is an individualistic approach which characterizes much Western society and religion. 'In our Western culture, "self-awareness" is often just self-obsession, too much "me, me, me".'[20]

Spirituality can be criticized as vague: a dictionary entry states that it 'is difficult to define'.[21] Yet a pioneering study found, contrary to conventional wisdom, that there was nearly unanimous agreement on a definition of spirituality as 'the basic desire to find ultimate meaning and purpose in one's life and to live an integrated life'.[22] A common theme among spirituality writings is our interconnectedness. Howard and Welbourn refer to four connections: to self, others, nature and higher power.

Religious language is often used in a business context: charisma, faith, saviour, transformation, values, vision.[23] Not all are sympathetic, although Georgeanne Lamont has commented[24] that those who are uncomfortable about allowing a spiritual dimension at work will nevertheless refer to a task as 'soul destroying' or of feeling 'dispirited'. A NHS trust convened a meeting on spirituality, but omitted to invite chaplains on the grounds that it wouldn't be of interest to them.

One important consequence of such an approach is that two topics that are often treated separately – Business Ethics and Corporate Social Responsibility (CSR) – can naturally be linked in an integrated way. Gerald Cavanagh notes the opportunities for cross-fertilization between spirituality, corporate ethics and CSR.[25] As an example, the scope and meaning of the sustainability agenda can usefully be explored from this perspective.

Not all are positive about spirituality at work. A Business School professor dismissed the 'tree huggers'.[26] Richard Roberts is scathing about managerialism and commodification of the soul.[27] And Dennis Tourish has highlighted the dangers of coercive persuasion in leadership.[28]

Bringing work to the worshipping community

We are now in a position to consider some of the avenues whereby aspects of work can be integrated into church life. As we saw in our theological introduction, there is a profound link between work and worship, so this provides a good place to start.

Work in worship

Liturgical resources vary. In comparison with some provision, where the world of work tends to invisibility, the Roman Catholic *Book of Blessings* deserves special mention. A glance through the table of contents of the Abridged Edition[29] reveals resources relating to a building site, office, shop or factory, boats and fishing gear, and tools or other equipment, to name but a few.

The churches' year

The rhythm of the churches' year provides specific opportunities to highlight the world of work. Some are recent (Victorian) inventions, but Harvest Festivals (autumn), Plough Sunday (winter), Rogation-tide (spring) and Lammastide (summer) all provide opportunities for a focus on work. The Church of England has recently dipped its toe in the water for the first time, reflecting a rural provenance, with 'The Agricultural Year' in its *Times and Seasons* volume.[30]

Another possibility is around the traditional link with May Day: the Industrial Christian Fellowship promotes denoting the Sunday before 1 May as Industrial Sunday. But consideration doesn't just have to be at these high points. For those struggling as the summer holidays draw to a close, the feast day of St Bartholomew on 24 August provides plenty of opportunity. For he is the patron saint of book-binders, butchers, cobblers, leatherworkers, plasterers, shoemakers and tanners.

Preach what you practice

Despite the growing number of lay preachers and ministers in secular employment, Mark Greene reports that 50% of the Christians he surveyed had never heard a single sermon on work.[31] A few examples from my own experience give a glimpse of the endless possibilities:

- **Shepherd**. A great opportunity was provided in a rural setting by having a shepherd in the congregation: this led to a practical dialogue during the sermon.

- **Potter**. A visit to a pottery in a neighbouring village produced several examples of misshapen pots to illustrate Jeremiah 18.
- **Salesman**. A risk during a wedding sermon, given that this was the groom's occupation. But the feedback from [non-churchgoing] guests at the reception indicated they were at least listening.
- **Supermarket**. The Feeding of the 5000 is hard to spiritualize from the setting of a supermarket coffee shop.
- **Airport lounge**. Separating sheep and goats is as nothing compared with the ends airlines go to to keep business and economy passengers apart.

Prayer: 'heaven in ordinary'

Once again, the opportunities are endless and there are plenty of opportunities to be creative. It is important to beware of subtle hierarchies (caring professions first, then educators, and so on until business people get mentioned at the end). And beware making a big fuss of the Sunday School teacher, who spends perhaps an hour a week with children, while ignoring the teachers who spend most of their working life with children.

Eucharist

Eucharistically centred communities have particular opportunities. Historic sensitivities about eucharistic sacrifice should not obscure the power of the words in the traditional thanksgiving for the bread, 'which earth has given and human hands have made' and wine, 'fruit of the vine and work of human hands'. Indeed, the whole presentation of the gifts, sometimes referred to as the Offertory,[32] provides boundless opportunities to offer our whole selves. Note, too, the opportunities provided at the Dismissal.

Coffee

After-church coffee provides endless opportunities for discussion starters . . . fair traded, organic, decaffeinated, low carbon footprint.

Symbolism

From harvest sheaves to hospital beds, from banners to bikes, from votive candles to voting slips, churches offer excellent space to explore multifaceted aspects of the world of work.

Pastoral insights

Chapter 31 on 'Sustaining a Process of Change' notes how insight from pastoral counselling can help see change as a grief journey: this can be highly relevant to people dealing with redundancy or other major change in their work. The much vaunted 'work-life balance' is another topic where the church could convene an exchange of useful insights.

Ethics

'Perhaps one of the most significant things, something that we might tend to overlook, is the power of our liturgy, worship and community prayer (or *Opus Dei*) to form an ethically sensitive community.'[33] The Church can provide opportunities to discuss not just the simplistic challenge of choosing between right and wrong, but the more nuanced occasions – defining moments – which occur, in the words of Harvard ethicist Joe Badaracco, 'when managers must choose between right and right'.[34] And the consistency of approach demanded by faith means that these ethics are not just for the board-room, but for the front line as well. Badaracco also emphasizes the importance of small events, of messy everyday challenges dealt with by the people working away from the limelight. 'There are no little things'.[35] Parallels with the incarnation are suggestive.

Political debate

Christian leaders and interest groups can contribute to local, national and international debates about globalization,[36] trading and employment practices.

Ministerial training

None of the above exists in isolation, and none will suddenly appear. One area where it is vital to see consistency between different areas of church activities is that of training. Seminaries, colleges and training schemes need to ensure that attention is given to the world of work as part of ministerial formation. The growing trend for people to enter different forms of ministry later in life suggests that there ought to be a store of experience to share.

Closing reflections

How to relate to the world of work? Some will advocate getting the world of the Church into the world of work; others will see the movement in the opposite direction. For those who hold that our lives should be integrated, there will be no dichotomy, at least in theory. Having started with an unholy conspiracy that has led to mutual marginalization, we can see glimmers of hope as we close with a plea for involvement in ministerial formation. For this author, at least, has been able in the past year to present the same material to both business school and theological college audiences. The worlds of faith and work may yet discover that they relate to – and can learn from – one another.

Notes

1. Silvoso, 2002, p. 63.
2. Higginson, 2002, p. 1. Higginson is Director of the Ridley Hall Foundation.
3. Grundy, 1992. Grundy is Director of the Foundation for Church Leadership.
4. The Jubilee Group. See <www.anglocatholicsocialism.org/jubilee2.html>.
5. Volf, 1991; Cosden, 2006; Wright, 2004.
6. A point duly noted by Stephen Green, Chairman of HSBC, in his talk at the Foundation for Church Leadership conference, King's College, London, 1 February 2007. See <www.churchleadershipfoundation.org/conferencesand-courses/postconference.htm>.
7. Moule, 1961, p. 80.
8. Ibid. For a similar idea, though written in a rather different idiom, see Greene, 2001, pp. 32–3. The absence of any such consideration is a major weakness of Cosden, 2006.
9. For further details and references, see Harle, 2007.
10. See, for example: Costa, 2007; Stevens, 2006.
11. Silvoso, 2002, p. 181.
12. Wright, 2000.
13. Dollard, Marett-Crosby and Wright, 2002.
14. Tredget 2002.
15. For a historical survey, see Mantle, 2000.
16. Barrett, 1998, p. vii.
17. See, for example: Mitroff and Denton, 1999; and Lamont, 2002.
18. Hicks, 2003.
19. Nash, 2005, p. 10.
20. Zohar and Marshall, 2004, p. 84.
21. Kroll, 2002.
22. Mitroff and Denton, 1999, p. xv.

23. For example, in two books applying complexity theory in a business setting: Lewin and Regine, 1999; and Owen, 2000.
24. At a seminar on 'Living Spirit at Work', University of Surrey School of Management, 9 November 2005.
25. Cavanagh, 2000.
26. In a personal conversation.
27. Roberts, 2002.
28. Tourish, 2005.
29. International Commission on English in the Liturgy, 1992.
30. Church of England, 2006, pp. 593–633.
31. Greene, 2001, p. 17.
32. See Buchanan, 1978.
33. Tredget, 2002, p. 6.
34. Badaracco, 1997.
35. Badaracco, 2002, p. 9.
36. Heslam, 2004; Jenkins, 2000.

References and further reading

Badaracco, Joseph L., Jr. (1997), *Defining Moments: When Managers Must Choose between Right and Right*, Harvard Mississippi: Harvard Business School Press.

Badaracco, Joseph L., Jr. (2002), *Leading Quietly: An Unorthodox Guide to Doing the Right Thing*, Harvard, Mississippi: Harvard Business School Press.

Barrett, Richard (1998), *Liberating the Corporate Soul: Building a Visionary Organization*, Woburn, Massachusetts: Butterworth-Heinemann.

Buchanan, Colin (1978), *The End of the Offertory: An Anglican Study*, Liturgical Study 14, Cambridge: Grove Books.

Cavanagh, Gerald (2000), 'Spirituality for Managers: Context and Critique', in Jerry Biberman and Michael Whitty (eds), *Work and Spirit: A Reader of New Spiritual Paradigms for Organizations*, Scranton, Pennsylvania: University of Scranton Press; originally *Journal of Organisational Change Management*, 12, 1999, pp 186–99.

Church of England (2006), *Common Worship: Times and Seasons*, London: Church House Publishing.

Cosden, Darrell (2006), *The Heavenly Good of Earthly Work*, Bletchley: Paternoster; Peabody Mississippi: Hendrickson.

Costa, Ken (2007), *God at Work: Living Every Day with Purpose*, London and New York: Continuum.

Dollard, Kit, Anthony Marett-Crosby and Timothy Wright (2002), *Doing Business with Benedict: The Rule of Saint Benedict and Business Management: A Conversation*, London and New York: Continuum.

Greene, Mark (2001), *Thank God It's Monday: Ministry in the Workplace*, 3rd edn, Bletchley: Scripture Union. See also under LICC in resources section.

Grundy, Malcolm (1992), *An Unholy Conspiracy: The Scandal of the Separation of Church and Industry since the Reformation*, Norwich: Canterbury Press.

Harle, Tim (2007), 'Religious meaning', in Antonio Marturano and Jonathan Gosling (eds), *Leadership, the Key Concepts*, Abingdon: Routledge.

Heslam, Peter (ed.) (2004), *Globalization and the Good*, London: SPCK.

Hicks, Douglas A. (2003), *Religion and the Workplace: Pluralism, Spirituality, Leadership*, Cambridge: Cambridge University Press.

Higginson, Richard (2002), *Questions of Business Life: Exploring Workplace Issues from a Christian Perspective*, Carlisle and Waynesboro, Georgia: Authentic Media.

Howard, Sue, and David Welbourn (2004), *The Spirit at Work Phenomenon*, London: Azure.

Jenkins, David (2000), *Market Whys and Human Wherefores: Thinking Again about Markets, Politics and People*, London and New York: Cassell.

Kroll, Una (2002), 'Spirituality', in Wesley Carr (ed.), *The New Dictionary of Pastoral Studies*, London: SPCK, pp. 356–7.

International Commission on English in the Liturgy (1992), *Book of Blessings: Abridged Edition*, Collegeville, Minnesota: Liturgical Press.

Lamont, Georgeanne (2002), *The Spirited Business: Success Stories of Soul-Friendly Companies*, London: Hodder & Stoughton.

Lewin, Roger, and Birute Regine (1999), *The Soul at Work: Unleashing the Power of Complexity Science for Business Success*, London: Orion.

Mantle, John (2000), *Britain's First Worker-Priests: Radical Ministry in a Post-war Setting*, London: SCM Press.

Mitroff, Ian I., and Elizabeth A. Denton (1999), *A Spiritual Audit of Corporate America: A Hard Look at Spirituality, Religion, and Values in the Workplace*, San Francisco, California: Jossey-Bass

Moule, C. F. D. (1961), *Worship in the New Testament*, Ecumenical Studies in Worship 9, London: Lutterworth Press.

Nash, Laura (2005), *Reframing Faith and Work for Lasting Success*, 16th Hugh Kay Memorial Lecture, London: CABE.

Nash, Laura, and Scotty McLennan (2001), *Church on Sunday, Work on Monday: The Challenge of Fusing Christian Values with Business Life*, San Francisco, California: Jossey-Bass.

Owen, Harrison (2000), *The Power of Spirit: How Organizations Transform*, San Francisco, California: Berrett-Koehler.

Roberts, Richard H. (2002), *Religion, Theology and the Human Sciences*, Cambridge: Cambridge University Press.

Silvoso, Ed. (2002), *Anointed for Business: How Christians Can Use Their Influence in the Marketplace to Change the World*, Ventura, California: Regal Books.

Stevens, R. Paul (2006), *Doing God's Business: Meaning and Motivation for the Marketplace*, Grand Rapids, Michigan: Eerdmans.

Tourish, Denis (2005), 'Transformational Leadership and the Perils of Coercive Persuasion', paper presented at the 4th International Conference on Studying Leadership, Lancaster, UK.

Tredget, Dermot (2002), *Can the Rule of St Benedict Provide an Ethical Framework for a Contemporary Theology of Work?*, Belmont Abbey: Monastic Theology Commission. See <www.benedictines.org.uk/theology/2002/dermot_tredget.pdf>.

Wright, Walter C. (2000), *Relational Leadership: A Biblical Model for Leadership*

Service, Carlisle and Waynesboro, Georgia: Paternoster.
Volf, Miroslav (1991), *Work in the Spirit: Towards a Theology of Work*, Oxford: Oxford University Press; Eugene, Oregon: Wipf & Stock, 2001.
Wright, Clive, 2004, *The Business of Virtue*, London: SPCK.
Zohar, Danah, and Ian Marshall (2004), *Spiritual Capital: Wealth We Can Live By*, San Francisco, California: Berrett-Koehler.

A number of journals address the relationship between faith and work. Among them are:

Faith in Business Quarterly. Published by the Ridley Hall Foundation and the Industrial Christian Fellowship. See <www.fibq.org>.
Spirit in Work. Published by MODEM. See <www.modem.uk.com>.
Journal of Management, Spirituality and Religion. An international peer-reviewed academic journal. See <www.jmsr.com>.

Resources

A veritable alphabet-soup of organizations provide material. Some are listed below.

CABE (Christian Association of Business Executives). Publishes occasional papers and promotes annual Hugh Kay lecture. <www.cabe-online.org>. Has recently published *Principles for Those in Business*: see <www.principlesforbusiness.com>.

CHRISM (Christians in Secular Ministry). Cross-denominational group, arranging occasional papers and events. <www.chrism.org.uk>.

ICF (Industrial Christian Fellowship). Ecumenical organization, working to help Christians live out their faith in the workplace. <www.icf-online.org>.

LICC (London Institute for Contemporary Christianity). Their publications include Mark Greene's useful workbook, *Supporting Christians at Work: A Practical Guide for Church Leaders* (2001). <www.licc.org.uk>.

MODEM. Ecumenical body, 'the voice of leadership, management and ministry'. Publishes *Spirit in Work*. <www.modem.uk.com>.

RHF (Ridley Hall Foundation). Organizes regular conferences; publishes *Faith in Business Quarterly*. <www.ridley.cam.ac.uk/rhf>.

Transforming Business. Project linked to University of Cambridge's Theology Faculty and Judge Business School. <www.transformingbusiness.net>.

7. Setting up 'faith at work' programmes

DAVID CLARK

'Losing the plot'

In August 2005, the then Vice-President of the Methodist Conference, John Bell, wrote an article in the *Methodist Recorder* entitled 'Have We Lost the Plot?' As a person with a long business career behind him, his concern was that Methodism had so concentrated its endeavours on the home, family and local community that it had neglected to equip its lay people to fulfil their ministry in the world of work. This is little short of a disaster because it is the laity who are the Church's primary witnesses to the gospel within daily life.

What is true for Methodism would appear to be true for all denominations. Towards the end of the 1980s, a number of churches set up working parties to explore the ministry of lay people in public life. In 1985, the Church of England produced a report entitled *All are Called – Towards a Theology of the Laity*[1] and, two years later, a report *Called to be Adult Disciples*,[2] both documents relating to the ministry of the laity in the world. In 1987, the Synod of Roman Catholic Bishops in Rome published *Christifideles laici*,[3] an apostolic exhortation concerning 'the vocation and mission of the lay faithful in the church and in the world'. In 1990, the British Methodist Conference approved a report on *The Ministry of the People of God in the World*[4] and recommended it to its districts for study.

It was not long, however, before all these documents were gathering dust on ecclesiastical bookshelves. In 1993, the Christians in Public Life Programme carried out *A Survey of Christians at Work and Its Implications for the Churches*.[5] Four hundred lay people from all denominations replied to a detailed questionnaire. The responses revealed a dire situation in that well over half the respondents felt that the educational programmes and pastoral care of their local church did not adequately support them in their working lives. Furthermore, only just over half found worship met their needs within the world of work.

There are those who continue to believe that the Church's presence in the world of work is adequately represented by chaplains and non-stipendiary ministers who focus their ministry on the workplace (in Anglican terms, known as Ministers in Secular Employment and, in Methodist terms, as Sector Ministers). However, I argue in my book *Breaking the Mould of Christendom* that the Church here faces a dilemma.[6] Chaplains may well be of symbolic, as well as pastoral, importance in representing the public face of the Church in the world of work. But their very presence can lead to the neglect of the ministry of the laity who in numbers, experience and expertise are a resource far more significant for the mission of the Church in the world than a relatively tiny group of chaplains and non-stipendiary ministers can ever be.

So where do we go from here? There is no other way forward than the blindingly obvious, yet, for some perplexing reason virtually ignored task of 'liberating the laity' (the subtitle of *Breaking the Mould of Christendom*) to fulfil their calling as the people of God in the world. What follows seeks to address this task in two ways. First (Part 1), we look at how 'faith at work' programmes might be set up and developed in the context of the local church. Secondly (Part 2), we look at what the need for such programmes has to tell us about the kind of church leadership that is required in the years ahead.

Part 1: 'faith at work' within the local church

The ideas for a 'faith at work' programme within the local church sketched out below come from a number of sources. They are drawn from the experience of the very few churches in the UK that have engaged in such programmes, some of whose experiences are written up in position papers presented to the Christians in Public Life Programme which I headed up from 1992 to 2001.[7] A number of suggestions come from my own endeavours to set up a 'faith at work' programme in two Methodist churches, one urban and large, the other rural and relatively small. Other ideas come from a 'Faith at Work Programme' that has been underway within the Methodist Diaconal Order for several years, and notably suggestions from the members of that Order's Convocation in sessions on the same theme in 2005 and 2006. (Many of the ideas offered below are discussed more fully in *Breaking the Mould of Christendom*.)[8]

Getting started

Most churches have neither the experience of a 'faith at work' programme nor are aware that any such programme is needed. It is felt to be quite sufficient, by ordained and lay alike, that church members are exhorted (mainly through sermons) to 'go out into the world to preach the gospel and serve their fellows'. Thus the first task of the person setting up such a programme (we here call him or her 'the coordinator') is to begin to raise the awareness of the congregation to the potential value of such a programme.

Awareness raising of this kind is often best done by the coordinator speaking at strategic meetings about the importance of affirming the ministry of lay people in daily life, of supporting them in the ways in which they are seeking to live out their faith in the world, of enabling church members to know more about the work in which each of them is involved during the week, and of making their experiences and concerns an integral part of worship.

In this early awareness raising exercise a number of points need to be stressed. The support of the priest or minister for the programme (if he or she is not the coordinator) is essential. Secondly, it needs to be made clear that a 'faith at work' programme is not simply concerned with those in full-time paid employment, though their concerns are often the most obvious. It also includes those in the congregation, many retired, who have continued in part-time work, or who undertake voluntary work. Furthermore, the ministry of those who look after or visit family, friends or others in need, should in some way be recognized.

Thirdly, examining the value of such a programme and the way in which it might best be introduced into the life of the local church should be a matter of open discussion. There can be resistance from those who feel that people come to church to get away from the problems of daily life. Others may feel neither any sense of Christian vocation in their work nor any need to relate their faith to it, at least in an explicit way. Some, for professional or personal reasons, may not want others to know what they do during the week. For example, a doctor or counsellor may be afraid of attracting unwanted patients or clients. There may be those who, in smaller churches, feel that everybody already knows what others are involved in during the week. In fact this is rarely the case and does not allow for newcomers.

The coordinator's response is the same for all these and similar reactions. It is to emphasize that the purpose of the programme is to affirm what people are already doing, to enable them better to support one another (pastorally and prayerfully) in their working lives, to give them the opportunity to explore together how their faith can inform their world and their work inform their faith, and to be able to communicate that faith more effectively through word and deed. At the same time, the coordinator should assure people who do not want to participate in the programme that their wishes will be fully respected and that their contribution to the ministry and mission of the church remains as important as that of anyone else.

Awareness raising

The next stage in any 'faith at work' programme is to raise the *whole* congregation's awareness of the work, paid or voluntary, in which each of them is *already* engaged.

One way of doing this, in which I myself was directly involved, was the production of a booklet entitled: [*The name of the church*] *at Work*. The first step was to explain the purpose of a 'faith at work' programme at a number of services and through the church newsletter and notice board. Cards were then handed out to people as they left Sunday worship. On these they were asked to fill in their name, present paid occupation (if applicable) and voluntary work (for example, service to the wider community, work for charities, etc.). The information asked for was about work done with or for non-churchgoers, not about work done for the church as such. Though people were encouraged to fill in a card, it was stressed that it was their own choice. Where members missed out on receiving a card, one was mailed to them with a covering letter.

The cards were then gathered in. The information was collated and produced in an attractive booklet. Each page of the booklet had four columns – type of work (such as education, health, business, aid agencies, etc.); employment (paid) (which describes the person's specific work such as primary teacher, optician, nurse, etc.); voluntary work/concerns (such as School governor, Oxfam, Rotary, etc.); and their name. The booklet had an introduction that stated that it was meant to help people:

- become more aware of the impressive range of services to the community in which those attending their church were actively involved during the week;
- share experiences and insights about how the gospel could be communicated through these areas of work;
- reflect through worship, house groups and other gatherings on how faith could inform work, and how work could inform faith;
- support one another in these activities through prayers and pastoral care.

At the end of the booklet two or three prayers relating to the world of work were included. The booklet was then distributed free to the congregation. Each year the booklet is updated and revised as necessary.

There are, however, many others ways of raising the awareness of lay people to their calling to be the Church in the world. Here I simply list a range of ideas that have proved helpful at one time or another.

- Put together a 'map' of the work (paid or voluntary) undertaken by church members – this could be an 'occupational' map (people grouped by occupations or voluntary work interests), or a geographical map (showing where people work in the area).
- Give opportunities for people to display (photos, collage, etc.) depicting their work (paid or voluntary). Logos, badges or letter headings could be used for a collage – including school or college badges.
- Invite people to offer job profiles of their work (paid or voluntary) in the church newsletter (or put on a notice board) and to suggest what they would appreciate the congregation pray for in relation to their work situation.
- Publish short articles in the church newsletter about how people are trying to link their faith and their work (paid or voluntary), either written by lay people or put together from interviews with them.
- Set up 'a work forum' or 'a charities forum' where people are invited to display literature about the organizations or charities for which they work and to talk to others about these.

Worship

It is very important that daily work is celebrated, reflected on and prayed about in worship. This can be done on special occasions and at special services. However, it is far more important to enable the congregation to realize that their Christian faith and daily life are inseparable and to acknowledge this recognition in *every* act of worship. In one church in the United States, there is a time set aside during Sunday worship every week for people to share news or concerns about their working lives, often followed by intercessions.

To help 'faith at work' to become more an integral part of worship, the following suggestions may be helpful:

- Encourage lay people to write prayers about their work that could be used in worship, and perhaps printed out for church members to use during the week.

- Ask (and prepare) lay people to speak about their faith and their work at a Sunday service. This is often done best by means of interviewing them during the service.
- Bring people together in worship from occupational groupings – health, finance, business . . . Listen to and pray for their concerns.
- Hold a service where people are encouraged to talk about what it means to be unemployed, what it feels like to be working very long or unsocial hours, or what it means to be retired.
- Use work-related visual aids to remind the congregation that the whole of life belongs to God (for example, placing the tools of people's trades on the altar or communion table and using these to assist intercessions).
- Link people's working experience to Christian themes in the Church year (for example, getting a midwife to talk about preparing for a birth – Advent . . .).
- Have services on work-related themes and contexts – schools/ colleges, hospitals, shops, business, transport, local government . . .
- Refocus special services on the world of work (such as a Harvest Festival turned into a 'Harvest at Work' service).
- Ensure that family or 'all-age worship' does not neglect the themes stemming from living out one's faith in daily life, including the ministry of children and young people at school and college.
- Arrange an annual 'commissioning' service to affirm the ministry of the whole church in daily life.
- Encourage lay readers and local preachers to draw on their personal experience of the world of work (past or present) more often than they currently do to inform and enrich their leading of worship and their preaching.

Reflection and learning

Preparing and equipping lay people to fulfil their calling as the people of God in the world remains a huge omission in the educational programmes of most churches. It is a vital but demanding undertaking that needs to be led by those with the appropriate experience and skills (see Part 2). Two useful overviews of the field are those by Michael Greene, an Anglican, entitled *Supporting Christians at Work*[9] and by John Ellis, a Methodist, called *Let Your Light Shine*.[10]

Learning contexts can range from informal groups based on the local church to professional groups meeting in or near their workplace led by those with considerable expertise of the field concerned.[11] There is now a wide range of courses and resources (many produced in the USA) that can be used in the task of supporting 'faith at work' groups. Going to Google on the Internet and typing in 'Christian faith at work' or 'Christian faith and work' will access many such resources, though these vary considerably in theological perspective and educational quality.

It should be noted, however, that a gradual shift is taking place from courses set up to explore the meaning and nature of 'faith at work' in a more general context to ways in which lay people can be helped to reflect theologically on particular issues and concerns at work to explore how best they should respond to these. In this context, Peter Challen, formerly of the South London Industrial Mission, has pioneered a process called 'Theological Auditing'.[12] Also relevant to this development are sections of a useful book on methods of *Theological Reflection* published in 2005.[13]

What really matters, however, is that churches make a start on the task of linking faith and daily work, learn from their mistakes and then shape their programme in response to the needs of their own people. Below we set out a few starting points.

- Set up a support group for those who want to meet informally to explore faith at work.
- Set up a more structured course for church members to explore the theology/ethics of work and/or to explore the spirituality of work.
- Offer young people linked to the church the opportunity to reflect on their work at school or college in a faith context.
- Use Lent discussion groups to discuss issues Christians face in their working lives.
- Arrange an occasional breakfast or lunch club for church members to exchange and explore ideas about faith at work.
- Practise the art of communal living Benedictine style as a church – work (indoors and outdoors), eat, study the scriptures and pray together – for a day church retreat.

Pastoral care

Pastoral care must widen its perspectives. Lay people need care and prayer not only when they or their loved ones are ill or bereaved but also to support them in the many challenges they face in their work, or when they are without work. This means that those offering pastoral care or counselling on behalf of the church do not fail to enquire about the person's work situation and how the church can best support them in that context. It may be that the local church can appoint a person with the necessary expertise to assist in this task though, more usually, it can be integrated into the ongoing pastoral care of the congregation.

Part 2: leadership

The Church has for far too long neglected identifying and training leaders whose task it is to enable lay people to discover and exercise their calling in daily life. In *Breaking the Mould of Christendom*,[14] I set out the need for the Church to distinguish between leadership that is focused on the gathered Church and that which is focused on the dispersed Church, and to begin to train and equip leaders to fufil the latter role. I called those leaders who are primarily concerned with the life of the gathered Church 'presbyters' and those primarily concerned with the life of the dispersed Church 'deacons'. The exact titles do not matter. What does matter is identifying and training church leaders whose key task is to prepare lay people for their ministry in the world.

Such leaders will need experience and skills not yet on the agendas of our theological colleges.[15] Such expertise will include a first-hand knowledge of the world of work, experience that is sadly often left at the gates of our theological institutions when men and women begin to train for the ordained ministry. One way in which such experience can be gained or broadened is for 'deacons' to visit church members at their places of work, shadow them for a day/half day, or meet them over coffee or lunch if visiting the workplace is not possible. Other requirements are keeping up-to-date with issues that affect lay people's working lives, familiarity with Christian ethics, an ability to fashion worship which honours the world of work, adult education and group work skills, and the ability to meet pastoral needs related to the world of work.

Because this role is such a demanding one, it simply cannot be bolted on to the role of priest or presbyter. Nor does the priest or presbyter have the time to undertake this demanding 'diaconal' task in any but a superficial way. Thus the Church needs with some urgency to begin to develop a new form of ministry that majors on the experience and expertise (as well as the calling) needed to equip lay people for their Christian vocation in daily life.

This does not mean that every church should employ a 'deacon' (with the role indicated above). It could be quite sufficient, where churches are small, for one such 'deacon' to act as a coordinator of a (deanery's or circuit's) 'faith at work' programme, at the same time identifying a person in each church involved who could act as a local coordinator operating under the 'deacon's' supervision.

Beyond the United Kingdom

In this paper, I have focused attention on the church in the UK. However, raising awareness to the importance of 'faith at work' and preparing lay people to act as the Church in the world is now moving up the agenda of many Christian agencies in many other countries. I finish with one such example.

The Coalition for Ministry in Daily Life (CMDL) is an initiative that took off in the United States in the early 1990s. In 1992, the Coalition gave itself a name and adopted a mission statement that affirmed 'that all Christians have been called into ministry and that for most of them their arena of ministry is in and to the world'.

The Coalition currently consists of organizations and individuals from a range of Christian traditions, mainly from the USA but also beyond. Bodies involved include campus ministries, seminaries and colleges, church departments and independent organizations concerned with ministry in daily life. The Coalition publishes a newsletter entitled *LayNet*, holds an annual conference and makes full use of its web site to link participants.[16]

The Coalition has had its ups and downs over the years, but has steadily gained momentum. In 2006, it hosted a very successful conference attended by well over a hundred people at Fuller Seminary in Los Angeles. The Coalition's concerns reflect a growing movement within the USA, now being taken forward by numerous agencies and developed through a range of publications, aimed at affirming the ministry of the laity as of crucial importance for a church seeking to re-engage with the world of the twenty-first century.

It is high time that Christian agencies in the UK who have the same concern came together in a similar way. Attempts to do this have in the past met with limited success.[17] However, the need to 'liberate the laity' for their ministry in the world is now so urgent that another initiative to set up a coalition of such agencies that can facilitate the sharing of experiences, insights, expertise and resources is well overdue. Perhaps this should be the next item on MODEM's agenda!

Notes

1. Church of England Board of Education, 1985.
2. Church of England Board of Education, 1987.
3. Synod of Roman Catholic Bishops, 1989.
4. *The Ministry of the People of God in the World*, Methodist Conference (1990).
5. Clark, 1993.
6. Clark, 2005, pp. 210–31.

7. Clark, 1997, Sections 6 and 7.
8. Clark, 2005, pp. 273–95.
9. Greene, 2001.
10. Ellis, 2003.
11. Note groups of professionals meeting under the auspices of the Heythrop Institute for Religion, *Ethics and Public Life*, <www.heythrop.ac.uk>. See also Clark, 2005, pp. 254–64, on 'Evangelical workplace associations and agencies (UK)'.
12. See Clark, 2005, p. 222.
13. Graham, Walton and Ward, 2005.
14. Clark, 2005, pp. 110–20 and 273–95.
15. Clark, 2005, pp. 123–4 and 296–300.
16. Coalition for Ministry in Daily Life, contact P.O. Box 239, South Orleans, MA 02662, USA. Web site: <www.dailylifeministry.org>.
17. Clark, 2005, pp. 179–82.

References

Church of England Board of Education (1985), *All Are Called – Towards a Theology of the Laity*, London: Church Information Office.

Church of England Board of Education (1987), *Called to Be Adult Disciples*, London: Church Information Office.

Clark, D. (1993), *A Survey of Christians at Work*, Westhill College, Birmingham: CIPL.

Clark, D. (1997), *Changing World, Unchanging Church?*, London: Mowbray.

Clark, D. (2005), *Breaking the Mould of Christendom: Kingdom Community, Diaconal Church and the Liberation of the Laity*, London: Epworth Press.

Ellis, J. (2003), *Let Your Light Shine*, London: Trustees for Methodist Church Purposes.

Graham, E., H. Walton and F. Ward (2005), *Theological Reflection: Methods*, London: SCM Press.

Greene, M. (2001), *Supporting Christians at Work: A Practical Guide for Busy Pastors*, London: The London Institute for Contemporary Christianity, Sheffield: Administry.

Synod of Roman Catholic Bishops (1989), *Christifideles Laici* (simplified version), Pinner, Middlesex: The Grail.

Being Relevant in Preaching

8. 'Is there any word from the Lord?'

Connecting relevant preaching with effective leadership

PETER STEVENSON

There is, perhaps, no greater hardship at present inflicted on mankind in civilised and free countries, than the necessity of listening to sermons. No one but a preaching clergyman has, in these realms, the power of compelling an audience to sit silent and be tormented.[1]

Since Trollope poked fun at preachers in 1857, questions about preaching have continued unabated. Surely in our tolerant, post-Christendom context, the boring monologue needs to be replaced by something more interactive and less authoritarian?

In such a context, preaching may appear an unlikely candidate for inclusion in a book about creative Church leadership. For, as Michael Quicke observes, 'Leadership is red-hot, gaining loud applause from enthusiastic fans' while 'sermons seem to lie cold and blue at the opposite end of the spectrum from dynamic leadership'.[2]

Before concluding that preaching has little to do with creative leadership, it is worth pausing to pay attention to Peter's Brierley's comments arising from the fourth English Church Census. Amid some sobering findings the census revealed that larger churches are growing, and 'the larger the church, the more likely it was to be growing'. Reflecting on why this might be the case, Brierley reports that 'this is partly because the preaching is relevant (a very important factor), the welcome received is warm, there are suitable activities for children and adults midweek, and especially because there is likely to be strong leadership with a clear vision for the future'.[3]

All of which suggests that, far from being unlikely bedfellows, relevant preaching and strong leadership can and should operate in tandem. Thus we find Michael Quicke arguing that

instead of operating independently, eyeing each other suspicious-
ly, preaching and leadership must embrace and do gospel business
together. Preaching needs leadership as much as Christian leadership needs preaching. When Jesus Christ calls preachers he creates
unique leaders for his church – those who declare his Word today
so that by the grace of God people and communities are transformed.[4]

If relevant preaching has the potential to be an important element in
healthy church life, then what might be involved in creating relevant
forms of preaching in the local church context?

One response to current criticisms of preaching might be to move in
the direction of a greater use of contemporary forms of communication, involving data projectors and PowerPoint presentations.
However, although I regularly use PowerPoint presentations in the
context of teaching students at college, I have to confess that I do not
normally make use of PowerPoint when I am preaching in church.

This reluctance to use PowerPoint in preaching does not arise from
any Luddite technophobia, but from a suspicion that there is a real
danger that the technology might get in the way of the personal form
of communication we call preaching. Some of the issues are voiced
provocatively by Richard Lischer who claims that,

> The real benefits of projecting a clip from *Friends* or a series of
> bullet points on a screen are negligible. In themselves, these tech-
> niques only reproduce what we already have in our family rooms
> and offices. And that's the point! The very presence of such media
> serves to associate the sermon (and church and preacher) with the
> glamour, power and authority of the same technology that rules the
> world. The medium really *is* the message. Technology is the new
> symbol of power. If the old symbol was the high pulpit and canopy,
> the new power-symbol is the remote in the shepherd's hand.[5]

It is clear that a reliable data projection system can be used creatively
in the context of worship in all sorts of ways, but my conviction is that
the source of relevant preaching does not lie in expensive systems but
in costly listening for the Word of God.

Is there any word from the Lord?

Reflecting upon the nature of relevant preaching leads me back in a
different direction, to an Old Testament episode recounted in
Jeremiah 37.1–21, where a fearless preacher comes face to face with
the harsh reality of international politics.

This passage takes us back to Jerusalem in 588 BC, where Zedekiah has been installed as a puppet-king by Nebuchadnezzar, King of Babylon. With the approach of Egyptian troops, Zedekiah hopes that things will improve, and under the cover of darkness he approaches the prophet Jeremiah and asks, the haunting question 'Is there any word from the Lord?'

In response to that question, the prophet gives the answer, 'There is!' However, this is not the answer Zedekiah was hoping for, because Jeremiah went on to speak a word of divine judgement, saying, 'You shall be handed over to the king of Babylon.'

Humanly speaking, Zedekiah was caught between the two great military powers of his day, Egypt and Babylon, and whatever happens he will not be able to shake free from their control. Theologically speaking, he is caught in a much greater predicament because he is accountable to the Sovereign Lord of history and he is tragically bringing divine judgement down upon his own head by his disobedience.

In the midst of a political crisis the prophet Jeremiah speaks a word that is directly relevant to the situation facing Zedekiah and the rest of the nation.

Is there any word from the Lord today?

Week by week the preacher in the local church also asks the question 'Is there any word from the Lord?' However, what message can there possibly be for a fearful world facing the war on terrorism and the prospect of global warming? How can a preacher hope to preach relevant sermons which seriously address the problems of a complex, fast-changing world? How is it possible to preach sensitively to the same congregation on a regular basis when the preacher is painfully aware of the heartache and tragedy with which so many people live?

Humanly speaking, the call to preach relevant sermons sounds like a mission impossible, for how can we possibly have something relevant to say to such a complex world as this? Mercifully for us, preaching is not about inventing something clever and 'relevant' to say.

So what is preaching?

On a regular basis I invite students to write down a short definition of preaching. My current definition of preaching suggests that preaching involves:

Discovering the Word of the Lord from the Bible for this group of people at this particular time, and then delivering that Word in the power of the Spirit, in ways that people can understand so that they can respond in worship and service.

Discovering the word of the Lord from the Bible . . .

Thomas Long argues that 'Biblical preaching is the *normative* form of Christian preaching' because 'preaching that involves significant engagement with a biblical text is the standard over against which all other types of preaching are measured'.[6]

For some Christians such an emphasis on the centrality and authority of the Bible may seem dated and unhelpful. It is true that the biblical writers have little or nothing to say directly about contemporary issues such as genetic engineering, computing or global warming. The continuing relevance of the Bible arises from the way in which the biblical story narrates and reveals the character of the living God. Scripture invites its readers to enter the biblical story where all of reality is seen in the light of God who is the prime actor in the story.

Biblical preaching continues to be relevant because it is a means of bearing witness to the continuing presence and activity of the living God who is relevant to every facet of life.

. . . for this group of people at this particular time

Back in 1928 the famous preacher Harry Emerson Fosdick pointed out that 'only the preacher proceeds still upon the idea that folk come to church desperately anxious to discover what happened to the Jebusites'.[7] Relevant preaching does not mean giving long, boring Bible history lessons about something that happened thousands of years ago. So rather than feeling obliged to tell my congregation everything that is in the text, on every occasion, I believe that my task is to discern the specific Word of the Lord, from this specific section of the Bible, for this group of people at this particular time.

I suspect that Anna Carter Florence may be on to something when she suggests that part of the problem with a lot of contemporary preaching is that preachers feel that their job is to *explain* the text rather than to *preach* the text. In seeking to redress the balance she advises new preachers that

> their job is not to make the text understandable, or logical, or relevant, or fun. Their job is quite simple, really. It is to *preach the text*, because there isn't anything more interesting or sensible than that. Preach the text, offer it in all its thickness and inscrutability, and

trust that it will speak better than we could to the competing worlds of consumerism and militarism and individualism and anxiety that plague our people.[8]

. . . and then delivering that word in the power of the Spirit

Some years ago when I was designing an open learning module on preaching for a Master's degree course, I attended a conference where people expressed some surprise that there could be a Master's level course in preaching. The implication seemed to be that, intellectually speaking, preaching was not a very demanding business. Over the years, as I have struggled to preach on a regular basis, I have become more and more convinced that preaching is an extremely demanding task. Preaching with integrity not only requires me to handle scripture and theology competently, but it also calls for the ability to make connections to the lives of my listeners in an accessible way.

The booklist at the end of this article mentions some of the books which explore the sorts of skills involved in effective preaching. It is obvious that anyone wishing to preach relevant sermons will need to go on developing their homiletical skills throughout their ministry.

However, at the same time it is important to stress, as the definition above does, that preaching is supremely a spiritual process. Having discovered the Word of the Lord for this specific occasion, we are called to proclaim this Word *in the power of the Holy Spirit*. So preaching is not ultimately about skills and sermon formats, but about the Spirit who takes our human words and uses them to communicate that divine Word which transforms people and communities.

. . . in ways that people can understand so that they can respond in worship and service

According to Walter Wright, leadership is 'a relationship of influence – a transforming relationship in which the leader invests in the growth and development of the followers, empowering them to become what God has gifted them to be'.[9] Through preaching, Christian leaders seek to influence people in such a way that they are inspired and empowered to seek first the Kingdom of God. Preaching is not an end in itself, but something which aims to provoke people into practical discipleship.

Costly listening

If preaching has to do with discerning God's Word for today, then those who offer Christian leadership through preaching will need to learn to be good listeners. Such costly listening involves a range of factors; but at this point it is worth mentioning three key elements in the listening process.

1 Listening to God's word

The opening verses of Jeremiah 37 state that 'Zedekiah son of Josiah, whom King Nebuchadrezzar of Babylon made king in the land of Judah, succeeded Coniah son of Jehoiakim. But neither he nor his servants nor the people of the land listened to the words of the LORD that he spoke through the prophet Jeremiah.'[10]

Zedekiah's habit of turning a deaf ear to the voice of God stands in stark contrast to the experience of Jeremiah whose devotion to God's word[11] is expressed vividly in Jeremiah 15.16.

> Your words were found, and I ate them
> and your words became to me a joy
> and the delight of my heart;
> for I am called by your name
> O LORD, God of hosts.

At a time when we are constantly surrounded by all sorts of images and messages, one of the fundamentals for effective preaching will be making time to immerse ourselves in the counter-cultural world of the Bible, learning to listen to God speaking through it. In seeking to listen to God, it will be necessary to draw upon a wide range of spiritual resources.

2 Listening to the congregation

Some books about preaching talk about interpreting or exegeting the congregation. Preachers rightly spend a lot of time seeking to interpret the biblical text, but there is also a need to interpret our congregation in the sense of understanding the different kinds of people who are likely to be listening to the sermon.

Leslie Francis advocates the value of drawing upon insights which emerge from the use of the Myers-Briggs Personality Type Indicator. He argues that 'personality differences may . . . have important implications for teachers and for preachers. It has, for example, long been recognised that introverts and extraverts prefer to learn in different ways, and as a consequence of their own learning preferences may prefer to teach others in the way that they themselves would prefer to be taught.'[12] He suggests that *Sensing Types, Intuitive Types, Feeling Types* and *Thinking Types* will engage with sermons in very different ways. Preachers therefore need then to be aware of their own personality preferences, and make conscious efforts to communicate with people who think and feel in different ways. Otherwise, the danger is that we end up communicating effectively with just one in four within the congregation.

From a different perspective, Alice Matthews explores some of the issues involved in helping preachers connect more effectively with women. She offers six questions to help preachers think about the impact of preaching upon women.

- Do we typecast men and women in traditional stereotyped roles?
- Do we represent both men and women as whole human beings?
- Do we accord men and women the same level of respect?
- Do we recognize both men and women for their own achievements?
- Does our language exclude women when we talk about humanity as a whole?
- Do we use language that designates and describes men and women on equal terms?[13]

Neither of these approaches offers the magic bullet for relevant preaching, but they alert us to something which effective preachers have known for a long time: that we need to listen to our congregations and understand the concerns and questions which people bring with them to the preaching event.

3 Listening to culture

One of the ways in which David Day encourages preachers to tune into contemporary culture is through TV soaps. He explains that 'each week *Eastenders* and *Coronation Street* are watched by about 12 million viewers every time they are screened, and *Emmerdale* by around 10 million. Over one-fifth of the population is watching on any evening. Soaps regularly take the top 14 places in the BBC1 and ITV1 viewing leagues, and even the next positions are taken by quasi-soaps like *Casualty, Holby City* and *Midsomer Murders*. This is a phenomenon which should not be ignored or disparaged by the preacher. The Gospels say, 'The common people heard him gladly'.[14]

Now a solid diet of TV soaps does not guarantee relevance, and there are plenty of other ways of listening carefully to the voice of culture. However, Day's comments suggest one practical way of tuning into contemporary culture.

Integrity

Recent writing about leadership draws attention to the integrity of the leader. This concern is mirrored in discussions about codes of conduct for people involved in various forms of Christian leadership and ministry. In a reflection on recent *Guidelines for the Professional Conduct of the Clergy*, Francis Bridger says that,

> the character of the professional is as important as the code to which he or she adheres. The ethics of conduct must be shaped by the ethics of character and the ethics of integrity . . . What we do is governed by who we are . . . the Christian minister must *deliberately* cultivate Christian character and virtues and not leave them to chance . . . he or she must seek the fruits of the Spirit . . . our theological convictions and spiritual practices are crucial to professional life. We are formed by the beliefs we hold and the ways in which we relate to God. Doctrine, ethics and spirituality go hand in hand.[15]

Rewriting that paragraph with preachers in view, it might say something like this:

> The character of the *preacher* is as important as the *message* which he or she *preaches*. The ethics of conduct must be shaped by the ethics of character and the ethics of integrity . . . What we do is governed by who we are . . . the Christian *preacher* must *deliberately* cultivate Christian character and virtues and not leave them to chance . . . he or she must seek the fruits of the Spirit . . .

Such an emphasis upon integrity, or a Christ-like character, is a reminder of the vital importance of spiritual growth and development in the lives of all who are involved in preaching.

Being a fully alive preacher

Every 18 months or so, Mike Graves makes a pilgrimage from Kansas City to Spurgeon's College to contribute to Master's modules on preaching and narrative. Something of his infectious enthusiasm for preaching comes through strongly in his recent book, *The Fully Alive Preacher*.[16]

On the one hand, his book is a helpful guide to the preaching process, but, on the other hand, it is an unusual preaching book because it explicitly focuses upon the spirituality of the preacher. Scattered throughout the book are what he calls 'Ten Sacraments of Renewal', various ways in which we can experience the grace of God that can renew tired preachers.

The image which Graves explores is Irenaeus' vision that 'the glory of God is a human being fully alive' (*Adversus Haereses*, 4.XX.7); and in a variety of ways that is what he encourages preachers to become. You may not agree with all of his suggestions, but he is surely right to encourage preachers to be fully alive people, who are being renewed spiritually.

Perhaps preaching that is relevant is simply one of the by-products of that process whereby Christians are becoming human beings who are fully alive, filled and empowered by the Holy Spirit?

Notes

1. Trollope, 1953, p. 52.
2. Quicke, 2006, p. 24.
3. Peter Brierley, 2006, p. 10.
4. Quicke, 2006, p. 71.
5. Lischer, 2005, p. 27.
6. Long, 2005, pp. 51–2.
7. Fosdick, 1928, p. 135.
8. Florence, 2004, p. 99.
9. Wright, 2000, p. 44.
10. Jeremiah 37.1–2 (NRSV).
11. See, for example, Jeremiah 1.4–19; 2.3; 3.6.
12. Francis, 2005, p. 75.
13. Mathews, 2003, pp. 158–62.
14. Day, 2005, pp. 118–19.
15. Bridger, 2003, p. 20.
16. Graves, 2006.

References and further reading

Bridger, Francis (2003), 'A Theological Reflection', in *Guidelines for the Professional Conduct of the Clergy*, London: Church House Publishing, 2003.

Brierley, Peter (2006), 'Pulling out of the Nosedive!', *Ministry Today*, 38, pp. 6–16.

Childers, J. (ed.) (2001), *Birthing the Sermon: Women Preachers on the Creative Process*, St. Louis: Chalice.

Day, David (1998), *A Preaching Workbook*, London: Lynx.

Day, David (2005), *Embodying the Word: A Preacher's Guide*, London: SPCK.

Day, David, Jeff Astley and Leslie J. Francis (eds) (2005), *A Reader on Preaching: Making Connections*, Aldershot: Ashgate.

Florence, Anna Carter, 'Put Away Your Sword! Taking the Torture out of the Sermon', in M. Graves (ed.), *What's the Matter with Preaching Today?*, Louisville: Westminster John Knox, pp. 93–108.

Fosdick, Harry Emerson, 'What Is the Matter with Preaching?', *Harpers Magazine*, 157, July 1928, pp. 133–41.

Francis, Leslie J. (2005), 'Psychological Type and Biblical Hermeneutics: SIFT Method of Preaching', in Day, Astley and Francis (eds), 2005, pp. 75–82.

Graves, Mike (2006), *The Fully Alive Preacher: Recovering from Homiletical Burnout*, Louisville: Westminster John Knox.

Greidanus, S. (1988), *The Modern Preacher and the Ancient Text*, Leicester: IVP.

LaRue, Cleophus J. (2000), *The Heart of Black Preaching*, Louisville: Westminster John Knox.

Lischer, Richard (2002), *The Company of Preachers: Wisdom on Preaching, Augustine to the Present*, Grand Rapids: Eerdmans.

Lischer, Richard (2005), *The End of Words: The Language of Reconciliation in a Culture of Violence*, Cambridge: Eerdmans.

Long, Thomas G. (2005), *The Witness of Preaching*, 2nd edn, Louisville: Westminster John Knox.

Lowry, E. L. (2001), *The Homiletical Plot*, 2nd edn, Louisville: Westminster John Knox.

Lowry, E. L. (1989), *How to Preach a Parable: Designs for Narrative Sermons*, Nashville: Abingdon.

Mathews, Alice P. (2003), *Preaching That Speaks to Women*, Grand Rapids: Baker Books; Leicester: IVP.

Mitchell, Jolyon P. (1999), *Visually Speaking: Radio and the Renaissance of Preaching*, Edinburgh: T&T Clark.

Quicke, Michael J. (2006), *360-Degree Leadership: Preaching to Transform Congregations*, Grand Rapids: Baker Books.

Schlafer, D. J. (1992), *Surviving the Sermon: A Guide to Preaching for Those Who Have to Listen*, Boston: Cowley Publications.

Standing, Roger (2004), *Finding the Plot: Preaching in Narrative Style*, Carlisle: Paternoster.

Trollope, Anthony (1953), *Barchester Towers*, Oxford: Oxford University Press.

Webb, Joseph M. (2001), *Preaching without Notes*, Nashville: Abingdon.

Willimon, W. H., and R. Lischer (1995), *Concise Encyclopedia of Preaching*, Louisville: Westminster.

Wilson, P. S. (1995), *Practice of Preaching*, Nashville: Abingdon.

Wilson, P. S. (1999), *The Four Pages of the Sermon: A Guide to Biblical Preaching*, Nashville: Abingdon.

Wright, Walter C. (2000), *Relational Leadership: A Biblical model for Leadership Service*, Carlisle: Paternoster.

9. Importance of relevant biblical preaching

BOB CALLAGHAN

Imagine

Imagine a preacher, sitting down to prepare an irrelevant sermon for the following Sunday. On the desk is a Bible, open at the passage of scripture that will form the text on which the sermon will be based. The preacher has spent some time in prayer and contemplation, beseeching the Lord to assist in the writing of this irrelevant sermon. This preacher reads again the Bible passages that will be used in worship on Sunday, and turns to a number of resources that will assist in the preparation. The Greek text is consulted in conjunction with a lexicon and commentary. The resource material used by those who help with Children's Church is referred to and subsequently ignored, ensuring that the sermon shall be as irrelevant to as wide a group as possible. (It is important not to forget the children if you are trying to be irrelevant.) This minister of the gospel knows the congregation well, and works hard at ensuring that the message that will be brought on Sunday will speak to absolutely no one.

Of course this scene is imaginary. There has never been a preacher who has set out to be irrelevant in their preaching. They may achieve this by accident, never by design. Those who are called to this ministry, either as lay-preachers or as clergy, seek to proclaim the good news of Jesus Christ in as relevant a way as possible. This chapter aims to encourage those for whom the proclamation of the gospel is part of their Christian ministry. It sets out to ask whether, in this multimedia age, preaching is still an appropriate tool for Christian ministers to use. It will also encourage those who have to prepare sermons Sunday by Sunday to consider ways in which their preaching may be as relevant as possible to their congregations and the communities in which they are placed. It will also encourage preachers and church congregations to consider other opportunities for the message to be proclaimed at times and occasions other than the main Sunday service.

105

Did anyone sleep through the Sermon on the Mount?

A preacher once said from the pulpit to a woman in the congregation, 'Would you mind waking up that man next to you?' She smiled and answered, 'You wake him up. You put him to sleep!' Sermons and preaching in general tend to have a bad press, both inside and outside the Church. Politicians are encouraged not to preach at people, for fear of being seen by the electorate as overstepping the mark in their involvement in people's lives. A nanny state of preachers is not welcomed. Martin Wroe's books helpfully poke fun at the Church and what Christians get up to. In *God: What the Critics Say*, he includes a section entitled 'Church, Worship, Sermons and Boring Stuff like That'. It seems that even within the Church, there are not high expectations that sermons will be relevant, life changing or even life enhancing. They are too often seen as something to be endured by the listener.

There is a classic scene from Mr Bean, often used as a training resource in preaching and evangelism. Rowan Atkinson plays someone obviously unfamiliar with church. On entering the church, he sits next to a member of the congregation, played by Richard Briers. Mr Bean doesn't know when to sit down or stand up; neither does he know the tune to the hymn. The preacher drones on to such an extent that Mr Bean falls asleep, and slips to the floor. Although a caricature of what sermons and the experience of church may be like, it carries some truth and is a warning for any who preach.

It is hard to believe that anyone would have fallen asleep while listening to the Sermon on the Mount. Of course, in the New Testament, preaching has nothing to do with the delivery of sermons to the converted, which is what it usually means today, but always concerns the proclamation of the 'good tidings of God' to the non-Christian world. The word 'relevant' as a word is entirely absent from the New Testament, but there are three words used for preaching (*euangelizesthai*, to preach good tidings; *katangellein*, to declare, announce; and *kerussein*, to proclaim as a herald). These words for preaching must be distinguished from the word for teaching (*didache*), which in the New Testament normally means ethical instruction, or occasionally apologetics or instruction in the faith. This distinction between preaching and teaching is found within the ministry of Jesus himself. Jesus preached (that is, proclaimed the Kingdom of God) and he taught. The instruction that he gave to his disciples in the Sermon on the Mount is *didache* (teaching) rather than preaching. The apostolic Church took the message of the gospel and presented a *kerugma* ('thing preached', 'proclamation') to the world. This *kerugma* is the apostolic gospel that may be summed up as the message of the cross and the resurrection of Jesus Christ.

Jesus used a number of ways to preach the gospel; he didn't rely on one form. He used parables as a medium by which the mystery of the Kingdom message may be conveyed, drawing on images with which people would readily have associated. The message itself may have been a mystery, something to make people puzzle over. But the images and stories were life related. Jesus used images that would have been familiar to people living in a rural environment: sheep, shepherds, seed and harvests. He told stories that drew on life experiences of which all individuals and communities would have had first-hand experience: illness, children running away, difficult family life, mugging, poverty and death. Jesus took these pictures and stories and used them as a base in which to weave the gospel message. Here can be seen a model of relevant preaching that can help today's gospel messengers.

The importance of relevant preaching

Church growth specialists and researchers have highlighted the importance of relevant preaching for over 40 years. From work that began in studying the way churches were growing in the Developing World, a whole movement became established in North America that became known as the Church Growth Movement. As it became clear that church attendance in the United Kingdom was rapidly declining in all denominations, many during the 1970s and 80s received the lessons that American Church Growth practitioners could teach. At the same time as liturgical renewal began to impact on the major denominations, churches found themselves considering how they could maximize the impact they were having. Soon churches were having social and church mission audits, considering new ways of delivering the message, exploring ways in which the laity could be mobilized and spiritual gifts identified and used effectively for mission and service.

Within this culture of learning lessons from the Church Growth Movement, and experimenting with liturgical change, the role of the sermon and preaching in general was seen as key. 'Far too much worship in Britain is culturally irrelevant. Preaching is so out of touch with the ordinary man in the street that attending church has become one of the most irrelevant activities imaginable. The average preacher has lost the common touch' (Pointer, 1984, p. 77). The importance of relevant biblical teaching is a recurring theme in all of the Church Growth teaching. Research that examines why people join some of the larger churches suggests that finding preaching helpful and relevant is an important factor. The research also highlights the fact that people leave churches because of the lack of relevance. In 2005 the Ecumenical Research Committee published the results of a large piece of research in which 70% of 14,000 respondents cited lack of relevance as the reason why they left the church. While it is acknowledged that being relevant is more than just how good a sermon may be, if the preaching in a church is out of touch with the people, the people may well vote with their feet.

The importance of relevant preaching is a core component within a whole range of programmes and movements that have swept through British church life over the past 20 years. In 1984, the Anglican Consultative Council identified 'Proclaiming the good news of the kingdom' (*kerugma*) as the first mark of Mission, thus placing preaching and preachers at the heart of what the Church was about. Since the Decade of Evangelism, the Church in Britain has begun to grapple with the fact that the society in which it found itself was rapidly changing, and those inside the Church were often out of touch with that society. How could a Church hope to be relevant in any way, let alone in its preaching, if it was out of step and out of touch? Gradually the Church has begun to look at itself, and consider new ways of being Church. From the Willow Creek example of Seeker Sensitive Services, through to Building Missionary Congregations, Mission Shaped Church and 'Fresh Expressions of Church', churches in Britain have begun to face the reality of the present situation. Christians have begun to engage with the real society in which they find themselves.

Good News from the Dartford Tunnel

When I received the invitation to contribute this chapter, I immediately thought it was some form of a practical joke. With a little investigation, I discovered that the invitation was based on a view that I may have some experience worth sharing. Throughout my ministry I have had the privilege of working with colleagues who preach well, and have taught me much; and with congregations who have been open to exploring creative ways to proclaim the good news.

Since 1991, I have been Vicar of St Edmund's Dartford, in the Diocese of Rochester. In many ways it is a fairly typical council estate parish, situated next to the Dartford Tunnel, near the local sewage works. (The poorest communities are often placed near sewage works it seems.) The day after my induction as Vicar, a cheque appeared in the post with a note wishing me well in my new ministry, the money was to be spent on the purchase of 100 Bibles for the church. Part of my vision for my new parish was a desire to preach and teach from the Bible, in ways that were life related. Having a Bible for everyone was a helpful step and an encouraging sign. I drew together a 5-year teaching programme that would take the main church congregation through some of the central themes of the Christian faith. For many, this was the first time they had engaged with systematic teaching, and the congregation was responsive. With an increasing congregation it became clear that for some there wasn't just a need for teaching specifically about some of the basic tenets of the faith, but to approach the presentation of the gospel from a life-issue standpoint.

In 1995, as the church celebrated its fortieth anniversary, a new worship service was added into the pattern of Sunday worship. 'Sunday at 11' had as its starting point the presentation of the gospel, based on a number of life-related themes. These themes would direct not only the focus of the preaching but also the structure, direction and content of the worship. It was the themes that were advertised to the local community, rather than the usual description of a worship event. People responded positively to a service that was dealing with life issues, in a way that advertising 'Parish Communion' or 'Evensong' never did. The local press were always keen to print head-lines that referred to the church dealing with issues that were in the news. (Of course, the press would always run a headline if we ran a service looking at anything to do with sex!)

Examples of teaching themes

Who Cares	The Big Four	Why Bother?
Caring for the environment	Money	Why bother with God?
Caring for society	Sex	Why bother with Jesus?
Caring for the family	Love	Why bother with the Church?
Caring for relationships	Death	Why bother with Christmas?

Wishing	Celebrating	Remembering
Wishing I'd never done that	Celebrating our creation	Remembering the living
Wishing you weren't here	Celebrating our differences	Remembering the dead
Wishing I wasn't me	Celebrating ourselves Celebrating our faith	Remembering how I was Remembering how you were

Growing	A Sideways Glance . . .	Would Jesus Christ . . .
Growing out of loneliness	At other religions	Play the lottery?
Growing out of anger	At the Church	Vote Labour, Tory or Liberal?
Growing out of addiction	At families	Be in the Church of England?
Growing out of pain	At community	Live on Temple Hill?

These themes reflect issues that were relevant to the community in which we were placed. The most important rule in relevant preaching is that it is relevant to where you are, not where someone else might be. Relevant preaching has to be grounded in the relationships we form with people in our communities. It should spring out of knowing our people well. It is not difficult to see how themes might be grouped around a particular season or event. The autumn lends itself to issues related with loss, or war perhaps, as the nation marks Remembrance Sunday. A national or international event (for example, the war in Iraq, the Olympics) can often be a springboard to a teaching theme. The relevant preacher should not only know the people in their community well, they should also have an eye and an ear to the world around them. Relevant preachers should be firmly rooted in the world and not spend all their time and energy in the business of church. Keeping up to date with the soaps (try *Coronation Street* rather than *The Archers*), an evening spent in the local pub talking with people, or chatting to folk at the school gate will give enough material for a whole year's teaching themes.

Preaching isn't just for Sundays

Sunday has changed as society has changed. The pattern of work, leisure and family life have altered radically over the past 25 years. Sunday is now a day to shop, visit the family, return home after a weekend break, work on the garden or the house, watch or play sport. The Church is beginning to recognize that it lives in a changed society, and things will never be the same again. Congregations of all denominations are seeing Sunday church attendance change. A regular worshipper might have been someone who went to church once a week or once a fortnight. Now, regular might mean once a month. Whereas Sunday church attendance might be altering, there are many examples of church attendance at other times during the week. Churches that run midweek church are seeing positive results. This has been well researched and documented in both *Mission Shaped Church* and the *Fresh Expressions of Church* material. One of the results of this is that clergy and congregations are beginning to experiment with ways in which to provide worship at times other than Sunday, and for those charged with the responsibility of preaching, this means that they too are beginning to find new and creative ways of presenting the message.

To some extent churches have always operated outside the arena of the main Sunday service, offering a variety of opportunities for preaching. Every time a minister conducts a wedding, a baptism, or a funeral, a sermon would be preached. In these key pastoral situations ministers attempt to make the event as relevant as possible. Within routine church life, there are other similar situations that take place, regularly offering opportunities for preaching in a focused and relevant way. (Christmas carol services, Harvest Festival). There are also the routine contact opportunities that present the preacher with excellent opportunities to make the message relevant – toddler pram services, school assemblies, midweek services, sheltered housing/ nursing home services. Each of these, whether informal or formal, liturgical or unstructured, offer the opportunity to find ways of making the message as relevant as possible to the congregation. Material that is suitable for an infant school assembly would be different to that used in a sheltered housing complex. Preachers naturally modify their material for their audience in these situations; is it such a huge step to take the same amount of preparation and thought when preparing material for the main Sunday service?

These opportunities for preaching can be diarised and planned for. The preacher needs also to be able to present the message on occasions that are unplanned, and sometimes unexpected. Clergy are in a privileged position in dealing with individuals and groups and need to have an eye as to when it might be appropriate to present the message. This may be in response to a local or national event that touches people's spiritual consciousness. Churches that opened their doors for people to sign books of condolence or light candles around the time of the death of Diana, Princess of Wales, were offering people the opportunity to respond to that event in a way that touched them spiritually.

How churches manage these situations is an opportunity to present the gospel. A sermon may never be preached, but the use of our buildings, customs, liturgies and ministries is an important way of communicating *kerugma* to the people of our communities. A sudden or violent death in a community presents the local church with an opportunity to respond appropriately. A national event, such as a royal celebration, a sporting victory, or a tragedy such as the London bombing, presents local churches with an opportunity to encourage people to find ways to respond. However a church chooses to respond, there can always be an opportunity for a word or two setting the event in context.

Welcome to this event, the church rejoices today because God is a God of welcome and celebration.

Welcome to this event, the church shares in the pain people feel, because God shares our pain with us.

Ann Morisy has called this form of ministry 'apt liturgy'. She describes this as 'a specific liturgy which aims at including people with little faith and Christian knowledge and often focuses on a particular distress that has arisen within a community' (Morisy, 2004, p. 237). Clergy need to be aware of the opportunities that present themselves. Not that they behave as vultures swooping on people's grief, but that they respond with pastoral care.

John's story

A priest colleague exercised an excellent example of relevant preaching and apt liturgy. John, aged 17, had recently begun to hang around our church premises. He had left school and because of a difficult family situation had been placed in temporary accommodation. He was using drugs, and would self-harm when particularly stressed. His father died a year before, and the anniversary of the death was approaching. He asked if a ceremony could take place to help him remember his dad. The priest drew a simple ceremony together, and invited a small number of the congregation to join them. Carefully choosing the space where this event would take place, drawing together the right symbols and words it became an effective pastoral opportunity. No 'sermon' was preached, but good news was effectively proclaimed. In John's own words, 'The church changed my father's death ritual. Before I started to go to church I used to get extremely drunk and then self-harm. But this year was different. Instead of doing what I normally do, the church and members of the congregation held a special service for me and my deceased father. I cannot thank them enough for this.' John is currently preparing for confirmation.

References and further reading

Mission and Public Affairs Council (2004), *Mission-Shaped Church: Church Planting and Fresh Expressions of Church in a Changing Context*, London: Church House Publishing.

Morisy, A. (1997), *Beyond the Good Samaritan*, London: Mowbray.

Morisy, A. (2004), *Journeying Out: A New Approach to Christian Mission*, London: Continuum.

Pointer, R. (1984), *How Do Churches Grow?*, Basingstoke: Marshalls.

Warren, R. (1995), *Building Missionary Congregations*, London: Church House Publishing.

Willans, J. (2005), Church Survey, Ecumenical Research Committee, <www.churchsurvey.co.uk>.

Wroe, M. (1992), *God: What the Critics Say*, London: Hodder & Stoughton.

See also

10. Combining relevance with a timeless perspective

TIM HARLE

An unlikely parable

As sermon preparation goes, it was not ideal. Work commitments had devoured my week; family commitments meant that I was accompanying my wife and young children to the supermarket on Saturday morning. We did a deal – I could sit in the coffee shop as long as I was ready to load up the trolley. Grateful for a few moments' relative peace, I turned for the first time to discover what passage I would be preaching on the following morning. It was . . . the Feeding of the 5000. While not being proud of this example of work-life imbalance, or of a lamentable failure to provide time for prayerful reflection in the days before, the surroundings of the initial preparation certainly made sure the sermon was relevant to a congregation of ordinary people.

Beginning preaching preparation

This chapter does not aim to reproduce material on sermon preparation, which is well covered elsewhere (see, for example, the writings of David Schlafer under Further Reading). Nor does it pretend that being 'relevant' somehow means we can skip careful preparation – if anything, the reverse applies. Not all of us can be up to date with every nuance of the 'new perspective', or of narrative, reader response, feminist, post-colonial and socio-rhetorical criticism, but it does behove us to be aware of the pivotal position we hold at the porous boundary between word and world. Whether in homily or extended exposition, we have a responsibility to be relevant.

Where to start?

Where do we start? At the risk of oversimplification, some would say start with the biblical passage(s). Others advocate a topical approach. Others say we should start where people are.

Meeting people where they are may trip off the tongue, but those who experience our sermons are unlikely to be a homogeneous group. It is good to hold different individuals in mind – the truculent teenager, the Oxford professor, the single parent – while preparing. It easy to get one group nodding sagely, but a far greater challenge to find appropriate forms for the glorious diversity of people who make up the people of God.

We could do a lot worse than follow our Lord's example. He wasn't averse to systematic exposition (remember the road to Emmaus!), but excelled in conversing with ordinary people – sowers, shepherds, Samaritans – in their own language. Whatever the situation, he was steeped in the Hebrew scriptures and ready to engage with people where they were.

In deciding where to start, we need to recognize the accumulated wisdom incorporated in the churches' lectionaries. Michael Vasey was a passionate advocate, and coined the memorable phrase 'Better than Trainspotting' to describe how lectionaries could help in worship.[1] Commenting on his perspective, two fellow liturgists wrote,

> Far from an arcane pastime, the design of lectionaries is of crucial importance to the life of the church. 'Calendar and lectionary are actually about the life-transforming encounter between Bible and church. Together they are the mechanics of how the Bible gets into the worship of the church' [quoting Vasey]. When challenged, [Vasey] said the lectionary is not a spotters' guide, but the train timetable itself. We may not read it from cover to cover for relaxation, but we are grateful when our trains run to time, and connections are made.

Relevant?

So what constitutes relevance? Checking the news channels, web sites and podcasts for points of contact? Absolutely. Keeping up to date with some soaps and so-called reality shows? Of course. But we should be seeking something more. After all, those with whom we seek to communicate are likely to be on their own search.

We certainly need to keep abreast of the postmodern world we inhabit, but pandering to the latest trends may bring pity and contempt rather than offer true engagement.[2] We need to combine contemporary relevance with a timeless perspective. Writing in another context, John Baggley noted how timelessness can be a two-edged sword for the Church, 'either as a commendation of its sense of the holy and the continuing tradition of the church, or else as a condemnation of its failure to face up to political and social issues in a rapidly changing world'.[3]

We may need to combine simplicity with profundity. A trawl through entries for foolishness and wisdom in a biblical concordance will show that we stand in a well-trodden tradition.

What topics are relevant? The uniqueness of the incarnation surely suggests that nothing is beyond the interest of the Almighty. So let us not limit ourselves to the big ideas, important as they are. The Roman Church did many a favour when it coined the term Ordinary Time for the periods outside the pivotal Christmas and Easter seasons. Relevance may relate to the ordinary things of life. We are happy to sing of 'praise in the common things of life'.[4] George Herbert (1593–1633) offers us powerful imagery, whether of the divine drudgery of sweeping floors or the description of prayer as 'heaven in ordinary'.[5] Yet our sermons so often avoid the ordinary. Mark Greene of the London Institute for Contemporary Christianity reports that 50% of the Christians he surveyed had never heard a single sermon on work.[6]

Engage in conversation

Preaching is neither a solo performance nor a spectator sport. We need to engage in all sorts of ways. Expressions such as 'double' and 'triple listening' are used, the latter meaning we should listen to God's word, the world and God's people.[7] But triple listening doesn't convey the breadth of the listening we must engage in. We should be engaging, actively listening, with – at least – the God who cares, with the world he creates and sustains, with his word, with the company of saints, with the dynamic tradition of the Church, with our immediate listeners and hearers, with those who are absent (including through choice), with ourselves.

We need to engage in spirited conversation with those with whom we have the privilege and responsibility of sharing the Word of God. Advocating the importance of preaching as dialogue, Jeremy Thomson could ask if the sermon was a sacred cow.[8] Jesus engaged in conversation to understand, share, teach, encourage and challenge.[9]

Understand different learning styles

Buried away in the Church of England's *Common Worship* book is a note about the sermon. 'The term "sermon" includes less formal exposition, the use of drama, interviews, discussion, audio-visuals and the insertion of hymns or other sections of the service between parts of the sermon.'[10] While this can lead to embarrassing personal indulgence and 'Death by PowerPoint', the underlying thought is congruent with the idea of multiple intelligence[11] and different styles of learning. It is also interesting to reflect how there is nothing new in using different channels of communication. In the Book of the Twelve, we read that the prophet will 'keep watch to see what he will say to me' (Habakkuk 2.1 [NRSV]). How many of us listen with our eyes, or watch with our ears?

One of the gravest traps we can fall into as preachers is to attempt to reduce the almighty Word, the *logos*, to mere words.[12] Have those who direct the congregation to page 1178 of the pew Bibles forgotten that the word was first and foremost proclaimed? That the apostles, prophets and teachers spoke before they wrote?

Nor should we underestimate the power of images. The only occasion when I have (knowingly) reduced someone to tears during a sermon came when I showed a picture of one of the great vineyards of Châteauneuf-du-Pape. The dominant images were of arid stony ground and severely pruned gnarled old vines. Yet over a long period of time, much of it hidden from our gaze, this unpromising scene produces some of the world's noblest red wines. For someone facing an uncertain future following the loss of a loved one, or the cutting down of a relationship, such images can speak more powerfully than words.

Of course, this is nothing new to those who understand the power of icons. One of my most humbling experiences when 'preaching' was to stand before Rublev's famous icon one Trinity Sunday with, unknown to me, the family of a distinguished Calvinist professor of biblical studies in the congregation. The shared ground we discovered that day – as we were drawn in to share in the life of the three figures gathered around the table for a meal – is testimony to the power of the word in its widest sense.[13]

So we should not be surprised to discover that one of the common features of so-called Alternative Worship[14] involves the use of multiple senses to communicate God's grace. Those used to centuries of incense and icons may wonder what all the fuss is about. Acknowledging the risks involved in liquid[15] church, Pete Ward advises that 'By paying attention to what is communicated, we can seek to remain faithful to the dynamic and living word of God'.[16]

Integrate Word and Sacrament

Churches from different traditions may place their emphasis in different ways. A glance at worship space is often illuminating. What is the dominant feature? Altar, pulpit, projection screen or drum kit? A former Archbishop of Canterbury wrote passionately[17] of the need to re-establish the place of the Word, including silence (let it be noted), in worship.

A good place for preachers to visit is the road to Emmaus (Luke 24.13–35). Despite instruction in all things 'beginning with Moses and the prophets', Cleopas and his companion only had their eyes opened in the breaking of the bread.

We can note that there is nothing new in the call to see consistency between word and action. The eighth-century BCE prophet, Amos of Tekoa could rail:

I hate, I despise your festivals,
and I take no delight in your solemn assemblies.

Instead, he cried out,

Let justice roll down like waters,
and righteousness like an ever-flowing stream.
(Amos 5.21, 24 [NRSV])

Before moving on, we can reflect how many preachers may find a mirror in the vestry as they prepare before a service. But are these mirrors misplaced? Might it not be better if a mirror was placed in each pulpit? I certainly find it a helpful – if hard –discipline to hold up a virtual mirror to myself when preaching. Perhaps in our weakness, we find strength.

Be prepared to learn

Keith Grint, Professor of Leadership Studies at the UK's Defence College, uses the term 'inverse learning' to describe something he observed on training courses.[18] Just as parents can learn from their children, he found learning did not always follow expected paths. Reflecting on my experience of leading worship in a hospital, I wondered 'who was teaching whom?'.[19] My recent experience as a primary school governor reinforces the view. No amount of practice of dealing with government ministers, of being grilled on radio and television, could prepare me for the feeling of vulnerability as I stood in front of the whole school leading an assembly for the first time.

The trend away from speaking of training, in favour of learning, may simply be window dressing. Or it may be a recognition that the dynamics are not as linear as we previously assumed. If inverse learning can be seen in the traditionally ordered world of the military, how much more ought we to look for it in our churches.

Watch your language

Language evolves. So it is important to beware (be aware) of what people hear when we speak. This cuts both ways. 'Wicked' may have reversed its earlier meaning, but digging back to the original language can make passages come alive. When Jesus said to the Canaanite woman, 'Great is your faith!' (Matthew 15.28), it may help to know that the Greek word used is *megale*. 'Mega is your faith' may make some people take notice.

While considering language, it is important to be careful not to let casual phrases slip. Examples include 'The Bible says' (Which bit? Who? To whom? In what context? What form of scripture?). This may be a good place to add a note of caution about being wary of simply searching for a phrase on the web and taking the first answer returned.

Explore the margins

How often do we find ourselves viewing a passage of scripture from somewhere near the centre of the action? A few years ago, our family was taking a short pre-Easter break in a small village. We joined the congregation at the tiny local church for their Palm Sunday service. They had a tradition of reading the passion gospel together, each taking one of the roles. The 'meaty' parts were dished out: narrator, Jesus, Peter, Pilate. One or two nervous eyes were cast at the unfamiliar family at the back. As the final parts were being assigned, they turned to me. Would I mind being 'Bystander 2'? I read my two lines with all the gusto I could summon up. And I like to think that the Easter Sunday sermon I delivered the following week was enhanced as a result of this unfamiliar perspective on apparently familiar events.

As we follow one who was born in a stable and died on the edge of a city, we should not be surprised to discover how important the margins, or edges can be.[20] My own ministry has been enormously enhanced by working with those whom society does not always wish to embrace at the heart of their community.

Conclusion

We started in a supermarket coffee shop and finished in the shoes of 'Bystander 2'. This reminds us that, however invaluable and essential the time we spend in the study preparing, our commitment is to one who became flesh and lived among us. We should seek continually to offer his message of good news as timeless, fresh and relevant. Then perhaps we, and those with whom we engage in preaching, can be drawn to see his glory, full of grace and truth.

Notes

1. The expression originated in a chapter Vasey contributed to Trevor Lloyd et al., 1997. This addressed the Church of England's adaptation of the Revised Common Lectionary (RCL). The subsequent extract is taken from Cocksworth and Fletcher, 2001, p. 17.

2. Searching <www.amazon.co.uk> for books entitled 'Gospel according to' produces interesting results. In November 2006, the gospels according to The Beatles, Disney and The Simpsons, to Ali G and Chris Moyles, and to Biff (Christ's childhood pal) were outselling any of the conventional Gospels.

3. Baggley, 1987, p. xi. His comments were directed at the Orthodox Church, but have a broader application.

4. In the hymn 'Fill thou my life, O Lord my God', by Horatius Bonar (1808–89).

5. In the hymn 'Teach me, my God and King' and the poem 'Prayer', respectively. In the latter, Herbert goes on to refer to prayer as 'something understood'.

6. Greene, 2001, p. 17.

7. 'Double listening' is attributed to both John Stott and George Lings. Mark Greene promotes 'Triple listening' (see, for example, *Imagine*, <http://www.eauk.org/resources/publications/upload/Imagine.pdf>, p. 19).

8. Thomson, 2003.

9. See Shaw, 2005. Although not specifically geared towards preaching in its traditional sense, this book opens up several examples of Jesus engaging in conversation.

10. *Common Worship: Services and Prayers for the Church of England* (2000), p. 27, n. 7.

11. Particularly associated with the educationalist Howard Gardner. See, for example, Gardner, 2000.

12. This actually behoves us to spend longer in seeking understanding. My own appreciation of the Prologue to John's Gospel was helped enormously by Raymond E. Brown's magisterial Anchor Bible commentary (1966–70), where he devotes a modest 37 pages to these 18 verses.

13. I wonder how much a deep knowledge of the powerful Old Testament allusions to Abraham and his companions helped in this encounter.

14. Baker and Gay with Brown, 2003. See also <www.alternativeworship.org>.

15. The term is used in the sense used by the sociologist Zygmunt Bauman (2000): it reflects a form of society which is becoming less 'solid' and more flexible.

16. Ward, 2000, p. 71.

17. Coggan, 1996.

18. Grint, 2005, pp. 103–6.

19. Harle, 2004, p. 15.

20. The insights of complexity theory, including the so-called 'edge of chaos', are highly relevant. See Chapter 31, 'Sustaining a Process of Change', for further exploration.

References and further reading

Baggley, John (1987), *Doors of Perception: Icons and Their Spiritual Significance*, Oxford: Mowbray.

Baker, Jonny, and Doug Gay with Jenny Brown (2003), *Alternative Worship*, London: SPCK.

Baumann, Zygmunt (2000), *Liquid Modernity*, Cambridge: Polity Press.

Brown, Raymond E. (1966–70), *The Gospel according to John*, Anchor Bible, 2 vols, New York: Doubleday.

Cocksworth, Christopher, and Jeremy Fletcher (2001), *Common Worship Daily Prayer*, Grove Worship Series 166, Cambridge: Grove Books.

Coggan, Donald (1996), *A New Day for Preaching: The Sacrament of the Word*, London: SPCK.

Common Worship: Services and Prayers for the Church of England (2000), London: Church House Publishing.

Gardner, Howard (2000), *Intelligence Reframed: Multiple Intelligences for the 21st Century*, New York: Basic Books.

Greene, Mark (2001), *Thank God It's Monday*, 3rd edn, Bletchley: Scripture Union.

Lloyd, Trevor, et al. (1997), *Introducing the New Lectionary*, Grove Worship Series 141, Cambridge: Grove Books.

Grint, Keith (2005), *Leadership: Limits and Possibilities*, Basingstoke: Palgrave Macmillan.

Harle, Tim (2004), 'Lessons from the Margins', *The Reader*, 101, 4, pp. 14–15.

Schlafer, David J. (1998), *What Makes This Day Different?: Preaching Grace on Special Occasions*, Cambridge, Massachusetts: Cowley Publications.

Schlafer, David J. (2004), *Playing with Fire: Preaching Work as Kindling Art*, Cambridge, Massachusetts: Cowley Publications.

Shaw, Peter (2005), *Conversation Matters: How to Engage Effectively with One Another*, London and New York: Continuum.

Thomson, Jeremy (2003), *Preaching as Dialogue: Is the Sermon a Sacred Cow?*, 2nd edn, Pastoral Series 68, Cambridge: Grove Books.

Ward, Pete (2002), *Liquid Church*, Peabody, Massachusetts: Hendrickson; Carlisle: Paternoster.

Booklets on preaching can be found in Grove Books' Worship, Pastoral and Biblical series. For an up-to-date list, visit the website at <www.grovebooks. co.uk>, select the 'Titles by Subject' tab, and click on 'Preaching'.

Although this is not the place to list biblical commentaries in detail, mention can be made of the Interpretation series (Louisville, Kentucky: John Knox Press), which is aimed particularly at preachers. Fred Craddock on Luke (1990) is outstanding. Given the importance of understanding the original language, the Word Biblical Commentary (Nashville, Tennessee: Thomas Nelson) provides helpful transliteration, albeit within a rather repetitive format. Hugh Williamson on Ezra-Nehemiah (1985) and Andrew Lincoln on Ephesians (1990) are two fine examples. It is also worth following the Berit Olam and Sacra Pagina series on the two testaments, being published by Michael Glazier (Collegeville, Minnesota).

Thinking Strategically

11. Thinking strategically

PETER BRIERLEY

The well-known proverb states, 'Where there is no wisdom the people perish.' It is best, although not inevitable, that before you start to think strategically, you have a vision to think strategically about.

Other chapters in this book look at the ways by which a vision may be developed – two key ways are by extrapolating into the future from the past and present situation in your church, or by moving backwards from the more distant future to the near future. This chapter therefore focuses on how that stated vision may be enabled, and gives two diametrically opposed methods by which strategic thinking fulfils that brief.

Enabling a vision to be fulfilled is a function of leadership, but leadership operates in a variety of ways. The two ways described here are like the two extremes of a spectrum – you may be totally at one end or totally at the other. But most people will be somewhere in between. Knowing where you come on that continuum can be helpful, so we look at that after describing the two extremes.

Relating and delegating

Pastor John Thomas is the minister of Fishhoek Baptist Church in Cape Town, South Africa. In 1993, after he had been there for five years and seen his church grow in number to 150, he wondered how best to evangelize the local community.

He approached the local radio station and, asking if he could broadcast for 2 hours a day for a week as an experiment, was utterly taken aback to be given permission to broadcast on a given frequency for 24 hours a day for a whole month to the south-west corner of Cape Town. When he got the letter it also stated the designated month started in 3 weeks time!

What would you do, given such a superb but totally unexpected opportunity?

Next day, he visited one of his church members at work. 'How nice to see you, Pastor,' said Bill. (Names other than the minister, John

Thomas, have been changed.) 'Do come in. Cup of coffee?" John explained what had happened. 'That's tremendous', exclaimed Bill, 'but why have you come to see me?' 'I'd like you to take a month's unpaid leave from your work,' replied John, 'and make it happen – raise the money, buy the equipment, find someone to put all the programmes together, locate a place to operate from and coordinate the whole effort.'

'Phew!' said Bill, taking all this in. 'When do you want me to start?' 'Tomorrow,' said John, and Bill, to his credit, did. Owing entirely to Bill's clear managerial ability, which John knew about, the whole project was carried through successfully, on time, with all the necessary finances raised. This radio station was so much appreciated that some 13,000 letters were received that month encouraging them to keep going.

It was a big step to decide to do so, but they did and, by the time I visited them in 2001, Radio CCM, as it was called, was the largest community radio station in South Africa with over 200,000 daily listeners.

Indeed, it became so successful that the leaders of Fishhoek Baptist Church, now relocated in a new (warehouse) building, agreed to start similar ones in every African country south of the Sahara. An A3 news-sheet was produced to illustrate their vision for each country. It was illustrated by children and put around the walls of the church lounge.

When he showed me round the lounge, John pointed to one of the pictures and explained, 'This one is Namibia,' explained John. 'Pat is looking after that; it's gone well. The station is about to open, and some of the volunteers are coming for training next week.' Moving to the next sheet, John indicated that Angola was proving more difficult. 'The civil war has made it hard to know where best we should locate the station, but Bert is visiting the churches there and will make a decision soon.'

'This one is interesting,' said John, pointing to a sheet labelled Basutoland. 'We are going to build not just a radio station, but a hospital and Bible seminary as well, all paid for as Mike has already obtained agreement from the government which will buy the electricity from the dam we're building. Now this one is Kenya . . .'

I interrupted. 'You say you are building a dam?' I asked. 'How much?' 'Yes, we are. Oh, it'll cost about £10 million, but Kevin is good at raising money and has already more than half. Now in Kenya . . .' 'But there's not another Baptist church in the world building a dam,' I said. 'Probably not,' calmly replied John and he finally told me about the Kenyan project.

John kindly took me to my next appointment. 'You see this field, opposite the squatter camp?' he asked me. 'I came back from holiday, saw it was for sale, so immediately bought it. That's where the AIDS hospital is being built. Peter has prepared all the plans, Charlie is raising the money, and Ted is organizing the whole thing.'

South African fields are much the same as English fields, by the way, but John insisted on stopping. In one corner of the field, an old pub was being renovated and, in the grassy patch to the left of the drive, John pointed out where the entrance would be, the site of the consulting rooms, the operating table, the counselling area and so on. Two years later, when I wrote this up in *Coming Up Trumps*,[1] he told me the hospital was already open!

John is an exceptional man, but not unique in his particular gifts. It is obvious that he knows his people well, but his key virtue is that he simply gives away his vision. He sees what other people do not see (have you ever envisaged a hospital when driving past an empty field?), but asks others to take over his vision. That means that Ted gets the 'glory' for building the hospital, not John. John trusts Bill, Pat, Bert, Mike, Ted to do the job, and allows them to choose their own teams to help them finish it on time and to raise the needed finance.

Strategic thinking? It is certainly strategic insight, strategic vision, and ultimately strategic accomplishment. When the phrase, 'strategic thinking' is used, this is not the method that most readily comes to mind! It is, however, one end of the spectrum, a crucial part of the process by which vision comes to fruition.

> Relating and delegating is the ability to achieve multiple projects simultaneously through delegation of total vision fulfilment to those trusted people (often business people) deemed highly likely to be capable of carrying them out on time.[2]

The military model

The very name will immediately indicate that this method has a large amount of processing and organization. This model focuses on three broad areas: strategic significance, operational impact and tactical success. We will look at each of these briefly.

Strategic significance

Strategic thinking requires lateral thinking, outside-the-box or beyond-the horizon thinking, relating to issues of wider importance, spanning past and present. It can fall into two broad areas – the grand strategic and the local strategic.

Jesus gave us his grand strategy in Matthew 28 when he told us to go into all the world and preach the good news to everyone. Every church or Christian agency should be operating under this broad general strategy. For most of us, such grand strategies are beyond our scope; we simply don't plan across two millennia! But there is no reason why a church denomination or a diocese shouldn't have a 'grand strategy' for the next 5 or 10 years. Some, of course, do have an overarching vision.

A church or agency's individual local strategy needs to be worked out in the light of a grand strategy. That means thinking about the people who will be involved, the necessary communication, the finance to be raised (usually!) as well as the different parts of the project itself. This local strategy is then broken down into the next area of responsibility.

Operational impact

This is the level where particular responsibilities are key, and where the leader converts strategy into practical activity. This could include delegation in such areas as youth work, the evangelism committee or the worship group. The area covered is broad but specific, and for each of the activities functional not theoretical.

It is at this level that plans are needed to fulfil the objective. Is training required? Where will the money come from? Does special equipment have to be ordered? All the different actions which need to be taken must be identified in order to get some idea of the goals required to achieve the total project. It is at this stage that leaders look at which individuals, or groups or people are to be involved – that home group, or membership committee – the people who live in the street, or the folk who work in this broad area – those who have the expertise or whatever.

Having identified the goals to be achieved, the priorities for achieving them then have to be agreed. Which are the most important goals? In what order do they come? Does the achievement of one goal depend upon the success of another? What would happen if one of them didn't occur? Would anyone notice? Which carry the greatest weight? Which will yield the highest consequences for the overall project?

Then the timings for each priority need to be sorted out. How long will each realistically take to complete? Will the performance of that overlap with the performance of this? Are the same people used for both, or the same materials, or do they clash in terms of location? Should allowance be made for overrunning, or late starting?

There is another aspect of operational impact that is sometimes overlooked. A task is often begun with great zeal. What steps need to be taken during the life of the initial project to allow it to continue into the future? If a church employs a youth worker for the first time and finds his or her work useful and helpful, it is no good waiting for the end of the 3-year contract before working out how to raise the funds for his/her successor! It is easier to think about how to carry on a strategic piece of work while the enthusiasm and energy and excitement are still there to celebrate its success.

Tactical success

This is where the rubber hits the road, the nitty gritty of the sharp end of performance, the detailed, day-to-day, ground level of activity. It is where the Sunday School teacher gives such an enthralling lesson that her 8-year olds will be sure to return the following week. It is where the relevant sermon makes an impact on those who hear it. It is when the meeting with that couple proves to be the turning point in their life. Without success here, the best laid out strategies come to nothing. In military terms, this is the winning of the engagement, the neutralizing of the enemy, a favourable outcome for this particular involvement.

The invisible

There is one further key element in the military model. After the thinking and planning, there is one further question to be answered. 'Is there anything else we should be doing to try to ensure that what we have planned will be successful?'

In the mid 1990s what had been Yugoslavia exploded into civil war with several new nations coming into being, previously having been part of a united country. NATO was asked to intervene to try to bring peace and it approached the British Army, requesting that it be responsible for disarming the belligerent countries. The Army High Command (whatever it is technically called) discussed this request and agreed to do it and asked one of its generals to take on the responsibility. He did a fine job, and every day for several weeks on the evening news the BBC showed pictures of the Serbs handing over ammunition and the Croatians handing over guns, some days more on one side, some days more from the other. This had been a carefully planned operation involving strategic objectives, operational impact and tactical success.

It was, however, but one side of a highly visible action. The other side was the invisible part. When the Army's help was requested, it not only agreed to organize the disarming process, but also asked the question 'Is there anything else we should be doing to try to ensure that what we have planned will be successful?' The Army leaders concluded that disarming alone would not bring the objective of peace to the region.

After much discussion, they agreed that the people on the ground needed to be persuaded that this was the best opportunity for peace that they were going to get, so it would be sensible to take it. But who would convince the mullahs, priests and village leaders that they needed to tell this to the people in each community? They decided this should be done by some of the Army Generals. So, out of sight of all the TV cameras, key British personnel visited the leaders in village after village encouraging them to persuade each village community to accept the terms of peace being offered. They were successful and war between the former components of Yugoslavia has not broken out since.

The question therefore needs to be asked in your church context also. What else needs to be done to try and ensure that what you have planned will be successful? This is not an easy question to answer, but it is an essential one if what you aim to do is to be accomplished.

The 'invisible', or Centre of Gravity as it is sometimes called, may be defined as:

That essential action or actions which if carried out successfully will allow and enable the fulfilment of strategic, operational and tactical objectives.

A church decided to appoint a youth worker. The church leaders knew this person would need to run their existing midweek Youth Club, and be responsible for youth services, but what else might he/she do?

The minister decided to visit the head teachers of the five local secondary schools within two miles of the church, to tell them that the church was appointing a youth worker and to ask, if they were interested, whether they would be very happy for that person to be invited to take the occasional assembly in their schools. The youth worker therefore had a sphere of operation when he arrived and a ready avenue to approach local schools as a key to involvement and getting known. The minister had acted to allow the fulfilment of the objectives, but not to achieve them – the youth worker had to do that.

How can one go about trying to answer the 'invisible' question? Perhaps, by trying to answer an alternative question such as 'What do we *have* to do to retain a sense of identity and purpose for the church or organization?' Some may object that getting to that is just as hard! If so, perhaps trying to answer the following questions may enable a conclusion to emerge for this 'invisible question':

1 If you could change one thing about your present position, what would it be and why?
2 What is the biggest hindrance you currently face in evangelizing your local community?
3 If resources were no problem, what feature would you innovate in the next six months?

Where there is no vision, the Church perishes; where there is no vision the leaders perish. Vision is essential for planning forward but plans have to be made and enabled. They also have to be implemented by people with the courage to keep on going. 'Strategy', Sir Terry Leahy, Chief Executive of Tesco, says, 'is only part of the battle. The difference between success and failure is the difference between implementing, say, 80% or only 50% of your plans.' That is just as true for church leaders!

Notes

1. Peter Brierley (2004), *Coming up Trumps!* Milton Keynes: Authentic Media; and London: Christian Research
2. Ibid., p. 143.

12. Coaching

JENNIFER TANN

Coach: So what is your main concern about the hostel for the future?
Client: To iron-out seasonality in bookings and keep the place full.
Coach: If you were to dream dreams for the business what would they look like?
Client: Ah well . . . to run this hostel and the place across the road (with similar problems) as one unit.
Coach: What would have to happen to make this a reality?

Farm, church, housing association, college, hotel, gift shop, restaurant, tax accountancy and many others could be substituted for 'hostel' in the dialogue above; for they all experience seasonal variations in 'demand'. This example encapsulates much of what coaching is about. The coach is focused on and believes in the client and in his/her ability to solve their own problem; the coach does not provide an answer, nor 'cap' the client's insight with an example from elsewhere.

An increasing number of senior executives in industry, the public and not-for-profit sectors, the professions and church leaders are adopting coaching for their own and colleagues' support and development. So what is coaching? Jenny Rogers defines it as working with clients to achieve 'speedy and sustainable effectiveness in their lives and careers . . . The coach's sole aim is to work with the client to achieve all of the client's potential – as defined by the client.'[1] This definition encapsulates some important principles, namely, that the client has the resources to resolve his/her problems and it is the role of the coach to help release this resourcefulness. Coaching addresses the whole person – their past, present and future – and it concerns change and action. The agenda is set by the client. Robert Hargrove emphasizes the transformational role of coaching which 'involves expanding people's capacity to make a difference',[2] expanding the client's horizons of possibility. The foundation of effective coaching is a relationship based on mutual trust and respect. This requires the client to be consistent in what they say and the coach to be consistent, honest and adhere strictly to a promise of confidentiality.

Moreover, the coach needs to demonstrate his/her belief in the client's potential for transformation:

Coach: Your commitment to personal growth and organizational transformation is inspiring and I am sure it will yield results.

Coaching focuses on the individual (sometimes as a member of a team) – both in and outside their professional role – but emphases differ. Some people seek support for a specific task which is anticipated to be difficult (for example, a radical new business strategy or change within a large organization); others wish to enhance their leadership skills in the top team, to find focus and improve their relationship management; others, having moved to a new top job, seek holistic and challenging support as they find their feet in the new role; others (perhaps a person who has risen through the ranks of their profession quickly, or a parish priest who has been a long time in the same place) seek coaching because they feel vulnerable or stale. These interventions are not always called coaching; some prefer the term work consultancy, strategic conversation or creative conversation. In these situations the emphasis is more on the individual in their work role, their 'other' life, while not out-of-bounds, being kept at arm's length. The focus of coaching is on what the client most needs.

Coaching has many benefits. First, it is tailored to the specific as well as the general development needs of the individual (the client) at times to suit him/her; second, the methods employed are varied to suit the client; and third, the coach can be selected according to the level, needs and personality of the client. The greatest difficulty for executive coaches lies in the common assumption that one individual can change another's behaviour or attitudes. But the client must be receptive to the idea and reality of coaching; coaching imposed by a senior manager upon a colleague does not work. Successful coaching is not something which is done to another; it is a learning partnership undertaken willingly and with the expectation that the client will be prepared to work on agreed material both during and between sessions. And there may be a greater receptivity to coaching at times of transition, when an individual is experiencing major change and new challenges. While a typical coaching session may last from one and a half to two hours, an occasional focused but informal session of ten minutes either in person or on the telephone is legitimate, providing the coach avoids the temptation to rush in with answers.

A particularly effective approach to coaching is where the work overtly starts from the client's strengths. Organizations appoint people on the basis of their strengths but, in many situations, lead and manage people for their weaknesses. The difference between a strengths-based approach and one focusing on weaknesses is profound. Many Christian leaders have a tendency to focus on their deficits/weaknesses. And the temptation for the coach is to boost their own ego by 'sorting somebody else out'.

This is not to suggest that leaders should ignore what they and others are less good at but, rather, the coach can help them to use their strengths so well that they can be applied as a proxy in areas of less strength. Perhaps the most important thing to learn about less-strong areas is that when an individual has to use less-preferred areas of their personality for long periods it is psychologically costly. Managing to 'cope' (in the psychological sense) with tough work demands is a different attitude of mind from believing (or being encouraged to believe) that one should aim to be an expert in everything. In the somewhat overused expression, it is better to get a squirrel to climb trees than a turkey.

The concept of the coach as 'thinking partner' for the client is a way of defusing any initial client defensiveness. A thinking partnership is also a powerful way of releasing intellectual energy through the creative imagining of possibilities in a safe environment where 'half-baked' ideas can be explored and assumptions challenged. A thinking partnership is a place where a senior executive can share thinking and achieve insights which are often not achievable alone, as well as explore ways of communicating them, before sharing them with the top team.

In some situations, 360-degree feedback may be appropriate at the commencement of a coaching partnership. This may be at the suggestion of either coach or client and may be particularly relevant where the coach is working with a top executive team both collectively and individually. It can also be relevant with an individual client who is seeking to take stock of where they are, with a view to making some changes in their professional life. Much 360-degree feedback consists of a questionnaire form which is completed by senior, peer and junior colleagues. Around 60 questions with a 5-point rating scale is an effective number, and responses can be made by email. Alternatively, a qualitative approach can be adopted, employing as few as 4 carefully chosen questions with around 8 respondents selected by the client and contacted by the coach for purposes of confidentiality:

- What do you enjoy about X?
- What are X's particular strengths and contributions?
- What would be useful development areas for X to take forward in his/her
  a) professional life
  b) personal life

- Which are the top 3 areas you would like to see X focus on particularly in his/her ongoing development?

One of my professional clients deliberately included two respondents who were expected to be critical. And they were, in a constructive way. The coach, having received the feedback by email (although face-to-face or by telephone would be alternatives), collated the anonymous responses into a two-page report for the client. This formed the basis of a creative conversation in which the client explored new avenues for her professional work and her work–life balance overall. The advantage of 360-degree feedback is that it supplements the client's story with observational data. We are all capable of self-delusion, of inflated views of the levels of our own performance, and of explaining away difficult experiences.

Coach: How well do you know yourself?
Client: (*starts a long ramble about their family background*)
Coach: Why do you think you have difficulty with 'working the room' at receptions and conferences? (*followed later by*) What stratagems could you use to help yourself in these situations?

Non-pejorative, developmental psychometrics is a valuable means of offering the client objective data on what makes them tick. Many senior leaders and managers from different walks of life lack an understanding of their strengths and preferences and because of this cannot explain to themselves, their colleagues or family why certain activities energize them and others exhaust them. Psychometrics offers an objective means by which individuals can understand what they share in common with colleagues and wherein lie the differences. In situations where the coach is working with an executive team, a well-selected psychometric problem can provide the basis for an exploration of team complementarities and similarities. And, sometimes, an individual and his/her colleagues may come to recognize that he/she is in the wrong job. In one large organization, the Team Management System questionnaire demonstrated that the company secretary was required to be in coping behaviour much of the time, since the job requirements involved a large amount of detail, whereas his personal style preferences were for the big picture, going back to first principles and seeking off-the-wall solutions. Psychometrics provides a common language framework, to which reference can be made during coaching sessions, by way of offering a possible explanation for events.

One of the most popular psychometric methods for coaching purposes is the Myers Briggs Type Indicator™ (MBTI), based on an underlying Jungian framework (see Appendix for details of all psychometrical systems mentioned). MBTI offers hypotheses about the behaviours likely to be associated with each style. There are no right or wrong style preferences, although, as in the example above, individuals may find certain tasks (and behaviours) more or less comfortable. Although MBTI does not offer insights into coping behaviour, as such, the coach can help the client to identify areas of work and personal life which are likely to be more psychologically costly than others (the opposite styles to those preferred by the client) and to work on coping strategies. While most people who know about MBTI have taken the basic (Step 1) measure, there is a more detailed measure (MBTI Step 2™) which subdivides each of the four dimensions, highlighting where the person has an 'out-of-style preference' – an 'oops' – in one or more elements. This can offer helpful explanations of, for example, the shy extrovert, the person who likes order and systems but struggles to be a completer-finisher, or the logical thinker who has a strong sense of personal values.

Firo-B™ identifies the individual's need and presented (shown) style in relationships and can be helpful, for example, for a Chief Executive Officer (CEO) to understand the extent to which others perceive his/her need for control, or for an individual who keeps their need for affection hidden, using as a safer proxy their 'including-others' style preference. Some coaches use Strengths Finder, the psychometric method for which is taken online upon the purchase of Buckingham and Clifton's book (see References and Further Reading). If a coach has been approached to work in a particular area with a client, for example to enhance his/her confidence in leadership, the Inspirational Leadership Tool is a useful starting point; or when a key element of a company's strategy is to become more innovative, specific psychometrical methods such as the Innovation Potential Indicator or KAI can be helpful in identifying individuals with strengths for specific innovatory roles and, through coaching feedback, to develop them in these roles. Where a coach is working with a team, the Team Management Systems profile provides a means by which members can explore their relative style preferences – their complementarities and differences – the latter usually being where people annoy one another in team working.

It is important for a coach to ask him/herself why a psychometric method is being used. It could be a way of exercising power/control over the client and, if there is the slightest suspicion of this, the use of psychometrics should be avoided. Moreover, training, accreditation and licensing is required before using most psychometric tests. Effective feedback is crucial. It should allow for client scepticism, respect confidentiality and, following general feedback on the measure, the client should be asked for his/her self-perception on how s/he may have been described against the various dimensions – and be asked to give practical examples to illustrate their understanding. When employed as a way of starting a conversation at a new level with a client, psychometrics can prove extremely useful.

And what about competencies? In some walks of life they appear still to be alive and well. Careers (and consultancies) have been established on the basis of competencies. Large swathes of the public service sector went through job evaluation programmes in order to identify and define the required competencies. Training and development programmes have been devised to enable people to become competent. But then what is the incentive to become 'super-competent'? The CEO was surely right who, when asked by head-hunters in his search for a new finance director, what competencies he was looking for, replied 'I'm not into competencies, what I want are excellencies.' He has had a strategic coach for three years. The individual who seeks 'excellencies' in colleagues is likely to be sensitive to his/her own learning and development journey too.

It is important that both client and coach explore their expectations of planned coaching sessions (five or six are usual but some coaching relationships last longer). The coach needs to make clear his/her expectations that the client will focus on agreed issues between coaching sessions in order that a pathway becomes clear. It is always helpful for a record to be kept of each session – coaches become adept at taking notes while not losing eye contact – and the notes of the first session should record mutual expectations. Agreed next steps complete the notes. It is helpful if these notes are sent by mail to the client's home address or to a non-work email address in order to preserve confidentiality. In thinking partnerships where this has been practised, most clients value their notes as a record of their story at a certain pivotal stage in their careers and lives.

A key skill for the coach is deep and careful listening; listening to the client and also to his/her own intuition. Laura Whitworth et al. identify three levels of listening. Level 1 is appropriate for the client and reflects their focus on the self; but it is not appropriate for the coach. When the coach begins to ask for unnecessary facts, finds him/herself getting flustered and wondering what to ask next, starts to give advice or starts to tell their own story, they are at Level 1. When coach and client are working together in an absorbed and focused way, when there is clear rapport, the client is doing most of the talking and the coach is hearing not only what is said but what is not, this is Level 2 listening – and much effective coaching takes place at this level. In Level 3 listening, the coach uses all the skills of Level 2 and, in addition, listens for emotion, considers risks to take in the conversation and trusts his/her intuition. S/he listens for silences, hesitation and energy, as well as metaphors. There is an emotional as well as an intellectual connection between coach and client. When listening occurs at this level (and it may not be very often), the coach can harness the client's own energy for transformation:

Client: I've been working a 75-hour week ever since I began this new job. I don't even have time to plan. I can't go on like this. Everything suffers – the quality of my preaching (the client is a bishop), my colleagues, my wife, my friends, my health.

Coach: That is hard and could have serious consequences. How shall we work together on this?

Client: (*tight laugh, followed by silence*)

Coach: And? (*silence*) That laugh sounded strained.

Client: Yes (*client begins to go into the detail*) . . . It's a huge burden.

Coach: I'm hearing a willingness to explore other ways . . .

Effective questioning is crucial. Some questions elicit the story line, while others prompt the client to look for explanation and to identify possible actions. The effective coach listens for signals and uses his/her intuition to probe, when necessary. In the dialogue above, the coach resists the temptation to offer an hypothesis, preferring silence. Only then was an observation made: *that laugh sounded strained*, but no advice is given. That would have been to move too quickly and, crucially, probably to fail to get 'buy-in' by the client. In a situation such as persistent overwork, major attitudinal and behavioural changes are required. Only if the client identifies the necessary actions is there likely to be a change. For leaders who find themselves reacting to a seemingly endless stream of 'important' tasks, the coach can play a vital role in helping the leader to focus and stay centred on creating the future:

Coach: What proportion of your time is spent
    a) on making a difference?
    b) doing what is important?
    c) doing what is trivial?

And by gently challenging, the coach can help the client to identify alternatives:

Coach: The action you suggest is one possible alternative. What other possible alternatives are there?

One of the most difficult aspects of coaching is to resist giving advice. The desire to advise goes deep and resisting it runs counter to much of what it means to be a professional:

Client: I am currently doing a 70-hour week. It can't go on as I'm utterly exhausted.

Coach: Have you asked your PA for feedback on where your time is going? You might consider keeping a timesheet; several of my clients have found that to be useful. You could keep one between now and our next session.

Client: (*doubtfully*) I'm not sure that would help . . . (*it is, after all, yet another task*).

An alternative approach might be:

Coach: What do you think is preventing you from stopping work at a reasonable hour each day? [It is possible to disguise giving advice by framing it as a seemingly innocuous question: *Would it be a good idea if . . . ? Have you thought of . . . ?* Or the coach might go for the leading question: *Do you agree that, in the circumstances, it was foolish to fire the Director of IT?*]

At all costs, the coach must resist the temptation to tell his/her own stories, however relevant they may appear to be:

Client: I have just had a row with one of my senior managers.

Coach: Oh, that happened to me once and there was some awful fallout and it took weeks to re-establish good working relations. [Far from building rapport, this is a turn-off.]

Coaching is concerned with outcomes, learning and change, achieved through a client-centred process and usually paid for. It is not counselling. The coach has to accept the paradox of being fully present but never overwhelming; of having a large portfolio of techniques some of which may only rarely be used; of being centred, even when anxious; of being both powerful and powerless. Coaching is a very great privilege, in which the coach, an outsider on the inside, supports and enables clients through transformations both large and small.

Notes

1. Rogers, 2004, p. 7.
2. Hargrove, 2003, p. 15.

References and further reading

Argyris, Chris (1990), *Overcoming Organisational Defenses*, Needham Heights, Massachusetts: Allyn & Bacon.

Briggs Myers, Isobel, with P. Myers (1980), *Gifts Differing*, Palo Alto, California: Consulting Psychologists Press.

Buckingham, Marcus, Donald O. Clifton (2002), *Now Discover Your Strengths*, London: Simon & Schuster.

Goldsmith, Marcus, Laurence Lyons and Alyssa Freas (2000), *Coaching for Leadership*, San Francisco, California: Jossey-Bass/Pfeiffer.

Hargrove, Robert (2003), *Masterful Coaching*, San Fransisco, California: Jossey-Bass/Pfeiffer.

Kirton, M. J. (2003), *Adaption-Innovation in the Context of Diversity and Change*, London: Routledge.

Rogers, Jenny (1998), *Sixteen Personality Types at Work in Organisations*, London: Management Futures.

Rogers, Jenny (2004), *Coaching Skills: A Handbook*, Maidenhead: Open University Press.

Whitworth, Laura, H. Kimsey-House and P. Sandahl (1998), *Co-active Coaching*, Palo Alto, California: Davies Black Publishing.

Whitmore, J. (1996), *Coaching for Performance*, London: Nicholas Brealey Publishing.

Appendix – A note on psychometric instruments

The contact points indicated below are the suppliers of the psychometric questionnaire materials as well as providers of the requisite training and accreditation.

Myers Briggs Type Indicator (Steps I & 2)™. Further information from OPP Ltd, Elsfield Hall, 10–17 Elsfield Way, Oxford OX2 8EP.

Firo-B™. OPP as above.

Innovation Potential Indicator. OPP as above.

Inspirational Leadership Tool. Developed by Caret and the DTI. Caret Ltd, Lancaster House, 67 Newhall Street, Birmingham B3 1NQ.

KAI, Occupation Research Centre, Highlands, Gravel Path, Berkhamsted, Herts, HP4 2PQ.

Strengths Finder, developed by Buckingham and Clifton of Gallup. A code on the inside back cover of their book (see References and further reading) provides an ID number which, after entry to the Strengths Finder web site, allows access to the questionnaire and provides the top five (signature) strengths.

Team Management Systems, Water Meadows, 367 Huntington Road, York Y03 9HR.

13. A time for everything

The work of the Lord and the Lord of the work

PETER BATES

Time is probably the most valuable resource given to us by God. It is important, therefore, that we examine our use of time and consider how best we can and should use the hours that God has given us.

For those in paid employment, the use of time is generally fairly well defined but what measures of time usage can be adopted by the priest or the voluntary worker?

Each enjoys an element of freedom which other working people do not. This freedom carries with it the additional responsibility to manage the time available and to use it effectively. This requires that each person knows what to do, when they are doing it, when they have done it and, critically, when they have not done it.

A study of the use of time by clergy show that the average minister in parochial ministry 'works' for about 61 hours a week, made up of:

Public and private worship	16.0 hours
Reading, study and instruction	9.0 hours
Visiting and counselling	8.5 hours
Administration	10.0 hours
Meetings – formal and social	11.0 hours
Business travelling	6.5 hours

Shown as a chart, the clergy working week appears in Figure 13.1.

The work of the Lord

But what constitutes work for a priest or minister? Is private worship part of a priest's working week? Are semi-social gatherings such as the annual Harvest Supper treated as work or not? Such an assessment is totally a personal matter, although it can help to consult with

Figure 13.1 Clergy working week

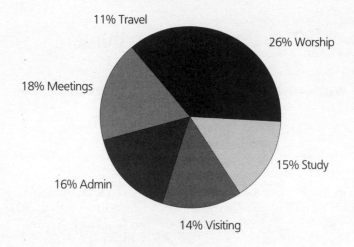

11% Travel
26% Worship
18% Meetings
15% Study
16% Admin
14% Visiting

others, perhaps members of the Parochial Church Council (PCC) and congregation, on whose behalf the priest's time is being expended.

One point to note from these figures is the 21 hours on average (34% of the working week) spent on administration and meetings. It is this area of the use of 'time' that the remainder of this paper will address.

Priorities and delegation – people or paper, mission or meetings

> If you want something done, ask a busy person to do it.

There is a lot of truth in this old adage, but it does mean that a lot of church folk, both laity and clergy, find themselves with too much to do and some difficulty in saying 'no'.

Many people tend to become 'too busy' and ultimately less effective. Busyness and hard working do not necessarily equal efficient or effective working. Time should be given at regular intervals, desirably every six months and preferably quarterly, to monitor one's work and either affirm or reset priorities for working.

Setting priorities

This can be done mostly in a process of self-appraisal using simple task-focused questions to analyse personal performance and effectiveness. Some years ago, the American management guru and writer Peter Drucker suggested the following questions:

1 What am I doing that that does not need to be done at all?
2 Which of my activities could be better handled by someone else?
3 What do I do that wastes other people's time?

These should be approached in a disciplined and methodical way either alone or with a peer or mentor depending on the level of appraisal conducted.

The appraisal may be a straightforward assessment of the day or week ahead, that is, the day-to-day administrative tasks, the in-tray, the emails, the phone calls, the bookings. Such appraisal can take place on a daily or weekly basis.

Higher levels of appraisal will consider the strategy of the work, the appropriate fit of the person (oneself or others) to the task. Such appraisal will consider the long-term goals and strategy of the ministry. It follows that the daily or weekly self-appraisal will provide a safety check to ensure that the work being carried out in the short-term period is fulfilling the strategy and thinking of long-term period.

Such a discipline will demonstrate the extent to which the 'busyness' of the minister or lay worker is serving the mission and ministry of the Church but more importantly it will also provide a check against drift in the strategy.

Only in this way will it be possible to make decisions about which jobs should be done at all and indeed who is the best person to carry out that job. The questions apply to every task, whether about people or paper, meetings or mission.

Effective delegation

Delegation is a critical strategic function, not merely the shedding of seemingly time-consuming and dull tasks. If the task is critical to the strategy, then it is a critical task and deserves appropriate priority. If the task is not critical to the strategy it should not done at all, and certainly not delegated to anybody else! Clergy have been too good at wasting their time and the time of others in this way.

I did it my way!

We all tend to have our own ideas on priority setting but the example that follows may be of use to some of you.

When Charles Schwab was President of Bethlehem Steel he confronted a management consultant with an unusual challenge:

'Show me a way to get more things done', he demanded. 'If it works, I'll pay you anything within reason.'

The management consultant handed Schwab a piece of paper. 'Write down the things you have to do tomorrow', he said. 'Now number those items in the order of their real importance. First thing tomorrow morning,' he added, 'start working on number one and stay with it until it is completed. Next, take number two and don't go any further until it is completed. Then proceed to number three and so on. If you can't complete everything on schedule, don't worry. At least you will have taken care of the most important things before getting distracted by items of lesser consequence.

'The secret is to do this daily,' continued the consultant. 'Evaluate the relative importance of the things you have to get done . . . establish priorities . . . record your plan of action . . . and stick to it. Do this every working day. After you have convinced yourself of the value of this system, have your staff try it. Test it as long as you like. Then send me a cheque for whatever you think the idea is worth.' In a few weeks, Charles Schwab sent the consultant a cheque for 25,000 dollars.[1]

It is an essential part of this system to prepare the list of the next day's priorities on the previous evening. It is then possible to proceed with the first item straight away in the morning rather than have to do the thinking and planning when it would cause delay in starting work. The intervening night gives some opportunity for reflection and for preparing the mind for the next day's tasks. The list of priorities may also be incorporated into intercessions for the day to come as well as forming the basis for thanksgiving at the end of the day. In a day when there are specific time appointments for services, meetings, visits etc., the items in the priority list will need to be dealt with in order in the intervals between appointments.

Following this practice can bring personal satisfaction, especially if items on the list are ticked off as they are completed. In addition, the discipline of making a list and establishing an order of priorities can provide a good basis for consultation and discussion between members of a parish or ministry team, or between clergy and their church councils and congregations.

Planned neglect

'Planned neglect' is a concept recommended to anyone wishing to make the best use of their time. It arises in the Rule of Life from the Companions of St Lawrence, as follows:

In order to live a fully rounded life, life as God intended it to be, we must include things other than our work. Almost inevitably this means leaving some things undone. For us, planned neglect will mean deliberately choosing which things we will leave undone or postpone, so that instead of being oppressed by a clutter of unfinished jobs, we think out our priorities under God and then accept without guilt or resentment the fact that tasks we had thought we ought to do we must leave. We shall often be tempted into guilty feelings when we do take time off, but we should then remind ourselves that such guilt is a sin against the generosity of the Spirit, and also extremely infectious.

The rule brings out the importance of activities other than paid work. In the context of this Rule, the question 'what is your job?' is of significantly less value than the question 'how do you spend your time?' There are so many activities undertaken, especially by church folk, that are additional or alternative to paid work, that the exhortation to include things other than our work is doubly important. For many people nowadays a fully rounded life consists totally of voluntary or non-paid activities.

Time off is an important part of 'planned neglect'. Time spent by oneself, with the family, with God in prayer or contemplation is just as important a part of the fully rounded life as are paid or voluntary activities, and we should make sure that our 'planned neglect' allows for this.

The importance of being people

The single most common outcome arising from being too busy is stress. The effect of analysing pending or current tasks, and consciously deciding those which do not need to be done at all, or which can be postponed, or delegated, however, can be the very opposite of stress.

Prioritizing, delegation and planned neglect will inevitably bring relief to the overstretched minister or lay worker. Of course, each must be a conscious decision taken in conjunction with others. Such decisions must be communicated, especially where other people are awaiting their outcome.

Administration for all

For a parish to run effectively, the clergy need to operate efficiently in the service of God and, to do that, the parish priest must have the right tools. Computers, emails, webs, blogs, Access and Outlook have helped many parishes, but not all clergy are computer literate, or even wish to be. It really is time for some clergy to wake up and shake up, even if they choose to delegate this area of work in order to take advantage of this critical tool!

All parochial clergy can make good use of secretarial or 'PA' services but not all parishes can afford it. Whether that service should be voluntary or on a paid-for basis must be considered. The paid employment should be given priority; some support should be in the reach of most if not all parishes. There is merit in sharing the full-time employment of a secretary between several parishes in a town or deanery, as this will both provide someone with a full-time job and also share costs which may not be affordable by one parish. There is no reason why the principle of 'administry' cannot function at local level.[2]

In places, this has been carried out effectively across denominations – an example at least of the offices of the Church being ecumenical if not the worship!

Money matters

In these times of financial pressures within the Church there is a real need for financial expertise and few clergy are likely to present for ministry with these. Management cost accounting is rarely to be seen within the training portfolios of most dioceses.

The more fortunate churches may be lucky to have a 'friendly' accountant in the congregation who can share with the parish priest in this aspect of ministry. It does not follow that such a person should automatically be assigned to the position of treasurer, a task which most numerate people can carry out perfectly well. Management of money should be seen as essential to the overall strategy and mission of the church.

In some parishes, where such expertise does not exist, the role falls on the clergy who generally have no appropriate training at all. There is a strong case for the diocese and/or deanery to identify people with such expertise; some dioceses have had the foresight to extend the role of stewardship advisor beyond that of merely fundraising, but these too are rare.

Conclusion – the Lord of the work

In the end, the key to the proper management of time, resources and people is rooted in the biblical concept of stewardship.

Stewardship is the proper care of all God's resources, not least the care of oneself as one of God's primary resources. Proper stewardship must begin with the stewardship of oneself. No one can manage others if they cannot manage themselves. Bound up in the biblical theology of work is the concept of Sabbath. Sabbath is the time when work pauses in order to enjoy the fruit of the work. It is the time when God walks about in the 'garden of his handiwork'. It is a most lovely symbol of God's plan and purpose for this world which is to be in relationship with his creation through those whom he has set apart to be stewards of that creation.

If, as Christian ministers, leaders and managers, we fail to grasp this critical concept then we have misunderstood the whole point of the work of the Lord. It is God's plan and purpose that we should find ourselves walking in the garden in the company of the Lord of the work.

Notes

1. Peter F. Rudge (1976), *Management in the Church*, London: McGraw-Hill, p. 126.

2. Administry was a small-scale but important national ecumenical church management training organization for lay church members. It was set up by John Truscott in 1981 and established a good reputation for the courses it ran and the research it initiated and carried out. John left in 1993 and Administry ceased business in 2000. One example of the type of course that it ran was on 'How to Produce a Church Parish Magazine'.

Part 3

People

14. Leading a team

GEOFFREY CORNELL

Ministers are not naturally collaborative. Their call to ministry is invariably rooted in a personal experience, marking them out for a distinctive vocation. Their role models, even biblical ones, are often 'lone rangers'. Moses is advised by Jethro to spread his workload, but pretty soon he is lugging commandments around on his own and coping with a golden calf.[1] The canonical prophets tread lonely paths. St Paul travels Asia Minor, founding churches single-handedly. My Methodist tradition was founded by John Wesley, a determined autocrat. In one of the early Methodist Conferences it was remarked, 'Mr Wesley seems to do all the business himself.' In contemporary culture, the TV series *The Apprentice* showed Alan Sugar as the leader making the essential decision alone, reinforcing the picture that leadership is about someone being decisive, visionary, ruthless. In churches, there is a yearning for leadership in a complex world and people who can know the ways of God in an authoritative way. Small wonder ministers are invariably people who work on their own – often bemoaning their lack of support. Small wonder some ministers see lay people, even church life, as things that restrict them from exercising their own God-given ministry.

But Jesus models a different style. From the outset, he calls disciples to be with him. He sends them out, nervously, to do his work. They fail, deny, betray, abandon. But Jesus does not give up on them. On the cross, he commits his mother to one of them. His resurrection appearances are limited to them. He leaves entrusting the future into their hands, aided by the gift of his Spirit. The New Testament offers no particular insight into church structure or strategy, but it offers the image of a body of believers, a collective discipleship, and spends time considering leadership within it and for it. The interaction between the team and the leader seems to be part of the Christian DNA. It is never easy, never resolved. At times, the Spirit calls for spiritual entrepreneurs, lone figures starting something. At other times, the collective experience and wisdom is crucial. Developing a movement requires more than one person, if ideas and actions are 'owned'. Leaders are only leaders, ultimately, if people are willing to follow.

I have been involved with teams throughout my ministry and, for the last six years, I have been superintendent of a team of full-time ministers and lay people engaging with mission and ministry in Central London. From this experience, I wish to engage with Tuckman's[2] work on team development in the hope that it will illuminate your situation.

Forming the team

Unusually within the Methodist system, the three ministers in my present circuit were appointed at the same time.[3] Someone foolishly referred to us as 'the dream team'. Alliteration has a lot to answer for! The circuit was, not surprisingly, as excited and apprehensive as we were. But, we discovered, their nervousness was because the last effective ministry *team* was over 20 years ago. Recent history included fragmentation, breakdown, people taking flight from each other. Lay people in the circuit did not know whether to trust ministers. But at the same time the team was laden with huge expectations. The team would sort it, whatever 'it' was. We felt washed up on a new shore watching the tide receding. If the team felt like this, gasping for breath and unsure whether we would survive, then the team leader felt even more exposed. But the task of a team leader is, initially, team formation.

A key initial question to ask is 'who is in the team?' It's by no means easy. I arrived at my present appointment with two other ministers, hence the team of three. But there was already another minister in the circuit with responsibility for the Chinese work. There was also a director of social work who had felt his gifts excluded by a cabal of clergy in the past. Then there were two lay workers, full-time in the circuit with specific responsibilities. Within the Methodist system, the responsibility for the oversight of a circuit is shared between ordained and lay – so the responsible officers, circuit stewards, were also part of the team, but clearly, as people with 'day jobs', with limited time available. I found myself part of a number of teams, relating to both circuit and to the principal church. Establishing clarity is crucial in order to remain true to circles of confidentiality and focus for action and communication. So I drew a map of circuit roles and teams and pinned it to the wall. People talked about it. There were overlapping and interlocking teams, and I needed to tread carefully. But I notice that Jesus was content to work with a team-within-a-team: there was the core of himself, Peter, James and John that he went away with, conversed closely with. It seems to have produced resentment[4] but Jesus resolved that. Having some close confidants, people on the same wavelength, was more important than some people feeling excluded. In the event our core team naturally evolved: the team of three gained the director and the Chinese-speaking minister, particularly when new people came into post for both those roles, and we now have a deacon. So there is a core team of six.

Before any grand plans, any developing of strategy, good processes have to be put in place. Time spent here repays a hundredfold. There is no substitute for people getting to know each other, discovering histories, experiences, gifts. People are valued for who they are, not for what they do. People are gifts God gives, not machines to be used. Early actions reveal whether as a leader you are serious about sharing or not. It seemed important that the ministry of my colleague newly emerged from initial training was affirmed from the outset, so we agreed to share the principal service at the main church wherever possible, alternating leading and preaching. We had an acid test of that collaboration very early on. Nine days after we came into post, the planes were flown into the Twin Towers in New York. I had preached on the first Sunday and so it was my colleague's turn for the one immediately following the attack. At such a time, in a church with many American links, it was assumed by many that the senior pastor would take the senior role and preach. Not only had my colleague just left college but English was not his first language. Moreover, he comes from South America and he and his country have suffered at the hands of American imperialist policies. We spent time thinking and praying together, but my colleague preached – and gave his distinctive slant to the sermon. Symbolic actions early on set the tone and are worth a thousand words.

Another key area that needs establishing early on concerns hierarchy. Is the team a flattened hierarchy where access is open, or is there more of a pyramid of power? More pertinently, is the former being announced but the latter covertly developed? Again, we faced a deceptively tricky decision early on – how were the ministers to be titled on publications? It was my probationer colleague who said that simply announcing that we were all equal was a deceit. He had just come from college, whereas I was an experienced minister. It was his suggestion (which my egalitarian side found uncomfortable) that I was titled 'senior minister' and he 'assistant minister'. When he was ordained in 2003 and with a pastoral role firmly established in the church, we moved to 'superintendent minister' and 'minister'.

Storming the team

Tuckman says that a team is not properly formed until it hits disagreement. Conflict is not the enemy of a team: it is its lifeblood. Conflict happens because people care enough about something to disagree. The first team I was a member of suffered because depth was rarely reached: we had to be relentlessly upbeat. My present team contains a number of strong personalities. We circled each other initially – polite, supportive, but looking for the kill. It wasn't long before fur flew! My instinct is to paper over, to hope things will go away. My two closest colleagues have a proper assertiveness and will-ingness to challenge. When one of them would sit down with me and begin 'you're not going to like what I have to say', I would brace myself and inwardly seek to rejoice. A good team leader will be alert to, will welcome, disagreement. It makes things real. But it is not easy because ministers have often been wounded by conflict in the past and have developed thick skins.[5]

Norming the team

Tuckman's rhyming headlines become a bit mystifying here! In this stage, he sees the initial conflicts resolved and the team establishing productive ways of working. Cooperation develops. Norms emerge. There is a team identity that is productive, not exclusive, but to which members are committed. There may be private storms, but there is public support of one another and of agreed policy. There is appreci-ation of the contributions of the others, a celebration of things well done. In my experience, the team leader contributes significantly to this through a consistency of practice, an attending to the process, and through consistent encouragement and availability. It helps provide a structured environment in which work can be productive. The leader also encourages this through delegation: in a close-knit team such as my present one it can be liberating for someone to get their teeth into a particular piece of work either on their own or with just one other. Gillian Stamp's work on ministry suggests it consists of three over-lapping tasks: trusting, tending and tasking. Good teams develop norms in each of these areas, ways of acting that are fruitful both for the team's work and for healthy development of both the individual and the corporate.

From the outset, we set structures in place. Being so close together geographically we committed ourselves to a weekly Monday morn-ing staff meeting for prayer, business and study. Sensing that prayer was at the heart of any work we could do we set up morning prayers each weekday. This has become a focal point not only for the team but also for other people working in the Mission offices.[6] We established structures that would enable us to flourish, whether ensuring each other took days off or keeping notes of our meetings. We kept the circuit stewards informed through a cycle of meetings with staff and stewards, and a half day away twice a year, externally facilitated, all these inviting people into a particular way of working.

Performing in the team

So far Tuckman's typology has alerted us to team composition and process and to the development of ways of working that are beneficial. But a persistent question is 'what is the team *for*?' Throughout, *purpose* matters. My experience is that teams are formed without clear agreement on their purpose. Even in those rare cases where the 'contract' is clear there are all kinds of expectations flying around. Acknowledging and then working with these takes time. Getting clarity as to purpose and strategy is vital. I'm not a supporter of mission statements: a group of people spending a day producing something succinct, usually involving a thesaurus and wrangling over the position of a comma. I have found a broader vision statement more useful. A clear idea of what a car is for is better than lots of time spent thinking up a fancy name for it and certainly enables you to get the right parts to move forward. Time spent exploring and refining the vision energizes a team, involves others if required and produces a common 'ownership' that will be invaluable in the implementation of strategy. Here we inherited a circuit review document – and the people scarred by producing it! We worked with it closely. After four years, we were clearer about what was working and embarked on another major review. A five-year cycle seems about right. But because reviews are destabilizing (putting a number of things up for grabs again, allowing people to ride old hobby horses again), they need to be managed well so as to provide an incisive 'snapshot' into the work and recommendations as to its development.

If process and purpose are important for a team, so is personality or gift. I have found two commonly used tools very helpful. The first is the Myers Briggs Type Indicator (MBTI).[7] People approach situations and work within them differently. MBTI offers 16 different types and explores the opportunities and tensions between them. In my circuit staff in North London, all were 'N' personalities (intuitive, looking for the possibilities) and only one was an 'S' (sensory, down to earth) and it revealed why she found the rest of us infuriatingly impractical. The second is the Meredith Belbin's analysis of team roles.[8] Some team members prefer thinking up ideas, others prefer putting them into practice, others checking how things are going, others finishing tasks and so on. Belbin identifies the skills needed to carry out a task successfully. If these are not found in the team then someone on the team will have to fulfil that function – and will find it difficult and exhausting to do so. When my present staff undertook this exercise, it revealed that we were great at dreaming dreams but no one was any good at putting things into practice. We could have countless creative sessions but it would get us nowhere. Equally we had no one who was gifted in finishing things off. If we managed to get started, we'd more than likely just drift! Allocating people to take on roles and support-ing them in it was key to performance. The team leader encourages this discernment and supports the development of gifts – and recog-nizes their own gifts and roles in the process and considers how that relates to the formal position of leadership. Fortunately, I am one of Belbin's 'Shapers', so I happily spend my time on strategy or trying to work out why something works or doesn't. I would prefer to do that than implement anything! Perhaps that is why I am spending my time writing this chapter! But it is also important that the team leader encourages a reflective process to accompany performance: not only 'how are we doing' but also 'what are we learning as we are doing this', what is sometimes called 'double loop learning'.

Mourning and the team

The category of 'mourning' does not appear in Tuckman's original typology but I find it a helpful addition. It reminds us that teams are always in flux and settled personnel cannot be taken for granted. Handling departures well is a skill few possess – and they must be marked within the life of the team and the church. Equally, facing failure is important. No team is perfect. How this is dealt with is key for the maturity and effectiveness of a team. In my present circuit, one member found the pressure of city centre living and the particular role she was being asked to take on was destructive for her and so she left. Exit interviews for individuals, autopsies for schemes can be painful but they can also reveal areas for development as almost no other feedback can. A loving but honest reflection from someone leaving the team is perhaps their greatest parting gift to it. Leaving gave our departing team member a distance to look at what we were doing and what we were being asked to do and to offer that back to us with care and clarity. It was hugely important for us.

Tuckman's theory illustrates the different stages of the life cycle of a team. However, it is important to notice that it is not a matter of simple linear progression. Teams may find themselves pushed back to 'storming' and may find themselves tackling more than one of the stages at once. I think we have struggled with having a superintendent, or this particular superintendent, who considers the responsibility of oversight entrusted to me involves the discovering of more information than is perhaps good for me or the work. I have had to learn, painfully, that people find me powerful.

As a team we have suffered from a breakdown of 'trusting' between two individuals so that the whole thing became a bit like a marriage in trouble, or a family where children squabble and the father dithers. I have not managed this well – not least because of my desire to paper over cracks. Even now the analysis of what went wrong is not shared by all in the team. My perception is that things got difficult because a particular piece of work required my whole-hearted extended attention and this produced a space into which conflict rushed. It was followed by certain key lay people who saw their long-established power threatened, were resolved to rock the boat, perhaps even capsize it.[9] But others see this as my paranoia. I am only partially comforted by the Woody Allen observation 'even if you are paranoid it doesn't mean that they're not out to get you'! But I see now, with the benefit of hindsight, that an external facilitator was needed to help us through this, with skill and neutrality greater than we possessed. I was wrong to try and handle it on my own. A team leader needs to know their own limitations and the skeletons in his or her own cupboard.

Leadership is not the personal responsibility of the team leader. It is to be exercised by all both collectively and individually. So the role of the team leader is to encourage growth in leadership in your colleagues. Just as a cricket captain seeks to bring out the best in bowler or batsman, so the team leader encourages, motivates. But equally there is a responsibility for the team leader to model good practice. How you handle yourself as a team leader is every bit as important as how you handle others. Just be grateful if your team watches over you in love too! And take satisfaction in the result – whether in the accomplishment of the task or in the growth of a team member.

Notes

1. Exodus 18–20, 31–4.
2. Tuckman, 1965.
3. Methodist ministers are appointed to groups of churches called circuits rather than to individual churches.

4. The dispute among the disciples about greatness in Mark 10.35–40 is given added strength because James and John were so often seen at the right and left hand of Jesus as part of the inner circle.

5. A fact of which most lay people seem remarkably unaware.

6. Working for a very active circuit we have an office staff of three secretaries, two working in finance, a married couple as caretakers and a cleaner. The demarcation of 'team' is thus very complicated. The acid test of who is 'in' and who is 'out' is simple: who gets invited to the staff Christmas lunch.

7. Retreat centres often run Myers Briggs courses. But there is great merit in doing the exercise as a team.

8. Belbin, 1993.

9. It is interesting that these people were those who considered themselves essential to the running of the church and circuit but who were not in the formal positions that entitled them to membership of any team. The team, however constituted, was thus a huge threat to them.

References and further reading

Adair, John (1987), *Effective Team Building*, London: Pan.

Belbin, Meredith (1993), *Team Roles at Work*, London: Butterworth-Heinemann.

Tuckman, Bruce (1965), 'Developmental Sequence in Small Groups', *Psychological Bulletin*, 63, 6, pp. 384–99.

15. Mentoring an assistant minister

SHAWN LAMBERT

The importance of mentoring and its development

The relationship between a senior minister and an assistant minister is a notoriously difficult one (Watts, Nye and Savage, 2002). This makes the task of choosing and mentoring an assistant minister crucial to the success of that relationship. Unresolved and ongoing conflict between staff members is very damaging for churches.

The number of ministers leaving the ministry within their first few years of ministry is also a worrying phenomenon. The front page of the *Baptist Times* (20 May 2004) headlined the fact that 50% of Baptist ministers leave the ministry before the age of retirement. Michael Hampson, a former curate, reported in *The Times* (Saturday, 23 September 2006) that, when he left the ministry after 13 years, only a quarter of his college year completed the same time period. Mentoring would help those starting out to manage what he calls the impossible expectations imposed on ministers.

Mentoring is apparently now one of the top three most widely used approaches by UK businesses, after on-the-job training and training courses (Parsloe and Wray, 2005). The history and development of mentoring is fascinating. In Greek mythology, *Mentor* was the trusted adviser of Odysseus. The traditional dictionary definition talks about a mentor serving as a trusted counsellor or teacher to another person. Mentoring was largely unknown until the 1960s when it began to develop, particularly in the USA (Clutterbuck, 1991). Parsloe and Wray (2005) report that even in the 1990s books on mentoring were rare in UK academic libraries. They also report there is no consensus on definitions and terminology and that we live in a semantic jungle as the learning revolution, of which mentoring is a part, continues to develop!

A number of writers recognize that mentoring has its roots in the old system of apprenticeship (Clutterbuck, 1991; Parsloe and Wray, 2005). There are three broad primary types of mentor: those in the corporate world, professionally qualified mentors and mentors who work voluntarily in the community (Parsloe and Wray, 2005). All three types can be usefully explored to help us in the area of mentoring within church leadership teams. However, if you look at the way curates are appointed in the Anglican Church, I think working with the apprentice model offers us the best way forward.

Two other important notes need to be made from the literature available on mentoring. Clutterbuck distinguishes between the North American model of mentoring and the European model (1998). The North American model seems to be more about helping the person make the right career moves and less about learning – with the mentor often being the line manager. The European model is more about learning, with the mentor usually not the line manager so that power differences can be shelved.

A number of writers urge against the use of a line manager as the mentor, because, as David Clutterbuck puts it, 'the boss/subordinate relationship, with all its entanglements of decisions on pay rises, disciplinary responsibilities and performance appraisal, may work against the openness and candour of the true mentoring relationship' (1991, p. 33). This is an important caveat; however, I feel that the senior minister/assistant relationship is closest of all to that of an apprentice moving towards a more equal relationship with the minister, as he or she gains relevant experience.

This means that mentoring should, in most cases, be the responsibility of the senior minister. All that I have to say about developing that mentoring relationship would apply, however, if you chose an outside mentor.

It may well be good practice to have someone outside looking at the relationship between the two leaders in order to overcome any problems that arise from possible judgemental line-manager entanglements. You would also need to work out the boundaries for male/female mentoring relationships.

Bearing in mind all the possible definitions of mentoring, I want to define it within the specific context of church leadership. A mentor in this context is someone who helps grow another church leader in character and competence.

James Lawrence, in his book *Growing Leaders*, identifies a mentoring matrix – the relationship between senior and assistant minister would in this matrix be a 'downward' one and intensive in nature – rather than occasional. That is not to say a leader couldn't work with a more equal type of relationship if he or she so chooses.

However, the complexity of the relationship between senior minister and assistant minister should not be underestimated. When we understand that complexity we can carry out the task of choosing and mentoring an assistant minister with much more confidence.

The development of my interest in mentoring

My interest in management and leadership and mentoring began over 20 years ago, when I joined Lloyds Bank (as then) as a graduate trainee. I greatly benefited from being mentored by more senior colleagues who took a personal interest in my career.

It was in my early years in the bank that I became a Christian and also met mentors within a local church who helped develop my involvement in local church leadership. After 10 years in secular management, I sensed a call into local church ministry and spent 3 years at Spurgeon's Bible College, a Baptist training college. That was an amazing opportunity to reflect on what I'd learnt in secular management from a theological perspective. What one learns in the secular world must be deconstructed theologically and not unthinkingly imported into the Church world. For example, Jim Collins, not a Christian, has written a monograph on why churches shouldn't try and operate like businesses (2006)!

However, we must engage with other disciplines. During the last ten years of ministering in a local church I have spent eight years conducting training courses in the fields of counselling and psychotherapy, at Roehampton University. Part of the creativity required of church leadership is to draw on different disciplines to help us become better leaders of local churches. It is from that discipline that I want to suggest a relational model of mentoring that draws on work developed by Petruska Clarkson (1995). This model has five aspects that Clarkson identifies in all relationships: the working relationship, the distorted relationship, the real relationship, the reparative relationship and the spiritual relationship.

One of the reasons for emphasizing a relational model is theological. We worship a relational God and, being made in his image, we are ourselves relational creatures. We often take relationships for granted but many research studies show that in psychotherapy it is the relationship between client and counsellor that determines the effectiveness of the counselling (Clarkson, 1995). What is true in counselling is true in any other helping relationship. In mentoring, it is the relationship itself that will bring about change, if consciously worked with in all its facets.

This is, therefore, the framework of the mentoring strategy that I am suggesting – the goal of the relationship being to help the mentee to become mature in their ministry. We can often focus as managers on techniques and solutions and forget the power of relationship.

I am also encouraged in this direction because, according to Clutterbuck, intense personal relationships often develop between the mentor and mentee (1991). Parsloe and Wray also argue that the success of the mentoring process depends on the development of the relationship (2005).

Church ministry is itself increasingly complicated and demanding and team work seems to be the best way to enable it to function healthily. This increased emphasis on team leadership has also given rise to new ideas of leadership styles. In their book, *Psychology for Christian Ministry*, Fraser Watts, Rebecca Nye and Sara Savage argue that the real work of leadership is raising up other leaders, not 'hugging' leadership to ourselves (2002, p. 227).

The five aspects of relational mentoring

This means the first and most obvious relationship is the working one – asking whether we can work together and how we are to do that.

This relationship also recognizes and safeguards the fact that there is a task to do, without forgetting the relational element in this. John Adair has developed a three-circle model of leadership, highlighting the overlapping areas of task, team and individual (2004), holding together the relational and task elements of leadership. Working out if you can work with someone and vice versa is not always obvious in initial meetings. Longer and more in-depth interviews along with personality assessments and other tools will help.

The other crucial question concerns the identification of the work with which the assistant is to help. Traditional models have often seen the assistant as a sort of clone of the vicar or pastor, doing the same things that the senior minister does. If this is the sort of assistant that you want then clear boundaries need to be drawn up.

There are a number of problems with this model: it doesn't necessarily take into account the individual gifting of the assistant; there are often problems that arise with comparisons being made between the senior minister and the assistant as they perform the same task (for example, preaching). If there are no clear boundaries when there is overlap then power struggles can often arise.

The strength of this model is that it can be set up as a genuine apprenticeship. Some churches appoint assistants with a more specialized role, for example, leading worship – here clear boundaries can be set.

Not only does the leader need to get to know the assistant but he or she also needs to know their own self. One of the issues around which there is often conflict is that of control and power. As a leader, it is worth asking yourself where you are on the continuum of control, how much control and power you are prepared to delegate, and how much responsibility your assistant is prepared to take. Mentoring is concerned with the development of new leaders.

This will involve real leadership rather than mere control of an organization or other people. Although these issues may arise – which is why in the European model of mentoring the line manager is often not the mentor – having to work through such issues can be developmentally important for both parties.

My experience of working for a major plc suggests that the working aspect of the relationship is often seen as the dominant one. However, I know there are other aspects of the relationship that need to be understood and managed.

Elizabeth Jordan in an unpublished doctorate suggests the theory that as managers we internalize a good manager and a bad manager. This brings us to the more hidden relationship which exists between people that distorts things. It's a complicated relationship, and there are different definitions, but it is generally called transference and counter-transference. For simplicity of language, I'll call it the distorted relationship. Jesus knew about this when he said, 'You hypocrite, first take the plank out of your own eye, and then you will see clearly to remove the speck from your brother's eye' (Matthew 7.3).

At different times the crowds and the Pharisees saw Jesus in distorted ways, either as a political Messiah or the devil incarnate. These distorted feelings can be positive or negative and are often exaggerated.

Alistair Ross says that transference occurs when a person, usually unconsciously, 'transposes onto the faith leader emotions which they had experienced earlier in life in relation to a significant person' (2003, p. 9).

This distorted aspect of the relationship has the power to destroy its working aspect and so needs to be something leaders can spot in others, or in themselves. This is not so easily done as it is usually unconscious. Every minister will experience such distorted relationships within his or her congregation. We all need to learn how to manage these. With someone with whom you are working closely, however, this is even more important. The clues to such possible distortions will be there even at interview. You either need to develop the skills for spotting this yourself or try and have someone as part of the interviewing panel who has such skills. If it flares up at a later date it needs to be tackled and not avoided.

If such transference is strong it needs to be worked through before the third aspect of relationship can really develop – and this is what has been called the real or person-to-person relationship. This is not necessarily the same thing as a friendship although it is a component of true friendships. Traditionally, it has been said that ministers cannot have personal friends within their congregation. Some leaders may feel that a friendship would get in the way of a working relationship with an assistant. In my experience, however, a real relationship is crucial in helping form strong bonds and trust between two people. One of the aspects of a good mentoring relationship that is truly accountable is that the mentee feels able to share their weaknesses and their more vulnerable side. This means that the mentor needs to model vulnerability in a real way. Expectations here may be problematic. Does the assistant expect there to be a friendship? Does the senior minister not expect there to be a friendship?

Once this relationship is established, the issues of character development can be addressed. Also in mentoring relationships as in others, regardless of the hierarchy, knowledge transfer can go both ways.

A counselling relationship is about helping someone to learn and change – and so is a mentoring relationship. The skills and principles that help you to be a catalyst in that change are very similar.

This relationship depends on four things. The mentor should be supportive, and people need to feel supported if they are to develop. The mentor needs to be able to help people to express their feelings. And on that strong basis, the mentor needs to be challenging – to get below the surface to bring out areas of discipleship or character or spirituality that need developing. This is a broad brush description of what are complicated people skills – but none of these areas should be neglected if the mentoring is to be fully rounded.

The fourth aspect of the relationship has been called reparative (Clarkson, 1995). One thing many church leaders suffer from is a lack of encouragement and affirmation. The mentor can help repair this deficit by being authentically affirming. Colin Buckland in his book *Freedom to Lead* (2006) points out that all of us come into ministry with a degree of personal wounding.

My experience in my own journey, and those I have worked with, is that being in ministry brings that personal woundedness to the fore. From his own observations, Colin Buckland believes that many ministering persons who have fallen into sexual sin have done so out of their personal woundedness (2006, p. 110). If we are merely task oriented then this hugely important area of a reparative relationship can be neglected. Having led a church through the fallout of one of my assistants having an affair with a member of the church, I know the pain that this can cause.

The idea of a reparative relationship fits well within Christian ideas of healing and growth and transformation. Key ideas in psychotherapy around the reparative relationship include the ability to 'hold' someone's pain and areas of personal wounding. The ability to be empathic and consistent is also really important (Clarkson, 1995). The ability to be empathic comes out of the self-awareness that we are all 'wounded healers' (Nouwen, 1994).

Churches can often import business models without careful analysis of their underlying assumptions. The heart of the relationship between mentor and mentee should be spiritual, which affects every aspect of the relationship. The spiritual dimension keeps the relationship rooted in biblical patterns and values.

I remember doing a placement with a senior minister while at Bible College and asking if he prayed, and being shocked when he said he didn't have time! It is important for any minister to be culturally aware and relevant but, as the Baptist Union of Great Britain (BUGB) guidelines point out, establishing the disciplines of a devotional rule and study are still the habits on which a fruitful ministry is based (Baptist Union of Great Britain, 1991, pp. 3–4).

There is a topsoil with prayer that we can all benefit from, that has been laid down over 2000 years of people praying. But we also need to take into account individual personalities in helping people to cultivate a discipline of prayer. It is here that you might need to draw in others who have more specialized skills that they can pass on, including, for example, those of a spiritual director.

Another important spiritual principle to try and pass on to the mentee is that of continued growth in all the areas of their life – including continuing professional development of particular gifts.

As well as passing on values that you feel are important, it is also a good idea to encourage the mentee to discover what values the Holy Spirit may be trying to bring back into the collective memory of the Church. For example, two of the values of the 24/7 prayer movement are creativity and rawness (Pete Greig and Roberts, 2003). Rawness is about being passionate about developing people rather than about being a slick organization.

Conclusion

Being a minister is a demanding job, and many clergy find their work stressful. I believe that a robust system of mentoring for new ministers would do much to help them manage the stress of their vocation.

There is a good fit between the apprenticing that has often gone on between a senior minister and an assistant, and the more recently developed strands of mentoring. I have found that working in the corporate world, as well as pursuing other disciplines in continuing professional development as a minister, have helped me develop a personal model for mentoring others.

That model is a relational one –both for theological reasons as well as psychological ones. It is the relationship in mentoring that will bring about change and growth in the person being mentored. Any relationship is complex and multifaceted but I have focused on five key aspects of relationship identified by Clarkson: the working relationship, the distorted relationship, the real relationship, the reparative relationship and the spiritual relationship (1995). A focus on these five key areas will also result in change and transformation for the mentor. The focus is on the development of character and competence as a leader.

The key to all of this is to help the mentee find their unique voice (Covey, 2005). In the Christian context, it is their God-given unique voice and purpose within the local church and the kingdom of God.

References and further reading

Adair, J. (2004), 'Overview: Passing the Ball to You', in J. Adair and J. Nelson (eds), *Creative Church Leadership*, Norwich: Canterbury Press, pp. 3–15.

Baptist Union of Great Britain (BUGB) (1991), *Ministerial Recognition: The Probationary Period*, Didcot: BUGB.

Buckland, C. (2006), *Freedom to Lead*, Farnham: CWR.

Clarkson, P. (1995), *The Therapeutic Relationship*, London: Whurr Publishers.

Clutterbuck, D. (1991), *Everyone Needs a Mentor: Fostering Talent at Work*, London: Institute of Personnel Management.

Clutterbuck, D. (1998), *Learning Alliances*, London: Institute of Personnel Management.

Collins, J. (2006), *Good to Great and the Social Sectors*, London: Random House.

Covey, S. R. (2006), *The 8th Habit: From Effectiveness to Greatness*, London: Simon & Schuster.

Greig, P., and D. Roberts (2003), *Red Moon Rising*, Eastbourne: Kingsway.

Jordan, E. M. (2003), 'The Professional Is Personal' (unpublished PhD Dissertation), London: Metanoia Institute.

Lawrence, J. (2004), *Growing Leaders*, Oxford: BRF.

Nouwen, H. J. M. (1994), *The Wounded Healer*, London: Darton, Longman and Todd.

Parsloe, E., and M. Wray (2005), *Coaching and Mentoring*, London: Kogan Page.

Ross, A. (2003), *Counselling Skills for Church and Faith Community Workers*. Maidenhead: Open University.

Watts, F., R. Nye and S. Savage (2002), *Psychology for Christian Ministry*, New York and London: Routledge.

16. Leading lay volunteers

Personal reflections – from a
Roman Catholic perspective

PADDY RYLANDS

While I was rummaging through the old family treasure box a few months ago, my attention was drawn to a tatty little pamphlet, well thumbed and stamped with my grandfather's name. It was entitled *The Help of the Laity* and dated 1900. Reading through it, I wondered what on earth my grandfather would think of parishes today!

The author defines 'lay' work as:

> Work not directly intended for one's own benefit in life, but work outside our own work in life, and intended in some way or other, sometimes directly, but often indirectly, to further the cause of God and His Church or the welfare of our neighbour.[1]

He then goes on to propose ways in which a 'loaded, and in many cases, overwhelmed' clergy might be helped by the laity. His proposal is somewhat tentative:

> I know that I am touching on precarious and much-debated ground, that I am walking on ashes that cover a smouldering fire; still, in all honesty, and with all due deference to the opinion of others, I venture to say that it is not impossible that some way might be found in which the help, which I am sure the laity would gladly give, could be supplied to the clergy . . .[2]

Over the past hundred years there has been what some describe as a radical explosion in the involvement of lay people in parish life – from a small number of volunteers 'helping Father' to parishioners consciously/intentionally taking up different ministries in the light of their gifts and talents to serve the Church – a living out of their baptismal mission.

In the following paragraphs, I hope to share with you some reflections. They arise from my experience of ministry – first working as a volunteer catechist in a semi-rural parish, then from working as an apprentice for 18 months alongside an experienced catechist. Six years as the Parish Religious Education Co-ordinator and member of the Parish Team in Our Lady and St Joseph's, Hanwell, offered scope for developing leading skills while working alongside a team of catechists. The last 21 years working with colleagues in the Diocesan Education Service has been a gentle (and at times not so gentle!) reminder that the ministry of leading, journeying alongside, parishioners volunteering their time and talents for the mission of the Church is neither static nor boring – rather an immense and humbling privilege. During this time, the focus for my work has primarily been in the area of catechesis,[3] the formation of parish ministry coordinators and parish pastoral council/team members.

Backcloth

'I've offered to help Father with Confirmation. What training is there?' Eileen requested enthusiastically.

'I saw a note in the newsletter asking for help with the new group for parishioners with disabilities. Can I help?' John asked, somewhat tentatively, one morning after Mass.

Two of countless examples of generous offerings from people wanting to give of their time and talent in response to need. Hopefully, within a short while, that 'volunteering' and 'helping' comes to be understood and owned for what it is – ministry, a natural outcome from Baptism, using gifts and talents for the service of the Kingdom of God, the mission of the Church. Over the last 40 years particularly, we have seen a radical change in the involvement of lay people in the mission of the Church. It has become the norm in parishes for 'volunteers' to be involved in ministry in the areas of liturgy and catechesis, in pastoral care, social justice, ecumenism and evangelization – ministry both within the Church and from the Church into the world.

This radical change has been in the movement from lay people being seen as 'Father's helpers' to seeing involvement as a flowing from a deepening understanding of the baptismal call to active participation in the mission of the Church – to transform the world according to the plan of God in view of the final coming of the Kingdom of God.[4] Such a change has its roots in the renewing of the Church ignited by the teachings of the Second Vatican Council, and subsequent Church documents, for example, *Christifideles Laici* and

Evangelii Nuntiandi.[5] This 'volunteering' of lay people in contributing to the life of the Church has come to be identified as 'ministry':

> the public activity of a baptised follower of Christ flowing from the Spirit's charism and an individual personality on behalf of a Christian community to proclaim, serve and realise the Kingdom of God.[6]

Following on from the Second Vatican Council – no doubt influenced by reflection on its teachings – the publication of *The Sign We Give* in 1995 invited, and continues to invite, serious consideration of, and reflection on, the effects of *how* we minister – whether lay or ordained, whether within the boundaries of the Church or in the broader setting of the world.[7]

> We are convinced that the manner and style of relationships in the Church are part of the sign it gives, and for this reason, we must develop patterns of collaborative ministry as a key feature of Church life to come.

> . . . the urgent need we have to establish patterns of working and collaborating in the Church – patterns which respect and cherish the essential dignity and consequent responsibility for the life and mission of the Church which belongs to every baptised Christian.

> . . . I believe that it [*The Sign We Give*] contains the seeds of a revolution in the way in which we live and work in the Church today. The revolution is not simply one which will affect radically our internal structures: it is a revolutionary insight into the way in which we exercise our mission, which is to proclaim the Good News in today's world.[8]

With renewed understanding of Church and the effects of *how* we minister, the ministry of leading volunteers willing to commit themselves to the service of the Church is slowly evolving.

The role of leading volunters

Concerning the what of leading

Reflecting on my experience of leading both in the parish and in the diocese, the main tasks emerging are:

To 'walk the talk' – to intentionally model a particular style of leadership

In a nutshell I see **Leading Lay Volunteers** as journeying with, nurturing, encouraging, supporting, coordinating lay people who desire to use their gifts and talents for the mission of the Church.

Very many of those volunteering will find that they are a part of a team and that, at some stage, they will find themselves to be in a leadership role – be it of a small children's liturgy team, or a larger group of confirmation candidates. My own style of leadership has been influenced by the experience of being led. How I relate to, work alongside with and form ministers will, however unconsciously, shape, for the better or worse, the way in which they in turn lead.

To offer formation – initial and ongoing

This continues to be one of the greatest challenges. People are coming forward with varied experiences, backgrounds and training which can be usefully built on rather than ignored. Likewise, they have a variety of commitments – family, work, parish, social – that inevitably put limits on to the time they can give. The challenge is to offer *appropriate* formation, with the relevant content of knowledge and skills training and geographically easily accessible. A pattern has emerged in the diocese for the catechists' formation, offering a series of *dimensions* of formation that catechists can access at their own pace. Fortunately, we are able to service it because of a growing team of experienced ministers willing to give their time to the formation of others. Experience shows that the same model is easily adaptable to other areas of ministry. At present, we do not issue a formal accredited ministry qualification. People grow into their ministry at different paces. However, it may be something we need to attend to in the near future as, increasingly, the day-to-day ministering of parishes is being led by ministers who are not ordained.

To journey alongside, supporting and encouraging

Yesterday, the phone went. It was one of the deanery coordinators, asking for a few minutes to chat through a situation. Reflecting afterwards, I realized how simply making time to be there is central to a style of leadership that is about enabling and empowering, working together with co-responsibility. A tension is how to avoid creating a level of overdependency. When facilitating new groups, it is recognized that the facilitator will probably work fairly hierarchically at first, then move towards a cooperative style and then finally with-

Dimensions of catechists' ongoing formation (Shrewsbury Diocese)
(Not necessarily sequential)

Request	Content	Formation level (1)	Formation level (2)
• Help! What do I have to do? Give me a programme!	An approach/ programme outline	– Day course – Help for individual parishes	
• Help! What is catechesis? What's a catechist?	Deepening understanding of catechesis	– 6-week course – CCRS module – Longer courses	
• Help! I'm working with People! Last time things didn't go too well. How do I work with people?	Skills development Working with groups Faith development Ways children/ adults learn	– Day course	– 4-week course – Facilitation training – Pastoral ministry – Co-ordinators' course
• Help! *What* is the faith I am sharing? What is the Church's story, teaching?	Exploring aspects of our faith tradition	– Evening sessions – Short courses – Study group	– CCRS* – Foundation degree – LIMEX** (Certificate/ Masters)
• Help! This 'faith sharing' business – it's turning my life upside down. It's making me see, think, feel, LIVE differently! What's happening?	Ongoing spiritual formation/ direction Developing personal prayer.	– Prayer experience – Retreat day(s) – Prayer guide	– Spiritual companion – Further formation – Skills of accompanying

*CCRS: Catholic Certificate in Religious Studies
*LIMEX: Loyola Institute for Ministry Extension Programmes

draw to a position where the group has greater autonomy and is less dependent on the facilitator. There are parallels in the Church when leading lay volunteers. It is frequently said that for some 400 years since the Council of Trent in the sixteenth century parishioners have been kept in a childlike role, expected to be extremely obedient. With the renewal of Vatican II, there is a strong call for adults to take seriously the responsibility that baptism and confirmation brings.[9] There is the expectation that, almost overnight, children will become adults! Too frequently the human, transitional stage of adolescence is ignored – and yet it is a reality. A challenge I continually experience is how to lead in a way that provides nurture and support through this adolescent-type period without smothering and stifling, at the same time not creating too many expectations that cannot be fulfilled.

To hold the reality of the context – Church and world – in which we are ministering, a context of missioning in a time of change, transition, diversity

The Church has been, is and always will be in the midst of transition, of becoming. Living in and with change cannot be avoided. The Church has a mission to, in and for the world – a world that is likewise in the midst of change. Its call to read, interpret and respond accordingly to the 'signs of the times' is central.[10] The temptation to establish a 'one size that fits all' approach can overwhelm the priority of discerning what is appropriate for *here* and *now*. One of the tasks in leading in such a situation is to keep to the fore the realities of diversity and change, working with the ability to be flexible, to adapt and yet be true to the task. For example, a model of parish pastoral council established in a situation where the resident priest is a part of this co-responsible team will inevitably require adaptation if the parish becomes one of a cluster sharing a non-resident priest – and so too will the formation of the members.

To keep the vision to the fore, yet allowing for its development in response to the needs of the times

St Matthew's Gospel ends with a clear mission: Go, make disciples of all nations . . . Our call is to work towards the final coming of the Kingdom[11] as the people of God, disciples living a gospel-centred life. New situations emerge. Theology develops. The Church's attitude changes. Rulings once seemingly set in stone have become more relaxed, more tolerant. Key in leading is the ability to incorporate this into working with volunteers – allowing informed discussion, questioning, the voicing of concerns, pointing towards sources of information, further reading. My experience of working with a colleague confident and gifted in this area is a bonus, let alone a reminder of how crucial it is.

Concerning the how of leading

The three key influences I describe are, more than likely, extremely familiar. Perhaps that indicates their centrality!

1. The Gospels – meditating and reflecting on how Jesus ministered; holding before the Scriptures for discernment and enlightenment the situations, struggles, challenges posed by day-to-day events. At the moment, I am finding much food for thought in the seven characteristics Marty Haugen uses to describe Jesus' ministry:

> Jesus was always present to those around him, and his words and actions were directed by his awareness of God's presence.
> Jesus' ministry began with a call to conversion and was marked by continuing conversion.
> Jesus' ministry was grounded in and guided by scripture.
> Jesus offered each person a compelling invitation, an invitation that evoked a genuine response.
> Jesus was faithful to his religious tradition while always critiquing and challenging it.
> Jesus' ministry focused on and identified with those at the margins of society.
> Jesus' ministry embraced the whole person, body and soul.[12]

One word that would link all seven is *relationship* – relationship with God, with those whom we lead, with the scriptures, with the Church, with wider society. For me, the invitation is to hold each of these at the core in the day-to-day ministry of leading.

2. When shared with other lay people, these words from John Dalrymple never fail to draw a smile of recognition.

> Christian action is done by you and me, ordinary people with weak and wobbly hearts who do not have the security of trained skills, etc. I think Christian action and the promotion of the Kingdom is done by those who are a bit afraid of what people will say, who are a bit cowardly, who are a bit diffident about standing up in public, do not have the security of plenty of practice, can be capsized by failure, hurt by remarks, hurt by being ignored; find themselves reacting jealously when they do not want to, are overcome by despair, yet go on loving and trusting. It is the weak and wobbly

173

hearts that Christ chooses, as he chose Peter, James and John – all the disciples. They were not the highfliers of Galilee or Judea. They were the ordinary folk, capable of love.[13]

They certainly echo the myriad of feelings surfacing when I first became involved in parish ministry. They serve as a constant reminder to ground all that I/we do in the reality of the experience of those with whom we are working. Some are volunteers, consciously choosing to give their time in this way. Others have uttered a reluctant 'yes' to please a parish priest desperately searching for help. 'Ministry' is often a completely foreign word – still something reserved for priests and deacons, and perhaps those who help with distributing Holy Communion. At this stage, being ordinary, with a weak and wobbly heart, yet willing to be of service is a more recognizable identity.

3. The experience of working with inspiring leaders, who, on each of the occasions I started new work, through their *style* of leadership taught me more than textbooks could ever contain. Each demonstrated the truth of the statement: 'We teach who we are.'[14] So, too, we lead by our very being of leaders. What I have learned from them can be summed up under the headings of: pray, recognize, respect, respond, support, cooperate, celebrate.

Pray
- our work is the mission of the gospel
- the Holy Spirit continues to speak
- each of us is responsible for our own prayer lives
- praying together supports, unifies, enables

Recognize
- uncertainty and hesitation
- any lack of confidence
- enthusiasm
- the desire to be of service
- the skills already there, previous training and expertise

Respect
- the wealth of life experience being brought
- time/availability
- family and/or other commitments
- the willingness to prepare, to learn
- the different motivations, reasons that prompt volunteering
- the faith root at the heart of volunteering

174

Respond with
- affirmation
- offering appropriate formation – initial and ongoing
- creating opportunities for discovering hidden depths, new skills
- nurturing, encouraging, enabling (empowering?), allowing each to discover their own strengths, weaknesses
- constantly rooting all that is being done in the Gospels, the mission of the Church
- working collaboratively at every level
- risking, allowing mistakes to be made
- being flexible, encouraging diversity,
- letting go

Support through
- being available for talking with
- creating structures for local 'networking'
- offering resources
- a good communications system
- offering opportunities for reflecting/reviewing/evaluating
- setting time limits on length of commitment (renewable)
- prayer

Cooperate with
- team colleagues
- others with more/different experience
- new initiatives
- the Holy Spirit

Celebrate
- significant moments
- creating opportunities for socializing together
- bringing all before God in praise and thanksgiving.

Surviving, maturing

The explosion of ministry is taking place in a time of unprecedented change in the Church. O'Meara describes many of the roles emerging as 'first generation'.[15] For myself, that is certainly true. In both appointments as a Parish Religious Education Co-ordinator and Diocesan Adviser for Parish/Adult Formation I had no predecessors on whom I could call. The whole area of working with and leading those involved in parish ministry was new. It has taken patience on behalf of all – team colleagues, clergy, parishioners – as the way forward has slowly emerged and evolved. The generosity of an increasing number of colleagues around the country (and the world) in sharing their time, reflections and experience has been invaluable. Searching out appropriate ongoing formation continues to be crucial – being challenged by, benefiting from, a much wider experience of theological reflection, styles of ministry, facilitation skills, working with change, spiritual accompaniment, to name but some areas. Building in time for daily prayer and an annual retreat is not an option but a must!

It is a continual challenge to set time boundaries around the work. Working with 'volunteers' means inevitably that times for meetings, formation, support are in the evenings or at weekends. Understanding friends, challenging the workaholic tendency, even welcoming, are pure gift! They are a gentle reminder that the gospel invitation is to 'live life to the full' (John 10.10). What models are worn-out, work-obsessed leaders?

One constant and significant dimension of support and ongoing formation has been regular (monthly, where possible) work 'accompaniment'/'supervision' – the space for reflecting on all that is going on with a skilled listener, not from the work situation. I have learnt the hard way that my leadership can be weak. Tiredness is one major enemy, lack of preparation another. I have become increasingly conscious of the responsibility for regular reflection.

People work in very different ways. For myself, I have discovered that working as part of a team is central. It is a witness to the way I am encouraging others to work. It keeps the work grounded. The relationships that a good team nurtures means that support, encouragement, questioning, development are there – sometimes a shoulder to cry on too. It serves as a constant reminder that the work is not 'mine'. In doing this work I am but part of a bigger picture – in this present situation, it is as a part of Shrewsbury Diocese. The diocese is mandating the work.

Finally

Leading lay volunteers is a role constantly evolving. It demands flexibility and energy and, even more crucially, a rootedness in the sources from which it flows. Probably most people involved in ministry discover early on the truth of the words of Jeremiah:

Blessed is anyone who trusts in Yahweh,
with Yahweh to rely on.
Such a person is like a tree by the waterside
that thrusts its roots to the stream;

176

when the heat comes it has nothing to fear,
its foliage stays green;
untroubled in a year of drought,
it never stops bearing fruit.
(Jeremiah 17.7–8 [NJB])

There will be struggles and disappointments as well as the good days. I have three quotations that together serve as 'motto':

I have come that they may have life and have it to the full. (John 10.10)

To know me is to know the Father. (John 14.7)

Go, make disciples of all nations . . . and know that I am with you always; yes, to the end of time. (Matt. 28.16–20 [NJB])

They serve as a foundation, an anchor as well as a reminder of the direction and vision. More importantly, they offer *hope*.

Many centuries ago, Augustine offered some words of advice. Although addressed to a deacon/catechist they have a relevance to all involved in leading lay volunteers – in fact, to all in ministry. I leave the last word with him.

Remember that we are listened to with much greater satisfaction when we ourselves are enjoying our work; for what we say is affected by the very joy of which we ourselves are aware, and it proceeds from us with greater ease and with more acceptance . . . The important thing is that everyone should enjoy catechising; for the better we succeed in this the more attractive we shall be.[16]

Notes

1. Norris, 1900, p. 5.
2. Ibid., pp. 10–11.
3. Catechesis: the process of formation for Christian discipleship.
4. John Paul II, 1988, Nos 1, 20, 23.
5. Paul VI, 1975.
6. O'Meara, 1999, p. 150.
7. Bishops' Conference of England and Wales Working Party on Collaborative Ministry, 1995.
8. Ibid., p. 7.
9. CFL, 1988, No. 23.
10. *Pastoral Constitution on the Church in the Modern World: Vatican Council II*, 1965.

11. *CFL* , 1988, No. 1.
12. Haugen, 2005, pp. 14–16.
13. Dalrymple, 1986, p. 132.
14. Palmer, 1998.
15. O'Meara, 1999, p. 261.
16. St Augustine on 'Catechising the Uninstructed', in Comby, 1984, p. 113.

References and further reading

Bishops Conference of England and Wales Working Party on Collaborative Ministry (1995), *The Sign We Give*, Chelmsford: Matthew James Publishing.

Catholic Church, National Conference of Catholic Bishops, Bishops' Committee on the Laity (1995), *Called and Gifted for the Third Millennium. Reflections of the US Catholic Bishops on the Thirtieth Anniversary of the Decree on the Apostolate of the Laity and the Fifteenth Anniversary of Called and Gifted*, Washington, DC: United States Catholic Conference.

Comby, Jean (1984), *How to Read Church History*, Vol. 1, London: SCM Press.

Dalrymple, John (1986), *Letting Go in Love*, London: Darton, Longman & Todd.

Dues, Greg, and Barbara Walkey (2003), *Called to Parish Ministry*, Ohio: First Academic Renewal Press.

Harrington, Donal (2005), *The Welcoming Parish*, Dublin: The Columba Press.

Haugen, Marty (2005), *To Serve as Jesus Did*, Chicago: GIA Publications.

John Paul II (1988), *Christifideles Laici, Post-Synodal Apostolic Exhortation of His Holiness John Paul II on The Vocation and the Mission of the Lay Faithful in the Church and in the World* (CFL).

Norris, John (1900), *The Help of the Laity*, London: Catholic Truth Society.

O'Meara, Thomas (1999), *Theology of Ministry*, New Jersey: Paulist Press.

Palmer, Parker J. (1998), *The Courage to Teach*, San Francisco: Jossey-Bass.

Paul VI (1975), *Evangelii Nuntiandi: Apostolic Exhortation of His Holiness Pope Paul VI to the Episcopate, to the Clergy and to all the Faithful of the Entire World*.

17. Delegating without abdicating

ROGER MARTIN

Sir John Harvey-Jones achieved a miracle at ICI and his success stemmed largely from his ability to transform the prevailing climate within the leadership structure of the organization. On becoming the chairman he scrapped the boardroom and all that it entailed, opting instead for working with a few specially chosen individuals whom he called 'the band of brothers'. He could see that the old pyramidal system of authority and the company's search for perfection was a root cause of unprofitability and so he engaged in a massive cultural change. He accepted the responsibility of vision-casting and explained to his core group what the new framework looked like. Their task was to go away, explain in writing to him what they understood to be the guiding principles and then, using their skills, get on with the business of management and leadership in an attempt to get 90% right. The company was turned round – delegation and accountability producing a culture of freedom and achievement.

The church scene

Across most of the denominations there is an acceptance in many circles that, in a church, the main leader needs to have ideas and is responsible for giving direction to the whole initiative. He or she is to preach and pastor but, in addition, is asked to 'set out the stall' and make it clear just how the goods are to be sold. This can and often does work well but normally only in the short term. Soon problems begin to surface:

- the leader doesn't have enough time and energy for the whole task
- they realize that they don't possess all the skills required for the wide-ranging agenda
- they desperately need 'critical friends' to enable them to evaluate competently
- ownership of the enterprise doesn't really occur at the grass roots
- some begin to resent the level of the leader's control.

As the result of these problems the water becomes more choppy than it might be and the rate of progress slows down dramatically – or the leader leaves!

Biblical case studies

A. Jethro and Moses – Exodus 18

Moses had obviously experienced the ups and downs of leadership but overall had known considerable success. He had

- led the Israelites out of Egypt
- taken them through the Red Sea
- overseen the daily provision of food and water.

But – he was working 24/7 and was constantly breaking commandment number four which he was about to be given.

Jethro, his father-in-law, seeks to help and he does so out of warm relationship and deep concern (v. 7). Jethro receives a full report from Moses detailing the magnificent activity of God among his people. It genuinely thrills him to bits. He receives the report and is really glad that God has been seen to be both sovereign and powerful (vv. 9–11), so he worships and as he does so he is joined by the religious and community leaders. There then follows, the next day, a 'reality tour' (v. 12) – he experiences 'a day in the life of Moses'!

Exodus 18.13–15

- Moses is sitting as a judge
- the courts are open from dawn to dusk
- Jethro is distraught

Key question v. 14

Why do you sit alone?

Key statement v. 17

What you are doing is not good.

Key reasoning v. 18

You'll wear yourself out and my daughter will have a pension crisis when you drop dead!

In this passage the case for delegation is based mainly on workload . . . but not just on workload. It is also based on the level of frustration that Jethro notices. He realizes that if accessibility to Moses is difficult, if there is significant delay, in justice there will come a 'tipping point' that will lead to anarchy and chaos . . . so he advises delegation with abdication (v. 19). He tells Moses that he has significant responsibility as the people's representative before God and that his task now is to work out just how he can fulfil this commission. He then mentions three key functions.

1 Moses will need to be a *trainer*.
   The others who are going to help will need to totally understand the principles which undergird the justice system. They will also want to know how they are to behave and have spelt out to them their tasks and responsibilities (v. 20).
2 Moses will need to be a *selector*.
   If these people are to represent Moses and therefore God, he will need to choose those who already seek to honour God, are spiritual in outlook and moral in daily living. They will need to be teachable and he will need to choose some who are capable of large responsibility and some who are gifted with dealing with smaller numbers. He will need to be a talent spotter (v. 21)!
3 Moses will need to be a *supporter*.
   While Moses needs to set the people free to do the task that God has gifted them for and he has chosen them for, he must make himself available for advice in tricky cases (v. 22).

Result

Putting all this into action will mean that the people will go home satisfied and Moses will not experience burn out (v. 23).

B. Jesus and the Disciples (Matthew 9 and 10)

Jesus had come from God and was on a mission for God. His methodology is described in Matthew 9.35.

1 He went to the places where people gathered to hear scripture read and explained (the synagogue).
2 He preached about the rule of God and in his healing ministry evidenced the fact that the rule of God had, in him, drawn near.

The crowds move him deeply. He experiences a deep churning within, equivalent to the action that goes on in a washing machine, and in the middle of this emotion (compassion) realizes that he can't meet the need by himself. The people are too many and the problems that they have are very complicated, so he asks his prayer team to pray for workers (9.38).

Jesus then launches into action and delegates:

- he calls a core group to spearhead the mission and gives them authority (10.1)
- he chooses different kinds of people for this task (10.24). There are extroverts and those who are cautious; there are those who are educated and those who are 'ordinary'. There are middle managers and manual workers and, as Luke 8 mentions, behind this group, totally involved in the ministry of Jesus are a group of wealthy women. Delegation to a mixed leadership group may be an important key to reaching a mixed target group and this may be the reason why the leadership in Antioch (Acts 13) contained such a variety of individuals.
- he organizes a *training day*. The agenda for the occasion is interesting. It includes

    1 The teaching of foundation principles. He talked about sticking to their primary task – reaching the 'lost sheep of the house of Israel' (Matthew 10.5). He talked about the need to rely heavily on God – 'do not take any gold or silver in your belts' (10.9 and 10).
    2 Honest analysis of the reception that they could expect:
        - 'if any does not welcome you' (10.14)
        - 'men will hand you over to the local councils and flog you' (10.17)
        - 'all men will hate you' (10.22)
    3 A clear indication of resources:
        - appropriate words will be given supernaturally to them (10.19)
        - the Holy Spirit will be present with them (10.20)
        - assurance of God's sovereignty will be experienced by them (10.30)

Jesus delegates but does his best to ensure the success of the venture. He also in his ministry engages in 'intentional apprenticeship' – in particular spending special time with Peter, James and John. In addition, he calls for accountability and receives reports concerning mission activities. In Luke 10 after sending out 72 workers he meets with them and, after they had shared with him their experiences, he told them how they were to interpret their activities, based on his supernatural understanding concerning what had happened (vv. 17 and 18). At the end of the Gospel record (John 21), there is a real moment of *appraisal* as Jesus and Peter meet.

Jesus knows that the success of the mission must not be hampered by his own physical limitations, so he delegates and trains and then engages in meaningful conversations at the end of each project.

C. Paul and Timothy

Saul of Tarsus, on his way to arrest Christians in Damascus, was himself, on the road, arrested by Jesus. The change was unbelievable. He believed, was baptized and started preaching immediately (Acts 9). On the day of his conversion, he received a commission and spent the rest of his life engaging in it. He was undoubtedly an aggressive and dynamic leader and probably was best suited to operate without a board of trustees! He quickly learnt, however, the importance of 'team ministry'. It was not all plain sailing, but he came to rely on his travelling companions. He formed apostolic teams and assumed the leadership role but needed with him experienced number 2s like Barnabas and young hopefuls like Timothy.

On Paul's first missionary journey he meets Timothy when he visits Lystra (Acts 14). It was an amazing period of ministry and it made an enormous impression on this young man. Paul recognizes that Timothy's mother and grandmother have made a significant spiritual impact on the young man and knows that here there is huge potential. On Paul's second journey, he offers Timothy a 'gap year'. The relationship deepens and this time is extended. Timothy becomes a respected, flexible helper. Paul delegates.

- Timothy is sent to Thessalonica to encourage persecuted Christians
- Timothy goes with Erastus to Macedonia
- Timothy accompanies Paul to Jerusalem
- Timothy is asked to engage in a more settled role in Ephesus where he specializes in pastoral ministry

Paul delegates – he can't be the pastor/teacher as well as the church planter. He can't be running the Alpha programme as well as the discipleship course. He can't be watching over people's lives and at the evangelistic cutting edge . . . so he delegates, but from time to time he steps back in to encourage and advise. This is what Paul's two letters to Timothy are all about. Timothy has obviously written and asked a series of questions.

There are issues about:

- leaders
- the fellowship fund
- false teaching
- money
- worship, and so on

Paul spotted Timothy and saw his potential. Paul gave him a chance and mentored him. Paul set him loose in Christian service. Now Paul keeps him on track and is especially keen to stress the importance of sticking to the task:

- Fight the good fight (1 Tim. 1.18)
- Watch your life and doctrine closely (1 Tim. 4.16)
- Keep yourself pure (1 Tim. 5.22)
- Guard the good deposit (2 Tim. 1.14)
- Discharge all the duties of your ministry (2 Tim. 4.5)

Paul delegates, gives Timothy his head, but supports him by reminding him of the importance of staying in touch with Paul and the others working with him.

Things that prevent delegation

1 The psychological need for control in many of us who lead.
2 The commendable desire to prevent our friends from falling over.
3 The sense that we alone are God's gift to the Kingdom and are therefore indispensable.
4 The knowledge that in the volunteer market most don't want to volunteer.

Things that prevent mentoring

1 The unwillingness to engage in any activity that gives the impression that we are involved in 'heavy-shepherding'.
2 Lack of a genuine, open, honest relationship with the member of the team.
3 An attitude among some that help from 'full timers' is not needed and that anybody can do anything.
4 A sense that the time commitment that is required would leave us in a worse state than we would be in if we did everything ourselves.

Important questions

1 Do I know what the DNA of my church is – do the leaders? Have all the members grasped the essentials of the VISION?
2 Am I constantly a 'talent spotter' and recruitment officer?
3 Do I give enough time to training and support as an alongside critical friend?
4 Have I worked out when I should give individuals a second chance and what I need to put in place so that success is achieved?

Conclusion

There is a biblical mandate for vision casting and over-the-top leadership but also a biblical insistence on delegation, teamwork and support. The biblical balance lies in both extremes. The age in which we live pressurizes us in the direction of achievement – Kingdom principles ask us to concentrate rather on contribution. Leadership is not ultimately about a system but about motivating people – people working together for the divine glory.

18. Relating to young people

ANDY WILLIAMS

'How do you relate to young people?' This was the question asked by a lady of a church congregation of the youth worker of her church. The lady (we'll call her Lesley), probably in her forties, found young people difficult to talk to and to relate to. They seemed to be completely different from her. They acted differently, they wanted different things and they even had a different vocabulary from her. How do you relate to young people when they seem so different and society seems so different from when Lesley was a young person?

In his book *Money, Sex and Power*, Richard Foster states that people crave after money, sex and power. They are driven by the necessity to have, to some extent or other, money, sex and power. Perhaps, what lies behind these temporary things is the human need for status, love and worth.[1] It could be argued that this need applies to young people as well as adults. When this is realized, relating to young people may not be as daunting as it seems.

In this chapter, I hope to dispel some of the myths about young people and to show that it is possible to relate to the next generation. In this chapter, the people in mind are people like Lesley who asked the question about relating to young people, the people in a church congregation who would like to be able to encourage young people, but feel a little intimidated by them.The chapter is for clergy and ministers in church who seem to have become detached from the younger people in their congregation.

Status

There are a number of books that detail the birth of 'the teenager' in the 1950s and 1960s.[2] Young people, with money to spare in the post-war boom, decided they wanted to be different from their parents. However, young people are not given the opportunity to be different before marketing managers cash in by mass-producing anything that is new. New music, new styles of clothes, new hairstyles are soon promoted as the new thing to have until everyone looks the same again.

This means that young people are forever searching for their own status and their own way of being young.

Subcultures

One of the myths when relating to young people is that of youth culture. People feel they cannot relate to young people because they do not understand the culture. The disheartening view, however, is that there is not one youth culture but many subcultures. Over the last few decades, young people have developed a new way of being different. They would develop their own dress style, hairstyle, music style and sometimes their own type of accessories. For example, the Mods of the 1970s had their own style of dress and all keen mods had a scooter. The Punks brought in a lot of colour but also an aggressive style of dance. Goths brought in chains attached to their jeans and rappers brought in jeans that are very baggy and have their crotch somewhere round the vicinity of their knees.

The reason for developing a new way to look different from other people is in order to stand out from other people. The young people want to be noticed. They want to be different. Therefore, I do not believe that you have to be like them to relate to them. If someone who is old enough to be their parent turns up trying to look like them then it is likely that more damage will be done than building bridges. It is not necessary to understand everything about their subculture in order to relate to them. A little knowledge maybe, but it would be very difficult to understand everything about each youth subculture before feeling ready to relate to young people. Let them develop their own culture and let them develop their own identity. This will help them to develop their own status.

Youth subcultures also provide a sense of belonging as well as a sense of being different. Those within the subculture feel that they belong to one another. This is not a bad thing and helps the young people to feel safe and to develop relationships. Rather than try and join their group, it is important to look past their style of dress and way of being and seek ways that will make them feel comfortable, safe and part of your organization. Young people will come to the culture of church if they feel they belong.

Use their expertise

One of the best ways for a youth worker to get to know the young people in the group is on a weekend away, ideally involving some activity like rock climbing, archery, canoeing, etc. This is because you are all likely to be inexperienced at the activities. I usually find that some of the young people are better at rock climbing, braver at abseiling, do not fall in the water and have a better aim at archery than I do. Adults are not better than young people at everything.

In an ever advancing technological age, young people will be better at the new gadgets than most adults. My four-year-old daughter understands the DVD player better than some of her grandparents. I do not understand the workings of iPods or how to download music from the web site, nor do I feel I need to or that I should so that I can relate to young people.

When setting up for a youth service, why not ask the young people what they want to do? They might need a bit of guiding, but they do have some experience. If the service is to use something technical they will probably have more expertise than you. At the youth service at our church we are privileged to have a PA system, lights and video projector. Some of the young people understand how the lights work better than I do, so I let them do it. I was trained by a young person how to use the software that projects the words onto the screen. Young people are able to do more with PowerPoint than I can. Whenever possible, I will use their expertise, which helps them develop their own status.

Love

This is a word that seems to have lost its meaning in today's society. Love often has desire as the undercurrent and focuses on the needs of one's self rather than sacrificial love that puts the needs of others first. We also live in a society where many people do not have a lot of experience of living in a loving family or in a family that does not know how best to display that love, for example, rich, busy parents who show love by giving gifts when actually time would be preferred.[3]

Commitment

Building relationships and cultivating trust take a long time. Young people will not spend time with people who are here one day and gone the next or with people who it is quite obvious are only giving a small amount of time to them. Relating to young people requires commitment. The more time you are prepared to commit to young people the easier it will be to relate to them. This is not necessarily in relation to hours per week, but it is in relation to consistency. However much people might want to help a youth group get off the ground or continue, being on a rota system will not help to build relationships with young people. It is far better for volunteers to commit to weekly for one or two years than it is for someone to commit to once a month until they drop dead. Whenever people say they want to help with the young people I am always looking for weekly commitment. This does upset people and needs to be handled sensitively, but so do young people.

Some churches realize that they are not always able to get people who can commit as much voluntary time as is needed and so look to employ someone. This step can show commitment to the young people from the church leadership. However, an employed youth worker cannot be expected to double the size of the youth group in 2 years, let alone 12 months. As already stated, building relationships with young people, indeed building a relationship with anyone, takes time and commitment. A new church leader would not be expected to double the size of the congregation in 2 years, so why is it expected of youth workers? If you are in a position to employ someone to run the youth work, commit to at least 3 years, if not more.

Stability

Without wanting to state the obvious, young people face many changes as they grow up. Teenage years see a lot of physical changes to their bodies. On top of this are the emotional changes that young people face. The opposite sex is no longer people who pull our hair or giggle in the corner. Instead, we cannot help ourselves but be attracted to them. Young people are finding out what sort of person they are going to be. Are they going to be macho or the quiet, silent type? Are they going to stick up for women's rights or are they going to subdue people with quiet confidence? Young people need to be offered relationships from adults that will acknowledge the changes they are going through and accept them for who they are. Of course, certain behaviour needs to be checked, but they need to be shown grace as they work out their identity.

On top of the physical and emotional changes, young people face an ever changing and demanding world. Long gone are the days when you followed your father into the ship builders or coal pit that was in the town. No job is guaranteed for life, let alone a career. Many people have career changes in their working life. Therefore, when a young person has to decide what subjects to choose at school very few know what it is they want to do as a career. This, I believe, adds to the instability they feel. Add to this the pressure that schools pass on to them to perform so that the government meets its targets and you meet some very stressed young people. In our relating to young people we need to provide stability. This can be achieved by deciding what purpose a youth group has and sticking with it. The book *Purpose Driven Youth Ministry*, by Doug Fields,[4] is excellent in explaining the need to have a focused group and helps the reader think through the purpose of the youth work and the different groups involved.

Boundaries

We live in a world where experience is respected more than knowledge and history. People do not believe something is good or bad until they have experienced it for themselves. There are no absolutes; there are no correct views, because everyone's experience is different. Some secular youth workers would almost encourage young people to experiment with drugs and same-sex relationships so that they can experience them and learn from them. To me, this seems ludicrous. Illegal drugs destroy lives and communities and young people have enough trouble understanding their emotions without being subject to other connotations. We would not expect a small child to put their hand in a fire just to experience pain and learn from it. We would set a boundary around the fire so as to protect the child. I believe it is only loving and caring to do the same for young people.

It goes without saying that we should not wrap young people up in cotton wool. They do need space to make their own mistakes. But I do think that young people do understand and respect rules and boundaries when they are explained to them. Being honest as to why boundaries apply, and sticking to them, helps with relating to young people. At the beginning of a weekend away I explain the rules that are necessary to help everyone enjoy their time away. This can be done in a positive way. One approach is to call them boundaries rather than rules. So that everyone gets a good night's sleep is the explanation behind having set bedtimes. It also means the leaders are fresher the next morning and more likely to enjoy the day and engage with the young people, which helps with relating to them. In the Sunday morning groups, we have recently had to explain the boundary that everyone respects each other and tries not to talk when someone else does. This was done by starting off with a comment that it is great that so many come along. However, so that the morning does not drag out and people get bored while others are being asked to keep quiet it is important that we have one person talking at a time.

Worth

The last few years have seen the emergence of 'Reality TV', particularly programmes that allow viewers to vote on who stays in the programme and who leaves. Programmes like *Big Brother*, *Pop Idol* and *The X Factor* have really engaged with young people. This is because young people want to engage with things and want to feel that they have the power to decide on how the programme unfolds. This helps them to feel that their opinion matters and that they are worth something. We might all be able to believe that young people matter to God, but do they really matter to us?

Responsibility

Relating to young people requires taking risks. But it also has rewards. This is definitely the case when giving them areas of responsibility. I have already spoken about using their expertise, but this is perhaps taking it further. The reason people sometimes shy away from giving young people responsibility, particularly within church circles, is the fear that they may make mistakes. Things may not go as well as we expect and others might get upset. This is always the risk, as we have to remember that they are still young people. But sometimes we can be pleasantly surprised.

Giving young people responsibility gives them a sense of worth, as it shows that you have faith in them and believe that they can pull it off. When time is spent with the young person working through their responsibilities it shows that you are investing in them and that you recognize that ultimately it will be up to them to carry the torch forward. Giving young people responsibility also helps with integration as they are seen by adults and in some cases meet with adults and even work with them.

Areas of responsibility often include being involved in readings, prayers, serving or being on the coffee rota. What about giving the young people a service to run? What about asking for their opinion, with the willingness to put some of it into action? These need to be handled sensitively, because sometimes too much responsibility can cause young people problems. Whenever I have been tasked with putting a service together with young people I always come armed with some suggestions. It is much easier for people to say what they don't want and develop suggestions than it is from starting with a blank piece of paper. When wanting to get the young people's viewpoint about your church, putting them on the church council may be too daunting for them (and they may find it boring). What about having a separate meeting with them and a couple of church representatives? Maybe even start the evening with some pizza. Do it the way they would want to. But remember, if the young people are valued enough to be given responsibility and asked their opinions, be prepared for a few mistakes and be prepared to put into action some of their ideas.

Not clones

So often, I get the impression that people want young people to come into church and learn how to behave in church. They want the young people to learn the hymns, to learn the different traditions and to learn how to understand the Bible as they do. They want to teach young people how to 'do church'. Unfortunately, despite some very sincere intentions to relate to young people, this does not give them any worth. This does not allow the young people to discover who they are. All that is achieved is that clones are made that keep the old traditions going.

This is a serious matter and will require some soul searching for us. Why do we want to relate to young people? Is it to make them like us, for them to understand the Bible like we do, to enjoy the styles of worship we like? Or is it to help them become the best people they can be, into the people God wants them to be? If it is the latter, then that means that they will be different from us. They may well have different ways of worshipping God and drawing close to him. In order to relate to young people and help them have a sense of worth let us explore these new ways with them. We can use our experience to encourage them to make sure the new ways of 'doing church' are glorifying to God.

Conclusion

When relating to young people, it is important to let them be young people. Let them be people who can still enjoy some of the freedoms of being young as well as people who are learning to relate to other people and learning to take responsibility. Let us remember that they may want to express themselves in new ways as they look for their identity in society, but ultimately they have the same basic needs as all of us. They need to feel that they are loved as well as being shown the real meaning of love. They also need to know that they are worthy as they are and that we are ready to accept them as they are. Relating to young people will mean that we need to be vulnerable and it will probably mean that we are hurt and cast aside occasionally. However, when we bear in mind some of these things, it may make the job a bit easier. And as we get to know the young people and see them grow, we will see that relating to young people is not as scary as it might seem and it is worthwhile.

Notes

1. It has been said that Foster wanted to title his book on these but it was felt the title would not be a seller.
2. Chalke, 1992, is still one of the definitive books, if it's still in print.
3. Chapman, 2000.
4. Fields, 1998.

References

Chalke, S. (1992), *The Youth Worker's Manual*, Eastbourne: Kingsway Publications.

Chapman, G. (2000), *The Five Love Languages of Teenagers*, Chicago: Northfield Publishing.

Fields, D. (1998), *Purpose-driven Youth Ministry*, Grand Rapids: Zondervan Publishing House.

Hickford, A. (2003), *Essential Youth: Why the Church Needs Young People*, Carlisle: Spring Harvest Publishing.

Kageler, L. (1996), *How to Expand Your Youth Ministry*, Grand Rapids: Zondervan Publishing House.

Moser, K. (2000), *Changing the World*, Sydney: Aquila Press.

Pollard, N. (2006), *Teenagers: Why Do They Do That?*, Milton Keynes: Damaris Books.

19. Resolving conflict

ALASTAIR MCKAY

Many church leaders think of conflict as negative or destructive and therefore something to be avoided. This chapter offers some keys that can help unlock a different understanding of conflict and an approach which can enable leaders to engage conflict as a source of creativity and transformation in the life of the church.

Think differently about conflict

How we think about conflict is important. At the beginning of Bridge Builders' training events we often begin by eliciting leaders' associations with the words 'church conflict', particularly the feelings and behaviours that come to mind. With almost every group of church leaders, whatever their denomination or role, the initial associations are overwhelmingly negative. We hear associations such as pain, a lack of understanding, hurt, anger, separation, power struggles and shame.

At the outset it is important to recognize the negative view that most of us have of conflict. If, as leaders, we are to engage creatively with conflict then we need to think differently about it. In trying to shift perceptions, it is worth reflecting on why conflict has such bad press. One teacher from whom I have learned, Carolyn Schrock-Shenk, suggests four common misperceptions.[1] First, we often restrict the use of the term 'conflict' to tensions where there are negative elements, and fail to include situations where there is a positive outcome. Second, we tend to view pain and struggle as negative and to be avoided, rather than as inescapable and intrinsic elements in growth and creativity. Third, as Christians, we often hold a theology that views conflict as wrong or sinful, instead of understanding that conflict is neutral and that it is our responses to conflict that may be sinful or ungodly. Finally, we'd like to think that it should be easy to get along together, but, in reality, dealing with our differences in Christian community is often profoundly challenging and demanding:

We have seldom been taught how to be proactive in conflict and to understand that conflict transformation is a deeply spiritual task that demands commitment, discipline, new skills, much practice, and constant vigilance from each of us.[2]

Further, the term 'conflict' is generally used by the media to indicate violence. Therefore we need to clarify what we mean by the term. One useful academic definition from the field of conflict studies is:

Conflict is an expressed struggle between at least two interdependent parties who perceive incompatible goals, scarce resources, and interference from others in achieving their goals.[3]

However, this is less user-friendly than the simple definition: 'Conflict equals differences plus tension.'[4] Whenever we encounter tension over differences, we are facing conflict. This broader use of the term helps open up the possibility of embracing and positively engaging with conflict.

Think theologically about conflict

As well as changing our thinking about conflict, we may need to change the way we read our Bibles. Many of the books in the Bible have grown out of situations of conflict, and most of the narratives are tales of conflict. The Bible can therefore be a wonderful resource as we seek to work creatively with conflict. One example from the early Church can illustrate the point. Acts 6 records the first community wide conflict within the newborn Church at a time of growth and change. There are two distinct groups within the Church, the Hebrew-speaking and the Greek-speaking believers. The Greek-speakers have a serious complaint:[5] their poor widows are being left out of the community's relief work. The leaders are under pressure, and now they're being accused of injustice and unfaithfulness.

How does the leadership respond? They *don't* get reactive and defensive. They *don't* just tell people what to do. They *don't* tell everyone to go away and just pray about it. What they do instead is recognize that the issues matter deeply to people, and so they call the community together to discern together how to proceed – to listen to one another and to work at problem solving. The temptation, when conflict comes, is to separate and avoid. The apostles resisted that temptation. They had the courage to face the issues and the feelings of hurt. They also provided clear self-definition, giving their perspective on where they thought their leadership priorities should lie: devotion to prayer and serving the word. They had a clear sense of their own call.

Having listened carefully to the community and taken their concerns seriously, the apostles made a proposal for the way forward: that the leadership team should be expanded. Both the community and the leaders recognized that the matter of justice for the poor was not the only issue. There was also a matter of justice in relation to the leadership. All the current leaders were Hebrew-speakers. Judging from their Greek names, it seems that all the newly selected leaders were Greek-speakers. Real justice was not just about attending to the needs of the poor but also about sharing power together.

The new leaders were commissioned by prayer and the laying on of hands. They were clearly endowed with spiritual authority. The mark of this is seen in the succeeding chapters as Stephen and Philip proclaim the good news to Jews dispersed around the Roman Empire, along with demonstrations of power. Interestingly, we hear nothing further of the seven's involvement in administering aid to the poor, but we do see them exercising the same authority as the apostles: they were not a second tier, or second-class leaders. Rather they were empowered leaders who shared fully in the leadership responsibilities and authority.

This conflict in the early Church contributes to God's purpose of drawing people into his kingdom. Acts 6.7 says, 'The word of God continued to spread; the number of the disciples increased greatly in Jerusalem, and a great many of the priests became obedient to the faith' (NRSV). This verse clearly seems to be linked to the story which comes immediately before it; there is church growth that results from the creative and constructive addressing of the conflict. And in many ways it is a preface to the bigger conflict which culminates in Acts 15, where the issues are not between Jews who speak different languages but between Jew and Gentile. Again, as Luke tells the story, the successful addressing of conflict opens up the Church's mission. So conflict can be the arena for discerning God's will for the Church and the world.

A first step: be aware of your power

Jesus offers some teaching for the Church in Matthew 18, which can provide a helpful starting point for the creative church leader addressing conflict. The start of the chapter, which alludes to the power struggles among Jesus' disciples, provides an important reminder that conflict is nearly always related to issues around power and influence. Within the Church, factors of power are all too easily ignored, either from embarrassment or denial. Jesus begins (vv. 1–5) by challenging the prevailing aspiration among us all to seek to rise or increase in power, and calls us to solidarity with the least powerful. For all leaders, this is a challenge. But the challenge doesn't stop there. Jesus continues (vv. 6–11) with an exhortation to those with power not to take advantage of those without. According to Jesus, the test of whether our use of power is redemptive or abusive is our treatment of the least powerful. We are called to constant vigilance about our potential for abuse of power. And we are called to look out for the weak who fall or are left behind (vv. 12–14). As leaders, an awareness of our own power, and how we use that power, is an important first step.

Accept conflict as normal

In the middle of Matthew 18, Jesus sets out what is generally seen as a disciplinary process. We should note that this is not a legal process, however, but about relationships and about being included or excluded from the community. While the process is designed to address issues where a member of the community sins, my experience is that in most situations of conflict there is normally a perception (often on both sides) that someone has sinned or offended in some way. Therefore, I think that we can legitimately draw out some principles for handling conflict from the disciplinary process set out in verses 15–22. Jesus' teaching here indicates that we need to expect to have to deal with sin in the Christian community. This points to the first principle, that conflict is normal, it is going to happen, and we need to expect it in the church. This is a message that leaders need to communicate to the church. By doing so, they help to reduce anxiety.

Learn to take the initiative

A second principle is the need to learn to take the initiative with someone who has hurt or offended us. Often our instinctive response is to distance ourselves but Jesus calls us to take the initiative, go directly and address it with the other person. This is a challenging demand. It will take courage to face the one we may see as our 'adversary'. It will also require us to engage in self-reflection ('What is my part in what has gone wrong?'), to be vulnerable ('What do I feel, and how have I been affected?') and to engage the other person in dialogue ('How prepared am I to hear a different perspective from my own?'). If we are ever in doubt about taking the initiative, Matthew 5.21–4 reminds us that, when we know someone else holds something against us,

Jesus also calls us to go directly to address it with them, a priority even higher than going to worship. Jesus catches us both ways. What he calls us to is counter-instinctive: moving towards the other with whom we have a difficulty.

Develop your communication skills and be ready to persist

A third principle from Matthew 18 is the need to develop our communication skills. As the repeated use of the word highlights, *listening* is at the centre of the process (vv. 15–17). This requires us as leaders to deepen our listening skills, to be able to demonstrate that we have heard the other, and not to brush people off with 'I hear what you're saying.' It also requires us to improve our ability to speak in ways which enable the other to listen – by avoiding blaming and attacking language, and instead speaking in a centred way, articulating our own feelings and concerns. All this points to a fourth principle from the passage: that often reconciliation requires hard work, and perhaps several attempts at listening and trying to achieve understanding. We need persistence in trying to restore broken relationships, as indicated by the multiple steps of the process (vv. 15–17).

Expect to encounter God

'For where two or three are gathered in my name, I am there among them.' This is one of the best known verses of Matthew's Gospel, often quoted in relation to the Christian community (and at poorly attended prayer meetings!). However, the context of this verse has been long ignored. Jesus is promising his presence when his followers gather together to engage in loving confrontation, good listening, and seeking agreement in the midst of their tensions and differences.[6] When we face conflict we can expect to learn new things about ourselves, and new things about the other with whom we are in conflict. Jesus points here to the principle that we can also expect to encounter God's presence in a new way when we have the courage to come together to face conflict. We certainly do need God's presence in such situations.

Know that you are forgiven

There is one last principle[7] to draw out from Matthew 18, which relates to forgiveness. It is important to note that Jesus' teaching on forgiveness follows the teaching on confrontation. Forgiveness is not a substitute for confrontation. However, in calling us to be ready to forgive 77 times, Jesus challenges us to develop a reflex of forgiveness. Martin Luther King put it this way: 'Forgiveness is not an occasional act, it is a permanent attitude.'[8] How can we develop such an attitude? Jesus addresses this (vv. 23–35) in the parable of the forgiving king and the unforgiving slave. It is only as we grasp the depth of how much we have been forgiven, that we will be motivated to keep forgiving others. So another principle for us as leaders is that our capacity to forgive and be agents for reconciliation is rooted in the acknowledgement of our own sinfulness and our experience of God's overwhelming forgiveness.

Learn from contemporary insights

In addition to biblical teaching, the creative church leader can learn from practitioners in the field of conflict transformation and psychology. The remaining principles emerge from these two fields.

Dig deeper

A basic idea for resolving conflict is the need to distinguish between the positions that people take and their underlying concerns. The challenge is to dig deeper, not to get stuck on the position (a person's solution to an issue, what they want to happen), but instead to explore underlying interests (a person's concern about an issue, why they want something to happen) and needs (what motivates a person's interests). This has been popularized as the approach of 'principled negotiation'.[9] The approach is often helpful because it means taking time to find out what really matters to people, and being creative in finding ways to address both their and our concerns.

Understand and explore style differences

No matter how obvious it may be, we all struggle to really grasp that people are different from one another: typically we generally expect others to be like us. Differences in personalities and styles of handling conflict can become tense issues of their own, and leaders can provide tools to help understand these differences. Fortunately, there are tools available. The Myers-Briggs Type Indicator (MBTI)™ and the Enneagram are two widely used instruments in the UK, and are both useful. I have found the Friendly Style Profile for People at Work produced by Susan Gilmore and Patrick Fraleigh[10] to be particularly helpful. Simpler than both MBTI and the Enneagram, its four styles are easy to grasp.[11] One of its greatest strengths is that it distinguishes between our functioning under normal circumstances ('calm') and our functioning under stress ('storm'), which I have not come across in other instruments.

Such personality style tools help our self-understanding as well as improving our understanding of others who are different from us. Whichever tool we use, it is important to know the tool well and use it regularly, and to work with it together as a leadership group. This gives a common language to explore style differences, which helps to reduce tension and enable constructive engagement around these style differences.

Understand emotional dynamics in the congregation

Have you ever been caught off guard by interactions between people in your church, and been left thinking, 'Where did that come from?' Typically, it may be behaviours that do not seem to make sense rationally. A key here is to appreciate that church congregations function as emotional systems.[12] They have much in common with the dynamics of a human family, therefore family systems theory[13] can help shed light on what happens in church groups. Some features of an emotional system include:

- The functioning of members of the system (such as the congregation) is profoundly interdependent with changes in one part of the system reverberating in other parts. Therefore one cannot change one piece of the system without impacting others.
- Interactions and relationships within the system tend to be highly reciprocal, and patterned. So people will respond to the behaviour of others out of a range of typical responses.[14]
- Emotional systems are constantly seeking balance (or homeostasis) and will react to any threat to that balance. Thus, there is always some level of resistance to change.
- Signs of distress or conflict may be indicators of the system's difficulties in adapting to change or loss.
- Systems are complex and organic, so problems or crises generally have more than one cause. Thinking systemically thus requires one to redistribute blame by seeking to address the multiple causes of a problem rather than 'fixing' or removing an individual or group seen as the problem. It is necessary to complicate one's understanding of the situation rather than simplifying it.

- The health of any system is more dependent upon the functioning of the leaders, those at the head of the system, than on any other single factor. So we as leaders have a key role, through our responses and self-management, in regulating the distress and anxiety within the system.

Family systems theory suggests four strands that are central for leaders to hold together if we are to help promote healthy group functioning, especially when emotions and anxiety are high.

1 **Offer and invite self-definition**: Healthy self-definition occurs when you openly express what you feel and believe, what you need and can give, what you hope for and where you feel disillusioned or hopeful. Often people wait for others to define first, and then define ourselves in reaction to them. When we, as leaders, clearly self-define it is much more likely that others will respond by defining themselves in a clear and positive way rather than in reaction to others.

2 **Foster a non-anxious presence** (or at least a less anxious one!): this is the opposite of being uptight and tense. It is about managing one's own anxiety and being fully present to other people. The goal is to create an environment where differences, hurts, feelings and issues can be expressed and explored in a safe space. We offer a non-anxious presence, not by detaching from emotions or issues, but by engaging with them without retreating or attacking. Engaging fully with one perspective and then another while managing our own anxiety reduces anxiety within the group.

3 **Maintain emotional contact**: when anxious, angry or hurt, people generally move away from the source of their anxiety by moving away from each other. Distance can take both physical and emotional forms. As a general rule, leaders should note anxiety and move toward it, maintaining emotional contact with the participants and helping them maintain contact with each other and with us as leaders.

4 **Stand firm when the going gets tough**: When a leader provides self-differentiation, it is common to experience resistance and pressure to move back to the way things were. The challenge for the leader is to stand firm, holding to your convictions and sense of direction, while being flexible and willing to adapt what shape your proposed changes might take in the light of others' genuine concerns.

Take a second look at difficult or extreme behaviour

Leaders sometimes ask in despair what they can do about 'totally unreasonable' people, who wear them down with persistent negative behaviour and leave them feeling blocked at every turn, or even under siege. In such circumstances, it is easy to get sucked into a spiral of blame and recrimination. The most important contribution you can make as a leader is to model a response that is both firm and compassionate. Here are some suggested steps, based on the work of Arthur Boers.[15]

First, separate the person from the problem. As soon as you label someone as a troublemaker, you tie together the problem and the person. It is then hard to solve the problem without rejecting the person. So, as a general approach, try to avoid that knot. Focus on how to respond to the difficult behaviour not on how to get around 'difficult people'.

Second, look below the surface. Try adopting a 'research stance'. This involves asking yourself what might be motivating the difficult behaviour, and why you are finding it so difficult. Recognize that it may be easier to act with grace towards another person when you are open to understanding things from his or her point of view.

Third, try examining your assumptions. Be slow to decide that this person has wrong intentions or is impossible to deal with. Rather than guessing at the person's motives, state your puzzlement and invite them to tell you *why* they are behaving in a certain way.

Fourth, examine the bigger picture. Assess the church's health and the functioning of the entire body. Where there are structural problems or skewed relationships in the congregation as a whole, the behaviour of difficult individuals may be a *symptom* rather than the *cause*. Why are other people not taking a stand against the difficult behaviour? The person perceived as difficult may be expressing concerns that others are avoiding articulating. Beware of allowing this person to function as a scapegoat, thinking that, if the 'troublemaker' is removed, everything will be all right. Instead, work at strengthening relationships in the whole and establish a common corporate response to the difficult behaviour, especially within your leadership group.

Fifth, take a stand against harmful behaviour. In the face of difficult behaviour, an aggressive response – being equally difficult in return – simply multiplies anger. But the opposite approach is also dangerous. Being passive, or just reasonable, will simply ensure that people get hurt, and then may leave. Instead, choose to be assertive, willing to confront and speaking the truth in a loving way. Unlike the other two stances, assertiveness requires careful thought and practice. It is likely to involve naming the problem behaviour, explaining why you consider it inappropriate in the context, and exploring alternatives which will build up rather than undermine. There may also be a need to establish clear boundaries, appropriate to the context.

Finally, it is worth recognizing that, in exceptional circumstances, extreme behaviour may be an indication of serious mental illness. Do not be quick to jump to this conclusion; and seek professional counsel from a trained psychologist or therapist before reaching such an assessment. However, if this is what you are facing, you may need to establish some firm corporate boundaries and take protective measures (which, if facing serious harassment, may include securing legal protection) for the sake of the group.

Develop a facilitative leadership style

How would you describe your leadership style? Ronald Heifetz and Donald Laurie offer this proposal: 'Rather than fulfilling the expectation that they will provide answers, leaders have to ask tough questions . . . Instead of quelling conflict, leaders have to draw the issues out.'[16] This suggests the need for us as leaders to avoid being the answer-givers and instead, to develop a more facilitative leadership style, welcoming conflict, inviting expression of differences, and helping the group to wrestle with the challenges that it faces. This does not mean that you will avoid providing clear self-definition: as we have seen, you need to articulate your values and convictions. But it does mean that you will hold back from offering 'the answer' or the way forward, and it will facilitate the engagement of everyone in the group, plumbing the depths of the different concerns that they bring. Developing your skills for facilitating groups and meetings is enormously helpful.[17]

Work at building consensus

Part of an effective facilitative leadership style is seeking to build consensus in reaching decisions, especially within the leadership group, but also within the wider body. Simply securing a majority vote is not good enough. Effective leadership will enable the group to move forward together, helping to ensure that people will not undermine decisions that are reached. It is important to be clear that consensus is not unanimity, which is an unrealistic goal in most situations. Rather, consensus[18] is the readiness to live with a proposed decision, to give one's consent to moving forward. Such agreement to cooperate is normally evidence of the Holy Spirit at work (see Acts

15.28). Different levels of consent can range from enthusiastic support to having significant concerns without standing in the way of making a decision. Those with very serious concerns can still give their consent if they are willing to do so for the sake of the group. However, they are much more likely to do so if their concerns have been adequately heard and noted and if the proposal can reflect their concerns in some way.

One method to test consensus before making a decision that Bridge Builders has found helpful is a graduated straw poll. Sometimes called the 'High Five' approach, this method helps avoid the trap of false consensus which assumes that silence indicates support. Once the facilitator has restated the tentative proposal, each person in the group responds to the proposal, indicating his or her level of support with a show of fingers on one hand, corresponding to the following scale:

5 I fully support the proposal. I can give an unqualified 'yes'.
4 I can support the proposal. It's OK with me.
3 I can live with the proposal, although I do have some concerns about it.
2 I have significant concerns about the proposal, but I will not block the group from making a decision (maybe because this seems the best decision that can be reached right now). And I will not undermine the decision once taken.
1 I cannot live with this proposal, and I need to block it.

When the group largely responds with fives, fours and some threes, they are probably ready to move to a decision. If there is a significant proportion of twos and threes, this suggests a need for more discussion as, obviously, does the presence of any ones.

Working to build consensus will take time, as the above suggests. But it is invariably time well spent, especially with major decisions. For example, the Mennonite congregation I was part of in the 1990s took over a year to consider the possibility of calling its first paid (part-time) ministerial leader. It was a real struggle for some, with plenty of agonizing, but the leadership stayed committed to finding a consensus, and this was eventually achieved. When the leader who was called left a few years later, there were no murmurs in the church about calling another paid leader, and during his whole time there were no concerns expressed about the decision that had been taken – both dividends of the hard work several years before. It is important to recognize that for most churches working at consensus-building constitutes a significant change to the way they have operated in the past and thus will take sustained and skilful leadership to effect a change.

Plan and agree decision-making processes

Decision-making can be a difficult time for churches for at least two reasons: first, because it often brings underlying disagreements (perhaps unrelated to the focus issue) to the surface; and second, because it means that the church is facing a time of change which can act as a focus for people's anxieties about changes elsewhere in their lives and in the wider world. Therefore, decision-making is likely to involve conflict.

It is unrealistic to expect everyone to be happy with the changes and decisions that are made. However, if people are not involved in the decision-making process they can feel ignored and marginalized. This can lead to bitterness and divisions that may not surface immediately but may sow the seeds of destructiveness later on. So it is important to obtain support for important decisions, including from those who may not agree with the final decision. An important principle of good decision-making, therefore, is that it requires the participation of all those who will be affected by the outcome. One first step that can make a big difference is to plan the process for a major decision carefully, and get ownership of the process from the group at the outset. If people own the process, they will be much more likely to live with the outcome, even if it is not an outcome they are particularly happy with.

Likewise, it is important to build in methods for people to respond in open and creative ways through the course of a decision-making process, promoting listening, reflection and problem-solving. Most people are familiar with surveys, small group discussions and panel discussions. Other, less familiar methods for eliciting responses, which Bridge Builders has found particularly helpful, include the Human Rainbow (which involves people standing along a physical spectrum between two extreme points); the Samoan Circle (a type of 'fish bowl' process with discussion only happening in an inner circle and which people can leave and join); and mapping needs and fears (of the different subgroups, on a large flip chart).

I have written at some length on decision-making elsewhere,[19] but the above hopefully provides a few important pointers to help reduce destructive conflict from decision-making within the church.

Understand conflict levels and intervention options

Conflict within groups ebbs and flows. It is helpful to be able to assess the level of intensity of conflict in the group. In my work with Bridge Builders, one model that I have found helpful is that developed by

Speed Leas.[20] Leas proposes five broad levels of conflict intensity and strategies for working with each level. Here is a brief summary:

Level 1: problems to solve

At this level there are real differences between people, but the people are problem focused not person focused. Communication is clear and specific and the people involved want to sort out the problem. Dialogue and discussion will enable the parties to do so. This is healthy conflict.

Level 2: disagreement

At this level people are more concerned with self-protection than problem-solving and may talk with friends about how to deal with an issue. Communication is more generalized and people withhold information they think may be used by those with whom they disagree. This level will need the leaders to facilitate more structured negotiation with active encouragement of participation.

Level 3: contest

At this level people's objectives shift to winning the argument and coming out on top. There is a win–lose dynamic and communication becomes more distorted, with personal attacks and emotional arguments overshadowing rational argument. While this level falls short of active hostility, it will require skilful leadership to find a way forward. Clear ground rules and a clear, agreed-upon process for problem-solving need to be established. Certain situations at this level may require an outside facilitator.

Level 4: fight or flight

At this level, the parties' goal is to hurt or get rid of others, or to leave if they cannot achieve this. Factions have solidified, with identified leaders, and the good of the subgroup (rather than the whole congregation) becomes their focus. Communication is characterized by blaming, negative stereotyping, self-righteousness and a refusal to take responsibility ('It's all their fault; they're the ones who need to change.'). At this level, no leader within the congregation will be perceived as impartial, no matter how hard they've worked at remaining so. Therefore a specialist outsider mediator or consultant is required to lead an extended reconciliation process for the group. (This is the level at which Bridge Builders is most commonly called in.)

Level 5: intractable

In a church context, this level is perhaps better referred to as 'Holy War' since conflict is out of the participants' control, and the goal of opposing parties is to destroy one another. In such situations, people see themselves as part of an eternal cause, fighting for universal principles with any means justifying the all-important ends. Communication is characterized by outright condemnation of others, extreme emotional volatility, compulsiveness, an inability to disengage, and with the issues lost from sight. At this level mediation and consultancy will be ineffective and short-term reconciliation is unrealistic. Authority needs to be exercised by those outside the congregation to determine clear boundaries and to secure an end to hostilities.

The key is making an accurate assessment of which level the critical mass of the group is at, as this will determine what type of intervention is appropriate. The appropriate approach at one level can be ineffective or counter-productive when used at another level.

Know when to seek help

As leaders in the church it is important that we understand our own limitations and recognize when we need outside help. The central need is to build-in regular mechanisms for support and review for oneself as a leader, well before a time of crisis is reached. This might include regular meetings with a spiritual director, an external supervisor (perhaps a trained counsellor) and/or a small group of trusted peers who are not afraid to give honest feedback. People such as these can help us become more aware of when we are getting overstretched and when we need further help. Another key is developing a good relationship with a denominational senior leader to whom you can turn when needed. When the time of crisis comes, know who you can turn to and do not be too proud to seek help: the capacity to do so is a sign of maturity, not of weakness.

A while back, after more than two years working together, one of my colleagues and I experienced some significant conflict between us. We both recognized that we had moved beyond our capacity to handle the situation ourselves without third party help. Fortunately, we wanted to sort things out between us. We both trusted the director of our centre, so we approached him and he was able to mediate successfully between us. We were able to continue working productively together until the end of my colleague's term later in the year, and to maintain a positive relationship following her departure.

Work at creating a culture of peace

I believe that everything I have set out in this chapter is part of what Alan Kreider calls building a culture of peace. It is important to acknowledge, as he does, that:

> It will not be easy, and the changes required will be numerous. They will take time – because essentially we are looking at a process of cultural change within the church. And such a change of culture can only take place over the medium- to long-term, through a range of strategies sustained over time.[21]

In this chapter I have tried to set out some of what is needed to develop such a culture of peace and peacemaking within the church. Leaders have a central role to play, especially when it comes to transforming the church's experience of conflict. As one executive has put it: 'The work of the leader is to get conflict out into the open and to use it as a source of creativity.'[22] But this is more than just about harnessing the creative energy in conflict. It is about our vision of the Church. Let me draw to close with a vision of the Church that I share, as set out by Robert Warren:

> Despite the forces at work which seem to have marginalised the church, we stand today faced with a great new opportunity to speak the good news of Christ into our culture by the way we live that truth in the life of the local church . . . The church is called to be the pilot project of the new humanity established by Christ, an outpost of the kingdom of God and the 'community of the Age to Come'. Not least is the world looking for models of handling conflict . . . A church where there is no conflict has little relevance to our society. A church that has found a way to handle conflict creatively will be good news to all around it and in it . . . the truth remains, that there is a longing to see relationships work, to see the truth of God's call to love being practised. Conflicts in the church can seem such a distraction from getting on with the real work; *but this is the real work*. When people come near such a community they will instinctively know how real the relationships are.[23]

If you share a similar vision for the Church, then join me in seeking to transform the way in which the Church engages with conflict and in the model that we provide as leaders, developing a new culture of peace.

Notes

1. Schrock-Shenk, 1999, pp. 33–4. This book is the single best introduction to conflict that I know.

2. Schrock-Shenk, 1999, p. 34.

3. Wilmot and Hocker, 2001, p. 41.

4. Schrock-Shenk, 1999, p. 23.

5. In the Old Testament prophets, doing justice for widows was shorthand for covenant loyalty; and in the Rabbinic tradition, doing justice was spelled out in terms of organized community giving to the poor, particularly widows. So the complaint relates to questions of justice and faithfulness to God's covenant.

6. Interestingly, there are three such promises in Matthew's Gospel. The first, near the beginning, is in the context of God's redemption of the world, where we are promised Emmanuel, God with us. The last is at the close of the Gospel in the context of mission and being sent out as God's agents into the world. The second is here, at the centre of the Gospel in the context of dealing with the tough issues within the Christian community.

7. I have certainly not exhausted the principles that could be highlighted from this chapter, but these few will suffice for this short chapter.

8. King, 1977, p. 38.

9. See Fisher, Ury and Patton, 1999.

10. Gilmore and Fraleigh, 2004.

11. For a basic introduction to the four styles, see Patterson, 2003, pp. 10–11. This booklet provides a well-written and accessible introduction to conflict in the Church.

12. The seminal book offering this view was Friedman, 1985. For a shorter introduction, see Steinke, 1993.

13. Or Bowen Theory, developed by the American psychiatrist Dr Murray Bowen.

14. See Gilbert, 1992, for a clear and readable introduction to family systems theory and the typical response patterns used to manage anxiety.

15. See Boers, 1999.

16. Heifetz and Laurie, 1990–98, pp.173–4. See also Heifetz, 1994.

17. Bridge Builders regularly offers a five-day course, Skills Training for Mediation and Facilitation in the Church, to equip church leaders in some of the skills set out in this chapter. See <www.menno.org.uk>.

18. In a pure consensus model, an individual who is unhappy, for example, because of questions of principle, can block a decision if they are unwilling to stand aside. Pure consensus can be an impractical ideal at times. Sometimes individuals abuse the power that consensus gives them, or their own inner struggles stop them from respecting the group as a whole. For this reason, I recommend a modified consensus model, where every effort is made to come to a consensus decision, but if the group gets stuck then, ultimately, it can proceed with a decision on the basis of a substantial majority vote, say 80%. This allows a church to proceed when there is a large majority which has worked hard to address the concerns of the minority, without having to be paralysed by those concerns. It also allows conscientious individuals to pre-

serve their deep convictions without feeling responsible for the outcome.
19. McKay, 1999.
20. Leas, 1985, esp. pp. 17–22.
21. Kreider, Kreider and Widjaja, 2005, pp. 91–2.
22. Jan Carlzon, quoted by Heifetz and Laurie, 1990–98, p. 182.
23. Warren, 1995, pp. 15–17.

References

Boers, Arthur P. (1999), *Never Call Them Jerks: Healthy Responses to Difficult Behaviour*, Bethesda, Maryland: Alban Institute.
Fisher, Roger, William Ury and Bruce Patton (1999), *Getting to Yes: Negotiating an Agreement without Giving In*, 2nd edn, London: Random House.
Friedman, Edwin (1985), *Generation to Generation: Family Process in Church and Synagogue*, New York: Guildford Press.
Gilbert, Roberta (1992), *Extraordinary Relationships: A New Way of Thinking about Human Interactions*, New York: John Wiley.
Gilmore, Susan, and Patrick Fraleigh (2004), *The Friendly Style Profile for People at Work*, 2nd edn, Eugene, Oregon: Friendly Press.
Heifetz, Ronald A. (1994), *Leadership without Easy Answers*, Cambridge, Massachusetts: Belknap Press.
Heifetz, Ronald A., and Donald L. Laurie (1990–98), *The Work of Leadership*, *Harvard Business Review on Leadership* (Boston, Massachusetts: Harvard Business School Publishing).
King, Martin L. (1977), *Strength to Love*, Glasgow: William Collins/Fount.
Kreider, Alan, Eleanor Kreider and Paulus Widjaja (2005), *A Culture of Peace: God's Vision for the Church*, Intercourse, Pennsylvania: Good Books.
Leas, S. (1985), *Moving Your Church through Conflict*, Bethesda, Maryland: Alban Institute.
McKay, Alastair (1999), 'Congregational Decision Making', in Schrock-Shenk and Ressler (1999), pp. 177–87.
Patterson, Colin (2003), *How to Learn through Conflict: A Handbook for Leaders in Local Churches*, Cambridge: Grove Books.
Schrock-Shenk, Carolyn (1999), 'Introducing Conflict and Conflict Transformation', in Schrock-Shenk and Ressler, pp. 25–37.
Schrock-Shenk, Carolyn, and Lawrence Ressler (eds) (1999), *Making Peace with Conflict: Practical Skills for Conflict Transformation*, Scottdale, Pennsylvania: Herald Press.
Steinke, Peter (1993), *How Your Church Family Works: Understanding Congregations as Emotional Systems*, Bethesda, Maryland: Alban Institute.
Warren, Robert (1995), *Being Human, Being Church: Spirituality and Mission in the Local Church*, London: Marshall Pickering.
Wilmot, William, and Joyce Hocker (2001), *Interpersonal Conflict*, 6th edn, New York: McGraw-Hill.

20. Extending a warm welcome

HEATHER WRAIGHT

A young couple and their two sons moved to a rural area as part of the husband's job. They decided not to commute into town to worship and so went to the village church. On their first Sunday, the vicar greeted them warmly at the end of the service, 'Nice to see you. Thank you for coming. Please come again.' They went away feeling good, and duly went again next week. At the end of the service, the vicar greeted them warmly, 'Nice to see you. Thank you for coming. Please come again.' For six months, they did 'come again', but he made no effort to get to know them, didn't ask their names or call round to see them. In fact, he didn't seem to realize that they had been before, and eventually they stopped going to that church.[1]

A colleague and I sometimes undertake deanery reviews, helping a group of Anglican churches in an area to evaluate where they are going and what they could do together. To get a feel of what is going on we try to visit each church, unannounced, for a Sunday service. One vicar assured us his church was very friendly, but we turned up when he was on holiday. Someone handed us each a prayer book and hymn book without a word of greeting and we duly found ourselves a place in an empty pew. We deliberately waited to see if anyone would offer us the Peace at the relevant point in the service – but not one did. Although it was announced at the end that coffee was available we were not invited to join in, nor shown where it was. We put our prayer book and hymn book on a shelf as we filed out and arrived on the street without having spoken to anyone. We looked at one another and said, 'If we really had just moved into the area and were looking for a church, we wouldn't go there again', even though we had liked the style of worship.

When on holiday, a family attended the parish church in the small town where they were staying. As they went in they were asked if they were newcomers, welcomed warmly and asked where they would prefer to sit. By the time the service started at least a dozen people had greeted them, but without being intrusive. When the service ended, the family were asked whether they would like tea or coffee and it was brought to them by people who then sat down and engaged in conversation. Not surprisingly, they discovered the church was growing and was especially concerned with families who were coming to join the church.

Getting to the door

People come to a church for the first time for a wide range of reasons. The most common is that they were going to church somewhere else and have either moved house or, for whatever reason, have decided to leave their current local church. About one-third of people who leave church do so because they move house to a new area[2] and many of them will look for another church near their new home. They may well turn up at your church, and will either consciously or unconsciously know what they are looking for. They may want a particular style of worship, relevant teaching, or provision for their needs such as a Sunday School for their children or a youth club for teenagers. If they are to come again they need to discover on their first visit that at least some of those hopes could be met in this church. A family with three young children moved house and went on their first Sunday to the church nearest to their new home. At the end of the service, a member of the congregation came up to them and remarked that they had brought their children to church. 'We are not set up for children,' he said, 'So this church is not suitable for you.' Well, at least they were left in no doubt, but it was rather discouraging! They went elsewhere the next week, but for some that would have been enough to put them off.

Other newcomers will be genuine visitors, perhaps staying with a family member who attends the church, or in the area on holiday. The minister of a Church of Scotland church in a tourist area encourages his congregation to use their gifts and experience for the Kingdom of God. The only significant employment in the area is tourism, and many of the congregation either work in the local hotels or run Bed and Breakfast establishments. He encourages them to offer lifts to church to their guests on a Sunday morning and on many summer Sundays the congregation is 50% larger than in the winter. Being in a much-visited part of Scotland, another of his churches now offers a wedding service with everything arranged. People come from far and wide to get married, and find a warm welcome from the small congregation. The minister regularly hears of people who, at the end of their holiday or after their wedding, have returned to church or have started going for the first time.[3]

Evangelistic activities and Christian witness bring in new people for some churches, but coming to a worship service on a regular basis may be a long way down the line for these people. An Alpha Course or similar may help them come to faith and draw them into relationships in a small group, but it is a big step from there to turning up on a Sunday morning to an event, the like of which they may never have experienced before. If they do eventually come, because they already know some people there, it can be easy to overlook the fact that they are actually new to Sunday worship.

Crossing the threshold

One minister announced that he wanted everyone in his church to go to the betting shop during the week and place a bet. Most were horrified, but a few did it. One agreed to explain how it felt from the pulpit next Sunday. He described how everyone else walked in and knew exactly where to go and how to place a bet but when he went through the door he didn't know what to do and felt completely lost. The lesson, of course, was that people who have never been to a church service before, except perhaps for a wedding or funeral, are likely to find the experience just as strange as the churchgoer did in a betting shop. Michelle Guiness described it this way,

> It's easy to forget what it's like to walk in through those doors for the first time – the indecision, that clutch of fear in the pit of the stomach, the deep inhalation of breath, the strangeness of those unknown faces.[4]

Identifying newcomers is straightforward in a small church where everyone knows everyone else, though it can be very difficult to break into the close-knit clique which such a group may have become. In a larger church it is much more difficult to spot who is there for the first time, and some kind of strategy for doing so is probably needed. It is all too easy to approach a person whom you don't know and warmly greet them with, 'Hello, I haven't seen you before, is this your first visit?', only to be embarrassed when the response is, 'I've been coming for six weeks' – or six months!

A welcoming team is a good step for a church, but the people involved do need some basic relationship skills combined with training in how to behave. In one church, a person who had not been for a long time turned up. An eager welcomer greeted her warmly and added the unwise comment, 'Haven't you put on a lot of weight?' The ability not only to identify newcomers but also to gauge how much interaction they want is a key qualification. Unfortunately, people get hurt in churches, and someone tentatively exploring whether this church is 'safe' usually wants to be left alone, while others want to be helped in any way possible.

A good welcoming team will not only have people who stand at the door to shake the hand of those who arrive and hand out hymn books or the weekly bulletin but also a team member might sit next to a person who is a complete stranger to church, explain what is happening, helping them find the hymns or Bible readings (if they are not on a screen on PowerPoint) and making clear that they don't have to give anything when the offering comes round. Someone else may be on the lookout for those with children and introduce the child and a parent to the leader of the appropriate Sunday School group. A disabled person may need not only help with access to the building but also to be shown where the toilet facilities are. Part of a warm welcome is to enable the visitor to feel as comfortable and relaxed as possible so that their focus can be on the service and not on practical issues such as 'I wonder where they've taken Lucy?', or 'Where is the loo?'

Coming back

A large, nationwide survey found that churches which were growing were more likely to give newcomers something.[5] It didn't seem to matter what that 'something' was, presumably because the act of identifying the recipient is in itself significant. However, what they are given does have to be planned and prepared and ideally should help to encourage them to come again. A large church of 800 people in New Zealand asks visitors to identify themselves during the service and then gives out visitors cards. If the visitor takes the card to the reception desk they are given a free porcelain mug. During the week, they receive a phone call from one of the pastors and a welcome letter which contains a voucher for a further gift if they come back the next Sunday – when they will receive a worship CD. In the first year of this programme, 300 people joined the church.

A number of churches now hold a 'newcomers meal'. Some larger churches, especially where there is a student community, have been doing it regularly for years. Those who are new or who have nowhere else to go for lunch are invited to a communal lunch laid on by the church, which is held either every Sunday or once a month. Holding such a lunch every three or six months is another strategy because a visitor, even on their first visit, can be given an invitation to the next such event.

Coming back may not be so much returning on a Sunday but moving from attending a mid-week church activity to coming to worship service. The level of involvement with a church varies from enormously committed to very loose. Does a mother who brings her toddler to a Tuesday afternoon group feel this is her church? What about the non-churchgoing parents of a teenager who comes to the youth group? Drawing people from the edge of the church into the heart of it rarely just 'happens', ways in have to be planned. The 'Leadership, Vision and Growing Churches' report showed that while 65% of churches had a parent and toddlers group this activity was least likely to result in new people attending church. It was only effective as a form of outreach if thought had been given to the steps such a parent might need to take in order to find out more about the church and its message. In other words, a Parent and Toddler group could legitimately be simply a valuable service to the community, or it could additionally be seen as a gateway through which some of those parents might start on a pathway to personal faith. If that journey is to happen, they need to feel that the rest of the church will welcome them, and indeed already sees them as belonging to the church community.

Beginning to belong

There is a huge range of strategies which can be developed to identify newcomers and help them to come back or to draw people from the fringe into the centre of church life, but one of the key things is that they need to feel welcome and not that they are intruding into a comfortable club to which they will always be an outsider. However, a friendly church may bring them back the first few times, but that is not usually enough – people are not looking for a friendly church, but a church where they can make friends.

What does belonging mean? It is somewhat different for men and for women. For a man, it often involves knowing that the whole family are happy to come to this church. He may be looking for a well-organized church, preaching that he can understand and which is relevant to his life, or a clearly defined sense of direction. For women, there is a definite process which is much more to do with relationships and acceptance than with spiritual reasons.

Being known

For women, it is more important than for a man that people know them by name, that they are not just Jamie's mother or even 'that new woman'. If someone has an unusual name, which is especially likely if they come from another ethnic group, their name may seem unpronounceable! An Afro-Caribbean woman went to a local, all-white, church and was asked her name. When she gave her full African name the response was, 'Oh, I'll never remember that, I'll just call you Joy'. But her name wasn't Joy; it would have been much better to ask what her friends call her! Being known by name helps with a sense of identity, which psychologists tell us is often weak in women. For a young mum, walking into church after the hassle of getting the children ready in time, it helps her relax to be called by name. For a single person living alone, it may be the first time they've talked to anyone since coming home from work on Friday, and for widowed or divorced people conversations at church may be the only meaningful ones they have all week.

Being valued

Belonging goes deeper than simply being recognized. It is being welcomed for whoever I am, and without reservation. Unfortunately, there are many in our society who feel that the church would never accept and value them. Perhaps their lifestyle is one they think the church would judge, or maybe they find reading difficult and don't want to have stand out as different in a service which involves hymns and perhaps liturgy. Those with physical or mental disabilities sometimes sense they are a 'nuisance', while people from another ethnic group wonder if they detect discrimination. One of the reasons there are so many thriving black majority churches in the UK, especially in London, is that the immigrants from the West Indies in the 1950s and 1960s were, by and large, not welcomed and so founded their own churches.

Being accepted

It can take a remarkably long time for a newcomer to feel they are an 'insider'. But they do not fully belong until they reach that point. There are four questions that people ask, often subconsciously, when they first join any new group, and these apply just as much to church as anywhere else.

1 Who am I? Am I the newcomer, the only non-white person, the one who doesn't know what to do? Do I have a right to be here or am I an intruder into your world? If this question cannot be answered, the newcomer will remain hesitant, fearful of committing themselves, and unwilling to trust themselves to others. It is the role of a welcomer to answer this question unobtrusively by, as it were, giving permission to the newcomer to become part of the congregation.

2 Who are you? Are you people like me, or are you so different that you'll never accept me? Are you used to visitors, or am I disturbing your status quo by turning up? Do you actually want me here and, if so, how are you going to let me know? As the new person gets to know others these questions need positive answers for the visitor to keep coming long enough to begin to belong.

3 What are we here for? The visitor may have come with a completely different agenda to the regular attenders. They are there to worship God, to receive some Christian teaching or encouragement, to meet their friends, to carry out responsibilities they have in the church or perhaps out of duty. None of these may apply to the newcomer. But do they find what they came for, nevertheless? If they return week-by-week they will discover what that particular church's priorities are and make a decision as to whether they are happy to share them.

4 How are we going to do it? Culture has been described as 'The way we do things round here', and every church has a culture. Why do we stand up for hymns and sit down or kneel for prayers (other countries do it the other way round!)? In an informal service, who is in charge, why do we have to stand up for so long? In a more formal service, am I supposed to read the liturgy with the others, should I take part in the Communion or Eucharist, is it expected that I put money in the offering? Some of the churches my colleague and I visit are very good at putting newcomers at ease by simple descriptions of what happens next, while others seem to assume that everyone present knows exactly what to do.

Welcoming people to church may start at the church door, but if it ends there that is a tragedy, because the newcomer probably won't come to your church again – and may not go to any other either. A warm welcome and really friendly people can be key factors in growing your church rather than turning people away.

Notes

1. Wraight, 2001, p. 9.

2. Private research for the Church of England Diocese of Rochester, London: Christian Research, 2001.

3. Wraight, 2007.

4. Wraight, 2001, p. ix.

5. 'Leadership, Vision and Growing Churches', 2003, private research for the Salvation Army Central Northern Division, London: Christian Research.

References

Wraight, Heather (2001), *Eve's Glue: The Role Women Play in Holding the Church Together*, London: Christian Research; and Carlisle: Paternoster.

Wraight, Heather (2007), *Back from the Brink*, London: Christian Research.

Part 4

Organization

21. Leading multiple congregations

BRIAN NICHOLS

Multiple congregation churches, like single congregation churches, come in all shapes, and are variously managed and led. The same basic leadership skills are needed for both single and multiple settings, but it is likely that the way they are exercised will be prioritized and delivered differently.

Asked what leadership meant to him, the retiring chairman of British Telecom, Sir Christopher Bland, described it as:

> the messy business of getting organisations and people to perform. I do not think there is a single leadership paradigm. They come in all shapes and sizes. One common feature is that you have to put yourself about. It is hard to lead invisibly![1]

'Putting oneself about' in a multi-congregational setting is not that simple. Much depends on the model of relationship being used and how much control or decentralization operates. In attempting to address some of the issues, I am aware that I write as a Baptist who has inherited and is reacting to a tradition of what is sometimes fiercely held congregational autonomy, fuelled by a strong commitment to every-member ministry. This tradition is instinctively anxious about questions of leadership. On good days, this produces exactly the kind of collaborative leadership which is essential in handling a large and diverse church. On bad days, it is like trying to quell a succession of leadership coups and uprisings as everyone determines to do what is right in their own eyes.

Defining a multiple congregation church is important. It is not just about having a multiple service pattern, or even grouping several autonomous small churches, although, as we shall briefly see, both of these can lead to the birth of a multiple congregation community. The kind of church we are talking about is one where different groups understand themselves to be part of one church in an area, but who function for worship, support, leadership and mission as distinct groups. Multiple congregation churches can be divided roughly into three groups, each of which anticipates a particular emphasis in leadership.

Multicongregational churches formed for practical reasons

These are churches that have a variety of services, but basically offer differing worship experiences for broadly the same group of people. As patterns of church attendance have changed in the UK over recent years so these services have increasingly taken on the characteristics of separate congregations and have forced leadership teams to rethink how unity can be maintained across the church. This involves either seeking to control more tightly what happens or moving to a model of subsidiarity which allows an increasing measure of congregational self-determination. Often when that transition is badly handled acrimonious disputes occur, often between traditionalists and those who enjoy the vibrancy and flexibility of new ways of meeting and being church.

Churches have long been grouped for economic and staffing reasons. It can be a difficult but necessary journey from the position of a single minister divided among several separate churches each with its own distinct programme to a culture of recognizing an essential oneness expressed in different contexts under a common leadership. Unfortunately, the demands on clergy and ministers in such contexts often cause them to burn out before any sense of becoming one church begins to emerge. Such a change often takes a generation before it becomes effective, but leaders often don't stay long enough to bring it about. Anyone assigned to such a group ministry needs from the outset to develop a team around them so that the load is shared creatively and new and sustainable patterns of collaborative ministry are established. As new people join the church (and often creative patterns of leadership provoke growth), a further problem emerges as some of them identify with only one congregation, fail to understand the history that brought them together, and therefore carry no allegiance to the whole church.

Methodism has long experience of such ministry. In this case, the raison d'être for grouping is not primarily economic, but ecclesiological. The connexional nature of the church guarantees a continuity of ministry, but unless good relationships are established between local and circuit leaders and there is a strong circuit identity, the movement of ministers at regular intervals disrupts purposeful collaborative working and they can find themselves chairing a proliferation of meetings, in which their leadership is not really accepted, and preaching vision to unconvinced and disconnected audiences.

Leadership in these settings is often characterized by strong administrative and managerial themes. The sheer complexity of ensuring the continuance of worship, maintaining pastoral contact with people, caring for premises and administering budgets dominates the timetable. There are often low expectations about what can be achieved. Unless they are able to operate astutely in this organizational maelstrom ministers may find themselves marginalized into being the deliverers of the 'spiritual bit', adjuncts to the real world, with little influence to bring about fundamental change in their congregations, yet frequently scapegoated as the congregations increasingly become dysfunctional for lack of clear leadership. Alternatively, they become ecclesiastical paper shufflers, maintaining a smooth-running organization, while the spiritual health of the congregations gradually declines around them.

Multicongregational churches formed as a reaction to growth

The reasons for growth may be quite varied and therefore the way in which congregations develop their relationships will differ, calling for different approaches in leadership.

The rationale for developing more congregations may be in order to cope with overcrowded premises. A shift system is devised, although the logistics of servicing two or more services in close-time proximity soon becomes quite debilitating without good administrative skills and lots of pastoral patience. Increasingly, each service develops its own identity and purpose, and in the worst cases leads to a competitive approach to the use of resources.

An alternative rationale comes from the desire to accommodate niche interests. These may be to do with conflicting preferences in worship style, or more fundamentally to do with creating distinct meeting points for people of a similar age, culture, ethnicity or language group. If these new groups begin to exhibit congregational characteristics beyond simply being additional services, questions soon emerge about the location of power, release of leadership and use of resources. The congregation that was there first will tend to try and hold on to the control of resources instead of seeing itself as having become one among several expressions of church.

Sometimes, growth occurs because of the charismatic style of leadership. The congregations hold together around the presence of a strong figure until he or she moves or there is a successful challenge to leadership. Once they have moved or been removed the church flounders, and in the end looks for a transactional leader who is able to bring strong mediation and pastoral skills to try and hold together the disparate groups. Significant energy is expended in this way, but as a result the circumstances that brought about growth diminish. The congregations lose confidence and, as numbers decline, reunite, or split off, impatient with the lack of progress. The effect on such second generation leaders is one of decreased morale as they perceive little reward for a lot of effort.

Those who find themselves at the centre of rapid growth therefore need to move swiftly to a collaborative style of leadership, and together the emerging team then has the task of enabling the congregations to gather around common values rather than personality. Planning for succession is important. Although the received wisdom is to offer the church the opportunity of a complete change without any interference from the retiring leader, in the complexity of a multi-congregation church this may be a mistake. While the incumbent ought not autocratically to appoint his or her successor, there needs to be some good consultation and an adequate handover period if the church as a whole is not to suffer serious setbacks.

Intentional multiple congregation churches

Churches of this type deliberately set out to be multi-congregational as a way of exercising their missionary nature. Leadership in these contexts tends to be much more entrepreneurial with a strong sense of the importance of evangelism and what might be described as an apostolic confidence born out of clear missional vision. A fundamental task is that of developing and supporting emerging leaders for each new expression of the church's life.

Three examples of this type of church come to mind. First, there are those churches which intentionally plant a new congregation in order to contextualize their mission activity in a new geographical or cultural setting. Either during a transitional period towards independence or as a deliberate policy of continued relationship, parent and child coexist and share common values and resources. Are the leaders equally leaders of both, do they have separate fiefdoms, do the senior leaders remain in the heart of the planting congregation with new leaders being found for the plant, or does the parent give away some of its key leaders to the child? Whichever direction is chosen, significant requirements of leadership are the ability to manage change well and to be able to live within a fluid organizational structure.

Second, there are those churches where there is an intentional pattern of breaking down growing groups into manageable relationship patterns – the traditional church growth ideology of cell, congregation and celebration – in order to ensure that growth continues. The starting end is usually at cell level, cells dividing as they grow, with clusters of cells forming congregations. Congregations meet with each other for less frequent celebrations. Occasionally, existing churches join the network as already formed congregations, in which case the challenge is to redefine their life in cell form and surrender a measure of autonomy so that they can benefit from the larger network. This kind of multi-cell/congregation sometimes acts as church and sometimes as churches. Usually networks of this kind are held together by a strong core leadership team. Many new church streams operate models of this and the next type.[2]

Another type is the church that deliberately sets about a strategy which leads to several congregations emerging and being held together in mature interdependence. Ideally, the maturation of the congregations is characterized by a confidence in their own identity, able to pursue their own agenda and nurture and disciple their own people in mission. With that maturity they responsibly hold relationships with their sister congregations, possessing a strong allegiance to overall vision and values and an interdependent sharing of resources and engagement in elements of mission and ministry which are best done together. The language of covenant is often used to describe this kind of network.

Four strands of leadership

To function healthily every church needs at least four broad strands of leadership running through every aspect of its life, either implicitly or explicitly. These strands might be described using the following biblical terms:

- Servant (slave/assistant labourer/orderly/general factotum)
- Shepherd (pastor/parent/nurturer)
- Steward (housekeeper/keeper of the memory)
- Overseer (bishop/helmsman/elder. Note: never 'ruler')

In congregations grouped for expedient, resourcing reasons the first strand of leadership often becomes the dominant one, while the shepherding models often dominate second generation leadership in situations which have arisen out of growth. Intentional multi-congregation churches often look for a combination of the shepherd and overseer, desiring a strong apostolic leader to aid their intentionality, but then becoming anxious about how such a diverse outfit is cared for. All groups tend to neglect the importance of the steward role of facilitating the sharing of resources, including people, of providing adequate training which invests in fresh leadership, and particularly of keeping the vision alive together with the memory of how that vision emerged.

Super-glued or held by elastic?

Research has shown that missional churches, especially those which include fresh expressions of church, tend by nature to be relational and are keen to reproduce.[3] This culture favours fluid structures which allow for individual congregational growth within a framework of wider relationships. Almost all the church streams which have emerged in the last 20 years are at least strongly networked, sometimes to the extent that they operate almost as one church in several locations. However, the material from which such growing churches are made is often quite raw and flimsy. The temptation is to make the relationships rigid and strongly dependent on the centre so that control can be maintained, rather than to decentralize.

Decentralization implies a delegation of power from an all-powerful centre. As constituent congregations grow, the elastic that holds them becomes quite taut, as insecure leadership tries to manage the diversity. Charles Handy[4] offers an alternative model of federalization. This model implies that power really lies with the constituent parts which then cede part of that power to the centre for the benefit of all. Leaders, as part of that federalization, would serve strongly and perhaps primarily in their local congregation yet have a confident relationship with peers in other congregations in order to offer oversight to the whole. This provides a level of elasticity which means that leadership can be exercised according to where the need is, rather than according to where controlling structures dictate.

Most multiple congregation churches seem to adopt a pattern which lies somewhere between federalization and a centralized control approach. The more 'emergent' in nature, the more likely it is that the church will be confident in a relational rather than an organizational model. In their book on emerging church, Gibbs and Bolger[5] list several transitions which take place in this more relational model. From stifling control we move to creative freedom, where the vision of the leader becomes the vision of all. Instead of having powerful group leaders, consensus-led groups emerge. Those who exercise leadership are there not because they are willing but because their gifts become apparent. Their role is not one based on position or status, but is characterized by passion and has influence because they have a proven track record. Such open leadership will include some who are new to the group and are welcome to contribute to the whole group discernment processes as the congregations set their own agendas rather than having them set for them.

Gibbs and Bolger note that, as a community grows, open leadership is not straightforward. Presumably, this is partly due to the size of the group making consensus harder to reach, together with the presence of people who are at very different stages of the Christian journey and with very different abilities in understanding and interpreting information. Therefore, there seems to be a necessary transition to be made to a community of representational leaders. What they do is then to release the gifts of others, rather than to construct a role of being the dominant mediators of God to the people. They operate not as controllers but as spiritual directors, mentors and facilitators.

Shared vision and values

There still has to be good reason why congregations would want to hold together as one church. So the glue or elastic is not just about exercising collaborative leadership. Perhaps it is the role of the steward to keep bringing before us our shared vision and values. Here are some of the themes that might hold us. There is usually a particular theological ethos, and common expectations of what values will permeate all congregations. In my own setting,[6] the common ethos is that of Baptist evangelicalism. There is a common strapline, 'Building Community in Christ', and we have found that the work done by the Baptist Union[7] on core values has been helpful in shaping our thinking. Each congregation may then have either implicit or explicit subsets of values which reflect the core ones. Part of the role of the leadership teams is to articulate and rearticulate these 'givens' of our life. This then takes us to the next bit of 'glue'.

Shared oversight and the glue of a common culture

In multiple congregation churches, oversight or episcope operates in several spheres at once and, as might be expected, this can be a source of misunderstanding and confusion. At least three stumbling blocks occur. First, however federalist the church might be there is often an undeclared hierarchy which has no formal description, but in practice operates throughout. Typical layers include the ministry team (staff), elders, deacons, managing trustees, congregational leadership teams, small group leaders and project team leaders. Where that hierarchy exists but is not recognized, either by the leaders or the led, assumptions and decisions are made which in practice cannot be carried through because authority is disputed and the community is not sufficiently helped to own decisions that are made. The connections between leadership teams need to be explicit, and where lines of management and accountability exist they need to be agreed and made public.

Second, multiplicity of leadership risks the development of a multiplicity of visions unless core vision and values are taught well and reinforced with each emerging group of leaders. This underlines the need for a good 'stewardship' strand of leadership, always setting the core objectives before the congregations. One way of doing this is to work on establishing the culture of the church, with a common vocabulary and instantly recognizable vehicles through which the vision and values are communicated. St Thomas's Church in Sheffield has successfully done this through the teaching of 'LifeShapes' at every level of their life. Rather than trying to reinforce a set of objectives and strategies, or attempting to reinforce an all-inclusive organizational structure, they have majored on discipleship as a way of being. This creates a culture which holds across a very large and diverse community.[8] 'LifeShapes' is designed to equip the believer for Kingdom life by linking the discipleship principles of Jesus to memorable images. At every level of church life, and wherever that church life is expressed throughout South Yorkshire and beyond, individual members and groups should be able to articulate fundamental principles for growth, using similar vocabulary and images. Intrinsic to this is the understanding that, in discipling, Jesus was equipping a fresh generation of leaders with the skills to mentor and release others into their ministries.

In this model, leaders are free to lead according to the particular context of their congregation, project or group, and with their own skill and gift areas, but are bound by a common understanding of what both church and individual life shape look like.

Shared resources

Another uniting factor is that of a common purse. This has considerable advantages with regard to the management of resources. Not only are there economies of scale but also the relative merits of each congregation's requirements and opportunities have to be carefully balanced, and spending assumptions can be more effectively challenged and tested against agreed mission criteria. With congregations of different abilities contributing to a common pot, the strong can resource the weak without a sense of patronization. The management requirements imposed by charity legislation can be dealt with more effectively – rather than having to find several treasurers and prepare and file separate accounts, there is one accounting system. To avoid a single point of failure (that is, one person handling all the financial affairs with all the attendant risks), a team-based approach is essential, but within that team different skills can be applied.

Skilled people are also a common resource. In South Parade, all Ministry Team members (staff) and elders (volunteers) are appointed by the whole church for the whole church. Each then has the task of working in three ways. First, according to specialism, a team member may work across the whole church facilitating an area of mission which is best done collaboratively. Second, each works within their skill area with each individual congregation as projects specific to those congregations develop. Third, the paid pastors take responsibility for working alongside leadership teams in designated congregations, and some elders are appointed, having first been elected specifically to their congregational leadership team in order to serve as congregational elders. The weekly staff team meeting and monthly elders' meetings are essential ingredients in ensuring good communication and cross-fertilization between congregations as well as enabling mutual support between key leaders.

Working towards mature interdependence

The glue that holds has to be elastic enough to enable continuing growth, otherwise too much energy is expended in maintaining central structures and values systems which become increasingly brittle or rigid with age. The Anglican report, *Mission-shaped Church*[9] encouraged the importance of enhancing congregational identity by allowing the dynamics of distinct worship patterns, dedicated leadership, focused mission, discrete pastoral structures, and good representation in the whole of church life. Additionally, it called for the abolition of all language that called one congregation 'the main' or 'mother' congregation.

By doing this, congregations should become stronger and healthier and more aware of being church where they are. There is a possibility that this may encourage some congregations to move towards independence as they grow in strength and confidence, but leaders ought not to fear this, especially if it continues the theme of growth. At the same time, if congregational identity is healthy, it may also lead to a greater sense of security and responsibility towards sister congregations in what we might describe as mature interdependence, just as a healthy family grows through adolescence into responsible adulthood.

Common pitfalls

There is not enough time to consider all the pitfalls. Among many perceived weaknesses of multiple congregation churches the following seem to be the most common.

Restrictive control from the centre

At first, there may be huge advantages in having a common 'house style' and branding. The core leadership work hard to maintain the standards and vet the emerging leaders to ensure quality. But eventually this works against growth. God's creation has a 'house style' which is marked by glorious and energetic diversity. A growing church will be characterized by such creative diversity and will work at liberating its constituent parts rather than restricting and controlling (and ultimately stifling) the work of God.

An unwillingness to let babies grow up

This is where new congregations never get beyond the stage of being heavily dependent mini versions of a parent congregation. These 'church-within-church' communities often implode. Their reason for being is usually not sufficiently distinct to sustain continued life, and their reason for being fades over time.

Shopping mall church

Consumerism guides how the church develops. Congregations emerge not as missional communities but as niche interest groups dedicated to serving particular groups of existing Christians. Believing becomes disjointed from belonging as privatized spirituality seeks to build a life with minimal commitment and little engagement with those not yet in church.[10]

Undue haste towards independence

The transition from being an integrated congregation in a flourishing and strong church to becoming independent is massive and very costly, both for the emerging church and those congregations left behind. If handled without care and planning, it can leave all parties quite debilitated and unable to make much headway in mission. If congregations are pushed towards independence without a clear mission purpose, they may also begin to turn in on themselves and become frustrated as they discover that what they have arrived at is not as vibrant as the community where they once belonged.

Lack of clarity about leadership and accountability

This is perhaps the greatest area of weakness. Individual church members do not know who pastors them. Contradictory visions emerge. Congregations hunt around for the permission givers. Core leaders grow more and more insecure and become the target of discontent as every group begins to do what it believes is right in its own eyes.

Summary

Multiple congregation churches have an important role to play in reaching a diverse and fragmented society, provided that they are intentionally developed for mission purposes. As Christopher Bland is quoted as saying at the beginning of this chapter, leadership is 'the messy business of getting organisations and people to perform' whatever the size of the organization. There is no single leadership paradigm. Leaders come in all shapes and sizes, as do multiple congregational churches. Leaders as ever need to put themselves about, not as charismatic loners, but as collaborators who recognize their responsibility of mentoring and releasing other confident leaders to be authentically spiritual, engaging in what Jesus talked about and did.

Notes

1. Interview by Elizabeth Judge, *The Times*, Monday, 14 August 2006.
2. For example, Ichthus Fellowship, described in Forster, 1986, pp. 48–71.
3. See, for example: Gibbs and Bolger, 2006; *Mission-shaped Church*, 2004; Moynagh, 2004; Jackson, 2005.
4 Handy, 1993, pp. 364–7.
5. Gibbs and Bolger, 2006, Chapter 10, 'Leading as a body'.
6. South Parade Baptist Church, Leeds (five congregations worshipping on three sites).
7. *Five Core Values for a Gospel People*, n.d.
8. Described effectively in Breen and Kallestad, 2005. See also <www.lifeshapes.com>. LifeShapes is significantly subtitled 'The Language of Leadership'.
9. *Mission-shaped Church*, 2004, p. 62.
10. See Gibbs and Bolger, 2006, p. 157.

References and further reading

Adair, J., and J. Nelson (eds), *Creative Church Leadership: A MODEM Handbook*, Norwich: Canterbury Press.
Breen, M., and W. Kallestad (2005), *The Passionate Church: The Art of Life-Changing Discipleship*, Colorado Springs: Cook Communication Ministries.

Croft, S. (ed.) (2005), *Explorations: Evangelism in a Spiritual Age*, London: Church House Publishing.

Five Core Values for a Gospel People: Prophetic, Sacrificial, Missionary, Inclusive and Worshipping, Didcot: BUGB.

Forster, Roger (ed.) (1986), *Ten New Churches*, Bromley: MARC Europe.

Gibbs, E., and Ryan K. Bolger (2006), *Emerging Churches: Creating Community in Postmodern Cultures*, London: SPCK.

Handy, Charles (1993), *Understanding Organisations* 4th edn, London: Penguin.

Jackson, R. (2005), *The Road to Growth*, London: Church House Publishing.

Mission-shaped Church (2004), London: Church House Publishing.

Moynagh, M. (2001), *Changing World, Changing Church*, Oxford: Monarch.

Moynagh, M. (2004), 'Introduction', *Emerging Church*, Oxford: Monarch.

Rowdon, H. (ed.) (2002), *The Church Leaders Handbook*, Carlisle: Paternoster.

22. Leading projects

ALAN HARPHAM

Introduction

What is a project?

A project is any one-off initiative that includes the following characteristics:

- Has a start and end.
- Has a purpose, usually to
  - deliver output(s) that enables some benefit(s) to the organization, and/or
  - change the way that the organization works, and/or
  - solve a repeating or ongoing problem.
- Will deliver an output that the owner can then put to use to achieve a desired outcome for the organization.
- Will involve change:
  - is a way of managing a change to the organizational status quo.
- Will typically create changes for people in the organization and the way that they will work in future.
  - will use resources
  - will cost time and maybe money
  - will involve a few or lots of people
  - will represent an 'investment' for the organization, hopefully with a payback
- Will be complex
  - that is, not a simple task, but a number of interrelated tasks
  - requiring a number of people to be informed of what they are tasked to do
  - over a significant period of time
- Will go through a series of sequential stages
  - with a life cycle, and
- Is usually innovative – never been done before (at least not here and in this way!)

Why use projects?

Projects are bigger than a task. A task or an activity is an effort of short duration, usually not complex and undertaken by one or a few people. We usually manage to do these without a lot of forethought or planning. Projects are more complex, different from day-to-day activities and usually need planning, coordinating and managing if they are to be successful. Most organizations use projects to differentiate them from day-to-day activities and to set them apart as change agents for the organization. Examples in a church or religious context might be: designing a new church liturgy, establishing a new process for marriage or baptism preparation, a major repair to the building, an extension to the church plant (buildings and equipment), determining a new hymn book to procure and use, reorganizing parishes or uniting them, establishing a new mission initiative, reorganizing church governance and committees, and designing and launching a new church magazine. Some would be called 'hard' projects because they lead to physical outcomes such as a new building or magazine, others are often called 'soft' projects because the outcome is softer, such as a new organizational framework or marriage preparation process. This should not be confused with the soft skills so essential to good project managers, such as the ability to communicate one-to-one and one to a larger group, the ability to influence and manage conflict and other organizational skills.

Project Management

What is a good project?

One that is properly led, with:

- a thought-out purpose – the 'why'
- a developed and properly defined scope – the 'what'
- a worked and thought-out plan – the 'how', that covers:
  - the timescale of events
  - with milestones for measuring progress
  - an estimate and timed budget
  - a resource schedule
  - defined work packages
    packages of work that can be delegated to individuals or small teams as part of the overall project, and
- a project strategy (high-level plan) that covers:
  - an organizational plan setting out who will do what (sub-parts or work packages of the project)

- a governance structure for the project
- a purchasing and/or contract strategy for sub-projects that will be bought in
- clearly defined roles and responsibilities for the key organizational parts:
  - a sponsor who is accountable for:
    the 'investment' funding
    obtaining organizational approval to undertake the project
    watching the project environment or context and constantly revalidating the purpose and making any necessary changes (including stopping it where the reason for doing it has now gone)
    ensuring that a project leader (usually called the project manager (PM)) is appointed
    enabling the PM to undertake the project by making available the necessary resources and unlocking any organizational blocks
    establishing (if necessary) the project board (the highest level governance for the project) to assist the PM to deal with critical issues and risks arising
    ensuring the organizational outcome is achieved with benefits delivered
  - a project manager who is accountable for:
    delivering the agreed project outputs
       to time, cost and quality
    planning and organizing the tasks and activities
    ensuring the work is properly delegated where necessary
    owning and managing the plan
       ensuring work packages and activities are delivered to time and budget
       managing the interfaces between work packages and activities
       devising strategies to overcome slippages and cost overruns to the project
    monitoring progress on time, cost and quality, and reporting on it to the sponsor (and project board) on a regular basis
    forecasting the new end-date and cost of the final outputs or deliverables of the project, and devising strategies to bring the project back on track or mitigating overruns of time or cost
  - an end user/operator who is accountable for:
    agreeing the organizational requirements for the project from the outset, but having these possibly reduced by the sponsor to make sure the project outputs are 'affordable'
    receiving, testing and accepting the project outputs

and, above all else, taking the project outputs/deliverables from the PM and putting them to work in order to deliver the planned outcomes of the project for the sponsor and sponsoring organization

What is good project management?

As already stated, projects are complex and made up of interrelated tasks. These tasks may or may not be able to be accomplished using internal, existing resources, or external resources may need to be bought in temporarily or for some significant length of time. This process of 'procurement' needs to be properly managed and the whole project will require some management to accomplish it. This may be possible using existing resources and adding it to the day-to-day tasks already being undertaken, as a part-time additional role. Alternatively, significant projects may require some dedicated resources to manage them (a dedicated team in the ultimate) or any arrangement between these two extremes. Clearly the overall importance and significance to the organization of the project and its affordability will affect the chosen approach. There are many PM books on how to select the right organizational and contract strategies (see links at end) – not always as simple as it at first seems. Basically, if time is of the essence, the project may proceed to a next stage before being fully defined and this usually requires external resources to be hired in on a reimbursable cost basis; if minimum cost is of the essence the project must complete the definition stage before proceeding, with evaluated tenders to get the best price and have it fixed. The latter will take longer but the price will be known; the former is likely to cost more but may be quicker (I say 'may be', because in the slower example more planning may shorten the timescale of subsequent stages).

The Life Cycle of a Project

What is a typical project life-cycle?

The project life cycle is the set of stages or phases the project goes through. Typically these might be:

1 Inception
   • During this stage the initial idea for the project is conceived. This could be in response to a problem or opportunity that presents itself. It could come about from a broader strategic plan for the organization or from a bottom-up initiative. At this stage, very

few people are involved, often only one or two; the outline of the idea may be worked up and a summary 'why', 'what' and possibly even a 'how' may be developed. The end of this phase is usually a proposal in some form to carry out a feasibility and definition phase and, if this involves significant expenditure, a plan and budget for the next phase, and possibly a guesstimate for the total project.

2 Feasibility and definition
   • In this stage the various possible solutions are considered and compared to see which offers the best option in terms of costs and benefits to the organization.
     The chosen solution (project) is then fully defined with:
     – a **business case** owned by the sponsor, the 'why',
     – the fully defined **scope**, the 'what', is included and excluded from the project, defining the specific outputs to be delivered, and the boundaries. This is owned by the sponsor but agreed with the PM and user(s), and
     – the how, the **plan**, owned by the PM, covering time, cost, quality and the strategy for organization and contracts.
     These three documents form the basic set used to obtain the necessary approval of the level of organizational governance authorized to approve the start of the project.

3 Design
   • This stage is used to carry out any design work needed to enable the construction or assembly stage to take place. During this phase, the detailed design work will be carried out and further alternative detailed ideas to solve the problem, or take advantage of the opportunity, will be considered and determined. By the end of this stage, all the necessary design work will have been concluded to enable the procurement and assembly or construction stage to proceed.

4 Procurement
   • This stage is optional and for use where the major part of the project is to be procured and supplied by others. During this stage, alternative bidders may be sought and invited to tender, sometimes with a pre-qualification stage to ensure they each have the capacity and capability to undertake the work. By the end of this phase, a preferred supplier will have been identified, a price agreed (or a basis for arriving at the final price agreed) and the basis of payment (or terms of payment) agreed so that work can start.

5 Assembly or construction
   - During this stage, the procured parts and pieces are assembled and constructed and delivered and put together to produce the final project output(s). By the end of this stage, the project deliverables are complete and ready for testing/commissioning.

6 Test and commission
   - During this stage, the PM tests the final deliverable(s) and shows through its commissioning that the project output(s) can be used by the user to enable the organization to obtain the benefits used to justify the project at its outset. The user is usually highly involved in this stage to make sure that s/he and his/her team are ready to utilise the outputs to the full.

7 Handover and lessons learnt
   - This is the end of the PM's responsibility when he hands over the project outputs to the user. At this final point it is usual for the PM to review the overall project to identify and record lessons learnt during the life of the project – good and bad.

Project life cycles may have stages and phases with many different names and titles to those used above, and there are no predetermined names of stages. Typically, they would relate to those shown above, but not necessarily. The important thing about the life cycle is to be aware that each phase gets to be an increasingly expensive one as we move through the life cycle. This means that, unless money is no object (or the benefits far outweigh the costs), we should get each phase thoroughly completed before moving on to the next stage. In addition, the sponsor should check that the latest information is used to update the 'business case' to ensure the project still makes financial sense and that the context has not changed in such a way as to invalidate the project continuing.

Elements of good project management

What is the 'business case'?

This is the financial model of the whole project giving the costs and benefits of spending the initial investment in the project. This model has to take account of the 'capital cost' of the project, the operating costs of running the project outputs (deliverables) and the benefits (income/savings) from the project. These cash flows can be compared using various financial models from 'break even', through 'return on investment', to 'discounted cash flow' techniques. In more social or public sector type projects, one might have to resort to 'cost/benefit analysis', where every cost and benefit (financial or not) is notionally priced, which involves deriving an equivalent financial value for each benefit and cost involved in delivering the project outputs and operating them. Economists have developed a range of techniques to enable this to happen.

What is the project team?

The definition of the project team is all the individuals who make a contribution to the project at any stage of the life cycle, for any length of time. The importance of recognizing the team is to do with letting each individual member understand their role and how it contributes to the overall project, and making sure that they understand clearly what they are expected to produce for the project, for how much and by when.

What is the project management team?

These are the members of the project team who carry a managerial function for the project. At its minimum, this might be a part-time project manager accountable for developing and managing the project plan. For larger projects, there may be a dedicated team comprising the project manager and a support office looking after planning, progress reporting and developing recovery plans. On a task force style of project organization, there may be a large part of the project team that is dedicated full-time to the project. Clearly the latter is the most expensive – if most effective – type of project organization, and is usually reserved for organizationally mission critical projects.

What is a 'benefit'?

A benefit is the final outcome of the project, or the programme in which the project sits, and there may be a number of them. They are used to justify the 'investment' in the project at its outset as part of the 'business case'. The intended benefits should outweigh the project costs, albeit there may be exceptions to this rule, such as in the case of 'regulatory projects'. The project typically produces outputs that the organization then puts to work to derive the benefits, that is, the required 'outcome'. Benefits may be financially measurable or not. Where they are not, a typical economist's way of weighing up the investment is to use 'cost-benefit analysis' – see above. In other words, the business case should cover the capital and operational costs of the project.

Good projects would produce a list of Key Performance Indicators (KPIs) for the project at the outset. These would typically provide a list of indicators to answer the question – 'what will project success look like?' These will often link to the project benefits and each can help in generating the other.

What is a 'programme' of projects?

Many organizations now use programme management. This is the idea of converting the organization's forward strategy into a series of related programmes (of projects), each of which is focused on delivering specific organizational benefits required in the 'corporate strategy'. Some describe it as the 'glue' that relates the projects to the corporate strategy. Projects that cannot be related back to the corporate strategy should almost certainly be dropped.

What is the schedule?

The word 'programme' has a number of meanings in project management. It can mean the 'programme of projects' described above. It is also used to refer to the overall time schedule of the project, which may be based on 'logic diagrams' used to ensure the tasks of the project are being undertaken in a logical fashion. These then have a time analysis carried out to get to the overall likely timeframe for the project. These are sometimes referred to as 'critical path' programmes when the analysis leads to the longest path through the logic diagram which is the critical path. Critical, because any task on this path which takes longer than planned will lengthen the overall project time-line. Another related technique is the use of the 'precedence diagram'[1] which uses another way of drawing the diagram. Most computer planning techniques are based on using a logic diagram of some kind. The most familiar programme output is the bar chart (or Gantt chart)[2] which represents time horizontally as 'bars' against each activity in the programme. These do not necessarily demonstrate the logic of the programme, albeit some (such as MS Project)[3] show vertical lines to show the logic, that is, what must be completed before the next activity starts.

Who is the project leader?

There are two key roles involved in project leadership – the project sponsor, responsible for the original investment and delivering the benefits, and the project manager, responsible for delivering the established project outputs to agreed time, cost and quality. Both have to exercise leadership skills and both could be said to lead the project – albeit in different ways.

What is risk management?

Projects are full of uncertainty, usually about the future. Typically, they involve making assumptions as to how long something will take, what it will cost and the likely outcome. As we make assumptions, we can see they represent risks to the project outcome if we get them wrong or things around the project and its context change. We know we live in an ever more rapidly changing world. A good project manager and his team generate lists of the risks that could affect the project, and analyse them by likelihood of occurrence and their impact (on the project outcome usually in terms of time, cost and quality but sometimes on the chances of successfully realizing the projected benefits). High-probability, high-impact risks are then designed out of the project – we do not want them and cannot afford them. High-impact, low-probability risks are laid off through insurance or by hiring a more experienced 'contractor'. High-probability, low-impact risks are typically managed by the team. The triggers indicating that they are arising as 'now issues' are identified and used to try to head them off, and if this does not work the impact is mitigated though mitigation plans. These mitigation plans will typically cost money and so all projects should have a contingency fund set aside to deal with risks that become issues. The fund may be administered by the sponsor and/or the project manager.

Conclusion

Project management can be great fun. It is certainly always a learning opportunity and should be used as such. The fun comes from the fact that they are often an innovation (at least in that place and at that time) and seldom go as planned (that is, risks become issues). The project manager role is an opportunity to try out new ways of managing and leading and to learn from them. When projects are completed there should always be a review to identify the lessons learned. These should be shared with the project management team, the project team and the host organization (the owner and client). The next project is an opportunity to use the lessons learned to try out new ways and experiment to get even better next time.

Projects lead to change and change is how we grow and develop. For some of us, this is what Christ's teachings were and are all about. We should also note that, the bigger the risks we take, the more we learn; the smaller, the less we learn. So with big projects typically come big risks and big opportunities to learn. This should encourage us to take the lead on projects, and particularly church or better still spiritually-based projects, because, with them, we can learn even more about ourselves and our meaning and purpose in life or our spirituality.

I wish you every success in all your projects undertaken to further your life's work and the life and the work of the Church and hope this starter on project management will get you started on learning more about managing projects.

Useful places to find out more about programme and project management are:

- The APM Group – <www.apmgroup.co.uk> — 01494-452450 and, in particular, its bookshop <www.apmg-businessbooks.com>.
- The Association for Project Management – <www.apm.org.uk> – 0845-458-1944.
- The International Project Management Association – <www.ipma.ch>.
- The Office of Government Commerce – <www.ogc.gov.uk> and, in particular, <http://www.ogc.gov.uk/programmes_and_projects.asp>.
- The Project Management Institute – <www.pmi.org>.

Notes

1. The precedence diagram is an alternative to an 'activity on arrow' diagram which was the original format for the Critical Path Method. The purpose of the Critical Path Method is to find the longest sequence of activities in a project which paradoxically gives the quickest (shortest) path to complete the whole project. In precedence diagrams the activity is on the 'node' with the arrows between nodes showing the sequence of the activities. Precedence diagrams give more choice of links as they can show more logical links than activity on arrow.

2. Gantt was the person who developed the idea of the bar chart and it is an alternative name. The bar chart lists the activities in sequence in a list of activities, usually to the left-hand side of the diagram. Then the duration of each activity is shown as a horizontal line (or bar) to the right of the diagram under a calendar of dates. Some 'linked' bar charts show the logic too, that is, vertical lines linking prior activities that must be completed before subsequent activities can start.

3. MS Project is Microsoft's proprietary product that carries out a 'critical path' calculation provided all the activities are fed together with their durations and logical sequence.

23. Leading a multicultural church

CAROL RICHARDS

After this I looked and there before me was a great multitude that
no-one could count, from every nation, tribe, people and language,
standing before the throne and in front of the Lamb. (Revelation 7.9
[NIV])

St John's in Stratford, London E15, is a large building that dominates
the town centre. It's home to a congregation that numbered 550 at
Easter 2006 – from about 50 different nationalities. While the worship
is, no doubt, far from the perfect worship of Heaven, the experience
of worshipping with so many from 'every nation, tribe, people and
language' (seemingly) is truly amazing.

Stratford is in the London Borough of Newham, which is said to
be the most multicultural area in the world. Other areas have large
concentrations of people from one or two cultures; Newham is completely mixed, with people from all around the globe. This was one of
the selling points for the successful bid for the 2012 Olympic and
Paralympic Games, which will take place largely in Stratford.

I am a lay reader and my husband, Dave, is vicar. We moved to St
John's in 1990 and the congregation then averaged 40 each Sunday.
We had no experience of working in a multicultural area – our previ-
ous parishes in Wales and outer London were monocultural.

St John's had welcomed black people since the 1960s, in contrast,
sadly, to some other churches. Yvonne Bailey, from Antigua in the
Caribbean, came here in 1961 on a British passport, prior to Antiguan
Independence. She recalls attending a church where the vicar took
her aside and said that, while he wasn't prejudiced, members of the
congregation would be upset if she continued attending and would
she please find somewhere else to go. Several years later, Yvonne
moved to Stratford and was welcomed by St John's. She has served
faithfully as verger and a church council member.

Sheva Williams from St Vincent in the Caribbean and Rosemond
Isiodu from Nigeria (Igbo tribe) were the churchwardens who interviewed us, and there were many other black faces in the congregation
when we arrived, but the majority were white – traditional Eastenders

and some young professionals, who had moved into the area to be near the City.

A steep learning curve

We both knew that St John's was where God wanted us to be, but were very conscious of our complete lack of experience of working with people of different cultures. Dave did find that it helped to be from Wales – he could empathize with people living in a different culture from where they grew up.

We started by spending time listening to people and their stories, many of them very moving. As we visited people in their homes, we began to understand more about them and their backgrounds:

- We learned to avoid stereotypes, 'You're black, so you must be good at sport' – well, not necessarily.
- We made an effort to learn how names work in different cultures and how to pronounce them – for example, a Nigerian person (Yoruba tribe) might be named 'Oluwafunmilayo', but friends will use a shortened version, perhaps 'Olu', 'Funmi' or 'Ayo'. People will often have an English name they use at work (sadly, but probably correctly, fearing discrimination). It would be a bit insulting to ask to use the English name at church, if people want to be known by the African name – it would signify that we couldn't be bothered to learn their proper name, which is not exactly welcoming.
- We learned to understand people's accents. As with any accent, it's a case of listening and getting 'tuned in' to it.
- We started to read the World News more carefully – when there's a disaster in a distant country, it's the friends and relatives of our church members who are affected.
- We were blessed by the hospitality we received. In many cultures, it would be considered impolite to leave without refreshments. On occasion, we have eaten three meals in one evening! Now, when we arrange to visit someone, we say that we will have already eaten (if we have) so just light refreshments would be nice.
- We learned that the vicar is expected to pray for the family at the end of the visit, and adults and children who have been scattered around the house are brought into the room for prayer. We were used to praying for people who were sick or in other need, but this formal time of prayer at the end of a visit was new to us. People want prayer for all aspects of their life – their job, business, exams, family life – everything is subject to God's sovereignty. For this reason, people also like a house-blessing when they move into a property.

- We discovered that people in the congregation loved their Bibles, but hadn't been encouraged to read them. They thought that reading the Bible was something that was part of church life in the Caribbean or Africa, but didn't happen in the Church of England! They had read their Bibles at home, but now they started bringing them to church as well.

Set for growth

St John's started growing as soon as we arrived and we were conscious that this was because God was at work, as we weren't doing anything that could have resulted in such dramatic increases in numbers. Tolu Babarinsa's story is interesting. Tolu tried to attend St John's, his local church, several times but found it closed (not unusual when there's no vicar). He made the effort to get to church on Christmas morning – there would definitely be a service then – but the service had been at midnight on Christmas Eve. He gave up, until one day he had to take a different bus home from work and passed St John's. He saw lights in the church. There was a bishop standing outside, who told him a new vicar was being licensed, so Tolu stayed to the service and joined the church at the same time as us. Tolu is Nigerian (Yoruba) and he was concerned about other young Nigerian students who were becoming disillusioned by the secularism in this country. They had been brought up in Nigeria to believe that Britain was a Christian country and were deeply shocked by what they found when they arrived here to study. For many of them, their faith was not on solid foundations, but based on the habit of churchgoing and it could not withstand the realization that people generally didn't go to church. Tolu brought these people to St John's and we helped them develop a real faith. Tolu is now churchwarden and has been a wonderful support over the years – it has been particularly useful for us to consult him about procedure for various Nigerian cultural events.

In the early days, the growth was almost all from Nigerians joining us, but gradually other people started coming – from China, Pakistan, Russia, most African countries, most Caribbean islands, Canada, Australia, The Seychelles, Malaysia, various Middle Eastern countries and Europe. My geography improved rapidly. The reaction of the existing English people was interesting. A small number left, because the church was no longer small and quiet and there were too many children. Others welcomed the change. One elderly lady, who had attended St John's all her life, rejoiced at what was happening, because she had watched the church decline over the years. It was also interesting that many more English people joined the church. People believe the media reports that churches are empty and it deters them, because they don't want to feel exposed in a large building. A growing church is an amazing witness. The fact that we are in the middle of the town centre helps, because passers-by see all the cars parked on Sundays and the people spilling out of the building after the service.

At one stage, we worried that the church building was two-thirds full, because the experts say that churches stop growing at this point. Our African members said this is not the case in a multicultural situation, because people look to join a thriving church and it doesn't look as if it's thriving until it's two-thirds full. The growth continued.

Children first

On the second Sunday at St John's, I started a group for children, meeting during the middle of the service. Initially, there were five children and grandchildren of church members and we met in one mixed-age group. The group grew rapidly, with the children of the Nigerian families joining the church. One Sunday, as I was telling a story, I looked at the sea of black faces in front of me and realized that Jesus wasn't white. Of course I knew this already – he was Jewish from a hot country and spent most of his time preaching in the open air – but it had never really struck me before, probably because my mind was influenced by pictures I had seen as a child that portrayed Jesus as a white man. We don't know what Jesus looked like, but we do know he wasn't white, and I now try to give the children books and pictures that are accurate in this respect. I also try to have resources that are multicultural; so, for example, we have white dolls and black dolls in the creche, to demonstrate equality and give positive affirmation. It's essential for all the children, whatever their colour, to know they are loved unconditionally, so they grow in faith together. We now have six different age groups, with more than eighty children and young people attending each Sunday.

Services + special events

The principle of wanting to give people from different cultures positive affirmation is carried forward into our services at St John's. It would give the wrong message if all the people 'up front' doing things (reading, leading intercessions, etc.) were white. We always try to have a balance; but this isn't difficult, because we have some very talented people from all cultures.

We try to involve everyone in ministry. Revd David Ibiayo told me that he traces his path to Ordination back to a letter I wrote him many years ago, asking him to be a welcomer at the evening service. He felt honoured that we trusted him with such a responsibility. I had forgotten about the letter, but David kept it. (David is one of a number of people, both black and white, men and women, who have gone out from St John's to full-time ministry in the Church of England in recent years).

We aim to make people feel they belong. It's important to take care with the language used – avoiding negative uses of the word 'black' and colloquialisms that will not be understood by someone for whom English is a second or third language. As with children's work, we aim to represent all cultures in our posters and printed resources. We also advertise St John's as 'Anglican, Church of England'. People from the worldwide Anglican Communion are now living here and they look for the word 'Anglican' when seeking a church.

Our Sunday services are fairly traditional in many respects. Many of our members are lifelong Anglicans and *Hymns Ancient & Modern* made it round the globe! However, their children want something more lively and we have a music group as well as the organ, and sing modern worship songs. It's interesting that some modern songs work better than others – lively songs with a good rhythm are popular, but quiet, reflective Celtic music doesn't work so well. We also sing music from different cultures. Church members will teach us a song in their own language, often accompanied by African drums.

Sundays are important. Current thinking in the Church of England is that we need to find fresh expressions of church and engage with people during the week, because they do other things on Sundays.[1] Not in Stratford. Large numbers of our congregation are working and studying during the week, and often work anti-social hours. We do most things on Sundays – music practice, meetings, discipleship courses, youth activities – because that's when people are around. We have just a few mid-week groups, attended predominantly by the English members of the Church.

A challenge we faced soon after moving to St John's was a funeral for someone from the Caribbean. We consulted Yvonne Bailey about the service – there may be small differences in different places, but generally they follow a similar pattern. An Afro-Caribbean funeral is an amazing occasion – full of hope. Usually, large numbers of people attend and the singing takes on a life of its own. Hymns are often old Pentecostal gems like 'When the Roll is called up Yonder' (we have a collection of old hymn books that are very useful for these occasions). The service will usually include many hymns, a eulogy by a family member, and a viewing. Towards the end of the service the funeral

247

director will open the coffin. The congregation files past slowly to say a final farewell, before the coffin is closed again. The singing (now unaccompanied) continues at the graveside, while male relatives fill the grave (called a 'witness-fill'). Usually, these days, after the grave has been partially filled, the cemetery staff will assist with the digger. The women decorate the grave with flowers, before people move to a local hall for refreshments.

African funeral services are very similar, though often the body will be flown back home after the funeral in church. We tend to have more African memorial services than actual funerals. When someone dies back home, people will do all they possibly can, even putting themselves into debt, to travel back for the funeral; but it isn't always possible. Not being able to get to the funeral is something new; something people can't cope with, and they find a memorial service here helpful as part of the grieving process.

New Year is a big event. Christmas Day is important for Africans, but there is no tradition of carol services or midnight services on Christmas Eve – though people will support them. The big midnight service is at New Year, and it's often the largest service of the year. A Nigerian preacher we invited one year said it's important to challenge people's commitment because some Nigerians think they can bribe God to give them a good year by being in church as the clock strikes 12! We have a standard Communion Service, but make sure the prayers lead up to midnight. Then we listen to the chimes of Big Ben and people celebrate with party poppers and balloons, as they wish everyone 'Happy New Year' and we sing a hymn to the tune of 'Auld Lang Syne'. Afterwards, someone will have a party, so we manage to combine elements of English and African culture.

One difference with a multicultural congregation is the pattern of holidays. Individuals will go to see relatives back home for several months every two or three years, often leaving their family here. There is no large-scale exodus in July and August, so we have lots of people around. One of our most popular ventures is to take the whole service outside into the churchyard (weather permitting) every Sunday in the summer. We have a good sound system and the emphasis is on lively songs and simple drama. Over the years, open-air services have been extremely successful outreach events, both with lapsed Christians and with people of other faiths and none. During 2006, we were meeting lots of Eastern Europeans, so we have literature in their languages.[2] We have a simple Bible study after the service for people who want to know more, and show the *Jesus* video in different languages[3] as necessary – Dave's particular favourite is the Farsi version.

We hold a One World event in October to promote different

cultures. The hall is decorated with flags for every country represented by a church member, and people bring food from their own culture
to share. Different groups prepare items for the entertainment. The
Welsh 'hold their own' with welsh-cakes and a small male-voice
choir, but the English people struggle. They usually fall back on a
Cockney theme, which is at least local. In 2002, we had a very successful street party for the Queen's Golden Jubilee and emphasized
the Queen's role as Head of the Commonwealth – an important theme
for our church members.

Problems

Yes, of course there are problems, but we work hard to overcome
them. A representative church council is very important, to discuss
matters as they arise. Sometimes we have to agree that something is a
cultural issue and find a compromise – for example, African church
leaders want a noisy, personal welcome for newcomers, but Dave
points out that many English newcomers want to be anonymous. We
compromise with a noisy, general welcome for all newcomers, but no
one is singled out.

Time-keeping is an obvious problem – it wouldn't work to do the
notices before the service! African and Caribbean people are aware
of the problem and will often advertise the time of an event like a
wedding half an hour before it actually starts, so people arrive for the
beginning (this causes problems for good time-keepers!). For an event
like a quiz night we advertise 'Doors open 7 p.m., Quiz starts 7.30 p.m.
prompt'. But quiz nights are a problem in their own right, because the
questions are often very English. We have questions about Caribbean
cookery or African football, to give everyone an equal chance.

People are moving out of East London because they can't afford to
buy here. We encourage people to go to their local church, but they
often come back, saying there's no children's work, or sometimes that
the service is too early. One Nigerian family moved to a town in north
Essex (about an hour's drive from Stratford) but the service at their
local church was at 9.30 a.m. so they decided they could have an extra
half hour in bed and get to St John's for 11 a.m.! In time, the children
made friends at school and wanted to attend church with their school
friends, and the family settled into their new community.

Conclusion

I am aware that I have hardly scratched the surface of some issues and have left many questions unanswered, but this is inevitable in one brief chapter. I have tried to tell our story and draw out the things I have learnt along the way.

- It is important to examine ourselves honestly and be aware of our prejudices, which are owing to our upbringing. We may need to challenge our own attitudes.
- It is important to treat people as individuals, to listen to them and learn from them.
- It is vital to give people positive affirmation and make them feel they belong.

I enjoy life in Stratford – it's an amazing, vibrant place. I enjoy meeting people from around the world. I feel privileged to be invited to share in people's family occasions, but I don't think I'll ever develop a taste for goat curry!

Notes

1. *Mission-shaped Church*, 2004.
2. Available from Lifewords (formerly Scripture Gift Mission) <www.lifewords.info>.
3. *Jesus* (1979), Inspirational Films. Available from Agapé <www.agape.org.uk>.

References

Mission-shaped Church: Church Planting and Fresh Expressions of Church in a Changing Context (2004), London: Church House Publishing.

24. Relating to the local community

Mapping the area and bicycle power

PETER STEVENSON

The first challenge to being a creative leader in the community is to identify who that community is. Within a parish system, this may not be the prior question, but for those in other denominations this becomes a real and necessary enquiry. Nevertheless, given the ever increasing number of multi-congregation pastorates within the Church of England, leaders here need to decide what are to be the boundaries of their interest and concern for the purpose of community working. Some time ago, I worked in a Cambridgeshire village and it was easy to align the community to the village boundaries. Today, I operate in a city with a population of 300,000 in the West Midlands. The pastorate includes three congregations and naturally fits within the north-west quadrant of the city.

After 'mapping' the area using a combination of census returns, local library statistical information and bicycle power, I established that there were 17 different centres of education, from pre-school nurseries to sixth form colleges within existing state and private senior schools. It also became clear that there were a large number of residential care homes.

Additionally, I arranged to meet the manager of the neighbourhood partnership team set up to coordinate the City Council's response to the area's needs, in conjunction with the government initiative of social inclusion.[1] Naturally, this avenue of enquiry is dependent upon local reaction to the Government's agenda. As a result of this meeting, I was able to evaluate the social priorities of the area and discuss the funding packages that existed. It was also a valuable start at networking with those outside the congregation who had a heart for the community.

I cannot stress enough the need to be in the community if a church leader wishes to be creative in their approach to the community. This might include a degree of 'loitering with intent' outside the local school, introducing yourself to the parents and carers meeting their

251

children; or eating lunch outside the local bakers ever mindful of others who pass by at that time; or using the local public house for personal relaxation and getting to know the landlord/lady and regulars. All these encounters add to the store of community networking and goodwill, and remember – few doors are ever closed to the church!

One section of the census return mentioned above details the largest employers in the area and the average distance travelled by people to their place of work. From a study of these statistics I was able to establish with a degree of certainty where people from the neighbourhood were employed. With the help of the local Industrial Mission it was possible to contact the largest employer in the area and arrange to meet the human resources manager to discuss the possibility of offering chaplaincy to the company. This aspect of community ministry will be considered in more detail below.

The final piece of initial investigative work was to assess the prominence or anonymity of the congregation within the neighbourhood. I soon established that the community described the church as the building opposite the supermarket and I asked for a person within the congregation to concentrate on getting the church's name into the local newspaper as often as possible in order to promote the congregation to the local neighbourhood. He did a fantastic job, and people in the community started to tell me how prominent the church had become. In reality, little more had happened but the self-promotion created a sense of movement in the mind of the community and there was a greater interest in the events and services that took place at the church.

As stated above, the initial research established that there were many centres of education in this quadrant of the City. Undaunted by the numbers, I began to arrange to meet head teachers of infant schools to establish what provision for religious education existed, and how extra input could be utilized. It soon became apparent that many schools failed to have a daily act of collective worship and some staff felt ill prepared to organize such assemblies. Although there was a degree of suspicion from a few head teachers as to my motivation for offering to lead assemblies, it was agreed that we trial one and I offered to show a script beforehand. In the event, no censorship was required and I arranged a broadly moral/ethical message which was generally acceptable to the school authorities.

As a result of these initial assemblies it was possible to develop the relationship with the schools. I became aware that the Religious Education (RE) syllabus[2] for infant schools included lessons on Christian Baptism, signs and symbols, and the nature of ministry [in general terms]. Offers of help were positively welcomed, particularly by those school RE coordinators who confessed little insight or knowledge in this area of the Christian Church. It also meant that children could be taken offsite to visit the local church and enjoy the interactive method of learning. The congregation have become increasingly involved in these visits, offering hospitality and support to the children and their attendants. Mutual respect and trust has resulted and three schools now use the church building for their Christmas carol service, recognizing the church sanctuary as the best setting for this annual celebration.

Bolstered by this success, I contacted the local secondary schools to establish relationships with them. Again, the door was almost closed; but gentle reference to OFSTED requirements and an assurance of sensitivity to the multifaith culture persuaded the schools to trial assemblies. Although they have been positively received, it is not so easy to operate routinely in secondary schools because the space (usually a hall) is often used for examinations and few other areas are large enough to accommodate a year group of 300. Nevertheless, the RE syllabus again offers opportunity for the creative minister to offer help to a small and often overstretched department. There are lessons in the curriculum on the Christian understanding of marriage and the Christian's view of God. It has been a privilege and a challenge to engage with the young people in these areas. After a while, some from the primary school children have made their way into these classes and it is exciting to follow them through their school life from one key stage to the next. Naturally, the children tell their parents about seeing the minister from primary school and the interest in the local congregation grows as a consequence.

Another and quite different relationship has developed in a special educational needs schools for children with other abilities. This has become more akin to a chaplaincy role, showing pastoral concern for staff and children alike. The initial approach was the same as before, but the need was different, and I have learnt that creative ministry calls for flexibility and adaptability in equal measure. In this setting I have found it easier to make a regular fortnightly commitment to the school, thus building close relationships of trust. As a result, I have been afforded the privilege of looking after a couple of families following the death of their child, and been available to comfort and support their school colleagues and the staff. As some of the children cannot hear or understand verbal communication, a greater degree of creativity is needed in portraying an assembly message. It has been a challenge and a joy to find other forms of communication using sight, sound, smell and touch.

These skills can then be used in residential care homes for those who have lost their sight or hearing. This is the next area of community ministry that I wish to investigate. I stumbled into this expression of ministry after visiting a member of the congregation who was convalescing after a period of hospitalization. New standards have been introduced that require care homes to establish with the resident what their spiritual needs might be, and to record them in an individual care plan that must be discussed with the resident. Some older people lose contact with their own church when circumstances require them to take up residency in a care home. The individual care plan can indicate that the person would like to continue contact with church, and if there is opportunity to worship on a regular basis some will be glad to participate regardless of the denomination of the worship leader. Over time I noticed that these regular services inside the care home become The Church for those who take part, and a 'planted' congregation flourishes.

It is also possible to build relationships beyond the worshippers, with members of staff, the care home management and the friends and families of the residents. These relationships often find expression at the time of bereavement, and the creative minister involved in the community is already in the best place to offer support, care and compassion from a position of trust and knowledge of the situation. As a result of these contacts, some family members have found comfort and support in the Sunday worshipping community, and a small number have remained with the congregation.

Essentially, this form of creative church leadership adds to a growing reputation that the congregation cares for those around them and is a place that can be relied upon when a person is in need. Whether the residents of the neighbourhood worship with the congregation or not, they know that this group of people can be trusted. In this respect, the church is re-earning its right to be taken seriously as a place of refuge, and can gain the trust of the neighbourhood to speak out against injustice and unfairness in the area. Or, put another way, its light to the nation burns brighter!

Opening a door into the industrial setting was more difficult and needed a lot of help from the Holy Spirit. As previously stated, it was possible to establish the major employer in the area from the census statistics, available from the central library. In this neighbourhood, it was Jaguar Cars who employed over 2000 people in a plant bordered by two of the congregations within the group of churches that I serve. The initial approach was made to the Chief Medical Officer (CMO), offering an additional resource to his team concerned with the well-being of the workforce. He referred the idea to the Director of Human Resources (DHR), and two pieces of fortune then came together. First, the CMO was training to be a reader in the Church of England and therefore sympathetic to the possibility and secondly, the DHR was challenged by the senior management in Detroit, USA, to introduce work place chaplaincies across all the plants of the Premier Automotive Group, of which Jaguar Cars was one. Interestingly, I took up the post in September 2001, as they both left their positions in the October.

The first year of workplace chaplaincy was dreadful and I thought that I was wasting my time. Few people acknowledged my presence and even less spoke. I was visiting every two weeks and was considering whether to give up on the ministry in the car plant when a couple of things happened. I was invited to become a member of the plant Diversity Council which explored issues of dignity at work and work–life balance; and I decided to wear a clerical collar while walking around the plant. Combined, they gave me a greater profile, and the medical centre started to refer people to me who needed to talk to someone outside the company structure.

These meetings proved helpful, and I began to get used in other areas, such as chairing focus groups and being asked to comment on issues of wellbeing. The result of all these interactions was a greater personal profile in the plant. When the company announced the cessation of car production I was best placed to offer the support that was needed. After that, the plant reduced to 500 employees and it would finally close altogether within a year, at the time of writing. It has been a privilege to serve the community at a time of change. I have met a number of the workforce in the neighbourhood and it has been good to be available to them, as many chose to take early retirement and redundancy when the car production ceased.

It is rumoured that another company will take over the site when Jaguar Cars finally leaves the plant and it is my intention to offer the new company my support, and I am hoping that they will want to maintain a chaplaincy service in the factory.

So far I have described three areas of community ministry that have involved gaining access to an organization. The approach has been to offer to each something that might encourage them to start a relationship with the representative person of the congregation. The approach has been to establish what government or company requirement exists and then to use these as the 'door-openers'. It is essential to build relationships with the people inside an organization and work at becoming an inexpensive and invaluable asset to them. However, this only represents one side of the equation and needs to be connected to the congregation if it is to be seen as a piece of relative and relevant community ministry.

The congregation in this setting described themselves as diffident toward evangelism. I have since realized that they had a certain understanding of evangelism that involved street preaching and high-profile community campaigns designed to 'win' converts for the Lord. I may even have expected this to be the nature of evangelism myself as I joined the congregation and set about working toward a more outward-looking expression of faith. Experience has taught me that evangelistic campaigns are unlikely to build sustainable relationship, even if they manage to achieve temporary interest in the congregation. Growth has occurred when the network of relationships has combined to confirm the congregation as a serious stakeholder in the neighbourhood within which they are set.

The work of opening doors into the community is wasted if there is no support and enthusiasm to engage fully with the people who come through those doors. While the community involvement work was being developed, the congregation embarked upon a programme of self-examination to assess what God's purpose was for them at this time in this place.[3] They resolved that the congregation's purpose was to Worship God, to Welcome people into the church, to Witness to and to Serve the community, and to Develop the whole people of God. This enabled the leadership to proceed with confidence into a phase in the life of the congregation that has been more concerned with looking beyond itself to the wider neighbourhood outside its doors. The result has been a 50% increase in church membership in five years.

In this chapter I have avoided adding the necessary encounters that link most church leaders with the community, such as births, deaths and marriages, but these can never be wholly separated from the other activities because they add to the growing network of relationships that the congregation can have with the neighbourhood. These opportunities to turn strangers into friends afford the best chance for the influence of the faith community to extend beyond itself.

In this final section I want to consider some theological reasoning for this expression of ministry. At the beginning of my ministry, an influential book was *Beyond the Good Samaritan*, by Ann Morisy,[4] who considered the value of partnership ministry as a form of *venturesome love*. It was a term that made me want to ask how the church showed the compassionate, caring and loving Jesus to the people in today's context. At first, I suspect my motivation was driven by a view that the 'end is nigh' and it was my task to get as many people to proclaim that Jesus is Lord in the hope that more would be saved as the day of judgement arrives. Some of this view has changed, following my reading of Raymond Fung in *The Isaiah Vision*, who suggests that 'our job is not to convince others that Jesus Christ is Lord but to convince them that we believe that Jesus Christ is Lord'.[5] From this perspective, evangelism looks very different and is more about living our lives in ways that look attractive to others, thus giving people the chance of finding out what the difference might be.

I have been drawn more and more theologically to an understanding of *missio dei* which has been helpfully summarized by David Bosch in his majestic and seminal book on mission studies, *Transforming Mission*. He writes,

> In attempting to flesh out the *missio dei* concept, the following could be said: In the new image mission is not primarily an activity of the church, but an attribute of God. It is not the church that has a mission of salvation to fulfill in the world [Christ's death has achieved that – *my addition*]. The church is viewed as an instrument for the mission. There is church because there is mission and that mission is to participate in the movement of God's love toward people, since God is the fountain of sending love.[6]

Now you can love people all you wish, but if they do not know they are loved and we fail to communicate love to them they may just as well stay unloved. There is plenty of evidence to suggest that people are not going to seek out the church and, if the growing sense of irrelevance is to be reversed, the church, through its creative leaders, must find innovative ways to keep the rumour of God alive and point people to the mere possibility of God's existence and desire to be part of their lives.

Checklist for opening doors in the community

1 Research your community, using census returns, the historical recollections of the congregation and your own physical observations.
2 Decide the geographical area which will involve the congregation.
3 Establish contact with the local authorities responsible for the neighbourhood to discuss current concerns, available funding and the identity of those already working in the area.
4 Investigate whether there are any aspects of industrial legislation which would make a church leader's input into the day to day operation of a workplace desirable.
5 Make contact and offer expertise and support to the organization.
6 Build the relationships within the organization and look out for opportunities to enhance those relationships.
7 Remain aware of the links that connect the congregation to the organization through the community and affirm, wherever possible, this triangulation.
8 Be persistent and consistent so that the organization can trust the relationship.

9 At regular intervals, review and evaluate the relationship to ensure that it remains of mutual [and reciprocal] benefit.

Notes

1. For more information on the Government's agenda visit <www.commu-nities.gov.uk/corporate>.
2. For further information about syllabus requirements visit the web sites of the local SACRE committees.
3. The church and elder's meetings were greatly helped in this programme by the work of Warren, 1995.
4. Morisy, 1997.
5. Fung, 1992, p. 21.
6. Bosch, 1991, pp. 389–93, p. 390.

References and further reading

Bosch, David (1991), *Transforming Mission*, Grand Rapids, Michigan: Orbis.

Fung, Raymond (1992), *The Isaiah Vision: Ecumenical Strategies for Congregational Evangelism*, Geneva: WCC.

Morisy, Ann (1997), *Beyond the Good Samaritan*, London: Mowbray.

Warren, Rick (1995), *Purpose-driven Church*, Maryknoll, New York: Zondervan.

Further reading – in specific areas

Moynagh, Michael (2004), *Emergingchurch.net* , Oxford: Monarch.
Moynagh describes characteristics of the *emerging church* as contextual, customized, diverse, flexible and experimental (p. 11). He suggests that many bite size, unobtrusive examples exist already. He considers an e-church as a mindset rather than a set of rules and argues that they are to be culturally authentic – arising from a culture rather than being imposed onto a culture (pp. 24–5). The main emphasis and particularity of an e-church is that mission be considered the clearly defined task of the church. A great deal of the book suggests that an e-church (or the e-church) is a separated congregation from the *inherited* church.

Murray, Stuart (2004), *Church after Christendom*, Milton Keynes: Paternoster.
This is an excellent book, looking at the relationship between inherited and emerging church traditions. It took the 'believing-and-belonging' question into new directions with consideration of belonging before (and without) believing, and also those who increasingly believe but no longer belong. On p. 25, it lists those who might be described as semi-, de-(or non-), pre-, post- and anti-churched, and speaks about listening to people at both doors of the Church, meaning that we hear the story of those leaving the Church as well as those who are joining. The author, Chair of the Anabaptist network, explores whether we understand members better as stakeholders.

Sedmak, Clemens (2002), *Doing Local Theologies*, Maryknoll, New York: Orbis. The writer was Professor of Epistemology and Religious Studies in Salzburg, and the book has been adopted by Bob Schreiter to the corpus of work in the Faith and Culture series that includes Stephan B. Bevans (2002), *Models of Contextual Theology*, Maryknoll, New York: Orbis. The greatest influence of this book on my thinking has been in the notion of being a local community theologian, likened to a Dr Dolittle, reflecting theologically on the differing practices of the people, doing theology as if people matter. In a sense, the book accepts that we cannot change the big things so we should work harder on the little things that can make a difference. Good theology is therefore about personal and communal transformation, based on a relationship with God. Theologians must be accountable to their communities and that relies on being in relationship with those communities.

25. Relating to the local community

A lifeboat in the community and not a yacht for its members

KEITH WILLIAMS

Introduction

The Church in Western Europe is in crisis and has been experiencing a steady decline over the last 40 years. In some areas, however, there are signs of new life and energy, as fresh and radical models of Church are emerging based on mission in the local community. In this chapter, I will be giving practical examples and case studies to help church leaders answer some key questions:

- Why are we called to relate to the local community?
- Who are the local community and what are their needs?
- What are the different ways in which we can relate to the local community?
- How can we transform our relationship with the local community?

Why are we called to relate to the local community?

Most churches meet on Sundays in buildings that most members of the community never step foot in. The main activities are worshipping God and listening to his word, but we are also called to spread the Good News and 'go out and make disciples of all nations' (Matthew 28.19 [NIV]).

Many people think of the Church as a building, whereas the Church is God's people and their main mission is to reach those who don't know him. Jesus ate with sinners and tax collectors and, when challenged about this by the Pharisees, he said, 'It is not the healthy who need a doctor, but the sick. I have not come to call the righteous, but sinners' (Mark 2.17 [NIV]). The Church is a lifeboat in the community and not a yacht club for its members.

Jesus said that the second greatest commandment was this – 'love your neighbour as yourself' (Mark 12.31). How can I show my love for my neighbour in my local community? Church leaders must look outwards to serve the needs of the community they live in. Church members should be involved in the community, acting as salt and light, as an expression of God's love for all the people – 'let your light shine before men, that they may see your good deeds and praise your Father in heaven' (Matthew 5.16).

> Then the King will say to those on his right, 'Come, you who are blessed by my Father; take your inheritance, the kingdom prepared for you since the creation of the world. For I was hungry and you gave me something to eat, I was thirsty and you gave me something to drink, I was a stranger and you invited me in, I needed clothes and you clothed me, I was sick and you looked after me, I was in prison and you came to visit me.'
>
> I tell you the truth, whatever you did for one of the least of these brothers of mine, you did for me. (Matthew 25.34–40)

Jesus is our model for life balance. He 'lived out his life in three relationships: Up – with his Father; In – with his chosen followers; Out – with the hurting world around him' (Breen and Kallestad, 2005). In our personal lives and in our churches we are also called to get the right balance.

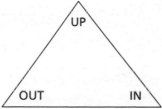

Who are the local community and what are their needs?

The local community is the people who live around or relate to the geography where the church is located, whether it be in a large city, a town, rural village or industrial estate. All communities are different and every church needs to define its local community and understand its needs.

In many communities there are individuals who struggle with meeting the basic material needs of life, for example, food, water and shelter. In Stuart Murray's book, *The Challenge of the City* (1993), he talks about the problems of poverty in inner cities, with Christians moving out to suburban areas and a concentration of resources on overseas mission. However, he also refers to studies about the different problems faced in suburban areas with 'too much socialising, useless hyperactivity in voluntary associations, competition and conspicuous consumption. Many of these evils are thought to be the result of boredom.'

In all communities, however, there are common needs that arise as a result of old age, sickness, disability, mental illness, addiction, loneliness, exclusion, family breakdown, or struggles with parents or parenthood. Some communities have large numbers of adults who are unemployed, whereas in others there are many who are stressed because of excessive work. There are also people in detention and ex-offenders who need to find a way back into society, people who lack self-esteem and the skills to find work.

When we consider how to relate to the local community we also have to see the needs of individuals in the context of the world in which they live. The local people are inextricably linked with wider communities through their work and other activities, and also the impact of world events is lived out in their lounges each night on their television sets. The world is a global village with instant access to people thousands of miles away through mobile phones, e-mail and Internet cyber cafes.

All of us are bombarded with the news daily and most of it is bad news because good news does not sell so well. There are famines, wars, terrorist atrocities, natural disasters, crime, depravity, and longer-term threats of climate change and global warming. Most of us get upset as we see the suffering of so many millions of people around the world. We feel sad, angry, helpless, and many respond generously through appeals, but it is so difficult to see hope. What is the role of the church in helping members of their local community to relate to the wider needs of the world?

What are the different ways in which we can relate to the local community?

People in our communites need to know that God is in control and have confidence that he will overcome all the turmoil and pain in the world. The ultimate mission for the Church is to help individuals to find Christ so that they can know the victory of his death on the cross and the hope of eternal life.

The problem is that we cannot preach the gospel to people with whom we do not have contact, and they will not listen unless we have a meaningful relationship with them. The Holy Spirit can touch anyone and anywhere but God calls us to reach out and make the contact.

The church must be relevant to the people in the local community and must engage in day-to-day life and issues to make a difference.

Social action

There are many ways in which the church has traditionally reached out to serve the local community. We can maintain contact with older people through lunch clubs; we can meet young people through schools work or by running youth clubs; we can visit people who are detained in prisons or immigration detention centres etc. Some churches serve the poor on the streets by providing food and shelter.

King's Arms in Bedford <project@kingsarms.org> – in my own home town of Bedford there is a project for the homeless run by The King's Arms Church, a plant from Woodside Church (Bedford). Both churches are part of the New Frontiers network.

The project was started in 1989 when Philippa Stroud returned to England after working with Jackie Pullinger-To in Hong Kong. She shared a vision with David Devenish (2005), and the other leaders of Woodside Church, to meet the needs of homeless people living on the streets of Bedford, many of whom suffered from drug/alcohol addictions or mental illness. In 1992, they established a hostel which can accommodate 14 residents, who can stay for up to 2 years, and in 1993 they established an 18-bed nightshelter, providing 24-hour support, the only emergency direct access accommodation in Bedford. They also established a discipleship house and a halfway house back into the community, which later became the base for support work.

The King's Arms Church was planted at about the same time in that part of Bedford and now the work of the project is integral to the life of the church. Some of the residents of the project attend the Sunday evening church services and many of the church members volunteer to help in the project. Mid-week meetings for residents are also held at the shelter and the hostel, involving members of the church, and an open meeting is held each Friday night in the town centre for all those who have links with the project.

Since 2002, the project has been providing one-to-one resettlement and development work for individuals. This has included life skills training, for example, budgeting; finding accommodation; and resettlement into work, with voluntary work as the first step. The next step is finding paid employment. There are many other work issues in which the church can relate to the local community.

Fresh expressions

Many of these activities have involved the existing church reaching out into the community or the community being invited into the church. In recent years, as attendance at many traditional churches has fallen, there are a number of examples new churches being established among different groups in the community as 'fresh expressions' of Church and the 'emerging Church'. Examples can be found in the books (Moynagh, 2004; Stoddard and Cuthbert, 2006) and DVD (*Expressions*, 2006) referenced at the end of this chapter, and they include:

Legacy XS in Benfleet – a church created for skateboarders, who can worship God through their skateboarding.

Sunday 4:6 in Devon – a church plant in an isolated rural community where people, with an average age of 50, meet in the village hall.

Nightshift in Hereford <herefordbaptistchurch.org.uk> – where night clubbers are served refreshments and are able to chat with Christians in a non-judgemental environment.

Messy Church in Portsmouth – where young people and their parents can get together once a month and 'make lots of stuff', have fun and listen to a short talk.

Taste and See in Kidsgrove – a café church where people who are typically in their 20s to 40s are able to worship and attend Alpha courses at the heart of the community.

Somewhere Else in Liverpool – a community church where everybody is included, and people can tell their story while making bread, with two services a month in the church building.

Sanctuary in Birmingham <eastandwest.co.uk> – which provides personal space for individuals to connect with God and share Asian food.

Cable Street Community Church in Shadwell, London <urbanexpression.org.uk> – where a team of Christians has moved in to inner-city estates to meet the needs of the local people. One of the activities they run is a 5-a-side football tournament for a whole week in a local park during the school holidays to make contact with young people and their parents.

In all of these examples the church has created the right environment for individuals in the community and enabled them to connect with God in ways that they are comfortable with.

In the workplace

Although people live in the local community, most of them spend their waking hours in other communities, for example, work or school, that exert a variety of different pressures on them. There are many people in work searching for meaning and purpose in life and trying to maintain a work–life balance that does not compromise their family life. There is peer pressure, bullying and stress caused by the ever-intensifying competitive pressure and speed of modern life, and in many environments there is an absence of shared values. What role can the local church play in the local workplace community?

In their study on *Working in the Twenty-first Century* (2005), Michael Moynagh and Richard Worsley ask questions about how work is developing and what employment will be like in the future in the UK. The study predicts that there will be a continuing, possibly widening, gulf between good and bad jobs, with initiatives to increase social inclusion focused on not just getting people into work but on improving job quality at the bottom end. An increasing range of tools will exist to support disadvantaged people into work, for example, mentoring. Action is needed to prevent people sliding to the fringes of the labour market. This includes measures to combat work-related stress, with even more emphasis on the early years of life and improving the quality of parenting.

For many years the Church has provided support to those at work through industrial mission and chaplains. In Hertfordshire and Bedfordshire, the main Christian denominations work together and provide over 40 chaplains (mostly volunteers) to a wide range of different organizations such as the Police, Fire and Rescue, London Luton Airport and companies in the manufacturing and retail sectors. They support individuals in situations where there is tragedy, uncertainty and stress.

The core team leader of Workplace Ministry in Herts. and Beds., Randell Moll, believes that chaplains should also minister to people in their strength. Work provides the goods and services we all need to live. For the individual worker and for the working community, this may be experienced as constructive, creative and collegial. It can provide a means not only of economic support but also of personal growth. Chaplains regard work not only as an economic but also as a spiritual activity. It is not peripheral but essential to human living and an essential element in the divine purpose of the created order.

He believes that chaplains should engage not only with personal pastoral concerns but also, when invited, with the issues of the working community – local, regional, national or even international. This 'prophetic' work goes hand in hand with personal care for all engaged in the process of providing, through the economic process, for the needs of all. Demand has been boosted by the new search for 'spirituality in the workplace' (Buckingham and Clifton, 2004) as employers are looking for ways to improve employee motivation and demonstrate social responsibility; and employees are seeking meaning and purpose in their work.

The WELL Centre <well-centre.org> in Oxfordshire is transforming work. The centre was set up by the Diocese of Oxford and draws on professional expertise and spiritual wisdom to deliver creative and innovative staff care, support, training and consultancy tailored to:

* develop the potential of people and organizations;
* develop work patterns and approaches to enhance wellbeing;
* enrich the working culture;
* engage the issues of meaning, value, beliefs and diversity.

The work of industrial mission relies heavily on the support of volunteers from local churches. Also, there are opportunities for all working church members to get involved in workplace ministry in their own place of work. The local church has a role to play in providing them with encouragement and support as they live as salt and light among their colleagues.

There are other creative ways in which the local church has provided direct support to the local working community by stimulating enterprise and building the skills of individuals.

HURT social enterprise in Alfreton <genesisenterprisecentre. co.uk> – HURT (His Upper Room Trust) Ltd is a Christian organization that is run by local church leaders. It owns a group of social enterprises in Alfreton, with activities including: a book shop, conference centre, learning centre and even NHS dental training. HURT's purpose is to express Christianity through its commitment to the community and its support to regeneration through social enterprise. It has encouraged local economic growth by not just providing jobs but also seeking to buy local services and products wherever possible, thus encouraging the local economy. The Genesis Family Entertainment Centre includes a soft play area, ten-pin bowling, community café known as Benedicts, sports hall and community rooms as well as business office incubators.

King's Church in Loughborough <kingschurch.co.uk> – Its aim is that, inside and outside of Sunday meetings, the church is alive and kicking and making a difference. It is involved in projects that reach outside to the community, by education, evangelism or practical help, for example, it runs an Energize <energize-solutions.co.uk> lifeskills centre to encourage young people into education, training or work. The curriculum contains elements such as basic skills, personal effectiveness (Lifeskills), work-related skills and team building. The students can gain qualifications on the courses.

It offers an NVQ level 1 qualification – Getting Connected. This is a personal and social development course and is accredited by OCR. Students can also obtain level 1 and level 2 qualifications in literacy and numeracy via the Adult Tests – again accredited by OCR. It now has a portfolio of established work experience placements in career areas such as childcare, care for the elderly, motor mechanics, administration (delivered 'in house'), youth work, retail, warehousing and plastering.

WorldShapers Ignite project in Hemel Hempstead <worldshapers.org.uk> – The aim of the project was to give young people, aged 16–25, a positive learning experience and increase their employability through Skills for Life training and qualifications to become Level 1 FA coaches. Most of their students had low academic achievements at school and a need to develop social skills and self-confidence. The studies were introduced to organizations dealing with the unemployed, ex-offenders or homeless.

How can we transform our relationship with the local community?

If you believe that your church is being called to transform the way that it relates to the local community, then where should you start? As I have considered the different successful examples provided above, I have looked for the 'nuggets' of best practice. I have also talked to some of the leaders and asked them to identify those factors that have been most significant. The top four are:

- seek God's vision and mission for the Church in the community (UP);
- understand the needs of the local community (OUT);
- mobilize talents and resources (IN);
- innovate and collaborate – being part of the whole body of Christ.

Seek God's vision and mission for the church in the community

'Growth was not the product of a clever strategy or gifted leaders but evidence of the grace of God' (Murray, 1993).

This does not mean that we don't need a strategy or good leadership but it means that God must be at the start, end and in every part of what we do. We can work ourselves into a froth by worrying about whether we need a strategy before we do anything, or whether we have the resources to commit to a particular activity. God knows what needs to be done and he will provide the right resources at the right time if we listen and obey.

The first step is to discern what God is calling us to do in our local community. Sometimes, God gives us the big picture in a vision and helps us to understand what actions to take as we travel towards it. Sometimes, he shows us specific actions to take and creates something much wider and/or more significant than we could possibly have imagined as we move forward in faith. Either way, we should be open to revelation of an overall strategy but also be prepared to take isolated actions, even if we can't see to where they are leading.

In 1998, God called Arno Andreasen from Denmark to establish the **New Horizons Christian Fellowship in Hemel Hempstead** <nhcf.org.uk>. He showed Arno a vision of fire from Hemel Hempstead spreading to other nations. The vision of the Church has developed since then and is presented as 'FACTS':

- Fair trade – how to be fair with your money
- Activity centre – the church as a centre for use by the community
- Church planting – for example, Hyderabad in India
- Transforming lives – seeing people healed, saved, delivered
- Specialist ministries – for example, a debt counselling centre; and WorldShapers, which has been set up as a charity in its own right to support the vision of the Church by carrying out ministries in the community and raising funds.

Service to the community is at the core of the vision and mission of the church and it is lived out in all that the church does. Visions and missions are sterile unless they are embedded in the ways in which those involved in the church think and act. In every service in New Horizons Christian Fellowship, there are reminders that 'we are here for the community' and church members talk about it constantly.

One of their key principles is inclusiveness. When the church was being named they sought advice from 80 local people, including non-Christians, who recognized what they had as a community in the way they had fun and demonstrated positive expressions of their faith. People from 16 nationalities are now involved in the church.

The church services are conducted in the community centre and members sit and worship around tables, where they share food and drink together. 'Their way' is also applied consistently. So when Arno was the Mayor's Chaplain for the year the civic service was held in the same way, with VIPs seated with the community around tables instead of in reserved rows.

On the Sunday in 2006 that the Buncefield oil terminal exploded in Hemel Hempstead the church service was shortened, because the congregation saw it as part of their worship to offer support to the local community. Five hours after the explosion, leaflets were distributed to 2500 houses with the message 'we are here to help' and offering practical support.

The King's Arms project, mentioned earlier, is integral to the life of the church. The main reason given for the lasting success of the project was the clarity of the call from God. As a result of this, the work of the project is embedded in the vision of the church – to serve the poor (Isaiah 58 and 61) – and all the leaders and members support it through prayer, time and other resources.

Understand the needs of the local community

I am sure that God can point us at needs in the local community if we pray from our pews or the comfort of our homes. The experience from many projects is that God talks to us as we get out and listen and learn directly from the people we are called to serve. This may entail a dieing to live experience, as you let go of your original ideas in favour of those generated by the local people.

Listening needs to be in partnership with local people so that they become stakeholders before the project starts. So many projects start as a bright idea of an enthusiast which has not been adequately tested on the people whom the project seeks to serve.

When Philippa Stroud started her work in the King's Arms project in Bedford, she spent a lot of time in Church (Pigeon) Square with the homeless, alcoholics, drug addicts and mentally disturbed who congregated there. She listened to them to understand their needs, and built relationships with them.

When Jim and Juliet Kilpin started their mission in Shadwell, East London, they took time talking to local residents and serving them in many different ways. They made a commitment to live in the local community for five years but it took them three years to earn their respect and trust.

Somewhere Else, the community church in Liverpool, discovered the needs of the community by walking the streets and talking to the local people.

Mobilize talents and resources

If the work in the local community is an important part of the overall vision and mission of the church then the talents and resources of the whole body of Christ should be available to support it. It should not be left to individuals to carry out the work on their own because the talents and resources available to them will be limited and unable to sustain the long-term commitment and sacrifice necessary to make a real and lasting difference. In every church there are a wide range of talents available, and God will provide the resources that are required.

The church leaders have a critical role in selecting, releasing, equipping and supporting those who will carry out specific initiatives and actions.

When selecting leaders it is important to recognize that different leadership styles work in different situations and that leaders need to be chosen carefully to play to their strengths (Williams, 1999). It is difficult and disruptive to change leaders when the work has started. The people selected need to have a heart for the work and the stamina to get it started and keep it going. This is more important than having all the right skills, and in many cases the jobs can be constructed around the people selected.

When the right people are selected then it is important to release them to carry out the work. The time they spend must be prioritized against other activities, and sometimes this may mean that they need to let some other things go. They must also be allowed the freedom to shape what they do and how they do it within appropriate boundaries, for example, the budget.

All those involved in the work need to be equipped with the right resources and supported through training, coaching, mentoring and prayer. They should be encouraged to seek opportunities for personal development and growth through their work in the community, and to develop others through peer mentoring arrangements where skills and experience can be passed on to others.

For some activities it may be necessary to set up specific governance and support structures, even separate legal entities, such as charities or trading companies, for example, WorldShapers was created as a charity to support the vision of New Horizons Christian Fellowship in

Hemel Hempstead; HURT Ltd was set up to run the Christian social enterprises in Alfreton; The King's Arms Project is part of a charity called The King's Arms Trust – which includes the church; the WELL Centre has been set up as a registered not-for-profit company limited by guarantee to address the needs of the work community in Oxfordshire.

Innovate and collaborate

Sometimes, God inspires us with a vision that seems too big, difficult or risky for us. He may be challenging us to be innovative by doing new things or doing existing things differently. In either case, we may be well outside our comfort zone and we may be worried about failure and the potential consequences. However, God calls us to have faith and be foolish because he provides for our needs. We need to remember that we are part of the whole body of Christ.

Often, this means looking outside our own limited resources and collaborating with others. It is likely that what is new to us has already been done successfully by others and we can learn from them. There may be many organizations or individuals outside our church who would be able and willing to share expertise or funding. We need to pray that God will show us how our needs will be met and be open to unexpected offers. There are many possible sources of help from other churches; Christian organizations; Government – both national and European, for example, European Social Fund; or businesses, through bodies such as Business in the Community. Involving them may be part of God's plan to spread the work more widely.

When seeking Government funding, it is important to take a longer-term view of the needs and initiatives and, where possible, to develop a portfolio of projects which are holistic and enable continuity of funding, leadership and infrastructure. This is more effective than being dependent on individual funding initiatives, which tend to be piecemeal, narrow and time limited.

Many church leaders find that they plough a lonely furrow, particularly when they are embarking on changes. They find it useful to 'buddy up' with leaders from other churches and establish peer mentoring relationships where they can share experiences and provide each other with coaching in different aspects of their work. This can be extended to other members of the church who have specific skills and expertise or a need to develop them. It can also be extended to include individuals in the community and business. The church can become the hub of a collaborative network of individuals growing together to serve a greater purpose.

Conclusion

In this chapter I have given examples of traditional and new ways of relating to the local community. I hope you will be challenged by the possibilities, but there is also a danger that you may feel overwhelmed.

There will always be clear direction to move forward but sometimes we don't spot it or we don't respond obediently. Sometimes we need to test the direction by laying a fleece. Sometimes we need to stop and check that everyone is getting the same signals from God – he will never send us in different directions, but he may give different people different pieces of the same jigsaw. We must ensure unity of purpose and be prepared to challenge personal ambition or interest if it creeps into our deliberations. He will call us to be foolish and look at situations with the wisdom of the Holy Spirit.

God will equip us to do the work he calls us to do. Creative church leaders are focused on God's word and allow him to lead them to action, mobilizing the talents that he has given us to serve the local community sacrificially. As individuals, we cannot meet all the demands, but as the body of Christ each of us has a role to play and the unique God-given talents to play it (Ahmed, Finneron, Miller and Singh, 2006). Different Christians will be called to different ministries.

God's timing is perfect and sometimes we are surprised how rapidly things happen and sometimes how slowly. He will not push us faster than we can cope with, but he does need us to be patient and also to be open to unexpected developments as he works through his plans.

Checklist

Seek God's vision and mission for the church in the community:

- in social action to meet local needs;
- in fresh expressions of Church – connecting the community with God;
- involving God in the workplace; and
- living out God's vision consistently as part of the Church's worship.

Understand the needs of the local community:

- by listening to those you are called to serve;
- letting go of your ideas in favour of those from the community; and
- developing local partnerships to take action.

Mobilize talents and resources:

- make all the resources of the body of Christ available;
- select the right leaders;
- prioritize activities and be prepared to let some things go;
- equip and support those involved in the work;
- set up the right governance and support structures.

Innovate and collaborate:

- be innovative;
- have faith and be foolish;
- look outside your own resources;
- take a longer-term view;
- collaborate with others.

Pray

Further reading

Ahmed, Rumman, Doreen Finneron, Steve Miller and Harmander Singh (2006), *Tools for Regeneration: Practical Advice for Faith Communities*, Faith Based Regeneration Network UK.

Breen, Mike, and Walt Kallestad (2005), *The Passionate Church: The Art of Life-changing Discipleship*, ???: NexGen.

Buckingham, Marcus, and Donald O. Clifton (2004), *Now, Discover Your Strengths: How to Develop Your Talents and Those of the People You Manage*, New York: Pocket Books.

Devenish, David (2005), *What On Earth Is the Church for? A Blueprint for the Future for Church-based Mission and Social Action*, Milton Keynes: Authentic.

Fresh Expressions (2006), *Expressions: The dvd. Stories of Church for a Changing Culture*, London: Church House Publishing.

Moynagh, Michael (2004), *Emergingchurch.intro.* 'Fresh Expressions of Church; 'Examples That Work'; 'The Big Picture'; 'What You Can Do', Monarch Books.

Moynagh, Michael, and Richard Worsley (2005), *Working in the Twenty-First Century*, Economic & Social Research Council and The Tomorrow Project.

Murray, Stuart (1993), *The Challenge of the City, a Biblical View*, Lancaster: Sovereign World.

Stoddard, Chris, and Nick Cuthbert (2006), *Church on the Edge: Principles and Real-life Stories of 21st-century Mission*, Milton Keynes: Authentic.

Williams, Nick (1999), *The Work We Were Born to Do: Find the Work You Love, Love the Work You Do*, Shaftesbury: Element.

26. Enabling church activities to be integrated into a strategic plan

IVOR TELFER

Introduction

Is this a chapter about business or the Church? I think it is about the business of the Church. Please don't be put off by the words strategic plan. Simply put, God had a plan when he created the world, and I believe the ministry of the local church is integral to that plan.

I hope that this chapter will enable you and your leadership team to look closely at what you do as a church and to put together a plan to take your local church where you feel God wants it to be and how best to make disciples.

My opening comment regarding the title of this chapter must be 'some of our activities may not be able to be integrated'.

We may find that they are not effective or necessary – but please read on!

In the summer of 1988, I became involved with a strategic plan for The Salvation Army in the region to which I had been appointed. A church consultant was asked to lead the group through an initial planning exercise. The most memorable piece of advice was this:

> Vision is 5% of strategy, aligning the organization to the vision is 95% of strategy!

This aligning of the organization – the local church – is where having a strategy is vitally necessary, but it is all too often missing from the local church.

I won't quibble about the percentages, but my heart warmed to this indicator of 5% vision and 95% alignment. So often we have a clear vision but, when we look at our weekly, monthly and annual programme, we don't seem to be achieving that vision although we have still been very busy and working hard! Additionally, as we see numbers dwindle, we tend to work harder doing the same things we used to do and the result is, all too often, a continuing drop in numbers and an increasing number of tired people in our congregations.

As our congregations in many situations are smaller than they once were, we need even more to be strategic in what we do, making the best use of the resources of people, of gifting and of available time.

I want to walk us through a process towards formulating a plan for the local church, which I have used and am still using with church leaders both within The Salvation Army and in other denominations.

- Scratching where people are itching
- Being intentional
- Measuring quality not just quantity
- Are we moving northeast and if not, what can we do?
- How long will it take?

Scratching where people are itching

A former boss of mine and good friend, Chick Yuill, frequently used to ask the question of church leaders: 'If your church closed, how long would it take the local community to realize?'

Sometimes our church activities and programmes don't actually relate to the people where the church is situated. We can fall into the culture of running the programmes for our own people – a club mentality – instead of a mission mentality. Let me explain using the tried-and-tested ENGEL Scale (see Figure 26.1)

My contention, which is supported by many church leaders with whom I have shared it, is that 50 or 60 years ago most of the UK population was probably around the –3 to –2 spot on the Engel Scale, that is, they knew about Christ and simply had to decide whether or not to accept or reject him. Christianity was taught in schools, church attendance was high, the laws and government of the country were based on Christian principles. Our methods then as churches reached out to the population and scratched where they itched. We were relevant.

However, in asking church leaders and congregations today where they think most people in the UK are on the Engel Scale, the answer is always somewhere between –8 and –10. The problem here is that many of our activities are still the same ones that we used when people were at –3 or –2 and that's why they don't often work today.

Another part of this process is to ask the congregation to evaluate all the individual programmes of the church, using a simple SWOT analysis. (See Figure 26.2 for simple SWOT sheet.)

S – strengths
W – weaknesses
O – opportunities
T – threats

Figure 26.1 The Engel scale

Spiritual decision process

God's role	Church's role		Man's response
General revelation		−10	Awareness of the supernatural
		−9	No effective knowledge of Christianity
Conviction	Presence	−8	Initial awareness of Christianity
		−7	Interest in Christianity
	Proclamation	−6	Awareness of basic facts of the gospel
		−5	Grasp of implications of the gospel
		−4	Positive attitude to the gospel
	Persuasion	−3	Awareness of personal need
		−2	Challenge and decision to act
Regeneration		−1	Repentance and faith

(Rejection ↕ shown alongside −5 to −2)

A new disciple is born — **Matthew 28.19–20**

Sanctification		+1	Evaluation of decision
		+2	Initiation into the church
		+3	Become part of the process of making other disciples
		●	Growth in understanding of the faith
		●	Growth in Christian character
		●	Discovery and use of gifts
		●	Christian life-style
		●	Stewardship of resources
		●	Prayer
		●	Openness to others
		●	Effective sharing of faith and life

Note: Adapted from James F. Engel and Wilbert Norton (1975), *What's Gone Wrong with the Harvest?*, Zondervan.

Figure 26.2

Strengths	Weaknesses
Opportunities	Threats

I have found that congregational involvement is best achieved by placing large flipchart sheets for each activity around the room and giving people a felt-tip pen to mark their thoughts about the activities on the sheets, without their names being known. Then, with the leadership team (and, if you wish, involving the congregation again), conduct a PESTEL analysis. This analysis looks at external factors which may impact the church in the performance of its mission. The different sections of the PESTEL include:

P – political – the political arena in which the local church must work
E – economic – the earning capacity of the local population, whether the area is deprived or rich etc.
S – social – the number of single parent households, the age profile of the population, their earning capacity, the number of households without cars or with two cars, the number of children per household etc.
T – technological – specific technology which affects the area and its population.
E – environmental – the major concerns of the local population regarding the environment.
L – legal – any issues of law which may affect the population and could impact on the local church.

In conducting this PESTEL it is advisable to check local statistical and demographic information that could be available from the web or through public libraries or other local research projects. Very often people's perception of their area is very much removed from the (statistical) reality.

The question to ask then is how many of our church activities actually relate to the people around the building as identified in the PESTEL analysis? The results often show that we are not scratching where people are itching. For example, we may be catering for the youth but the real need is the elderly or we may be in an area with an extremely high single-parent family population and, as the church, we are doing little if anything to address their needs.

Being intentional

I think much better in pictures and, in an attempt to come up with a standard process for mission which would enable each local church to do what is relevant in its own area, I devised the Process Diagram which my good friend Michael Carson and I developed (see Figure 26.3).

Running along the bottom of the diagram is the ENGEL scale. All the sections of the diagram are placed carefully at the appropriate point on the ENGEL scale and the scale (Figure 26.1) should be referred to when to looking at the Process Diagram. The process of the diagram from left to right is the 'intentionality' of making disciples, the Great Commission. While it looks neat and tidy, real life will show that no individual flows neatly from one to the other, but the intention is to move from left to right along the diagram and therefore along the ENGEL scale.

Multiple entry points (MEP)

On the left hand end of the diagram, you will note **Multiple Entry Points**. These are programmes and activities which are *targeted* at the unchurched, those who are between –10 and –8. Some hard questions need to be asked and answered about these activities. For example, if we run a luncheon club, are we actually targeting those at –8 or is it really for those who are already in the church? If it is for the churched, then it cannot be classed as an Entry Point. That does not mean it should stop. If it is meeting a need, then at whom is the luncheon club targeted? Is it those who are at –3 or –2 or is it those who are at +2? What may need to be introduced into the luncheon club so that it serves the intention of the Process Diagram – which is to make disciples – depends on our answer to the question of targeting. Then we need to ask how are we moving those who attend the luncheon club further on in their spiritual experience?

If the luncheon club is successfully targeting those who are between –10 and –8, the next question is what processes are in place to move

Enabling church activities to be integrated into a strategic plan

Figure 26.3 Process diagram – generic

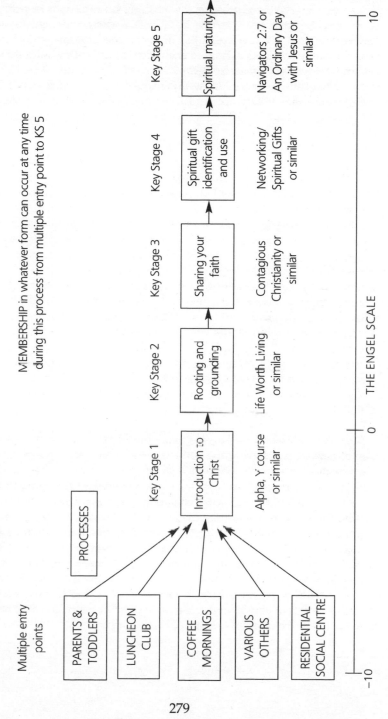

these people to the right along the ENGEL scale? Instead of only coming in for lunch, how can they be GENTLY warmed up spiritually during their lunch experience? For instance, are vibrant Christians, who have been trained in how to share their faith, eating with them and building up relationships?

At these Multiple Entry Points, you should record all the activities and programmes which are actually scratching the people in your community who are at –10 or –8. If you haven't got any, don't worry, keep reading.

Processes

Once the MEPs have been identified, what Processes are in place to move people towards **Key Stage 1**?

If we can get the processes right – and processes involve both method and motivation – we will immediately have more Kingdom success.

Note: I want to stress at this point that winning people to the Lord and discipling them is not a mere mechanical process, that is, follow the process diagram and it will all work. The power of the Holy Spirit can do anything, despite us, and, if he is not in it, it will not work.

What I am attempting to show is that if we have a clear understanding of what we are trying to achieve in mission terms and a visual process to help us document our plans, this will be of great help in ensuring that our motivation is matched by our method.

Back to Processes. How do we relate to people who are at –8 and move them onwards? For example, if we are running a parent and toddlers group which is populated by people who are mostly at –8, how do we warm them up? One idea may be to introduce a parenting course and encourage the parents to look after each other's children for half an hour or encourage them to keep coming on the normal Wednesday morning parent and toddler day even when their child starts preschool. Serve them coffee and juice and chat with them about parenting. This will enable relationships to be built and through this, will help us then to look GENTLY at what the Bible has to say about parenting. A movement to the right along the ENGEL scale should be evident and at some stage they may be happy to come to a Key Stage 1 (for example, Alpha Course) activity.

Key Stage 1 - Introduction to Christ

This stage is asking if you have an activity or programme which is targeted at people becoming Christians. You will see it sits above the ENGEL scale at about −2. I suggest that the Alpha Course is a good example of what can be used at this stage. At the end of this stage, it is hoped that the person will have become a Christian and the other stages are to enable them to become disciples.

Key Stage 2 - Rooting and grounding in the faith

This stage seeks to explain the outworking of becoming a Christian. Now I am saved, how does this affect my life? If *Alpha* is used at KS1 then *Life Worth Living* is a good KS2 course.

Key Stage 3 - Sharing your faith

The idea here is to enable the new Christian to know how to share their faith naturally with their non-Christian friends. Those who are newly saved still have unsaved friends whereas many who have been churched for a while have few if any un-churched friends. A course that could be used here is *Contagious Christian* from Willow Creek.

To clarify, this stage is not about winning people to the Lord. This stage is about training our people so they know how to win others. Once they have been trained, we can then place them to serve in the Multiple Entry Point and Processes stages.

Key Stage 4 - Spiritual gifts identification and use

At this stage, it is necessary for the believer to know how God has specifically gifted them, and they will now be mature enough to be taught more about spiritual gifts. Various spiritual gifts surveys abound but particularly I would suggest the 'Network' course from Willow Creek or the Houts-Wagner spiritual gifts survey from the Fuller Theological Seminary. This latter survey does not include teaching notes, so these will need to be developed independently and used before completing the questionnaire. The most vital part for the church leadership team is to make sure people are then used in their area of giftedness.

Key Stage 5 - Spiritual maturity

This stage keeps on going with lots of additional courses and work until we see the Lord Jesus face to face. Lots of courses exist for small

281

groups and there should be a clear plan of which one to progress to in this section.

> Note: I want to stress again at this point that winning people to the Lord and discipling them is not a mere mechanical process, that is, follow the process diagram and it will all work. The power of the Holy Spirit can do anything, despite us, and if he is not in it, it will not work.
>
> What I am attempting to show is that if we have a clear understanding of what we are trying to achieve in mission terms and a visual process to help us document our plans, this will be of great help in ensuring that our motivation is matched by our method.

The Process Diagram is simply a tool to assist the local church in being intentional. How the model is implemented will depend on each local church situation and the differing skills mix of the leadership team. It is also not necessary to start at the Multiple Entry Points. If the worshippers would benefit from starting at Key Stage 2, do that – or if Key Stage 4 is more appropriate, great, start there.

The 'intentionality' of the diagram is vital and, if we are planning to commence a new Multiple Entry Point activity, we should ensure we have thought about the Processes which should be used to move people towards faith before the programme is commenced.

> Now pause and draw a Process Diagram for your current church activities and discuss this at your leadership meeting. Then take time to plan your response to what you find. You may be able to integrate programmes but you may see the need to stop some!

Measuring quality not just quantity

How can we determine the quality of our existing and new programmes? Many of us have collected statistics for years but these largely are quantitative and don't tell us anything about the quality of the programme. Sometimes we assume that numbers attending indicate great quality and that the converse is also true – small numbers means bad quality. This translates sometimes into our 'measurement' of churches – big churches must be good and small churches must be bad. Not so! Often large churches are able to keep going owing to their own momentum rather than because of good leadership and intentional discipleship.

Michael Carson and I developed what we call the **Qualitative Matrix**. (Much more in-depth comment can be given about the

MATRIX and its uses but this is not the appropriate place for such in-depth information.)

The MATRIX, as we will refer to it, was developed from a strategic tool which we have interpreted to use in the church setting (see Figure 26.4).

Figure 26.4

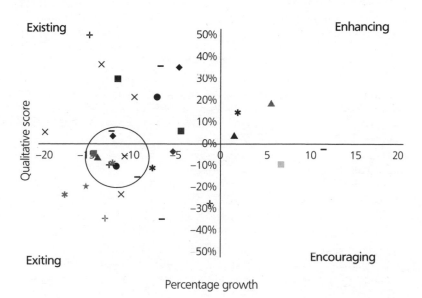

The 'x' axis – the horizontal one – measures the quality of the programme and the 'y' axis – the vertical one – measures the percentage increase or decrease in attendances during this period compared with the last period. (For example, the church had 1000 attendances last period and 1200 this period so there has been a 20% increase in attendance.)

Michael and I developed a questionnaire which we ran past our Strategy Group in my previous appointment and the revised version is in Figure 26.5.

This questionnaire has eight sections. The first section looks at leadership and warmth. The other seven sections are based on each of the seven sections of the Process Diagram working from left to right – Multiple Entry Points through Process etc. to Key Stage 5 (See Figure 26.3).

Members of the leadership team of the local church are encouraged to complete this together, then – in The Salvation Army system – it is

Figure 26.5

QUESTIONNAIRE

A. Overview

1. What is the church leadership structure?
2. What is the frequency of leadership meetings?
3. What are the priorities of the leadership team for the next 12 months?
4. Do you have worship targeted at the unsaved?
5. How many people have attended worship for the first time in the last 12 months?
6. How many of these have subsequently attended worship more than 6 times?

B. Multiple Entry Points

1. How many activities do you have that are *targeted* at unsaved people?
2. What are they?
3. How many *individual people* go through these activities on a weekly basis?
4. What age ranges are catered for in these activities?
   0–5   6–12   13–18   19–30   31–40   41–60   61+
5. How many paid local leaders run these activities?
6. How many unpaid local leaders run these activities?

C. Processes

1. How many processes are in place for each activity listed in B above to bring people to Key Stage 1?
2. What are these processes? (specify age ranges where appropriate as detailed in B)

D. Key Stage 1 – Introduction to Christ

1. Do you have a Key Stage 1 activity/ies in place?
2. What is/are it/they? (specify age ranges where appropriate as detailed in B)
3. What is/are its/their frequency?
4. How many *individual people* attend?
5. How many people have come to Christ through it in the last 12 months?

E. Key Stage 2 – Rooting and grounding in the faith

1. Do you have a Key Stage 2 activity/ies in place?
2. What is/are it/they? (specify age ranges where appropriate as detailed in B)
3. What is/are its/their frequency?
4. How many *individual people* attend?
5. How many people have had a noticeable increase in their passion for the Lord through this/these activity/ies over the last 12 months?

F. Key Stage 3 – Sharing your faith

1. Do you have a Key Stage 3 activity/ies in place?
2. What is/are it/they? (specify age ranges where appropriate as detailed in B)
3. What is/are its/their frequency?
4. How many *individual people* attend?
5. How many of these people have brought new people to a Key Stage 1 activity or to faith in Christ in the last 12 months?

G. Key Stage 4 – Spiritual gift identification and use

1. Do you have a Key Stage 4 activity/ies in place?
2. What is/are it/they? (specify age ranges where appropriate as detailed in B)
3. What is/are its/their frequency?
4. How many *individual people* attend?
5. How many of these people, within the last 12 months, have started to use their dominant spiritual gifts in the corps?

H. Key Stage 5 – Spiritual maturity

1. Do you have a Key Stage 5 activity/ies in place?
2. What is/are it/they? (specify age ranges where appropriate as detailed in B)
3. What is/are its/their frequency?
4. How many *individual people* attend?
5. How many of these people are spiritual elders and leaders in the corps?

Ends

sent to our Divisional Headquarters where each section is independently marked out of 5 by three different people who each have responsibility for work at the local church and bring a variety of skills, knowledge and personality to their marking. This makes a total score of not more than 40 marks (8 × 5) per 'marker'. The mean of these marks is then applied to the 'x' axis of the graph, giving a score which is shown as being a minus figure if under 20 and a plus figure if over 20 (this is so that Microsoft Excel can plot the graph, for no other reason).

Figure 26.4 shows a sample of what the Matrix looks like for 35 churches.

The enhancing quadrant

This top-right quadrant indicates where churches are scored who have good quality programmes and increased attendance. It is our belief that, if a church is running good quality and targeted programmes, the attendance will increase.

The encouraging quadrant

This bottom-right quadrant shows churches that have good quality programmes but decreasing attendance. This may be a temporary arithmetical or seasonal blip or may indicate either a lack of relevance and interest in the existing programmes or it may reflect the fact that a church has stopped a programme which isn't working, that is, isn't moving people forward along the ENGEL scale. An example of this could be the luncheon club which was providing lunches for 50 people 5 days weekly and where all the people are church attenders at other churches in the town. The church leadership then decides to stop this programme as three other churches and community groups offer a luncheon club, and instead the church decides to commence a debt counselling programme with a coffee shop. The attendances will decrease but the quality will increase as the church scratches where people are itching.

The existing quadrant

This top-left quadrant shows churches that have increased attendance and a varied quality of programmes from extremely poor at the left-hand end to fairly good towards the right of this quadrant. A church here needs to watch that it is not playing the numbers game but doesn't have any quality. We have all too often seen new people coming in but just as quickly going out the back door as we haven't been building relationships with them or moving them on in their faith.

The exiting quadrant

This bottom-left quadrant shows churches where programmes vary from extremely poor to fairly good but who have declining attendances. Continued time in this quadrant may lead to the church needing to be closed.

What our work with the Matrix has shown us over the last four years (at the time of writing) has been confirmation of what many have thought and voiced:

1 Big is not always beautiful – all the large churches except one were in the coloured circle in Figure 26.4
2 The three churches in the top-right quadrant – Enhancing – were all new church plants which had been operating for five years. This shows that it is often easier to plant than to transition
3 Churches which are high up in the top-left quadrant – Existing – will lose people out of the back door if they don't improve their quality and type of programmes
4 Leaders of churches who are in the top-right quadrant – Enhancing – are under much more pressure to keep growth going, and, if they and their leadership team do not have good management abilities and systems, these individuals and systems can become a blockage which affects churches much more in this quadrant than in any other.
5 Clergy who take their church from bottom-left to top-right are often tired. We ask them to do the same again for another ailing church, but we should not ask a third time without giving the clergy a respite – a sabbatical or a different type of ministry for a period.

Figure 26.6 shows the type of strategies that can be implemented with and in a church in one of these quadrants, for example, instead of trying to take the church in the top-right quadrant from 200 people to 300 people on a Sunday, why not plant a new church?

Are we moving northeast and, if not, what can we do?

Wherever a church is positioned in the MATRIX, if it is moving in a generally north-easterly direction over successive years this is good. Wherever a church is moving in any other direction this needs to be examined closely and some serious questions asked. Sometimes a consultant is the best person to do this for the leadership team.

Figure 26.6

IN SUMMARY

Existing	Enhancing
Planting	Planting
Increase profile and presence	Increase profile and presence
Better or different programmes	Better or different programmes
Takeover/replant/merger	Improved management
Stop some programmes and concentrate on effective ones	Increased freedom from DHQ/THQ
	Takeover/replant/merger
	New similar programmes
Exiting	**Encouraging**
Merger	New similar programmes
New similar programmes	New programmes for present congregation
New programmes for present congregation	New programmes in community
New programmes in community	Mergers and networking
Stop some programmes and concentrate on effective ones	
Close	

Annually, a new Process Diagram should be completed and a SWOT and PESTEL may also be helpful to ascertain whether the church has drifted from its primary purpose or whether the local community has changed and the church hasn't realized. Then one or more of the strategies need to be implemented.

How long will it take?

If you are starting out on this process, please don't think it will all happen in a year. I worked with one church that had lots of things happening at all the stages and lots of processes in place but it took them nine years to achieve appropriate activities at each stage. Then they saw the need to improve these and to change some. It doesn't need to take that long but the shortest period of time that this could be in place is, I suggest, four years and that depends on the abilities of the leadership team and the drive and the quality of the change process with the existing congregation.

Conclusion

As I suggested at the start of this chapter, the title 'Enabling Church Activities to be Integrated into a Strategic Plan' may actually mean that some activities cannot be integrated! Considerable energy from the leadership team will be needed if an activity that has lots of people attending but which cannot be changed into being mission focused has to be stopped.

As the church consultant mentioned, however, 'Vision is 5% of strategy, aligning the organization to the vision is 95% of strategy!'

Aligning the church to the vision is what will take the energy and the time but if we are able to make this happen, I firmly believe – and I have seen evidence to support the fact – that churches will grow when their activities and programmes are carefully planned, bathed in prayer, intentional and support the mission God has given to them.

Finally, may I suggest a strategic plan with alignment from scripture:

Jesus undeterred, went right ahead and gave his charge:

'God authorised and commanded me to commission you: Go out and train everyone you meet, far and near, in this way of life, marking them by baptism in the threefold name: Father, Son and Holy Spirit. Then instruct them in the practice of all I have commanded you. I'll be with you as you do this, day after day after day, right up to the end of the age.'' (Matthew 28.19, 20 *The Message*)

27. Chairing a church council and when not to

ALAN HARPHAM

Introduction

Many of us have endured at least one dreadful church meeting where the 'saints' gathered together and proceeded to behave like a bunch of sinners! Perhaps that is where Ghandi got his idea that he loved Christ but was less sure of his followers?

Have you ever seen that well-known poster with a picture of Jesus and underneath the words – 'God so loved the world that he did not send a committee'? However, he did choose 12 disciples – his team. Matthew 18.20 suggests, even assures, the presence of Christ in decision-making as Christians sit together. The word 'ecclesia' is used by Christ on only two occasions in the context of discernment – 'binding and loosing' – as to what should be forbidden (binding) as opposed to allowed or permitted (loosing) in the rabbinic tradition.

How is the chair chosen?

Who is the chair of a church council? Many chairs of church councils are elected, others are appointed.

For example, in the Church of England, the vicar is the de facto chair of the parochial church council and may or may not decide to have an elected lay co-chair. The chair of the Anglican deanery synod is appointed, namely, the rural (or area) dean: whereas the chair of the house of laity in a deanery synod is elected (incidentally, there are co-chairs with equal status in deanery meetings). In diocesan synods, similarly, the chair of the House of Bishops is the diocesan bishop who is appointed, while the chairs of the houses of clergy and laity are elected. At General Synod the chair is an Archbishop who is appointed while the chairs of the Houses of Bishops, Clergy and Laity are all elected.

Other denominational church councils have other appointment rules for the chair who has two functions: first, to act as the titular and working head of the council and, where there is more than one chair, this may be a shared role; the second is to chair the meetings of the church councils. This chapter focuses on this second role and the running of effective meetings. The former role is usually set out in the governance documentation of the particular denominational church organization and is usually different for the various denominations and church councils within that denomination.

Chairmanship and the resolution of conflict

Christians are often fearful of conflict, believing it may lead to aggression or severe disagreement. The truth is that conflict explored by trying to put yourself in the other person's place (perception) can be wholly positive and enable a better understanding to develop and grow and from it a solution to a perceived impasse.

I remember a meeting that I was both chairing and strongly proposing a change of direction. I got into such a 'perceived' impasse with a church colleague, where we were both unable to see a way out, when the secretary announced, 'It was the best meeting of this church council he had been to for a long time – at least important matters rather than trivia were being discussed'! Out of this, we agreed to leave some time for reflection before coming back to the debate at a future meeting.

Christian decision-making should seek where possible to hold together the two views, to seek the reasons for the differences, to seek reconciliation where necessary, and to acknowledge rather than hide situations where offence has been taken. Prayer time taken over difficult decisions, leaving space for more information and some debate over issues and, in some cases, deciding to defer decisions until a further meeting to give time for reflection before making the decision are all useful ways forward in difficult meetings. Meetings should not be a chore to be endured but to be enjoyed as a lively part of the gathered people of God.

Chairing church council meetings

Meetings are like most activities in life – to be effective they need a purpose, intended outputs and outcomes, be planned ahead, managed so that everyone is heard, their ideas and opinions captured, discussed and a consensus reached, so that at the end of the meeting there is agreement on the outcomes and everyone can go home content to have been heard, committed to the council's decision and empowered to go and do their part of any agreed activities. At least, that is what the rational (logical) manager expects.

Of course, in all walks of life, there is an ongoing battle between mythos and logos and never more so than in religious activity. So there may be those who prefer their meetings to be less logical and rational, more fuzzy, an opportunity to (just) talk, to try out their 'soft management skills' and, perhaps, to come away satisfied by a good open chat with no particular resolution. And, of course, there are many meetings run somewhere between these two extremes. However, the remainder of this chapter focuses on running 'business-like' meetings that follow as much as possible the use of the rational and the logical.

There may be moments, as in any organization, where the interests of the council may be better served by a period of quiet reflection, in silence, prayer or a led meditation, to ponder where God is leading the church and his desire(s) for it. A good chair will sense that moment and propose it to the council for its consideration. This may be during a 'rational/logical' meeting when there is an impasse and the way forward is very unclear, or indeed planning a purposeful quiet day (or part day) when the council agrees to meet in prayer and silence, perhaps with an appropriate facilitator.

Getting started and planning ahead

The key decision of course lies in the stated purpose of the meeting, the answer to the question: why meet? This decision usually rests with the person who calls the meeting, usually the chair for the meeting; although more formally organized churches may have a standing committee responsible for planning and calling meetings.

Having determined the purpose of the meeting, the next step is to agree an agenda: the items to be looked at and some idea of how much time is needed for each item and thereby for the whole meeting. Again, the agenda is usually determined by the chair(s), or a standing committee if one exists. The secretary to the meeting may prepare the first draft, often agreed on a standard agenda template (see typical agenda below) including items carried forward from the last meeting. The chair will then add other key items s/he believes need dealing with, and will seek the agreement of the key attendees to the agenda before issuing it.

A key question for the chair(s) in planning the meeting is to ask the question as to whether 'visioning work' has been done on where the council is trying to get to in the longer term and whether time should be given occasionally to think about this. Or is the meeting just

---

Typical Meeting Agenda for a Church Council
Place, Date and Time of Meeting

Item No.	Item	Speaker	Time
1	Opening Prayers	ANO	0.00
2	Apologies for absence	Secretary	0.10
3	Minutes of last meeting – corrections of fact	All	0.15
4	Matters arising from last meeting (not on agenda)	All	0.20
5	Specific item A – with paper	ABC	0.30
6	Specific item B – no paper (to be presented at meeting	XYZ	1.00
7	Specific Item C – with paper	PQR	1.30
8	etc.		
10	Any Other Business (AOB) [please notify chair in advance]	GHI	1.45
11	Date, time and location of next meeting	Secretary	1.55
12	Closing Prayer – e.g. The Grace	Chair	2.00

'MOTS' – more of the same? Has the council been challenged to think ahead and envisage what it should be doing to order the church's future purpose?

Usually, the penultimate agenda item is AOB – Any other business. This provides the opportunity to add for discussion items not included in the original agenda. A prudent chair asks members to notify him/her in advance of their AOB so s/he can build this into his time planning for the meeting (and perhaps with a time limit for each).

Some people, of course, have so-called 'hidden agendas', and the chair must be alert to these and try to get them 'out on the table' beforehand in the agenda or at least during the meeting if they arise.

Together with the location, time and venue of the meeting, the agenda should be issued to the attendees well before the meeting date (of course the date, time and venue for the meeting should have been booked with the attendees some time beforehand, perhaps with a set of dates for a year ahead, sometimes on a fixed day in the month or quarter – if, however, it is an ad hoc meeting, sufficiently in advance to get it into people's diaries – ideally at least a week beforehand so that they can prepare for the meeting.

Ideally, some of the agenda will be supported with specific item 'papers'. Some of these may be reports from subcommittees, hopefully with 'decisions required' noted and set out as a proposal to the council. Ideally such reports will be as succinct and clear as possible to aid the council to make decisions quickly without rerunning the work of the subcommittee to which it has delegated a task!

These papers and reports should accompany the agenda, along with the draft minutes of the previous meeting, if appropriate, so that the attendees can come properly prepared, having had time to read them. Also, with the agenda and attached papers, if this is one of a regular and repeating meeting, will be the draft minutes of the last meeting with 'matters arising' to be discussed at this meeting listed as part of agenda.

In a typical church council meeting the main agenda items will be specific matters/issues and a reasonable amount of time should be scheduled for each of them. More than two or at the most three in a two-hour meeting is usually enough; most attendees at church council meetings have had more than enough with a meeting lasting between two and three hours.

The timescale of each agenda item is a variable, and the prudent chair will know to leave enough time for each item and not create an incredibly busy agenda with no hope of completing it. Better to cut it back and defer less urgent items for future meetings.

If there is a large amount of business to be covered at every meeting of a committee and insufficient time in which to do justice to it, there are two alternative solutions: either to increase the number and frequency of meetings or to delegate some of the items to a standing committee (or some other name) that deals with the more mundane and less-urgent items and which meets regularly, or can be convened at short notice, between church council meetings, on behalf of the whole council. The council should be informed of decisions made by this sub-group at the next available meeting.

If one of the purposes of meetings is to arrive at a consensus decision, some members of the committee may be encouraged to meet beforehand to 'lobby' each other on their preferred outcomes. As in most management activities, preparation and planning usually attract major benefits when it comes to actually running the meeting: people are well prepared, know the issues to be discussed and come with their opinions well ordered.

Running the meeting

So we come to the meeting itself. The role of the chair is to facilitate the smooth running of the meeting. The aim is to run an orderly meeting where people listen and respond civilly to each other, and arrive at consensus decisions. This means that the chair must make sure that all are heard and, in particular, the quieter members, while the noisier, more assertive ones are encouraged to listen to others as well as to speak.

This means that the role of the chair is, first, actively to listen and watch the rest of the group's body language, to pick up clues of agreement, disagreement and hostility, and to use this to bring other members into a discussion or to move the meeting along. In other words, the chair should also be looking for 'what is not said', particularly when a 'blocker' is at work trying to prevent change that has generally been agreed to by the group, most of whom are remaining quiet while the 'blocker' holds the floor of the meeting.

Secondly, the chair should run the meeting to an effective timescale so as to finish on time, having given due consideration to each item on the agenda, and without the attendees feeling too rushed or feeling that the meeting has dragged.

Sometimes, when the chair wants to take a more active part in debating the content of an agenda item, it can be helpful for him/her to hand over the chair for that particular item. Indeed, if the chair has a lot to say or get across in a meeting it may be helpful for him to hand over the chairing of the whole meeting. Obviously, where there are co-chairs they can share the role easily. Where there is not a formal co-chair, it may make sense to elect a co-chair to run the meetings in the absence of the chair or when the chair wishes to do a lot of speaking.

One common phenomenon to be avoided, particularly in voluntary organizations, is the 'action replay'. This is where someone who has missed a previous meeting decides to have a go at reopening a decision made at a previous meeting and with which they are unhappy. The chair may get a clue from a participant who asks whether it is his intention to run a total replay of the last meeting. Better still, s/he should spot what is happening and head it off.

At the outset of the meeting, the chair should make it clear as to who is going to take the draft minutes and record the committee's decisions. This may be part of the role of the elected secretary and, if not, the chair should have asked someone beforehand who will be at the meeting to undertake this task. The secretary's role is not to record a verbatim transcript of the meeting, but just the key points made, decisions made and any agreements made about actions to be taken by individuals, plus a note of when these actions are to be completed (usually before the next meeting).

After the meeting

Within a few days after the meeting, the draft minutes together with agreed actions (by whom and when) should be circulated to all the members of the council. Most of us forget what we have agreed to do between meetings unless we are reminded. If the reminder appears only a few days before the next meeting, that is, with the agenda, it will usually be too late for those responsible for doing things from the last meeting to get them done in time. If it is not possible to get the draft minutes out within one week of the meeting being held, then at least a list of the delegated actions should be issued to those responsible for them.

The final role of the chair(s) is to make sure that those charged with leading or taking actions are getting on with them and are sufficiently resourced to be able to deliver their actions on time. This is an ongoing role between meetings, along with planning the next meeting, any additional meetings and, from time-to-time, calling a special meeting to deal with very significant items. This type of meeting may have to go on for longer than is usual – and may be scheduled to take place during the day at weekends.

Longer meetings

From time to time, or on the formation of a new council, or after major changes to its membership, or when a major decision is looming, the council may decide on the need for a longer meeting (more than two hours) and may ask members to set aside a half-day, a day or a weekend to give more consideration to getting to know each other better, to do some team-building and/or to have the time to address a major issue.

A reasonably regular major issue would be to produce a five-year plan for the local church which would almost certainly require a change of format, a new location possibly, perhaps with a professional facilitator and, as mentioned above, perhaps with time for reflection and meditation on a decision.

When not to . . .

Clearly by standing for the role of the chair there is a (tested) presumption that the person has some idea of what they are letting themselves in for. This is usually because they have been a member of the council before being asked to consider becoming the chair.

When I told my father that I had been elected churchwarden of my local church his reply was unrepeatable, despite the fact that he had himself been a loyal churchwarden for 35 years in two churches. The fact was that he knew it was a 'role' with little thanks, lots of work (between as well as at meetings) and it was the place where many churchgoers bring their complaints. (As many of us know, that is what goes with the role of leader.)

So, if you have agreed to undertake this role, I wish you every success in it. On a more serious note, 'when not to' is if it begins to undermine your faith or desire to belong to a church. I would seriously suggest that, in those circumstances, you should consider resigning and/or finding a new church.

Further reading

Behrens, James (1998), *Practical Church Management: A Guide for Every Parish*, Leominster: Gracewing.

Dudley, Martin, and Virginia Rounding (2003), *Churchwardens: A Survival Guide*, London: SPCK.

Macmorran, Kenneth, and Timothy Briden (2001), *A Handbook for Church-wardens and Parochial Church Councillors*, London: Mowbray.

Pitchford, John (2003), *An ABC for the PCC*, London: Continuum.

28. Putting fun into being involved

LEN SIMMONDS

From time to time I come away from something I am involved with and say to myself, 'Why on earth do I keep going to this? It's not fun any more. One thing is for sure, unless things change they are going to lose me!'

Wanting to achieve an element of 'fun' from the things we do appears to be an important part of our psychological make up but trying to bottom what that really means is the challenge. It is apparent that 'fun' means different things to different people. The dictionary describes 'fun' as amusement, jocularity, pleasure, gaiety, merriment, a diversion, and yet I know accountants who would consider deliberating over a difficult set of numbers as 'being a bit of fun'.

Over the years people have recognized that 'fun' should be an essential feature of our day-to-day lives. Indeed, British actor, Noel Coward, suggested, 'Work itself should be more fun than fun', and the French poet, Paul Valéry, enlightened us with the thought, 'Serious minded people have few ideas. People with ideas are never serious minded'. He is putting forward the notion that there are some important benefits associated with 'having fun'. Indeed, the Austrian philosopher, Ludwig Wittgenstein, goes so far as to say 'If people never did silly things nothing intelligent would ever get done'.

These are just a few people who over the years have made a case for 'having fun', and yet I find it very surprising that in my quite extensive library of management books not one includes the word 'fun' in the index. Why should this be?

Possibly it is because 'fun' is difficult to define, could be difficult to supervise and might involve an element of risk. I suspect that some managers are more comfortable with 'fun' being something that happens outside the organization's precincts.

'Having fun' does not have to mean that there is slack organization, poor discipline and that people are not accountable. Some of the organizations and groups I have had most 'fun' in are the ones that are very professional, well organized, achieve the desired outcomes and have the ability to be always celebrating success of one kind or another. In these organizations, everyone understands their role and consequently strives to move things on. A few years ago, when I was visiting organizations working towards Investors in People recognition, I developed the knack of getting a feel of the company as soon as I walked through the door. Those that had it right showed it through people's voices and their positive approach and manner. People expressed enthusiasm for what they did and what the organization was about and were obviously enjoying themselves. They had what I call 'The X Factor' – but an explanation of that is for another time.

In contrast, the tension that you feel in disorganized organizations and groups does not allow scope for much 'fun'. Everyone is so often 'fire fighting'.

It is depressing that, in some organizations, 'having fun' is nothing to do with management at all and often staff take it upon themselves to organize their own thing. They do this because they subconsciously recognize the importance of building bonds with the people with whom they are associated. The Christmas party and possibly the birthdays of colleagues are the only times when they can lighten up – and that is off site.

This need of management to be separate from the 'fun' and the 'social' element of the organization is quite new. The social club was once an important part of the structure of business and was often used as a benefit to attract new employees. Sadly, in too many organizations, social and relationship building activities and events have been programmed out through cost-cutting exercises. Some senior managers would go so far as to say that it is impossible to fulfil this role nowadays as there is so much opportunity for people outside of the organization. They can't compete. This means, of course, there is competition for people's time and other ways have to be found to solve the problem. Not getting this right can have dramatic implications, the most evident being staff-retention problems.

I recognized a long time ago that people don't leave an organization – they leave people. People work for people. I worked my hardest (and had the most 'fun') when it was in support of an individual or for a group of people. My driver was that I wanted what I did, and the end result, to make a difference to them. I find it difficult to do the same for something corporate.

Only a foolhardy manager/leader ignores the importance of building relationships and forgets that in the end people do things for people. It is not surprising that staff turnover within call centres is so high. People come in, sit at their station, put on the headset and start taking calls. They have little opportunity to get to know the people sitting in front, at the back and on either side of them. The job itself restricts building relationships. Some are trying to overcome this by sending people for their breaks in teams as they realize that it is in the breaks that relationships start to be formed.

A workplace chaplain once told me of a comment made to him by a member of staff of a retail business that was going through a difficult time. This was bringing about a great deal of stress among the employees. When asked why they stayed, the shop assistant said, 'I stay because I like the people I work with.' Exactly!

We should never underestimate the power of communication when trying to create an environment of which people will want to be a part. Someone once said, 'When you get right down to it, it is our ability to communicate that makes us human', and Victor Borge went so far as to suggest that 'laughter is the shortest distance between two people'. Effective communication is critical if there is to be an element of 'fun'. It is not much 'fun' being kept in the dark on issues that you feel are important.

It is important to create space to allow people to communicate. One committee of which I am a member is so organized that no one has time to talk, either before or after meetings, and consequently the committee's social relationship is non-existent. Creating time for people to get to know each other is an essential part of a leader's role. From time to time I also come across chairs of meetings who never (and I mean never) create opportunities for people to make a contribution – they have missed the fact that some people need encouraging and be invited to give a view. I can only think that these people leave the meeting feeling that they have not been involved and have just been a part of a process – and that's not much 'fun'.

Successful communication also helps achieve better involvement. People can have 'fun' through involvement with people who have something in common with them. The need to share, listen and tell is a vital part of our make up. People coming together provide an opportunity to be involved, get excited, to learn, to share positive as well as negative thoughts and, most importantly, to get to know and understand other people better. Unfortunately, all too often, doing things that develop involvement gets programmed out because we are too busy. The challenge for the leader is to create space for people to discover common interests, goals, and to share concerns.

As I go into organizations I am always surprised how little people really know about the organization of which they are a part. No one has taken the time to create space to 'excite, stimulate and enthuse' them about what the organization is about. Indeed, all too often people cannot even articulate the importance of their role to the success of the organization. They do not know where they fit.

Some organizations get this right. I once visited a company that makes the soap dispensers that we often see on the walls of toilets in hotels and public places. On the production line, I spoke to a young lady who spent the day putting a small spring into the push-button control mechanism. Within minutes, she convinced me that she had one of the most important jobs in the factory. She said that if she did not correctly insert the spring it would have major implications for the business. She explained that after the dispenser left her it is packed and sent to the customer. Once there, it is mounted on the wall. If on testing the dispenser there is no soap coming out the whole thing has to be taken off the wall and is returned to be fixed. The young lady then told me that the customer would not be happy and the chances are that there would not be any future orders. The effect of this was that targets would not be met, she said.

Here was someone who completely understood the importance of her job and was excited by the fact that, if things were done properly, then the dispenser would work, the customer would be happy and the invoice would be paid. Someone had spent time explaining how important she was to the success of the business. It is vital that everyone involved in an organization recognizes that what they are doing is important and that their contribution does indeed make a difference to the organisation's success. The role of the leader is to get them excited.

I am reminded of the story of the visit of a US President to NASA. The sweeper-up told him that he was part of the team that would be putting a man on the moon. The sweeper-up was fixed on the end result and was proud to be a part of the team that was going to achieve it. Someone excited him about the vision and expressed how important his input was to the team effort.

I come from the school of thought that believes that everything we are involved in should make a difference. A test I apply to the things with which I am involved or to the meeting to which I go, is this – 'did that couple of hours make a difference?' If the answer is no, I get really frustrated. The difference I am looking for could simply be that something got advanced, a decision was made, I feel more informed, my contribution was needed, or quite simply I now know other people better than before I started. Sadly, too many meetings end with a negative feeling because somewhere along the way we have lost the plot and there is not much 'fun' in that!

Getting people involved in things and, more importantly, keeping them involved are key challenges for the leader. To be successful there is a need to appreciate and understand what is important to other people, and this means knowing why people are likely to get involved, what it is that drives them, and identifying what they will want to achieve personally through their involvement.

Having a marketing background, I realize that people buy benefits and not the technical things that are inherent within products or services. We don't buy the motor and the drum in the washing machine, we actually buy what the washing machine will do for us – it washes our clothes and saves us time. Using this thinking, we can work out and understand what the benefit will be of being involved.

Actually 'doing something' is an essential element of involvement because most people don't want to be a part of a talking shop. Someone once wrote, 'Don't measure yourself by your goals, but rather by what you are *DOING* to achieve them', and it is my belief that the real 'fun' and 'sense of achievement' is derived from what is being done and the way we go about it. It is important 'to do and not just to be'.

I have worked in organizations that believe that the end result is the be all and end all and do not recognize that, at the end of the day, it is people that gets them that end result. Of course the end result is important. Experience tells me that, unless people have an overarching feeling of involvement and enjoy what they do, they will not 'have fun', and this will eventually impact on the required end result – however that is expressed.

People want to be involved in things that are successful so it is vital the leader finds things to celebrate on a regular basis. This creates a reason for people to rejoice, have 'fun', to enjoy themselves and feel a sense of achievement. Far too often the reasons for celebration just pass us by. However, there are organizations that create space to identify some achievement to celebrate almost every day – even more so when there have been disappointments. The positive impact on people is really noticeable.

We should never underestimate the negative impact that 'not having fun' has on other people. If a person's family, for example, feels the negative impact then they are mostly likely to put pressure on for them to disengage. One organization of which I know was going through a great deal of inevitable change that would cause some stress, making it necessary for people to work late nights and weekends for a while. The managing director commissioned a monthly magazine that explained everything that was happening, the accomplishments and failures. This was mailed to the homes of employees so that everyone in the household could gain an appreciation of what was happening. At the end of the exercise all the families were invited in to see the achievements for themselves.

So what does all this mean for the church leader?

For a start, there is a need to be a creative church leader and this effectively means being imaginative and inventive; innovative and resourceful; inspired and productive.

Putting 'fun' into something is not easy. A church leader needs to create a structure where the congregation develop skills so that they can, with confidence, seize the opportunity to develop mission strategies and actions. This should be done in such a way that they have some 'fun' in the process.

The church leader has to be someone who has the ability to set the style of involvement, and this has to do with method, approach, manner, empathy, technique and, above all, wisdom.

One of the strongest emotions of all is PASSION and it is a motivator, which drives us to incredible limits. Kevin Thomson, in his book *Passion at Work*, tells us that passionate people are enthusiastic, excited and stand out a mile. He goes on to say that 'when people have passion you can see it in the way they work and behave; even more uplifting is when you can see the smile on their face, or the joy of a job well done' (Thomson, 1998, p. 4). Thomson's book helps people understand what makes them and others tick and provides a framework that can help create a culture of success around them. It is my experience that passionate people always have 'fun'.

Understanding what switches a person on or makes them tick is something the church leader has to appreciate. This helps them to guide the right people into the right roles. For some people, it is being in the background and possibly leading on an administrative role. For others, it could be simply rolling their sleeves up and using their hands. Some may even enjoy being a front person and others will be switched on because they have the chance to make things happen.

I have become involved in some things because there was a learning opportunity and the chairman of the committee provided that opportunity. It was a win/win situation. The church leader has to stretch people, create opportunities to experience new things and develop win/win opportunities.

The church leader also needs to recognize when it is appropriate to have a lighthearted approach to things. I know of lots of people who would find it difficult to manage this and indeed would, because of their style, be most likely to make a meal of it and become too bureaucratic. Sometimes these people forget that people are involved on a voluntary basis and they quickly switch them off. I know of one voluntary committee secretary who resigned because people nit picked over the minutes that had been produced. To her it wasn't 'fun' any more and she walked away – the end result being that there is now no secretary.

The church leader has to put some individuals in check – unfortunately some people do have the ability to turn people off because they have a passion for something that others do not share. They become the self-appointed expert and make things difficult for the person who has got the job. We will all know of a person who makes the job of the treasurer or churchwarden more difficult than it need be. That is when the treasurer or churchwarden will perceive that the 'fun' has gone out of the job.

The effective church leader knows that there are some people who are good at keeping morale up, can motivate and encourage, and they know how to use those talents. The church leader has to understand the importance of identifying people who have gifts and strengths that complement theirs. They would then have to have the wisdom to front those people when it is most appropriate. If the leader finds the going tough on something because it does not come naturally to them then the tension will be felt by everyone else involved. Before too long someone will say, 'This is too much like hard work – it's not fun any more'.

The church leader has to be an effective networker. They have to develop the skill that is similar to that of the conductor of an orchestra. The conductor brings together a lot of talented musicians and makes music. The church leader has the challenge to bring together a disparate group of individuals and to let them discover their individual strengths and collective responsibilities. This is not an easy task, as they may need to grow people, help them to learn new skills and even make them feel comfortable with taking risks.

Effective church leaders will always make time for people. They do not let the structure and the administration of the job take over and they make time for themselves and others. I am aware that over the last ten years or so many pubs in the UK have lost (or, dare I say, programmed out) the role of 'mine host'. I go to pubs where the team has never made any attempt to get to know their customers. I have not the faintest idea who runs the place and everyone has been far too busy to build relationships. However, there is a restaurant my wife and I go to on a regular basis. The food is OK but that is all. We keep going back because the hospitality is superb. We are always greeted like long-lost friends and the team have taken the time to know our likes and dislikes. They always make us feel special and extend this to any friends we take along. We always have 'fun' when we are there.

Quite recently, I read somewhere a comment that suggested that there is a feeling that some people in the church relish being 'amateurish' and that 'professionalism' is for others. I have personal experience of that and have lost count of the number of church roles I have taken on where I have not had the benefit a job description and/or some sort of formal handover of responsibilities – and I can tell you there is not much 'fun' in that!

The problem with being amateurish is that it will disengage some people simply because they are already experiencing best practice elsewhere. So, the church leader has to be concerned about developing people into roles that are well defined.

The church leader has to be the custodian of 'fun'.

However, 'fun' to one person might not be 'fun' to another, so achieving the right balance is vital. We have all heard the comment made by an enthusiastic leader 'Let's go and have some fun' and we dread the thought of what that means. So the trick is not to talk about 'fun' at all but to let people discover that they quite enjoy what they are a part of and take great pleasure out of being involved in something that makes a difference.

It is important that the church leader creates a sharing, caring environment that people can excel and develop in. It is also the effective church leader who finds time to say thank you and takes steps to recognize achievements.

One of the problems in the church is that we often get wrapped up in things that allow and encourage us 'just to be' when 'just to be' is no longer good enough. How many church meetings have an agenda that is focused on things that enable the church just to be? David Osborne, in his book *The Country Vicar*, suggests that 'a well-constructed meeting agenda can help church members recognise different aspects of their church life, and encourage them to occasionally reappraise matters which might otherwise go unconsidered for years' (Osborne, 2004, p. 88). He goes on to suggest an agenda that moves 'matters arising from the last meeting' to the back end and brings up front four key headings. These are 'Community', 'Worship', 'Discipleship' and finally 'Resources', where management and fabric matters are dealt with.

The church leader should see that space is created for things that really matter.

In conclusion, the challenge for the church leader is to provide the opportunity for meaningful involvement, to create space to enable the development of relationships, to excite, to stimulate and to enthuse others.

Everyone has to know and appreciate the difference they make through their involvement.

It is my experience that if these things are done people will discover it can be 'fun' and being involved is an enjoyable experience.

When people are 'having fun' and 'enjoy what they do' the benefits are enormous. There is greater retention, a reduction in internal politics, more willingness to share and help others, a better sense of achievement, a more relaxed environment, openness, a reduction in conflict; people become more visionary; there is higher morale and a lot less stress.

What more could a church leader want?

What follows is a checklist designed to make you think.

Putting Fun into Being Involved
A church leader's checklist

- Don't be tempted to do everything yourself
- Do things that help others build relationships
- Make time for people
- Always remember that, at the end of the day, 'people do things for people'
- Never underestimate the importance of effective communication
- Make communication a high priority
- Don't keep people in the dark
- Before meetings create an informal opportunity for people to get to know each other
- If you chair meetings make sure everyone has an opportunity to contribute
- Make sure people have reasons to become involved
- Create space in church life for people to discover common interests
- Remember the need that people have to share, listen and tell
- Find things that will excite, stimulate and enthuse
- Make sure that people understand that their role is important and know how it contributes to the overall mission of the church
- See that people feel that what they do does make a difference
- Remember people are involved because of the benefits derived from the end result
- Do rather than 'just be'
- Regularly remind people of achievements
- Celebrate success and involve a wider audience
- Never underestimate the negative impact of people not having 'fun'
- Involve the wider 'family' in what is happening and the achievements
- Learn from others – pick up best practice
- Don't reinvent the wheel – be a copycat
- Create an environment that is imaginative, inventive, innovative and resourceful – who wouldn't want to be involved?

- Set the style of involvement – be inspiring and productive
- Do things that will help people develop passion
- Create win/win situations – for example, learning opportunities and new experiences
- Have a plan to grow people
- Keep in check people who make life difficult for others
- Use the skills and talents of others
- Develop effective networking skills
- Get out and about
- Be professional in everything that is done – there is no future in being amateurish as it will disengage people
- Be the custodian of 'fun'
- Do some silly things from time to time – and encourage others to do the same
- Don't be too serious otherwise you might just stifle ideas
- Do not measure yourself by your goals but by what you are doing to achieve them

References and further reading

Alder, Harry (1995), *Think like a Leader*, Piatkus.

Davis, William (1987), *The Innovators*, Genesis.

Egan, Gerrard (1993), *Adding Value*, Jossy-Bass.

Feinberg, Mortimer R., and John J. Tarrant (1995), *Why Smart People Do Dumb Things*, Simon & Schuster.

Garrett, Bob (1987), *The Learning Organisation: The Need for Directors Who Think*, Fontana.

Glutterbuck, David (1994), *The Power of Empowerment*, BCA.

Holbeach, Linda (1998), *Motivating People in Lean Organisations*, Butterworth-Heinemann.

Honey, Peter (1994), *101 Ways to Develop Your People, without Really Trying*, Honey.

Kiernan, Matthew J. (1995), *Get Innovative or Get Dead*, Douglas & MacIntyre.

Osborne, David (2004), *The Country Vicar: Reshaping Rural Ministry*, Darton, Longman & Todd.

Pedler, Mike, John Burgoyne and Tom Boydell (1991), *The Learning Company*, McGraw-Hill.

Ries, Al (1996), *Focus*, HarperCollins.

Thomson, Kevin (1998), *Passion at Work: Six Secrets for Personal Success*, Capstone.

Part 5

Vision and the Future

29. Projecting an inviting image

DAVID HEWITT

Most people would agree that the Church in the United Kingdom has an image problem. In spite of the wealth of good work that is going on, still the Church is considered by many to be negative, out of touch and irrelevant.

From where do these ideas come?

I think that it likely that they stem from one of two sources. Maybe people have had a negative personal experience of a particular local church or group of Christians. Having plucked up the courage to turn up one day, they find the building unattractive, the people unwelcoming, the sermon unintelligible and the service boring. Or perhaps, more commonly, they haven't got that far. They have just swallowed the media image and the negative news stories.

Most people have no time for, what they see as, the fine distinctions between one religion and another, let alone the more esoteric divisions between denominations. For them, religion is a bad thing 'per se'. They see the destructive activities of religious extremists and sign up to John Lennon's philosophy and 'Imagine no religion'. It may be a Roman Catholic priest, a Church of England vicar or a Free Church minister who has dreadfully abused his position, but as far as they are concerned we are all the same. The world would be a better place without religion as far as they are concerned. We all live in the shadow of bad publicity.

Again, whenever a man or woman of the cloth makes an appearance in a soap opera or television drama, they rarely do the cause any favours. How often the corrupt vicar is the murderer in the 'who-done-it'!

Where do we start to change the image that people have in their minds of the Church of Jesus Christ?

First impressions are important

First impressions may be almost totally wrong but they can be very deep and long lasting. An individual's first contact with their local church can come in a number of ways. It will often come from a view of the building. Already, a picture will be forming in their minds. Does it look well looked after? If there are grounds, are they well kept? Are there clear and understandable notice boards? What impression do your premises give to the passer by? J. B. Priestley wrote of a church that looked like 'a rich man that gives but never smiles'. Does the building convey virtue but lack warmth?

What about the publicity we produce? So much of it can be so very worthy but so very dull. Does the publication or advertisement look good? Does it make sense to the outsider? I recall a church that advertised in the local paper that it offered 'body ministry'! How would this have read I wonder to someone who was not 'in the know'? 'Has the church gone into the massage parlour business?'

Let's take a closer look at some of these areas.

The building

There are obviously certain 'givens' about our premises. We would all love modern, purpose-built buildings that are light, airy and flexible! But we have what we've got and we should make the best of it. Is the building in good repair? Would a coat of paint make a real difference? Windows covered in protective grilles can make a church look more like a prison, a place you want to get out of rather than a place of warmth and welcome that you want to get into!

Is there adequate car parking? This is a problem for many of our town and city centre churches, especially now that charging for parking on Sunday is becoming more wide spread. We are in the process of doubling the size of our own car park. Some of the congregation have objected that we should be encouraging people to walk or cycle to church (by the way, do you have a safe place where people can leave bikes?), but I have tried to explain that this is an evangelistic car park! It is not for us, but for those who do not yet come to church. The visitor will not come unless he or she can find a place to park. We should do our best to remove any potential barrier to them coming to church and thence to faith.

There are some 48,000 churches in the UK according to Christian Research figures. That is one church for every 1200 people. That compares to one pub for every 1000 people. In other words, there are not quite so many churches as pubs – four churches for every five pubs, but the average pub has four times as many visitors per week than the average church.[1] Why does the local pub so often have a more attractive image in people's minds than the local church?

The web site

For more and more people, a church's web site will be the first port of call to get more information about a local church. More than just information, this is where people form their first impressions when looking for a local church.

Here are some important points to consider:

1 Does your church have a web site? Sometimes, no web site at all can be better than a bad web site! Not having a web site does not necessarily mean that you are out of touch but a well-presented web site can be a powerful tool for engaging with your local community.
2 If you do have a website, is it clear and uncluttered? Any web site that is full of pictures, text and annoying flashing signs will turn most people off within a few seconds, and they will turn away from your site. It is important to have a well-designed web site, at least as professional as your notice board or newsletter, free from church jargon and 'Christianize' language. Furthermore, is your URL (Uniform Resource Locator) memorable? Does it give clear contact information and directions?
3 Does your web site convey the message that Church is about people? Too often, the web site can be filled with information about meetings, finances, buildings. It should rather be a way of introducing people outside the church to people inside the church. It is often good to include photos of members of the church on the site. The web site's purpose should primarily be to build relationships with people and ultimately, through people, with God.

The notice board

A few years ago we updated our notice board. The new one was lively, modern and colourful. But there were two problems. It was very difficult to read and it didn't actually tell people when the services were! So now we produce an A4 notice for each of the three church doors that gives information about what is happening the next Sunday. This is changed each Monday morning and it is clear to the visitor that the information is current. There would be nothing worse than a visitor plucking up the courage to come one week and finding that there is no service for whatever reason, even though the wooden board outside says 'Evensong Sunday at 6 p.m.'

Our services are roughly similar most weeks, but I know that this is not the case for every church, often for very practical reasons. I often wonder whether the casual visitor is able to work out whether the next Sunday is the third in the month and therefore the service is at 11 a.m., or is it the second Sunday and therefore the service is at the other building! This is partly why we have decided not to go down the route of the occasional 'seeker-sensitive' service. Our thought is that it would be embarrassing to invite a neighbour one week to a service that has been weeks in preparation and is creative, exciting and interesting. They enjoy it and say to the friend that has brought them, 'That was really good, can I come next week?'!!! Embarrassed response: 'Er, no it won't be like this next week. Come again in three months'!

The entrance area

An outsider makes it across the threshold. What do they come across?

I have long been convinced that the only people who actually read the notices in the vestibule are visitors. Like many churches, our premises are used by many outside groups – the blood donor service, parental access groups etc. What impression do they get as they come through the door?

So many church vestibules are cluttered and dark. There are notices for events that took place several weeks ago. Papers totally covered with A4 typing. Full of helpful information that no one will ever read! Then there are the rotas!!! Many of our churches seem to be 'rota-driven' churches! There are rotas for flowers, for stewards, for coffee, for anything else you can think of. Does it all need to be on display in the first part of the building that people come into? Surely there is a better place for such internal information?

Much better to have a few essential items attractively introducing aspects of the church's life and work. Pictures are of great value; they tell the visitor that the church is about people and people just like them are part of it. I know of one church that takes a photograph of every new member and the pictures are then displayed in the entrance area. The impression given is one of life and humanity.

And what of the essential facilities – the loos! In one church, they were right down at the front of the church so the poor visitor has to take 'the walk of shame' in front of everyone. In another, they were in an awful state and needed a good clean. In another church, they were non-existent! If at all possible, toilets should be easily accessible from the entrance area and clearly signposted.

It's useful to take a look at your building through a visitor's eyes. We learn to live with things an outsider would notice straight away. We sometimes ask people who have begun to settle with us, 'What was your first impression when you came into this church?' Their answers can be revealing and helpful.

You're welcome!

Welcoming visitors is a key ministry and deserves the best people. Would it be more strategic for the church leaders to be in the entrance area than locked away in a back room in prayer before the service? Could the prayer take place at another time? (And, why do we put the people with the most limited people skills on the door?) It's about first impressions again. Some welcomers can be too pushy and the visitor has already decided, 'If they are all like this, I'm not coming here again'. In my experience, most British visitors do not want to be 'greeted with a holy kiss' quite yet! Other welcomers are so busy greeting their friends that they all but miss the newcomer. Already an impression of unfriendliness is communicated. Rick Warren has said, 'Long before the pastor preaches, the visitors are already deciding whether or not they will come back.'[2]

What information is given to the visitor as they arrive? Are they loaded down with a variety of books in various shapes and sizes that they are unsure what they are supposed to do with? Is there a simple welcome leaflet or a welcome pack? Many churches produce a relatively inexpensive publication that helps a person to feel a little less anxious and a little more at home. Our own welcome leaflet has brief information about the staff team, the church programme ('A typical week at ABC') and contains an insert that can be filled in and left at the welcome desk as they leave, if they wish to. The weekly newsletter also has a small box on the front each week that begins, 'If this is your first visit we hope you will enjoy your time with us', then it gives a few pieces of basic information. We also have rolling information on the projection screen, that includes all the little essentials like 'Please turn off your mobile phone!'

Some churches welcome visitors publicly during the service. This is probably inappropriate in our culture, although it may work in some places. Generally, people who are coming to church for the first time prefer not to be the centre of attention.

Many churches are able to offer coffee after the service. This can be really helpful as long as there are people from the congregation who are looking out for the newcomers. Many churches have a reputation for being friendly, but it is only a case of the members being friendly among themselves! Standing alone drinking a cup of coffee among a crowd of people who are happily chatting away to one another can be a very lonely experience.

After the service, contacts are followed up with either a phone call or a visit. We hold occasional newcomers barbecues or teas; this helps us to meet them, and them to meet one another. The best people at befriending newcomers are other newcomers.

The best/worst advert of all

The Church, of course, is far more than the building and the deepest impression that people will have of a local church will be gained from the people they know who are a part of it. Being minister of a church in a reasonably compact town, I often meet people in the community who know members of the congregation. 'Does "so-and-so" go to your church?' they ask. I am always fascinated by what they say next. Answers have varied from the best – 'What a great guy. He is so reliable. He's always there if you want to talk' – to the worst – 'What a weird guy. He's so unfriendly. He never joins in anything. He's always last to arrive and first to leave'. And everything in between.

Paul tells the Corinthian Christians that they are a 'Letter from Christ' (2 Corinthians 3.2–3). So are all God's people. This letter is being read every day. People are making a judgement. The criteria are the way we live our lives, do our job, treat our families, care for our friends. The most powerful way to change misconceptions people have about the Church is for them to meet representatives of that Church that are loving, sincere and Christlike.

Another image that Paul uses is that of the Ambassador (2 Corinthians 5.20). We are Christ's representatives. The United Kingdom has some 17,000 ambassadors based here, representing countries throughout the world. The Church of Jesus Christ has twice that number of ordained minsters plus an army of lay people who represent him. Jesus represents us before the Father (Hebrews 9.24). We represent him before the world. As well as this being done on an individual basis, the Church can take active steps to become more involved in the local community.

We have to do this in a number of ways. There have been litter picks, gardening projects, decorating of a community building as well as ongoing work among the homeless and needy. All these initiatives help to change people's minds about their local church. How good it is to hear someone say, 'Oh, that's the church that cleared the garden for the young carers home', or, 'that's the group that decorated that old person's home'. After a recent litter pick, the local paper reported, 'The church has already helped in the community and made a real difference'. A councillor, who had no connection with the church, is quoted as saying, 'Organizations such as Andover Baptist Church are making a big difference to our community'. (The church's mission statement is 'Making a Difference 4 God'!)

Press releases, particularly if it is possible to include photographs, can be of real value. Local papers are always looking for stories with human interest.

A reputation can be very easy to get but very hard to lose. I have a reputation for not being the greatest at DIY. This, of course, is completely unfounded(!) but stems from one or two disasters in earlier years. I think I will have to build my own extension from scratch to get rid of the reputation! In the same way, the Church has a lot of ground to recover, a lot of negatives to wipe out before we can start building the positives in people's minds. This is not about 'spin' or 'impression management' but about giving people a clearer, more honest picture of a community that, while being far from perfect , cares and can offer hope to people who desperately need it.

Check list

- The building – what impression do your premises give to the passer by?
- The web site – is it clear, accessible and informative?
- The notice board – does it tell people what they need to know?
- The entrance area- is it bright and welcoming or cluttered and untidy?
- The welcome – are the people and publications the best they can be?
- Christians – what kind of reputation do your people have in the workplace?
- The church – what kind of activities is the church involved with in the community?

Notes

1. Brierley (2005).
2. Warren (1995).

References and further reading

Beer, David (2000), *50 Ways to Help Your Church Grow*, Eastbourne: Kingsway.
Benyon, Graham (2005), *God's New Community*, Leicester: Inter-Varsity Press.
Brierley, Peter (2005), *Building by Numbers*, London: Christian Research.
Warner, Rob (1994), *21st Century Church*, London: Hodder & Stoughton.
Warren, Richard (1995), *The Purpose Driven Church*, Grand Rapids, Michigan: Zondervan.

30. Researching your local context

PETER BRIERLEY

How much do you actually know about the local community in which your agency or church ministers? The purpose of this chapter is to give the basic principles of effective local research. The first question is to ask is why the church wants to do the research. Is it to evaluate the needs in their area with a view to starting a project to help meet some of those needs, such as providing a youth resource or older people's lunch-club? Is it to identify the disparity between those who attend the church and those living nearby to see who is not being touched by the church?

One church did such a survey and found that a very large number of single mothers were living in their immediate area, and began a ministry specifically to welcome and provide support for them. Or is the purpose of the survey to identify the opportunities and challenges church members face and to provide suitable teaching over the months ahead? At the outset, therefore, it is good practice to write down a sentence along the lines 'The purpose of this study is to . . .', recognizing that the outcomes may well affect the work of the church or agency over the next three to five years. Research can provide several things:

- The foundation for strategic planning and thinking (which Chapter 26 looks at in more detail).
- Encouragement in what you are already doing. This programme *works*! Guidance for the future work, perhaps to help focus on one particular strength rather than another.
- Basic information about your community in terms of age, gender, marital status, an occupational breakdown which can impact your future ministry.
- Trends (if it is a repeat study) showing which way things have gone over recent years, and how they might continue to go in the future. Such understanding can be very valuable in terms of resource planning.
- The basis for vision by indicating what might be possible.
- An overview of your area, parish, town, or even county or country.

Some surveys have assessed, for example, the involvement of local churches in providing volunteers for community service in a region;[1] sometimes the findings are much higher than expected.

Expect your research to result in decision-making by the church, otherwise it becomes just an interesting exercise with no real point other than gaining some intellectual knowledge.

Asking the right questions

This is always the critical part of any piece of research. If you ask the wrong questions, you don't get the answers you are wanting! Whether the research is carried out on the web, or through interviews of local households, or by means of a questionnaire sent or given to people for completion, the principles of questionnaire design are fundamental and are largely the same whatever means of enquiry is adopted.

Some principles of questionnaire design are:

- Only ask questions to which you really need the answers, not questions for answers you would like to have. This requires a vigorous focusing on the purpose of the study. Too many questions put people off.
- Group questions on the same theme together, so you might wish to have a series of questions on 'the local area', 'health and safety issues', 'church life', 'transport policy', 'economic concerns' as well as having a group for control questions with a title such as 'About you'. Put these theme headings on the form itself, since it both breaks up the questions and enables respondents to get a flavour of what ground you are covering.
- Make the initial questions relatively easy to answer, so that respondents get drawn into the theme of the form.
- Ensure that the wording of the forms is easy to understand, unambiguous, as short and crisp as possible, focused rather than broad, asking one question not two, positive rather than negative, and generally not asking for a detailed recall of events.
- Where possible, base the questionnaire on a pilot form sent to a small number of people, or from interviews with sample respondents.

If the form is an interview schedule make sure that the date, time and name of the interviewer are on each sheet. You will also need to provide the interviewer with something to show they are bone fide. A letter to interviewees should be sent in advance so that the person concerned can expect someone to call. It is sometimes necessary to let the local police know that the survey is being undertaken.

If the form is for self-completion by the respondent, it needs to be well designed. Make sure that questions do not go over the end of the page, and are in a legible and modern typeface. For young people, a few clip art illustrations lighten the look of the form. Always print the form on coloured paper as this generates a better response (green is the best colour), but use different colours for different groups of the sample for easier recognition of which comes from which group. Always put on the form instructions for what to do with it when it is completed, and the address to return it to (with Freepost address or stamped addressed envelope if possible).

Asking the right people

Sample selection

Unless you are going to every individual or household in your church or community (so making the survey a census), you will need to choose a sample of people to be approached. It is very important for the validity of the response that these people are randomly selected. Perhaps you will need to make a list of all the roads in your locality and the number of houses in each (which can probably be obtained from your Council Offices), and then select, say, every tenth house, which will mean choosing 9 houses in a street of 90 residences, and could mean missing out completely a small road of only 8 houses.

Response

Getting a good response is the crux of any survey. If you get too small a response, you can never tell whether the people who have not replied would or would not have said the same as the folk who did answer. This is the value of interviews, since most interviews go through to completion. What is a 'good response'? There is no agreed answer; many market research firms are happy to get from 10 to 20% response, although in the 1980s 50% was the norm. A postal questionnaire to non-Christian people will usually generate a much lower response than one to Christian people, as non-Christians do not see the point of replying.

Incentives

Do incentives help? 'Provide your name and address on a separate slip of paper to enter a draw for £25 of books' is an incentive Christian Research used in one survey, with excellent effect; the overall response was 44%, and some 35% of these gave their details. Perhaps a voucher for a meal at a local restaurant would be appreciated.

Covering letter

Part of the incentive to reply to any survey is the covering letter that accompanies the form. This needs to be very carefully written. It should indicate clearly:

* The purpose of the study,
* That all replies will be treated in complete confidence,
* The final date by which replies should be sent, and
* The address to whom the form should be returned (or when it will be collected).

Number to be contacted

How many people should be selected? Ideally, you need to get a minimum of about 500 replies for the answers to be statistically reliable. If therefore the response is likely to be 25% then you need to select 2000 people.

Reminder

In a postal questionnaire, or one delivered by hand to selected houses in your area, a reminder will invariably increase the response, often by as much as a further 10%. Two copies of the address labels need to be made at the beginning and, when a form is returned, that address deleted; reminders can then be sent to all those left after say 3 weeks after the initial distribution. This means that returned forms will carry some form of identifiers (often a number). It is essential that the list which carries the identifying numbers for reminder purposes is destroyed once the reminder has gone out; you have to act with integrity when you promise anonymity. If the forms will be collected by hand then you could create a list of which houses were given them and the date they were collected.

Getting the right replies

Quantitative data

The replies have to be analysed. Usually, this will be done by entering all the data on to a computer, but it is best to ensure that the programme you use is one which is capable of producing two-way tables. Just having worksheets will not give you the flexibility necessary for a good analysis. Many surveys will ask for gender and age-group of respondent. Your computer programme needs not just to be able to tell you that you have 300 men and 200 women, and 150 under 40 and 350 over 40, but to break these numbers down so that you know how many men are under 40 and how many over, and how many women are under 40 and how many over, ideally in a table such as that shown in Figure 30.1.

Figure 30.1

	Age-group		
	Under 40	40 & over	TOTAL
Men	80	220	300
Women	70	130	200
TOTAL	150	350	500

The best computer analysis tables will also provide percentages for numbers in each row and column and usually some statistical tests of significance as well. SPSS is used by many professionals, but Microsoft Excel or something similar can do the job well enough. The value of having the ability to get such two-way tables is that they help in understanding the replies. So, in the above example, the number of men aged 40 and over who replied was nearly 3 times the number under 40, while for women fewer than double the number of replies were from those aged 40 or over, a much smaller percentage, so older people responded more than younger, and men more than women.

Qualitative data

If the data is in the form of interviews then the analysis needs to focus around the topics raised in each question, and to see if some of the replies made reference to other replies. Thus, if in response to a question about what a person liked about living in a particular area, the reply was given 'the older people are very friendly' then you might wish to make a cross-reference to that in your comments about how replies vary by different ages. What were the differences or similarities between old and young people, or between men and women, for example?

Getting the right answers

Analysing answers on questionnaires is the critical part of a survey. Get the number crunching wrong and the entire exercise is in vain. There are two levels to the analysis, however, and it is essential that whoever is compiling the eventual report goes beyond the first into the second (many do not). The first part is taking the mass of information supplied by the study and making some kind of sense of it. It is like sorting out the evidence. Until the task is begun, there is no sure way of knowing what answers it may yield or surprises it may show. How the analysis is undertaken will depend to some extent on the person doing it and their particular professionalism, as well as on the computer program they have available, and on the expectations of those who initiated the study.

How the findings are expressed is also very important. There are some helpful rules, based on the work of Professor Andrew Ehrenberg, for giving statistical information. These are as follows:

- Make sure that tables and graphs tell (or illustrate) a story, and put that story in words as well as numbers and diagrams. 'As can be seen from the Table . . .', though if nothing can be seen don't bother to print the table!
- Round numbers up or down to two significant places, and never use a decimal place in percentages unless the first number is a single digit. So instead of saying 'the number of women teachers in training rose from 29,942 to 94,347' say, 'The number of women teachers in training rose from 30,000 to 94,000.' It is then much more easy to see that it is a threefold increase.
- Order the rows *and* columns in a table, so that the total goes from the largest to the smallest (or vice versa), and the items from A to Z, or whatever is appropriate.
- Figures are easier to compare in columns, so tables should be arranged accordingly.
- In a table also minimize the use of space and lines. There is a whole science to this aspect of making tables look attractive and not off-putting. Labelling is important also, and DO NOT PUT EVERY-THING IN CAPITALS as this is far harder to read (every item is the same height). The columns also need to be spaced evenly, whatever this may do for the individual column heading.

- Make averages of table rows or columns (or other summary measures), or work out the average age or cost or whatever to give some kind of sense. So while you might wish to say that 35% thought the price should be 80p, 22% 90p, 41% £1 and 2% £1.50, also say the average price was 92p, and then indicate what was, say, the average price from male and female respondents.
- Use graphs to show patterns not numbers, and give a written summary of what the graph is showing. Some have suggested that graphs essentially communicate the qualitative aspects of numbers, or are for 'indicating relationships'.

Getting the right meaning

Getting as far as a report with tables and graphs is not the end of the work. That first stage reveals the answers, but does not tell you what they mean, so interpreting them is essential. The differences in the *quality* of the information at your disposal should be noted:

- There is a difference between 'hard' data which is supported by a reasonable response from the target audience and 'soft' data which may come from interviews of a smaller number; both types of information are valuable in ascertaining the 'big picture'.
- It may well also be possible to add to your findings by looking at what others have found, whether these be similar investigations written up in books or papers stored in a library or downloaded from a relevant web site. For example, local data from the Population Census is available on <www.statistics.gov.uk>.

Having analysed your data, what steps should you take next? Here are some suggestions:

1 Get the overall picture. Try summarizing the results of your study in one sentence: 'This study shows that . . .'
2 Look at both strengths *and* trends if you have trend data. You may find something like: 'More women are attending this church than men, but, in the previous survey 5 years ago, the gap between the numbers of men and women was much greater.'
3 Where you can, compare the information with other studies, or government population figures, or similar relevant information. 'In this church, 28% of those who attend are 65 or over, but in our neighbourhood the proportion who are that age is only 18%.'
4 Focus on individual areas of importance. If there are relatively fewer women in church now than there used to be, does this vary by age or occupation? Analyse this factor as completely as you can by getting

more two-way tables of questions broken down by gender.

5 Draw out the reasons 'why'. If there are relatively fewer women in your church, why is this? Have more left, or have more died in the past year than usual? Look at your church membership records and see if they have changed in a similar way. Are the women actually leaving the church or simply attending less frequently? If the latter is the case, is this because of a clash of priorities, such as children wanting to play football on Sunday morning or the need to visit aged parents?

6 Then think through the implications. If attending on a Sunday morning is difficult, should the church start a service at say 4 o'clock? Or a service on a day other than Sunday? This is looking at the 'so what?' question. Some will say this is difficult. Yes, it is! Note, however, that your interpretation, while it may be valid for you, is not necessarily the only perspective or conclusion that can be drawn. It is also important not to just read into your findings the results you expected: 'of course some of the older people have died'. It is the *consequences* of what that means that need to be spelled out.

7 Here are some questions which may be helpful in thinking through what the information might mean. Is the information new, that is, does it fill a gap in previously available knowledge? Does it solve an unanswered problem? Does it conflict with, or add to, previous understandings? Does your data define the boundaries into which previous thinking should be put? Does your data provide a new perspective on previous information? Does your data suggest more detailed research should be undertaken in one area? Does it throw open new questions, or even new research methods?

Getting the right conclusions

The interpretation of the data is as critical as the original analysis, but this should not be the end of the story. A study only helps the world along if the outcome is *action* of some kind; information is useful if it enhances your decision-making. However, while information is one of the most crucial elements in decision-making, it is not the only element. Data after all is but an interpretation of reality; it is not reality itself. Some people may react, 'I don't mind what the study says, we are going to do this!'

Some actions may be *negative*: 'Now we know what people feel, there is no need for us to consider starting a playgroup for under 5s.' But other actions will be *positive*. Some actions may be *suspended*: 'We will review the situation in 12 months' time (or do another survey then) before finally deciding.'

What are the criteria for trying to understand what actions should follow research? Here are some suggestions:

1 Who were the majority of the respondents in your survey? What actions are they most likely to want?
2 Which actions would lead to your church reaching the largest number of people, or enable your organization to survive longest, enable you to make the greatest profit, or do the most good? What is your key market?
3 What do people expect a church or agency like yours to do? In other words, are you wanting to improve your image or take actions which some might find surprising, even out of character?
4 What kind of resources do you have? Are they especially suitable for working in a particular direction? Do you have procedures for the kind of circumstances in which you now find yourself?
5 What are the long-term consequences of taking this action? In other words, if we do this now, what will we then have to do next month, next year or in 5 years?
6 Do our existing structures enable us to do what we believe we should be doing in the future?
7 Ultimately, most major decisions are controlled by the vision of the key person, minister or senior executive. What is their vision?

Getting the right communication

Whatever the result of your analysis, sensing the implications, and working out your interpretation, the results have to be communicated. A succinct summary of such might be 'Use simple words, simple figures, simple visuals.' The length of a report is not a criterion of its success; succinctness and relevance is. Include a summary of recommendations (which is not the same as a summary of findings).

The rules for simple numbers have already been outlined above. Good visuals (graphs, pie charts, bar charts) are those which tell a story. Use maps when suitable.

Think of the reader, or viewer, or whoever is hearing your message, when writing, talking or drawing. If necessary, buy a book on how to communicate!

Note

1. For example, Andrew Presland of the East Northamptonshire Faith Group conducted such a study in 2005; details from <andrewpresland@ harboroughroad58.freeserve.co.uk>.

31. Sustaining a process of change

TIM HARLE

Approaching change

One of the best-selling Harvard Business Review reprints of the 1990s was John Kotter's *Leading Change: Why Transformation Efforts Fail.*[1] Figures quoted for the failure rate of corporate change initiatives hover around the 60 or 70% mark. I am not aware of statistics for churches, but would be surprised if results are that different.

Which is a great shame. Because this chapter is written in the passionate belief that the Christian tradition has much to offer those engaging in change, whether at an organizational or individual level. It begins by outlining some theological pointers and goes on to outline a framework for understanding different reactions to change. Only then does it identify key elements of a sustainable change process. This approach is deliberate. For this is an area, above all, where ticking boxes will not produce lasting results.

In addition to a theological understanding, our approach will be informed by a number of perspectives. These include observations from the natural world, from the business scene, and from insights of complexity theory. Although the expression 'change management' is widely used, we should pause and ask how much we can actually manage change. The dominant Newtonian world-view implies a predictability – if 'management' (or the priest, deacons or eldership team) does this, then that will follow. Complexity theory (sometimes referred to as chaos theory) give a much more nuanced view: 'You can never direct a living system. You can only disturb it.'[2] Observations from the natural world illustrate self-organization (ant hills are often quoted). We are introduced to emergent properties, and taught to recognize the importance of boundaries where developments often take place (the so-called 'edge of chaos'):[3] a key church programme is named Encounters on the Edge.[4] The management ecology approach offers a stark reminder to those who long for permanence: 'Equilibrium is death'.[5] It is noteworthy how biological models of cells, involving growth and subdivision, are used among churches.

Commenting on the business scene, two respected strategists, Gary

327

Hamel and C. K. Prahalad, reflected that 'Enormous managerial energy . . . [has] been devoted to turnarounds, rescues, and massive "change" programs, yet isn't the real goal to avoid a crisis-sized transformation problem by creating a capacity for continuous renewal deep within the company?'[6] If we replaced 'company' with 'church(es)' – whether in universal or particular form – then 'a capacity for continuous renewal' looks remarkably relevant. We can reflect, too, on the need for continuous renewal at an individual level.[7] The last of Steven Covey's seven habits of highly effective people[8] was 'sharpening the saw', covering principles of balanced self-renewal.

Word association often reveals underlying attitudes. A group with whom I was working recently produced a typical list. On being shown the word 'change', they wrote down the first word that came into their head. The result produced the usual mix of powerful images – *panic, hope, obstruct, upheaval, positive, resistance, again, fear*. Note the strength of both positive and negative emotions (the latter typically outscoring the former by three to one). It is rare to get neutral words (though my favourites include 'loose' and 'wheel').

We have to ask whether churches contribute to this attitude. We can learn from liturgists, whose *lex orandi, lex credendi* loosely translates as how we worship shapes what we believe. So how does our worship shape up? We might start with the popular Victorian hymn, 'Abide with me'. One verse reads

Change and decay
in all around I see.
Oh, thou who changest not,
abide with me. (H. F. Lyte [1793–1847])

Change is linked to decay. But we are reassured that the Almighty does not change. Lest we think the problem is confined to Victorians, consider an altogether older tradition, that of adding the *Gloria Patri* to the end of Jewish Psalms. Since around the sixth century CE, many have added:

As it was in the beginning
is now and shall be for ever.

Added as part of a Christological debate, one wonders how many contemporary worshippers are aware of this subtlety. Constant repetition hardly encourages openness to change. Yet change is at the heart of the Christian gospel, so we turn to some key theological features.

Towards a theology of change

Although we cannot engage in detailed discussion, we can note some key themes that are relevant to our task of creating a sustainable process of change.

God. The Holy Trinity offers a dynamic model of identity and relationship. In a continually changing world, God is creator, redeemer and sustainer.

> When you send forth your spirit, they are created;
> and you renew the face of the ground. (Psalm 104.32 [NRSV])

We can reflect on transformational change as we try to comprehend the incarnation and transfiguration, and, supremely, the crucifixion and resurrection of Jesus.

Scriptures. The Christian canon has a powerful *inclusio*. In the opening chapter of Genesis, the earth was a formless void until the breath of God moved over the turbulent waters, bringing order out of chaos. In the closing chapters of Revelation, we hear of one who was seated on the throne saying, 'See, I am making all things new' (Revelation 21.5 [NRSV]; note the tense). In between are endless examples of change – some sustained, others not – in both communities and individuals.

Tradition. Books such as *Faith in Momentum* and *The Dynamic of Tradition*[9] remind us that this is anything but static.

Church. Pope John XXIII introduced the Italian word *aggiornamento*, 'bringing things up to date', which featured prominently during the Second Vatican Council. It has been heard less often recently. St Paul used a natural metaphor, the body, and we have noted the contemporary language of cell churches.

The individual. We are offered the chance to be ransomed, healed, restored, forgiven. St Paul emphasized the radical nature of the transformation offered: 'If anyone is in Christ, there is a new creation: everything old has passed away; see, everything has become new!' (2 Corinthians 5.17 [NRSV]).

Conversion. A multivalent word, its richness of meaning is diminished if it is applied in too narrow a context (for example, in confining it to those joining specific faith communities). One of the Greek words it translates, *metanoia*, covers an interplay between process, event and attitudinal change.[10]

A framework for understanding people's attitudes to change

First and foremost, we need to understand how, and why, people react differently to change. Without this, any change process will not be sustainable. With our theological background, we can also gain valuable insights from various disciplines, from management ecology to psychology.

S Curves

Figure 30.1 S curve

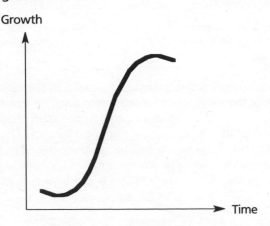

A natural pattern, which we can observe in many situations, from civilizations to relationships

The natural world offers many examples of cycles of growth and decay, for example, in seasons and crops (Figure 30.1). Such S curves can also be seen in the flourishing and decline of civilizations, in organizations and in personal relationships. Some never recover and cease to exist; others burst forth into new forms. Organizations (including churches) can become victims of their own success; exciting new initiatives become established routines and barriers to change. Others emerge from turbulence to new horizons. At any time, an organization such as a church will be at different stages of overlapping S curves, and leaders will be at different stages of personal S curves. Organizations and individuals that succeed understand how to recognize these different stages, and the different approaches needed.

For sustainable change, the transition from one S curve to the next is crucial (Figure 30.2). This is where powerful personal learning and

Figure 30.2

Breaking out of a previous growth phase may involve a
period of turbulence, before embarking on new growth.

development can take place. Studying leaders across generations,
Warren Bennis and Robert Thomas noted how profound personal
change often came from unexpected, outside, sources: they coined the
term 'crucibles' for such defining moments.[11] The Dutch management
ecologist, Peter Robertson, uses the metaphor of salmon leaps,[12] noting how salmon gain momentum by diving into points of maximum
turbulence. Parallels with church and individual life are compelling.

Attachment

> Two respected service organizations of long-standing were merg-
> ing. The leadership team was worried that a crucial group of
> professionals was not taking part in launch events. Conversations
> showed that attachment to their profession overrode their organi-
> zational loyalties. The merger went ahead successfully.

A major insight into reactions to change derives from John Bowlby's
work on attachment.[13] Attachment is an instinctive, if risky, process.
Of particular significance is the object of attachment: the ideal is safe,
or secure, attachment.

Behaviour driven by the attachment process will, in any new
situation, focus people on establishing connections with something
familiar and valued from the past. Recent research[14] has shown how
attachment may not just be to other people, but to ideas and forms

331

(referred to as 'matter'). We attach in varying degrees to people or matter; in a church context, examples of matter attachment might include denominational or local traditions, and liturgical forms.

Bridges notes the importance of letting go, before moving through the neutral zone to new beginnings.[15] When people are in an unfamiliar environment, it is important to promote – and, if necessary, re-establish – 'safe attachment'. Unsafe attachment occurs when we detect inconsistency in our object of attachment: our energy is directed to re-establishing safe attachment. Safe attachment occurs when we detect consistency in our object of attachment: we can 'trust' it. 'The consummation of attachment . . . [is] a relaxed state in which one can begin to 'get on with things', pursue one's projects, to *explore*.'[16]

Exploration

Exploration is an instinctive and equally strong process. Our need for personal growth, learning, etc. takes over once our need for security – safe attachment – has been satisfied. Exploration involves the drive to discover what we do not know without the need to know possible benefits. It occurs when we have 'safe' attachment, and provides the creative energy needed to deal with the challenges of change.

A vivid illustration of attachment and exploration can be seen by observing what happens when a young child is taken by its parent(s) or carer to a party full of unfamiliar people. Initially, most children will cling – often literally – to their 'secure base' (Bowlby's term). But when it is time to go home, the typical child cannot be found anywhere. The intervening steps are vivid examples of the interplay between attachment and exploration.

Emotional reactions

> A feature of life in former coalmining communities included the holding of quasi-religious ceremonies to enable the community to move on in their collective journey. A former bishop of Durham described addressing a demonstration at the closure of a coal pit as 'like conducting a funeral service.'
> See Jenkins, David, 2002, p. 123.

A significant contribution to dealing with change comes from the pastoral perspective on change as a grief journey (Figure 30.3). Elisabeth Kübler-Ross described five stages: denial, anger, bargaining, depression and acceptance (though not necessarily in this order).[17] Both individual and communal reactions to change can reflect these stages.

Figure 30.3 Change as a grief journey

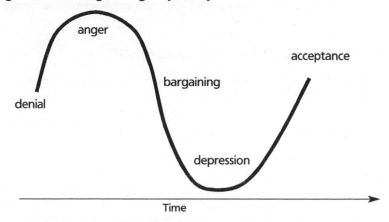

Insights from pastoral counselling help us understand people's reactions to change, and how to work through them.
Note: after Kübler-Ross, 1970

Figure 30.4 Emotions during change

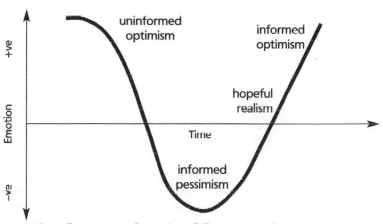

The roller coaster of emotions follows a typical pattern
Note: after Conner, 1998

Daryl Conner has developed the recognition of emotions in responding to change (Figure 30.4).[18] His journey starts with 'uninformed optimism', then moves on through 'informed pessimism' to 'hopeful realism' and 'informed optimism' to completion. In both schemes, it is important not to deny the early reactions, but work through them from a passive to an active acceptance of the situation.

Key elements of a sustainable change process

We are now in a position to draw out some key elements in a process to promote sustainable change.

Demonstrate relentless consistency

Change leaders need to demonstrate consistency[19] in all they do and say. Such behaviour creates safe attachment and demonstrates alignment with deeply held values. By doing so, we can build a foundation of trust from which the challenges of change can be confidently tackled in a mutually supportive environment.

Create a secure framework

We can use our understanding of attachment and exploration to provide a secure framework in which people can exercise their natural tendency to explore. Note the vivid contrast between this approach and some conventional change management writings. Far from creating 'burning platforms', the leaders' role is to provide the secure environment to encourage exploration.

Develop a compelling vision

Hebrew wisdom literature speaks across the centuries: 'Where there is no vision, the people perish' (Proverbs 29.19 [NRSV]) has passed into Anglo-Saxon culture. Yet it is based on a mistranslation in the King James Bible. The verb means something like 'lose constraint'; a good paraphrase would be 'without a vision, the people run around and do their own thing'. Two and a half millennia later, US researchers discovered something remarkably similar when studying companies which endured: they were *Built to Last*.[20] Whether for a company or a church, change needs to be aligned with the organization's vision.

We can identify the following components of a compelling vision:

- **Enduring components**. *Purpose* and *values* define an organization.[21] For change to be sustainable, it must complement and add to the organization's purpose and values. If it is at odds, it will ultimately wither on the vine. A compelling purpose must be worthwhile, so churches ought to be well placed. Values define

334

> An organizational prided itself on its investment in project man-
> agement training. Certificates and diplomas adorned office walls.
> But staff did not trust one another, or share information. A high
> profile change programme collapsed in a costly fashion.

what we will and won't do in pursuit of our purpose: they help us
resolve dilemmas.
- **Changing components**. *Big goals*[22] and *vivid descriptions* describe
  the changes needed, in line with our purpose and values. To be
  sustaining, these need to excite those who will be affected by the
  change. Big goals are mountains we climb in pursuit of our purpose. Vivid descriptions are mental images of what it will be like to
  fulfil our part in the journey.

Creating a strong vision is not about writing it down and sending
out a well designed newsletter. It is about fostering a conversation
which provides meaningful context for everything we do. It is about
consistent behaviour which aligns with the vision.

Live leadership

Many elements of a sustainable change process relate to leadership,
but two particular requirements can be highlighted.[23]
- **Lead quietly**.[24] Following up the *Built to Last* research referred to
  above, Jim Collins applied a similar approach to leaders in *Good to*

> A new leader began to engage the leadership team in a much-
> needed change programme by opening up about personal feelings
> on getting the 'top job'. Given the organization's macho manage-
> ment tradition, this involved an exciting mix of risk and trust . . .
> which was rewarded by the response of a majority of co-workers.

Great.[25] This produced some unexpected findings. In contrast to
headline-hitting Chief Executive Officers (CEOs), Collins found
executives who '[build] enduring greatness through a paradoxical
blend of personal humility and professional will'. It is hard to read
of such leaders without being reminded of one who described
himself as one who serves, who carried on while his closest
companions slept, who laid down his life for his friends, who ultimately endured.

- **Distribute leadership**. The idea of distributed leadership is well captured in a book subtitled *A Practical Guide for Ordinary Heroes*. In it, George Binney and colleagues outline the results of an Ashridge research programme. They echo Collins's research: 'Showing some vulnerability is a key element in leading'.[26] They write of leaders 'living with permanent transition'.[27] We have seen how important consistency is among leaders at all levels: change agents (see below) have an important role to play.

Identify key roles, and the right people to fill them

Three particular roles are crucial for building sustainable change.
- **Sponsor**. A respected leader who demonstrates the organization's vision and values. Depending on the scale of the change, they may be a local minister, area superintendent or (arch)bishop. They need to demonstrate consistent behaviour and provide visible commitment. They are crucial to good governance.
- **Project manager**. Managing projects is covered in Chapter 22. Here, we can note that change programmes need clear, realistic plans with clear responsibilities. The project manager's role is different from that of the sponsor: they should be encouraged not simply to deliver a change, but to ensure that it works in practice.
- **Change agents**. Irrespective of formal structures, a crucial contribution to success is made by involving a group of stakeholders, sometimes referred to as 'change champions'. These are individuals who tend to emerge through their commitment – or sometimes resistance – to the change. They are invaluable in making sure that ideas work on the ground, and acting as a focus for two-way communication.

A new manager started to introduce some much-needed changes to improve customer service. One member of staff complained passionately. Described as 'difficult' by their manager, they turned out to be one of the very best change agents.

Engage with those affected by change

It is important to engage people, working collaboratively at all levels, not trickling down through a hierarchy, but involving a 'diagonal slice' (from worship leader to youth group member). This is one area where change agents (see above) can come into their own. Stakeholder mapping can be a useful discipline to clarify out who will be affected – usually, more than you first expected.

The Benedictine tradition has an apposite view. Chapter 3 of the Rule of St Benedict states that, 'Whenever anything important has to be done in the monastery the Abbott must assemble the whole community and explain what is under consideration . . . The reason why we say that all should be called in council is this: It is often to a younger brother that the Lord reveals the best course'.[28]

Reverse three questions

The first contact people often have with change initiatives involves asking the question 'How?' How am I supposed to deal with the reordered church interior? How do I know when to stand/sit/kneel during the new service? They then move on to the 'What?' What can I do to help in the new coffee shop? What does being a lay pastoral assistant involve? But it is the third question that often surfaces when it is too late: 'Why are we doing this?'

In building a sustainable change process, it is helpful to reverse this order.

- **Why?** Until people can answer the question, 'Why change?', they are unlikely to engage fully. This is where a compelling case for change, aligned to vision and values, is important. Frankl approvingly quotes Nietzsche: 'He [*sic*] who has a *why* to live for can bear almost any *how*.'[29]
- **What?** Once people understand why a change is happening, they can move on to ask, 'What is involved?'
- **How?** If the first two questions are answered positively, the third, 'How do I . . . ?', becomes more straightforward to answer.

When any of these questions is ignored, change risks becoming bogged down in conflict and confusion based on different assumptions. When answers are shared, there is a better chance of reaching agreement and sustaining change.

Tell stories

Societies through history use stories for learning and building identity, as a glance through the pages of scripture demonstrates.[30] Many communities learn through engaging in conversation. Alastair McIntosh writes powerfully of the Celtic bardic tradition in *Soil and Soul*.[31]

Celebrate success

However small, early success breeds confidence. Encourage infectious joy. But do not forget that one of the errors listed by Kotter[32] was Declaring Victory Too Soon.

Grow through failure

A US stock exchange offers an unexpected parallel with the natural world, and highlights the importance of risk-taking. NASDAQ's Robert Greifeld reminds us that, 'For companies focused on organic growth, failure – in reasonable proportion to success – is a sign of health.'[33] Once again, substituting 'churches' for 'companies' is thought-provoking.

Honour the past

> A church had separate congregations for traditional and contemporary services. A Lent study group investigating ancient liturgies discovered shared riches. The Good Friday liturgy they created enthused a wide range of people and became a staple of church life.

Too many changes inadvertently imply that what is being replaced is somehow inferior. Recognizing where attachment may lie, it is vital to recognize our heritage, building on core strengths and values.

Work to people's strengths

There is a growing recognition in many fields – work, education psychology – that we concentrate on weaknesses and how to remedy them. In their book, *Now Discover Your Strengths*,[34] Marcus Buckingham and Donald O. Clifton report how Martin Seligman of the American Psychological Association found over forty thousand studies on depression, but only forty on the subject of joy, happiness or fulfilment.

Do a few things and do them well

This is one of the marks of healthy churches identified by Robert Warren.[35]

Summary: the paradox of change

We have seen the importance of safe attachment, providing a secure base to promote exploration. We have understood the importance of not getting stuck in S curves, of the turbulence encountered when jumping from one curve to another. We have learned of the emotional roller coaster involved in change. And we have outlined some key elements that contribute to a sustainable change process.

Herein lies an apparent paradox: creating a secure environment promotes exploration, growth and continuous renewal. We can note a remarkable parallel with two of the three Benedictine vows: of stability and conversion of life. Members of the Ampleforth Community sum up much as they write how 'the call to conversion of life is in effect a vow to change, to never remain still either in self-satisfied fulfilment or self-denying despair'.[36]

Notes

1. Kotter, 1995. Subsequently reprinted many times, for example, in *Harvard Business Review on Leading through Change*, 2006, Boston, Massachusetts: Harvard Business School Press.

2. Maturana and Varela, 1992, p. 162.

3. See, for example: Wheatley, 1999; Olson and Eoyang, 2001. Robertson, 2005, uses this perspective.

4. Based at Church Army, Sheffield. See <www.encountersontheedge. org.uk>.

5. Pascale, Millemann and Gioja, 2000, p. 19. Rendle applies insights from the new world of sciences, helpfully distinguishing between linear and chaotic change (1998, p. 101). However, in contrast to Pascale et al., he sees equilibrium as a state that systems naturally seek (p. 62ff.).

6. Hamel and Prahalad, 1996. The quotation is from the Preface to the paperback edition, p. x.

7. Black and Gregersen, 2002, bring out the links between individual and organizational change.

8. Covey, 1992.

9. Guiver, 1990; Allchin, 1981.

10. John Finney demonstrated how people came to faith through a long process in Finney, 1992. See also Wakefield, 2006.

11. Bennis and Thomas, 2002.

12. Robertson, 2005, p. 126.

13. Bowlby's work is hardly accessible: the Attachment and Loss trilogy extends to over 1400 pages: *Attachment* (1969), *Separation* (1973) and *Loss* (1980). Even someone who admires Bowlby describes it as 'hard going for the faint-hearted' (Holmes, 1993, p. 1).

14. Robertson, 2005, pp. 61–73.

15. Bridges, 2003.

16. Holmes, 1993, p. 67 (italics orig.).

17. Kűbler-Ross, 1970.

18. Conner, 1998. His development of Kűbler-Ross's work is on pp. 131–5; the 'uninformed optimism' journey on p. 137.

19. It is important to understand 'consistency' in context. Far from a uniformity which stifles creativity, consistency promotes exploration.

20. Collins and Porras, 1994. The following summary is indebted to this work.

21. Vision and Values are the first two of 'The Four Vs of Leadership', in Peter Shaw's book of that name (2006).

22. Collins and Porras coined the expression BHAGs – Big Hairy Audacious Goals – for these.

23. Leadership competencies are well described by Daniel Goleman in his work on emotional intelligence. See Goleman, Boyatzis and McKee, 2002.

24. *Leading Quietly* is the title of a book by the business ethicist Joe Badaracco (Boston MA: Harvard Business School Press, 2002). In it, he emphasizes the importance of small events, of messy everyday challenges dealt with by the people working away from the limelight.

25. Collins, 2001, p. 20.

26. Binney, Wilke and Williams, 2005, p. 48.

27. Ibid., p. 231.

28. Parry and De Waal, 1990, p. 15.

29. Frankl, 1959, p. 109.

30. Rendle (1998) refers to the Wilderness Wanderings and Exile as instances of powerful, if chaotic, change. Although he does not use the terminology, these are good examples of turbulent crucibles or defining moments for a whole people.

31. McIntosh, 2001.

32. See n. 1.

33. In Greifeld, 2004.

34. Buckingham and Clifton, 2004. The Seligman quote is on p. 129.

35. Warren, 2004.

36. Dollard, Marett-Crosby and Wright, 2002, p. 201.

References and further reading

Allchin, A. M. (1981), *The Dynamic of Tradition*, London: Darton, Longman & Todd.

Badaracco, Joe (2002), *Leading Quietly*, Boston, Massachusetts: Harvard Business School Press.

Bennis, Warren G., and Robert J. Thomas (2002), *Geeks and Geezers: How Era, Values and Defining Moments Shape Leaders*, Boston, Massachusetts: Harvard Business School Press.

Binney, George, Gerhard Wilke and Colin Williams (2005), *Living Leadership*, Harlow: Financial Times Prentice Hall.

Black, J. Stewart, and Hal B. Gregersen (2002), *Leading Strategic Change*, Harlow: Financial Times Prentice Hall.

Bowlby, John (1969), *Attachment*, London: Hogarth, repr. Pimlico 1997–8.
Bowlby, John (1973), *Separation*, London: Hogarth, repr. Pimlico 1997–8.
Bowlby, John (1980), *Loss*, London: Hogarth, repr. Pimlico 1997–8.
Bridges, William (2003), *Managing Transitions*, 2nd edn, London: Nicholas Brealey.
Buckingham, Marcus, and Donald O. Clifton (2004), *Now, Discover Your Strengths: How to Develop Your Talents and Those of the People You Manage*, London: Simon & Schuster.
Collins, J. (2001), *Good to Great: Why Some Companies Make the Leap . . . and Others Don't*, London: Random House.
Collins, James C., and Jerry I. Porras (1994), *Built to Last*, London: Random House.
Conner, Daryl R. (1998), *Managing at the Speed of Change*, Chichester: John Wiley & Sons.
Covey, Steven R. (1992), *The Seven Habits of Highly Effective People*, London: Simon & Schuster.
Dollard, Kit, Anthony Marett-Crosby and Timothy Wright (2002), *Doing Business with Benedict: The Rule of St Benedict and Business Management: A Conversation*, London and New York: Continuum.
Finney, John (1992), *Finding Faith Today*, Swindon: Bible Society.
Frankl, Viktor E. (1959), *Man's Search for Meaning*, London: Hodder & Stoughton.
Goleman, Daniel, Richard Boyatzis and Annie McKee (2002), *The New Leaders: Transforming the Art of Leadership into the Science of Results*, London: Little, Brown.
Greifeld, Robert (2004), 'How CEOs Manage Growth Agendas', *Harvard Business Review*, July–August.
Guiver, George (1990), *Faith in Momentum*, London: SPCK.
Hamel, Gary, and C. K. Prahalad (1996), *Competing for the Future*, Boston, Massachusetts: Harvard Business School Press.
Holmes, Jeremy (1993), *John Bowlby and Attachment Theory*, London and New York: Brunner-Routledge.
Jenkins, David (2002), *The Calling of a Cuckoo: Not Quite an Autobiography*, London and New York: Continuum.
Kotter, John P. (1995), 'Leading Change: Why Transformation Efforts Fail', *Harvard Business Review*, March–April 1995.
Kotter, John P. (1996), *Leading Change*, Boston, Massachusetts: Harvard Business School.
Kübler-Ross, Elisabeth (1970), *On Death and Dying*, London: Tavistock, repr. Routledge.
McIntosh, Alastair (2001), *Soil and Soul: People Versus Corporate Power*, London: Aurum.
Maturana, Humberto, and Francisco Varela (1992), *The Tree of Knowledge: The Biological Roots of Human Understanding*, Boston, Massachusetts: Shambala.
Olson, Edwin E., and Glenda Eoyang (2001), *Facilitating Organization Change: Lessons from Complexity Science*, San Francisco, California: Jossey-Bass/Pfeiffer.

Parry, Abbot, and Esther de Waal (1990), *The Rule of St Benedict*, Leominster: Gracewing.

Pascale, Richard T., Mark Millemann and Linda Gioja (2000), *Surfing the Edge of Chaos*, London and New York: Texere.

Rendle, Gilbert R. (1998), *Leading Change in the Congregation*, Herndon, Virginia: Alban Institute.

Robertson, Peter (2005), *Always Change a Winning Team*, London: Marshall Cavendish Business.

Shaw, Peter (2006), *The Four Vs of Leadership*, Chichester: Capstone.

Wakefield, Gavin (2006), *Conversion Today*, Evangelism Series 75, Cambridge: Grove Books.

Warren, Robert (2004), *The Healthy Churches Handbook*, London: Church House Publishing.

Wheatley, Margaret J. (1999), *Leadership and the New Science*, San Francisco, California: Berrett-Koehler.

32. Needing a change agent?

JENNIFER TANN

Lewis Carroll's Cheshire Cat was an elusive creature; quixotic, questioning, catalytic and with a habit of disappearing – leaving behind a sense of its presence. Lest this sounds scary, think of the occasions when innovation or organizational change hasn't worked out as intended. Hindsight is a wonderful thing and what often becomes clear after the event is that effective innovation and change demands several different roles. A key role is the catalyst, an individual who enables, rather than implements. This is the change agent. In what follows, Section A provides seven examples from a variety of sectors, including the Church, to show the change agent at work in different situations. Section B discusses the roles required in change, in particular the change agent, together with his/her behaviour and personality characteristics, from which it should be possible for organizations to identify their own Cheshire Cat.

Section A

Midway through 1999, a pharmaceutical advisor to a Manchester primary care trust (PCT) became aware of the possibility that a large number of unwanted pregnancies might result from the celebrations of Millennium Eve. At the time, pharmacists were not allowed to dispense the 'morning after pill' without a doctor's prescription. And the price charged was too high for people in an inner-city area of social deprivation. Acting as a change agent (external to the pharmacies in the PCT) the pharmaceutical advisor decided to initiate Emergency Hormonal Contraception. Outcry ensued – questions were asked in very high places nationally but, through persistence (change agents don't take 'No' for an answer), political networking, addressing local pharmacists' anxieties, recognizing what protocols had to be in place – and ensuring that they were – an initial group of ten pharmacies was ready to provide the service. What was an audacious move in 2000 is now a mainstream service, nationally.

A major UK manufacturer of underground drainage pipes for the construction industry had a product failure – a junction pipe. The trouble was made worse by the fact that, being underground, the fault was not immediately detected and a considerable number had been installed. An external change agent, a consultant, was asked to facilitate the development of a design brief for the replacement product. She requested that the original product development team be present. Having identified the perceived design faults of the original product, the group constructed a 'storyline' of how the product was designed and brought to market, identifying the design brief principles which should have been used, along the way. At the end of the day, working with their new design brief principles, the group produced the brief for the replacement junction pipe. There were other outcomes too: the original team, whose members had been engaging in cross-functional blame, stopped blaming each other; people recognized that failure (in a no-blame environment) provides excellent organizational learning; and the principles for the design brief were generic and could be employed for other products.

The managing director of a Midlands housing association recognized that a complete transformation of the organization was required. He held discussions throughout the organization and, after August Bank Holiday weekend in 2003, threw down the gauntlet to all staff to join him on the journey. He listed 15 points encapsulating what he had learned about the organization during the previous year – some good, some not at all good. He continued, 'We now know the extent of the job ahead and burying our head in the sand is not an option.' He appointed a change agent to facilitate major cultural change throughout the organization, with himself acting as sponsor. Each employee was given a copy of Spencer Johnson's (1998) *Who Moved My Cheese?*, a story about three mice whose cheese was provided in the same place for them each day. Until one day it wasn't. Each mouse behaved differently in response to this perceived threat. 'Finding the cheese' became the metaphor for change in the housing association as staff considered how they were going to engage with change and whether they were prepared to challenge the status quo. The managing director publicly identified the key tasks of the change agent and undertook to update employees fortnightly. One of the ways in which he challenged staff to compare their organization with others was to take them on a visit to what he considered to be an exemplar organization in London. He also wrote to local Chief Executive Officers (CEOs) of companies with reputations for outstanding customer relations, asking whether they would be prepared to second a customer services manager for a short period as part of their social responsibility agenda. The walls of the office building became picture galleries for a poster in cartoon style headed

'Achieving Centre of Excellence by 2007', besides flip charts from the many workshops on change. The results have been impressive. Part way through the planned five-year change programme the housing association group, of which this was a member, merged to become one of the larger associations nationally. But not before the Audit Commission had commended the 'strong, clear and passionate leadership creating a culture which supports continuous improvements'.[1]

Becoming a change agent in a large hospital trust is not easy. But one manager in a new hospital project became a change agent through her ability to identify multiple stakeholder needs and broker a high-trust relationship between managers and clinicians, an area that is often particularly fraught. 'Change agent' was not part of her job description but her skills in dealing with emergent issues and frequent design changes without alienating architects, engineers, other managers or clinicians were quickly recognized, and the project moved forward far more effectively as a result.

How about the change agent in church organizations? Is there a role? And is it necessary? The answer is emphatically 'yes'. From cathedral to Church of England diocesan officer to village church, change agents have enabled groups of people to think the unthinkable, plan new ways forward and implement change. An English parish church cathedral, which lacked the endowments of a medieval foundation, was faced with having to produce its annual budget in the context of an interregnum and a level of income which was not increasing at the rate of inflation. The projected budget was likely to be a replica of the previous year's – with cuts. The Chapter, encouraged by an archdeacon, charged the residentiary canons with the task of going back to the drawing board in order to develop a new strategy on which the budget could be based. The group planned two days away with a lay member of the chapter, the change agent, during which they constructed stories of the future which were informed by current contextual data on congregations, urban plans, as well as the role of the cathedral church and its staff in the diocese. The residentiary canons divided into two groups and worked in separate rooms to construct, respectively, realistic positive and negative stories of the future (on a five-year timescale). The positive scenario was built around increased giving by the business community, enabling new building and repair work to be undertaken. The negative scenario contained tales of woe from dry rot, to the dead pregnant teenager found propped against a tombstone in the churchyard one morning, while 'still the choir sang Palestrina'. Having shared their respective stories, the groups retired to their rooms to work out what they should do in the light of their respective scenarios. The positive

345

scenario group discussed improving cathedral facilities and the provision of a coffee shop in the grounds – both positive and needed projects . The negative scenario group sat in their room in silence. The change agent decided to let the silence run – and run. Eventually, the most senior canon hesitatingly said, 'We must let it [the cathedral] fall down.' A pin could have been heard to drop. But, when the two groups reconvened as one, it was the negative scenario which prompted the group to devise a strategy grounded in the cathedral facing outwards towards the community, rather than inwards. This scenario planning exercise fed into a fully-fledged strategy document and ultimately to an implementation plan. The new budget reflected this and many of the planned actions have now been accomplished.

A Church of England diocese wished to identify its priorities for the next five years, having undertaken an exhaustive 'bottom-up' approach of listening to the desired objectives of each parish and deanery. At the same time, it decided to make its values explicit. The Bishop's Council, at a 24-hours away event, went some way towards identifying both. The bishop delegated leadership of the task to the head of a diocesan function, who fulfilled the role of change agent. Further work was required and a small group was asked to take the project forward, under the same leadership. Membership criteria were implicit in the balance of ordained and lay members with different skill attributes. The task required big-picture conceptualizing, together with precision; risk-taking, with adherence to rules, in order to arrive at a series of clear but brief statements and descriptions. The change agent maintained the requisite pace in order to achieve the task within a tight time-frame, producing new iterations of the document before each meeting of the group. Midway in this process, the work-in-progress was represented to Bishop's Council as a sounding board and to ensure sufficient political support before the document was presented to Diocesan Synod.

The PCC of a small village church undertook an evening of visioning to explore what it should be doing within the next five years. One of the churchwardens acted as change agent, prompting and probing to help members ask 'what might be?' There was a wide range of responses from the high-risk suggestion of letting the chancel slip down the hill or demolishing the church social rooms and starting again, to more incremental changes such as celebrating parish breakfast at the back of the church rather than in the church rooms, despite one amazing complaint that the church smelled of bread. When, just over a year later, there was an Archdeacon's Visitation 23 innovations had been implemented.

Section B

The change agent can be either external or internal to an organization. In the first three examples, the change agent was an outsider, while the hospital change agent was an insider, as was the case in the church examples, although in the cathedral the Chapter member change agent was on the boundary between inside and outside. Insider change agents are much more likely to be found in large organizations. It is possible to behave like an outsider, while still being an insider – this is partly to do with the way the individual works in role and partly to do with behaviour and personality characteristics. This insider/outsider characteristic of the change agent is well captured by E. M. Rogers who describes him/her as 'a marginal figure with one foot in each of two worlds'.

There is no generally accepted definition of a change agent. Rogers (1995, pp. 235–6) states that the change agent 'influences clients' innovation decisions in a direction deemed desirable' by an organization, a view supported by Maidique (1988) who describes the change agent as positively influencing innovation/change decisions in a mediating role. Both Lichtenstein (1997) and Schuyt and Schuijt (1998) seem to be closer to Lewis Carroll's *Alice in Wonderland*: Lichtenstein focuses on 'grace, magic and miracles', namely the non-linear logic necessary to enable transformation, in addition to the rational logic of managing change. Schuyt and Schuijt liken the change agent to a magician who guides and structures important transitions, while Tann and Blenkinsopp (2003) use the term 'shakers and movers' to describe change agents in the NHS. Buchanan and Boddy (1992) usefully identify the political role of the change agent, highlighting the potential tension between the 'public performance of rationally considered and logically phased and visibly participative change, with backstage activity in the recruitment and maintenance of support and in seeking and blocking resistance' (Buchanan and Boddy, 1992, p. 27). The change agent, in these terms, is, among other things, a skilled political operator.

So what do change agents 'do'? In the above examples, the change agent acts as an outsider, even when on the inside, he/she is an influencer, a person who persuades and motivates; who networks, identifying coalitions and partnerships; brings people and resources together; a person who helps to make things happen; encourages self-reliance in others; doesn't take 'no' for an answer. And disappears (often moving on to the next project). The change agent must possess a high degree of expertise in the innovations to be adopted but he/she is primarily a facilitator who must also be able draw out ideas from others and identify sources of expertise both inside and outside the organization. The change agent works independently and works happily across functions. He/she is an effective collaborator, does not seek recognition for his/her activities and is characterized by 'self-confidence tempered with humility'.[2]

The change agent's role can be further explored in the hypothetical example of a parish church, some members of which think that it would be a positive step to abolish the pews and replace them with flexible seating – a contentious issue in many parishes. Assuming that an insider change agent emerges (this might be a churchwarden, PCC member or someone fairly new to the congregation without a specific leadership role), he/she will collect facts and figures on the age of the present pews and their value, besides the potential cost of replacing them with high quality, comfortable and moveable seating. Clearly a faculty will be required from the Deanery Advisory Committee (DAC) and it would be sensible to approach the appropriate diocesan officer informally to sound him/her out on the issue at an early stage. A PCC meeting might be convened to discuss the issue, and it is to be expected that there will be a diversity of opinions on the subject, including some vociferous and deep-seated opposition. A general congregation meeting might be held after the priest has, perhaps, preached on diversity (including a diversity of uses of church space). At this meeting people might be invited to write or draw on flipcharts around the walls, suspending judgement, to identify as many reasons as possible why it would be a good idea to replace the pews – or not. And then to address feelings issues through expressing hopes and fears of the proposed change. It might be helpful to have the support of an archdeacon at this meeting. The change agent might propose, taking a leaf out of the book of the managing director of the housing association, namely, taking a coachload of parishioners to churches where pews have, successfully, been replaced by chairs. If congregation members of these churches could be present to say 'how it is' and 'what we have been able to do', these opinions are more likely to carry weight than those of the respective incumbents. The most difficult part of the project will be to obtain a majority decision to proceed. The change agent will probably be the person who liaises with the church architect at an early stage to obtain his/her support. The change agent might also be involved in identifying funding possibilities, besides lobbying at deanery and diocesan level, should there be a possibility of concerted opposition in the DAC.

Behaviour characteristics of the change agent

- works independently
- works across functions/levels

- collaborator
- facilitator
- courageous – comfortable with discomfort
- builds high-trust relationships
- risk-taker
- sense of humour about self and situations
- social skills of empathy and giving effective feedback
- 'self-confidence tempered with humility' (Kanter)

Clearly there are many other tasks involved in project management. Change requires a senior sponsor. In a parish setting, this is likely to be the incumbent who may chair the PCC, can more easily convene activity groups and seek assistance from the congregation. In large organizations, for example, a diocese, it might be the bishop or an archdeacon. There is a need for an insider to hold the 'big picture' of the project and convene working groups and bring in other people as and when necessary. This role, the innovator, is more one of internal leadership than management. In smaller organizations, where there is an internal change agent, the same individual may fulfil both roles. But, as in the cathedral and the pharmacy examples, it is important to have an insider who holds the big picture. Change projects need to be managed. This requires a project manager who identifies milestones and monitors progress against them, as well as checking that the project is keeping to budget (and giving advance warning if this is not the case). An implementer (who in a small organization such as a church may be the same individual as the project manager) liaises with suppliers and checks work in progress. He/she is concerned with day to day practicalities (for example, such things as contractors gaining access to the building, and also identification of sources of power, heat and light).

It will have become clear that different change/innovation roles require different talents and skills. Some roles demand a big-picture approach with objectivity; others require precise attention to detail; some require clear structure and consistency in ways of working; some require excellent networking skills; others require the skills of involving people within an organization. These talents are optimized in people with different personality characteristics and behaviours. While it is possible for an individual to work across the grain in terms of personality style, rather than with it, to do so for any length of time demands a degree of psychological coping which causes stress and is likely to result in dysfunction. Change/innovation is best accomplished by a group of individuals, the members of which recognize their own and others' talents and play to their strengths.

Potential change agents can be identified in personality terms. They are highly motivated for change and need personal autonomy; they challenge currently held knowledge and beliefs and may be seen by some others as disruptive; they have less regard for the status quo and rules than others and frequently change their ways of working; they see the 'big picture' and have a low tolerance for detail – indeed, they are likely to make mistakes if required to work in project management mode for too long; they are impulsive. Within organizations, including church communities, people with these characteristics are relatively easily identified and are probably well known to the leaders. But these cognitive characteristics can be identified by psychometrics, in particular the Innovation Potential Indicator and KAI (see Appendix).

Is a change agent always required? Only, it is alleged (with apologies to Dylan Thomas) 'with change on a scale and of a scope beyond the manner in which pyjamas are folded' (Buchanan and Boddy, 1992, p. 24). Small-scale change in what amount to routines do not, but larger-scale innovation and organizational change requires a multi-talented team. The change agent being, by inclination, an outsider is not a natural team player. But it is hard to conceive of innovation or change being effective without one. And it's worth remembering that the Cheshire Cat left behind a very large smile in the sky.

Notes

1. Audit Commission quote from Baddeley, 2006, p. 116.
2. R. M. Kanter, *The Change Masters*, Hemel Hempstead: Allen & Unwin, 1985, quoted in Buchanan and Huczynski, 1985, p. 634

References and further reading

Baddeley, Donna (2006), *In Search of Midland Area Cheese . . .*, Birmingham: Midland Heart.

Balogun, J., and Hailey V. Hope (2004), *Exploring Corporate Change*, London: Prentice Hall.

Buchanan, D., and D. Boddy (1992), *The Expertise of the Change Agent*, London: Prentice Hall.

Buchanan, D., and A. Huczynski (1985), *Organizational Behaviour: An Introductory Text*, Harlow: Prentice Hall.

Carroll, L. (1885), *Alice in Wonderland*.

Johnson, S. (1998), *Who Moved My Cheese?*, London: Vermilion.

Kanter, R. M. (1985), *The Change Masters*, London: Unwin.

Lichtenstein, B. M. (1997), 'Grace, Magic and Miracles: A 'Chaotic Logic' of Organisational Transformation', *Journal of Organisational Change Management*, 10, 5, pp. 393–411.

Lundin, S., J. Christensen and H. Paul (2002), *Fish Tales*, London: Hodder & Stoughton.

McGovern, M., and D. Russell (2001), *A New Brand of Expertise*, Oxford: Butterworth-Heinemann.

Maidique, M. A. (1988), 'Entrepreneurs, Champions and Technological Innovation', in M. L. Tushman and W. L. Moore (eds), *Readings in the Management of Innovation*, New York: Ballinger, pp. 565–84.

Page, T. (1996), *Diary of a Change Agent*, Aldershot: Gower.

Rogers, E. M. (1995), *The Diffusion of Innovations*, New York: Free Press.

Schuyt, T. N. M., and J. J. M. Schuijt (1998), 'Rituals and Rules: About Magic in Consultancy', *Journal of Organisational Change Management*, 11, 5, pp. 399–406.

Senior, B. (2002), *Organisational Change*, London: Prentice Hall.

Tann, J., and A. Blenkinsopp (2003), *Shakers and Movers for Innovation in Community Pharmacy*, London: Royal Pharmaceutical Society of Great Britain.

Appendix

The Innovation Potential Indicator (IPI) is available from OPP Ltd, Elsfield Hall, 15–17 Elsfield Way, Oxford OX2 8EP. OPP also provide training/accreditation in the use of the measure.

KAI is available from KAI Distribution Centre, Ye Jolly Gardeners, Pleasant Place, Old Uxbridge Road, West Hyde, Rickmansworth, Herts WD3 9XZ. For accreditation to use the measure: Dr M. J. Kirton, Occupational Research Centre, Highlands, Gravel Path, Berkhamsted, Herts, HP4 2PG.

33. The necessary vision

TONY MCCAFFRY

This chapter was first drafted on the west-facing terrace of an old Andalusian olive farm house. Set on high hills, there was huge scope for focal shift and perspective transformation. Incredible skies above, sometimes cloudless, occasionally silvered with the vapour trails of aircraft heading to distant parts. Incredible depth, to a far-distant horizon beneath which the sun eventually set each evening, to the accompaniment of preprandial beverages. Incredible breadth, with hills folding in and away on both sides, ancient olive trees standing guard in serried ranks. In this panoramic scene there were the promises of purposefulness: roads, both major and minor; paths; trails . . . other houses on other hills; tractors and trailers of working people; smoke drifting from an unseen distillery. The place for me was significant, so different from my Surrey December home, but so was the time. The last days of 2004 were when the tsunami spread its destruction across so many lives, challenging the faith and generosity of all who felt its effect. Contrast the holiday reverie on the Spanish terrace with the death and destruction in Asia and Africa. Geography and history, place and time: perceptions are affected by such contexts. This final draft takes shape in the post-Pentecost, post-General Election England of 2005. In the story of my own religious tradition, a pope has died, another has been elected to the office.

There is a tension between the good news (of holiday terraces) and the bad news (of tidal-wave disasters). There is an uncomfortable paradox at work. But is that all there is to see? Is that tension the reality or just a symptom of a greater reality? Is my Spanish idyll cloud cuckoo land, the flood chaotic meaninglessness? For the believer, there is meaning, there is hope. Tensions persist between what was, what is and what might be or might have been. What is the nature of the vision which allows us to see beyond the customary partial parameters to a holistic appreciation of all that is?

Your pilot through these perplexing waters is no personal purveyor of miracle solutions. I have held responsible positions of management and leadership in Church-connected and other voluntary sector institutions. The experience has pushed me to see the problems more clearly – and to recognize the need for a more rigorous and radical response by the Church to their challenge if Church is to live up to its claim to be champion of the 'good news'. Let me share with you something of what I have found helpful: for you, then, to assess in your turn what your life experience has taught you.

The book of Proverbs puts it this way: 'For want of leadership a people perishes, safety lies in many advisers' (Proverbs 11.14) or, alternatively, 'Without deliberation plans come to nothing. Plans succeed where counsellors are many' (Proverbs 15.22). Wise words, these, about leadership as a collaborative endeavour. The isolated megalomaniacal leader is bad news, not least for the people being led. So, how does the leader get a sense of perspective, of purpose, of meaning? What is it that the good leader offers to others to comment upon, to take on board, to make all the more compelling to follow? I think it is *vision*, the bigger picture, having sight of something which is not as immediately obvious to others but which provides a context which offers a practical way forward. It is in this sense that I see vision as the sine qua non of effective church leadership. So, what is the content of this vision and where does it come from? Let us begin with a look at 'Church'.

There are many ways of considering 'Church'. The sociological, historical and cultural Church is a considerable and fascinating phenomenon but is not necessarily the same as the theologically understood reality. I like the starting point for my own tradition's policy view of Church, the premise of which is that Church is a mystery (Vatican II, 1964: 'Dogmatic Constitution on the Church' *Lumen Gentium*, Chapter 1). The cynic might say that this is all too true – for no one seems to understand what goes on within it. The less befuddled view is of Church as mystery because it is rooted in the Godhead, participating in some way in the divine life. This Church is called Christian precisely because it is the togetherness of the people baptized into Christ, dying and rising with him through the waters of baptism, putting on the Christ as one does the celebratory white robe, sharing the Lord's Supper in memory of him, going out in the Spirit to the whole world with the good news of forgiveness, redemption, restoration, salvation, affirmation. The pilgrim journey of the People of God is a triumph because of the victory of its leader, Jesus the Christ. We are God's through Christ: we are Christ's through the Church, its fellowship and its teaching.

Three texts from the New Testament carry for me the awesome nature of this mysterious Church relationship through Christ. Paul prays for his people at Ephesus that they might appreciate the multi-dimensional God-view, the definitive basis of all that we presume to consider real:

353

This, then, is what I pray, kneeling before the Father, from whom every fatherhood, in heaven or on earth, takes its name. In the abundance of his glory may he, through his Spirit, enable you to grow firm in power with regard to your inner self, so that Christ may live in your hearts through faith, and then, planted in love and built on love, with all God's holy people you will have the strength to grasp the breadth and the length, the height and the depth; so that, knowing the love of Christ, which is beyond knowledge, you may be filled with the utter fullness of God. (Ephesians 3.14–19)

This Christ is the head of all creation and its reconciling principle: Paul's prose poem catches the excitement of this divine profligacy:

He is the image of the unseen God,
the first-born of all creation,
for in him were created all things
in heaven and on earth:
everything visible and everything invisible,
thrones, ruling forces, sovereignties, powers –
all things were created through him and for him.
He exists before all things
and in him all things hold together,
and he is the Head of the Body,
that is, the Church.

He is the Beginning,
the first-born from the dead,
so that he should be supreme in every way;
because God wanted all fullness to be found in him
and through him to reconcile all things to him,
everything in heaven and everything on earth,
by making peace through his death on the cross.
(Colossians 1.15–20)

God's view is cosmic in scope. The Prologue to John's Gospel sings its praise (and, in the verses omitted here, plays with the temporal rootedness of the human John the Baptist as against the eternal divine Word):

In the beginning was the Word:
the Word was with God
and the Word was God.
He was with God in the beginning.
Through him all things came into being,

354

not one thing came into being except through him.
What has come into being in him was life,
life that was the light of men;
and light shines in darkness,
and darkness could not overpower it.
[...]
The Word was the real light
that gives light to everyone;
he was coming into the world.
He was in the world
that had come into being through him,
and the world did not recognise him.
He came to his own
and his own people did not accept him.
But to those who did accept him
he gave power to become children of God,
to those who believed in his name
who were born not from human stock
or human desire
or human will
but from God himself.
The Word became flesh,
he lived among us,
and we saw his glory,
the glory he has from the Father as only Son of the Father,
full of grace and truth. (John 1.1–5, 9–14)

One of our prosaic problems is that we muddle this Church as mystery with the Church as culturally conditioned tradition, any thing but godly in some of its aspects. The mission-minded Church of God seeking transformation can all too easily become the bureaucratic administrative organization with transaction as its outcome. Our credal recognition that 'we are Christ's' can surreptitiously mutate into 'Christ is ours'. 'We are God's people' can slide into 'God is ours'. Before we know it, we are appropriating and monopolizing the divine, falling into that most idolatrous of errors, making God in our own image and likeness, a *reductio ad absurdum* indeed! We must stay alert and critically sharp. We need to respect our diversity in the Church if we are to appreciate our unity. Our individuality is too important to be left to others to exercise on our behalf. This Church, with its myriad diversity, both is and is becoming: it is both institution and, in the Spirit of God, event. It is not too early to flag up the fact that exclusivity should not be allowed as an individuating note of the Christian Church rightly understood.

Church-vision must, then, be Christ-vision, which itself is God-vision, coming to the human Christ as the fruit of reflection and prayer. We can be grateful for the God who became human for showing us that we have nothing to fear or be ashamed of for being of a particular time and place, of a particular culture and people. That is how it is for humans. The error comes in making relativities into absolutes. 'My way is right because it is the one I know – so yours must be wrong.' Our perception is partial: to claim that it is definitive is to put ourselves in the place of the divine norm, a very dangerous appropriation.

The Lord's Prayer has a telling line for the seeker after the worthy vision: 'Thy will be done on earth as it is in heaven'. To get God's view, we have to see things in God's way of seeing – the view from eternity. This could be plain scary, because we are clearly out of our true league here. But remember this is a prayer addressed to a Father who loves us, even if we do not always understand why and what is implied by it. I like the cartoon of a benevolently smiling deity giving the globe of the world a loving hug. The caption? 'God so loved the world!' We'll understand more as we grow up, I think.

The God-vision is the heart of the mystery: all human life is there, all creation is there. The faith tradition shows the God-view by the God-works: the Genesis creation stories, for example, tell of the goodness of everything, even human diversity. This God is both the Almighty Transcendent and the Intimate Immanent, the God of earth and sea and sky, the God of the olive, the insect, the baby infant's windy smile. Through Jesus, the Son of God incarnate, creation itself becomes redemptive: through him all things were made, in him all creation will be restored. Everything, as well as everyone, matters. But people, fashioned in the image and likeness of God, matter for themselves precisely because of this close and potentially conscious participation in the divine purpose.

The astronaut Edgar Mitchell was the sixth person to walk on the moon: he saw things anew thereafter. On the occasion of the launch of the Year of Inter-religious Co-operation and Understanding in London (January 1993) he spoke movingly of his 'conversion':

For me, seeing our planet from outer space was a momentous experience. Five hundred years ago we thought our planet was the centre of the Universe. We now see that our Universe is fifteen billion light years in radius and is itself only one of billions and that we are way out on a spiral arm of a rather average galaxy which is only one of billions of galaxies.

As I saw this vision I recognised that our science was incomplete and flawed as it tried to describe our cosmology and I recognised that our religious cosmologies were incomplete and flawed as well.

As I looked at the earth, I could not see the political boundaries that so often lead to human grief, nor could I see the boundaries of thought that lead to so much misunderstanding and strife.

We went into space as technicians: we came back as humanitarians. Since then I have devoted my life to finding ways of healing this planet.[1]

Edgar Mitchell had clearly found something of the God-view and the Jesus-mission.

So what is the God-view of humanity? The most memorable formula I have yet encountered came to me from Brother Daniel Faivre SG, a friend in the ways of interfaith. Every human being, of every time or place, is a UMG,RBC – a unique manifestation of the Godhead, redeemed by Christ. Each one of us carries some aspect of godliness which no other person does – therein lies our dignity as well as our identity. We do not need to know it for it to be there – but it is heartening to be helped to appreciate that such is indeed the case and to help others to become alert to this same loving realization and so to a renewed enjoyment of their reality.

If church leadership is to be an effective articulation of the God-vision, what must it look to? I am greatly helped here by the esteemed work on theory of the American academics, Chris Argyris and Donald Schön (1974). They note the potentially disruptive disjunction between espoused theory (what a person professes to do) and theory-in-use (what a person actually does). I may profess to love God, neighbour and self but my lived-out life might tell a different tale, featuring a number of exclusions for all sorts of reasons. If we claim to live in accord with the God view, but actually use a different accord in practice, the tensions will show, there will not be the desired fulfilment in the partial achievement.

If the God-view is all-embracing and inclusive, the Church leader's view must be equally untrammelled. Exclusivity is unacceptable, even the exclusive consideration of the particular church membership. God's love is total and wholly relational: it does not admit of exception. The most excluded at this time of Make Poverty History campaigning are the materially poor, the exploited, the picked upon, the different. The exclusions prevalent in our world make the litany of our institutional sinfulness: racism; sexism; ageism; minority-bashing; trade rigging; economic exploitation of the poor; marketing arms to oppressors. There is little godly in these. The persecuted and oppressed, however, have a solidarity with the suffering Christ and need to know the hope his resurrection brings. The abused, the demeaned of all ages and genders, those struggling with illness or disability, the homeless, the unemployed, the refugees, the asylum seekers, the imprisoned. In the God-view, these are the important ones, the poor for whom the Church should make a preferential option. We ignore them at our peril: come the day of judgement, will we be surprised to find our puny value system upended (Matthew 25.31–46)?

The non-exclusivist God-vision raises a challenge for the church leader: what should the relationship be with faith traditions which do not share the Christian creed? We cannot claim a monopoly on God, unless it is a God on our own terms. There is still an unfortunate tendency to define others by the negative characteristic that they are not like us: Catholic and **non**-Catholic, Christian and **non**-Christian. Can this be godly? Does our scant regard for wisdoms which might be older than our own traditions truly reflect a godly view of reality? The vision we need is an all-embracing one. Best practice demands that we take interfaith (relations between faith traditions) seriously. This goes beyond (but does not preclude) being polite and attentive to others with whom we do not share fiducial agreement. What is required is dialogue, an honest and careful exchange of views in the cause of mutual understanding. The double danger inherent in this lies in the level of trust required (always risky in human relations) and the possibility that challenging or disturbing changes could be called for in our own thinking and practice. This meeting with the other, the careful listening and the serious effort to articulate faith understanding accurately, is not an optional extra: it is of the mainstream in church leadership.

The church leader with the God-view aspiration does not impose preset responses to problems: such fundamentalism, providing the answer to the question yet to be raised, gives little respect to the individuality of the Christ-bearer other who, like the leader, is a learner whose integrity is to be respected. This does not rule out the leader's prophetic role as the signpost pointing the way of the Lord to the pilgrim traveller. Clarifying the parameters is not the same as punitively judging the actual or presumed decisions taken. The leader is also a fellow-pilgrim: prayer and collective discernment are required to filter out the dross and extract the essence. Views get modified in the light of experience: back on my terrace, the daytime sky was not the same as the night, the dusk not the same as the dawn. I learned to appreciate each phase the more for recognizing the others were there by association. This human capacity to readjust the view in the light of experience has been described by the adult educator, Jack Mezirow, as 'perspective transformation' (1991). I see heavy parallels with the change-of-heart conversion evidenced in Edgar Mitchell's testimony earlier. As disciples of Jesus, all church people are by definition learners, necessarily on the move, learning with heart and intuition as well as head. Stagnation and decline are signs that learning has ceased – and true discipleship with it. Change is more of a life-indicator than a threat.

The leader with vision is aware that what is at one time perceived as the substance might in time be shown to be the shadow. The effort to share the God-view demands that the leader goads the complacent to restlessness: idling is not a Christian virtue. The Christian must be active, ever critically alert. There is a job to be done. The boat will indeed rock: tsunamis will indeed happen. Faith is not static.

All of which may give the impression that the brunt of the deal is dumped on the leader. Get a bunch of believers together and there will soon be moans about the pastor, the bishop, the leader by whatever name. Careful! To cast the leader in the role of baddy is to risk being exclusive, a not very godly trait, as we have tried to make plain. Much of what has been said of the leader applies to all members of the Christian faith tradition: each has a unique witness to contribute for the common good. There is a distinction in the leadership function, perhaps, but the essential unity is in the shared humanity and the need to learn of the developing human. Some lead; some are led; all are (or have the capacity to be) learners on the move. Our leaders need our encouragement, our support, our critical friendship, our prayerful discernment of the God-view for our times. As we learn together, we need not be afraid of honest mistakes or seeming failure. The mission is ongoing. Inclusivity is very political and will win enemies as well as friends: the task is to show whose side the Church is on.

I take some considerable solace from the thought that perhaps the agenda is only just beginning, that we are still only in the early days of Church history. Threats to life – and faith – will happen. Discerning the God-view of a tsunami is a tester for most. As with life, so with faith: the making of meaningfulness out of the givens of seeming nonsense is more than difficult. We have to work and develop this 'faithing' if our faith is not to fail, fall apart, or die. The 'good news' is given to us to be put on offer to all: it is our privilege and reassurance. The process is cooperative and collaborative rather than confrontational, competitive or even hierarchical: it is not a question of 'them' and 'us', more a search for the loving 'we'.

A final thought on the process of discernment of the God-vision for leaders: do not underestimate the value of thinking time on the job. Meditation and prayer are intrinsic to the public work, not private adjuncts to it. Membership of groups is also important: isolation is a form of exclusion. It is good for seekers of the God-view to hear ourselves articulate belief. Others' interest can draw this out of us without great pain. The wider community, seemingly beyond

'Church', offers a sense of balance by being precisely that wider context for what goes on in the Church community. God is smilingly present in both: relish recognizing the good news!

Notes

Biblical texts are taken from *The New Jerusalem Bible*, London: Darton, Longman and Todd, 1985.

1. Source not known.

References

Argyris, Chris, and Donald Schön (1974), *Theory in Practice: Increasing Professional Effectiveness*, San Francisco: Jossey-Bass.
Mezirow, Jack (1991), *Transformative Dimensions of Adult Learning*, San Francisco: Jossey-Bass.

34. Theology – a lifelong quest for meaning

TONY MCCAFFRY

The truism is that we can only start from where we happen to be. In this article, I would like to invite you to accompany me on a reflective journey. Allow me, if you would, to be your guide, pointing out features which those who have passed this way before have deemed of interest. Whether or not you consider them equally compelling will, of course, depend on you and your perceptions, which may well differ from those of others, mine included. Mine come from the bulk of a lifetime spent in education, either as a student or as a teacher. I have been taught and have taught theology and religious education at primary, secondary, tertiary and practitioner researcher levels. I have been taught and have taught at primary, secondary, tertiary and adult ages. What I have to offer as a guide is the cumulative awareness that my experience has occasioned for me. A number of things have taken on a coherence and cogency corroborated by further experiential verification. Learning and teaching at one level or age has proved to be informative and illuminative for learning at any other.

I have become shy of definitive claims since I have experienced, and still experience, movement in my own appreciation of how things are. Some might see this as a serious weakness for a self-professed guide, but I feel at ease with it: this particular guide is claiming no more than to be pointing out features considered of interest. There is no claim to be offering the definitive interpretation of their significance, rather it is the suggestion (based on an experience of and feedback from other travellers) that there are vantage points from which perspectives and panoramas can be the better appreciated. The proposed approach is more methodological than directly interpretative of content.

This approach is rooted in what experience has taught me about how adult human persons learn: our starting point is always where we are and as we are. Our imagination can take us out of and beyond our immediate physical incarnational location, but the fact remains that this springboard is rooted in us as and where we are, physically, emotionally, socially, culturally, morally, spiritually. Our perceptions

361

are informed by the experiences we have accumulated, sifted and wholly or partially integrated into our awareness of our self and our self's view. In this understanding, learning is more than absorption of information. Learning occurs when the new information enters into dialogue with the body of existing personalized experience and results in a reassimilation or readaptation which causes there to be some modification in the personalized experiential base: there is a new starting point for action. Change is, in this view of a learning experience, a distinctive characteristic. A Pauline conversion experience is more than the arrival of new information: it is the personal assimilation of the new information against the background of earlier established positions, the interchange between the two resulting in a revised position which will affect subsequent action. It is understandable that such learning is not contained in, although it may be occasioned by, a momentary blinding flash of insight. Weighing up the implications and ramifications calls for a time of serious reflection.

My own learning has been affected as I have changed in age, environment, opportunity and responsibility. One experience is weighed against (put in dialogue with) another, sometimes resulting in a modification of the principled stance as a shift in operational behaviour. As I get older I have noticed a greater reluctance to take on new learning because of the radical and possibly disruptive effect it has on my established patterns of thought and action. At the same time, I feel a greater confidence in the quality of what I have learned so far and a calmer strength in the degree to which I can assert my own learning in the face of challenge from others. Perhaps this is something to do with being nearer (in years) to the end of my life than to its beginning. Really knowing that I must some day die has a serious effect on the way I live. Am I perhaps beginning to see a link between cumulative consciousness and the wisdom we sometimes associate with our ancients?

I will ask you to pause at this point and question whether this is an adequate description of what happens when we human adults learn something, or whether some dimensions intrinsic to the learning process have been neglected. What we have sketched out here is an indication of 'how' we experience the learning process: what is not so clear is 'why' we should make the effort to learn. The feature to note here is motivation, what it is that pushes us to learn or at least to grapple with the more or less unknown. Again, experience tells me that sometimes the trigger is outside us (an encounter with a person, place or thing; an experience which rocks our perception of the way things are or should be); sometimes it is within us, some sort of restless urge which impinges on our conscience and consciousness, and is able to be ignored in the short term but is not as easily ignored in the longer term. This inner restlessness is a matter to which we will have to return later, but for the moment it is worth noting that it is not unconnected with the power which motivates the human person to be open to alternative perceptions and to be prepared to envisage a change in personal stance. Clearly, we are envisaging learning here as implying much more than the taking on of information. This deeper learning goes to the heart of our conceptual and value systems and the way we make sense of the broad sweep of existence. We are in the territory which many describe in God (*theo*) language: this has been done in various ways throughout human history, resulting in a variety of religions and faith traditions. A point to ponder here is the relationship between a faith tradition and our own individual human experience.

I take faith tradition to be a way of looking at human experience which has been tried and tested across time (tradition) and which has proved successful in offering adherents a way of understanding, making sense of and finding meaning in that experience (faith). Faith traditions offer meaning interpretations particularly to the enigmas of the human experience, the ultimate questions of: where am I from? what am I doing here? where do I go to next?

The problem of the individual's experience confronting the faith tradition is often a question of scale: the faith tradition is often widely respected for its wisdom acquired over a long history, articulated by institutional structures of impressive authority, and celebrated in ceremonies and rituals of awesome significance. By contrast, the devotee can easily feel insignificant and reluctant to offer a critical engagement (dialogue) when personal experience seems to offer perceptions which seem to be at some discord with the faith tradition, as perceived. The individual feels she/he no longer fits in the faith tradition: the only recourse seems to be in abandoning it, often with serious regret.

It is worth dwelling on this situation in order to extract some of its implications. The scenario described puts the faith tradition on a par with a body of information rather than a personalized perception. The adult as described does not see a way of exercising adulthood within the faith tradition, recognizing that either the adult must become as a child and do what she/he is told by their elders and betters, or must leave. The challenge for the individual and the institution is to provide ways in which the adulthood of the devotee (the 'where they are' dimension) can be appreciated and its particular energies utilized for the common good.

The weakness of the impasse lies with an intransigence in the faith tradition and a timidity in the devotee. In many years of working in adult religious education I have found the common denominator in what thwarts growth in adults' religious learning is lack of self-assurance. The reason for this can sometimes be found in a faith tradition's structures which militate against individuality and creativity and, by implication, claim a definitive hold on the truth. In fairness, however, the problem is sometimes elsewhere in the ignorance or false perception of just what the faith tradition is. Adults need to catch up with themselves and their patterns of understanding if they are to maintain a balanced perspective on life, and this cannot happen automatically – it demands some conscious (and often collaborative) effort.

Let us attempt an equation, at this point, between faith tradition and theology: it does not work out, of course, but the attempt is itself worthwhile because illustrative. The faith tradition offers a particular way of 'faithing' life (to borrow Fowler's use of the noun as a verb), giving meaning to life. For many faith traditions (but by no means all, hence the poverty of the proposed equation) the articulation of this meaning will be made in 'God' language, as a theology. Now there are two ways in which this theological articulation can be understood – statically, as a statement of fact or information, or dynamically as a contemporary experience of a still-living and developing tradition. Apply this to theology and the gap between theology as a predetermined content and theology as a process of engagement with experience becomes more apparent. In the one mode, theology is something done to you, something which you study and absorb as you would any body of information you consider of importance to you. In the other, you do the theology, you make it, using the tradition to help establish the pattern of personal meaningfulness. The one model treats the devotee as an outsider received into a pre-existent wisdom. The other model implies that the devotee has riches to offer to, as well as to take from, the tradition/the theology. The individual's personal experience can feed into as well as feed from the cumulative consciousness of the faith tradition/the theology. The first model treats the devotee as a child, needing to be told what to do, requiring formation of the approved behavioural patterns: the second allows greater scope (which implies greater responsibility and accountability) for the adult individual, acknowledging, by implication, that the adult may well have discovered a centre of gravity which allows the possibility of a balanced but fresh point of perception. The second view respects faith, as we have described it, as the giving of meaning to life. The first view reduces faith to belief, a codification of the faith tradition.

I have found the work of the American educator and theologian, Thomas Groome[1] to be helpful in understanding the relationship between the faith tradition and personal experience. Groome, focusing particularly on Christian religious education, sees the secret as lying in dialogue between perceptions. He takes two aspects of the perception, story and vision, and treats them as two starting points, two statements of where you are. The two visions he compares and contrasts are the Vision of God (big V), 'thy will be done on earth as it is in heaven', and the vision of the individual human (little v). The stories likewise are the God Story (big S) and the individual human's story (little s). It is not a question of one being good and the other bad: it is a question of accepting that there could well be difference and making constructive use of the energy which that difference creates. The faith tradition articulation offers an appreciation of the God perception, while the individual's experience can offer corroboration or counterpoint to it. The 'dialogue' suggested by Groome is based on mutual illumination. 'V' can help 'v' to see itself in a different light, while 'v' can also provide insight into what 'V' might contain or imply. The same applies to story: my experience of 's' can put new light on what the 'S' might be: my exploration of 'S' might help me see more clearly my own 's'. The method is not unlike the sharing of insight which is facilitated in any worthwhile group religious educational opportunity: it is by being made attentive to others' questions and their suggested answers that we can become more aware of our own; it is by hearing ourselves having to articulate previously under-expressed questions and suggested answers that we discover what our own position actually is, that we become aware of where we are at present. Who we are is the product of our givens and our accumulated experience, whether imposed and freely sought out, is the newness we have to offer to life: if we deny this to ourselves and to others, the whole of creation is the poorer.

The weighing up of different views in this way is not an academic exercise: implied in the exchange is the preparedness to change, should the case be sufficiently compelling. It is risky, dangerous and potentially disruptive. (Trevor Cooling[2] put the question: 'Surely theology carries a 15 if not an 18 certificate?') So why bother?

Take time to look around at this point. We are here at the heart of what it means to be human: to be lumbered with a life we did not request, to be slowly emergent to consciousness, to be faced with decisions at crucial times; to look for sense and purpose amid the uncertainties; to face up to finality. The restlessness of our spirit drives us to look beyond what we have and are for the realization of our aspirations. Many of us who have not yet won the National Lottery jackpot see that as an answer to our problems. Yet we note that those who have won and resolved some of life's problems seem to have acquired a new set in their place. The wisdom of those who can come to terms with the harsher dimensions of human experience we find admirable: they have learned somehow to hold in constructive balance the conflicting demands of different areas of their experience and being. Theirs is not a prejudged position but a principled appreciation of the everchanging present moment in all its complexity. The quality of the appreciation often comes from a long life of carefully considered experience, but not necessarily. Many of us have met young people with wise heads, just as many of us have met adult people whose approach to life is redolent of a spoilt child.

Time passed does not necessarily mean lessons learned. However, time does mark the passage of opportunities to enrich experience and to inform reflection. The young look at the wrinkled ones and hope to die before they get old: there is less evident rush to mortality when the wrinkled stage is reached by those who were once young and dogmatic! Time is a way to mark the development through phases of life, each of which provides a whole range of vantage points from which to assess meaning and purpose. What proves satisfactory at one time proves at another to be less than adequate. Coming to terms with physicality, individuality, relationships, social and economic identity varies at different times of life. A human existence is not very long, from womb to tomb, but there are myriad possibilities for choice-making between those fixed points, all of which leave their mark on the individual and the environs.

My view of meaningfulness at 4 years of age was different when I was 14, and again when I was 24, 34, 44, 54 and 64. What has altered is not just the date but the details of the environment to which I relate, and my perception of that environment. My story is chronological and will be recorded cryptically for posterity by the registrar in terms of birth, marriage and death dates and places. Others will see items in the spaces between. My parent, sisters, brother, spouse, children, colleagues, students, friends, neighbours (not forgetting 'readers') will all have their perceptions of me, as I have of me myself, but experience tells me very few of them will be the same. Are some right and some wrong therefore? I think it is unhelpful to question in those terms, implying moral worth in the position taken. That some may have an erroneous or distorted view is quite conceivable: everyone is working with a different set of data, resulting in different perceptions. It is not uncommon for an individual to have a self-perception that no one else recognizes. If our understanding of our 's' (personal story) is to be rounded, we need the benefit of the way others understand our 's' to be. It is difficult to get a clear understanding of ourselves using our own resources: for example, the self we see reflected in the mirror is not the same image of self as seen by those we encounter. (Check this out if you are not sure: the right-hand side of the face looking into the mirror is reflected back as the left-hand side!) In our early years, the love and affirmation of those close to us is crucial to our personal and social development. As teenagers, our peer opinions are often taken to be more important than those of the very people who were earlier so important to us. The development of personal relationships outside the group often leads to life choices of considerable moment, choices which have to be consciously maintained and reviewed if they are to last. And, finally, even the most important options are disrupted by our inbuilt corporeal impermanence. Life, like nature, has its seasons.

So my personal story is one of change in my physical and social situation, and in the perceptions of me by myself and others. Through these changes I can come to terms with the implications for the way I feel, what I consider to be of worth, how I behave – but I may not take that plunge. I can evolve a vision which more comprehensively embraces my experience – or I may stay with a vision which proved satisfying in the past, despite its uncomfortable fit with the present changed realities. My vision is fundamentally fixed: my answer is ready and predetermined, even before the question is posed by the changed and changing circumstances of my life. It is fixed, without movement. There may be a theological stance but no theology is being done.

There is, however, more to me than a personal and social life. Increasingly, we humans are being reminded that our context, our environment, is of immense importance to us. The context can be physical. My physicality is in contact, proximate or remote, with other physicalities. The scope for my experience is limited or expanded accordingly. My capacity for awe and wonder, for imagining beyond the immediately perceptible, will be conditioned by what is available to me. If I am hungry or thirsty, afraid or insecure, matters of truth, unity, beauty and goodness will be part of my vision only with difficulty. Physical, emotional and moral deprivation can be effective prisons of the human spirit, from which that spirit will have to be liberated if doing theology is to be more than a cynical exercise, almost an insult added to the injuries. We are beginning to recognize that the rich of this world can be just as much trapped in this way as are the poor – by the excess of material goods this time rather than from their lack. Vision can show the way out, but story must be informed anew if vision is to offer fresh light and realistic hope.

The environmental context is not only physical: it is also cultural. We humans all do things differently, have different tastes and aspire to lifestyles which cannot be easily corralled. Yet there are patterns of similarity. Language, for example, can unite as well as divide us (pet names for the ones we love, for example). Culture may be described as 'the way we do things around here' and this can be understood at all levels from the personal, through the domestic, to the neighbourhood, town, region, country, continent and world. Anyone with experience of family life will know that families are not monocultural: opinions will differ on what constitutes good music, good TV, tidiness in rooms, the advisability of doing homework, and an acceptable hour for homecoming from a night out. Much of this diversity of culture in the home is to do with age and position in society, which affect perception of the good. One culture impinging on another tends to lead to volatility, a tension which is potentially creative but, conversely, potentially destructive too. Racial and religious cultural differences (different stories) challenge the human capacity to envision a way of mutual acceptance and appreciation. The self-interested materialism of the industrialized and commercially sophisticated minority is increasingly appreciated as being a culture which is exploitative of the majority of humans on the globe and abusive of the world's resources. The cultures are in conflict. To live together in mutual respect and appreciation is a vision which demands some radical political, economic and personal decision-making. Cultures are complex and impinge heavily on our story and vision: the question of why we should make the major effort to divert and direct culture for the common good is to raise again the question of motivation. In a matter which is growing rapidly towards and beyond the cosmic in its significance, the relevance of theology (the use of the God dimension) is acquiring renewed significance as offering a conceptual scale commensurate with the task.

The interplay between 's' (personal story) and 'v' (vision) is expressed clearly in the ways in which experiences, opportunities and responsibilities affect the ways human develop. What happens to us (the 'givens' of our existence) and what we do with what happens both affect the way we look at things. Likewise, the way we understand our responsibility and accountability affects our choices of action. Making the effort is considered worthwhile because of the perceived greater good which ensues. The articulation of the vision, just as the perception of the opportunity and the responsibility, will be affected by the personal situation of the individual, as will the choice of actions emanating from it. World peace may be an envisioned aspiration shared by two people, one of whom may decide to live a life of prayer in seclusion, while the other chooses a path of direct political action. Both may well have used theology to develop both their vision and their choice of action. Interestingly, our times are raising questions increasingly about the permanence of decisions implying life-long commitments. It would seem that such decisions are being seen as personally relational (therefore open to evolutive development) rather than as statically definitive. It is helpful to consider the theological faith traditions and their developing (changing) appreciation (perception) of the nature of the God–human person–people, person–person, people–people relationships. The 's' can learn something from the 'S'; the 'v' can gain something from the 'V': the perceptions of what constitute God's 'S' and 'V' can be sharpened by our appreciation of our own 's' and 'v'. What results is a re-evaluation of the earlier understanding (perhaps that of a faith tradition), which might occasion a rearticulation of the position which, by its very nature, becomes a reinterpretation which itself then becomes exposed to challenge by past, present and future experience. History has shown that tidy theological summations do not always suit the messy reality of human existence. The establishment of a dialogue between the two can lead to new insights for both sides, providing that there is inherent in the dialogue courage to change, should it be shown to be imperative.

Theology, the recourse to God language to explain the mysteries of being, is only one response among many: not every faith tradition invokes deity. However, many people have found God language to be helpful in engaging with the anomalies and paradoxes of existence. It helps name the mystery which precedes and follows us, which is immanent and transcendent to us at any time. We have a capacity to question beyond our perceived certainties, in particular to ask: 'why?' It can be a 'why?' of wonder as we are faced with love or beauty: it can be a 'why?' of rage at the affront of the innocent suffering. The time of questioning can be strikingly memorable; the finding of an answer can take a longer time: the peak experience articulates the question; the response comes in the lowlands of quiet mulling. Any response is, however, relative: our capacity to question always outstrips our answers. Just as we change in size, shape and appearance throughout our life cycle, so we need to discover renewed answers to our newly formulated questions. This search will only happen when we feel the need to ask the question as our own and feel the need to provide our own answer. Ready-made answers can help, but rarely do they respond to every detail of our question: our personal perception provides a unique dimension.

The vistas become even more tantalizing as we near the end of this guided tour. You will have noted that we have concentrated on the human person and we have not particularized when we have spoken of faith traditions. We have spoken of theology as God language, seen by some people as commensurate with the task of making sense of existence. Christians use God language: the Word becomes flesh; God shows solidarity with the human condition and articulates a loving relationship which has the power to transform and reconcile all and

369

everything. There is mystery here: it defies understanding rather than insults it: it is possible to get into it, but not to embrace and contain it: and the more we get to the heart of it the more we see there remains to be known.

This God incarnate was born, lived a full life, suffered, died – and rose again. The 's' of this person tells us of the 'S' of God, Christians believe, and offers a new meaning to and way of understanding life. This experience of hopefulness, of new life coming from a seemingly bereft situation, is not the prerogative of Christians: it is, it would seem, a fact deep at the heart of the human psyche. Christian theology names it in a particular way. The individual Christian is able to take this construct, the paschal mystery, and use it as a tool to examine, evaluate and come to an understanding of some of the deeper anomalies of the human experience. In the individual perception, experienced actuality seems the reality of which the Christological is a reflected image; the faith of the Christian transforms this understanding; the reality is the Christological dimension, our experience the reflection. In linguistic terms, we could talk of metaphors – using the known to reach an understanding of the unknown. Is my experience the reality, or only a sign of the reality? Does my love of God indicate that God is similarly loving or is my love only possible as the reflection of the God reality of love?

The Christian tradition articulates a salvific redemption in terms of the reunification and restoration of all in Christ. The finality is not the immediately perceived finality of death and corruption: there is new life, renewed hope. The tenets of the Christian Creed offer theological tools for the believers to use to make sense of the life they experience, young and old, female or male, poor or rich, heterosexual or homosexual, well or ill, unschooled or learned – and every other variant which makes for the individuality of the human person. It is this reflected experience which can lead to a revision of the creedal statement too: the feminist critique has indicated, for example, a male bias in thought, language and organization which could well have seriously (if unwittingly) distorted the faith tradition it was seeking to uphold. The answer is not clear: it has to be worked upon and tried out for validity. It has ever been thus.

The wisdom we applaud in some of our elders is bred of a life lived and a richness of compassionate understanding of life and humanity's place in it. They have learned (and are continuing to learn) to keep in creative tension the potentially turbulent variables of human experience. Their 's' has helped them to develop a 'v' which provides meaning. The spirit of constructive criticism and solidarity ensures that perceptions are able to develop as long as life perdures.

Both human consciousness and theology in this sense are aspects of the journeying and means of transport rather than the point of arrival. In this article I have suggested some ways of appreciating people's restless questionings about ultimate meanings and their conjectural responses. I do not claim to have provided you with definitive answers: I hope to have helped you to consider more closely just what is going on.

Notes

1. Thomas A. Groome (1980), *Christian Religious Education: Sharing Our Story and Vision*, London: Harper & Row.

2. Trevor Cooling (1994), *Concept Cracking: Exploring Christian Beliefs in School*, Stapleford: Stapleford Project Books.

35. Habakkuk and four steps to visionary leadership

ROGER STANDING

So, how do you decide what to do? How do you plan for the future? If you are in business then a little bit of market research would not go amiss; if you are in education there is the National Curriculum to guide you and, for the politician, there is the heady mix of ideology and focus groups – that strange interplay between core values and electability. The marketplace is also full of strategies to be embraced and lived out from old favourites such as Management by Objectives and the ubiquitous '5-year plan', to more exotic strategies of leadership based on a whole variety of insightful role models from Jean Luc Picard of the star ship *Enterprise* to everyone's favourite man in red, Santa Claus himself.[1]

Should church be any different? Can we just take secular models of vision building and incorporate them into the Kingdom of God, or does being believers make a difference? What is the contribution of spirituality to discerning the future?

The prophet Habakkuk is a fascinating case study. One of only three prophets in the Old Testament to be actually designated as a prophet at the beginning of the book, he was very much a free thinker. Habakkuk did not hesitate to put God on the spot about things that did not seem to add up in his situation and experience.

How long, O LORD, must I call for help, but you do not listen? (1.2a) (NIV)

Why do you make me look at injustice? Why do you tolerate wrong? (1.3a) (NIV)

Your eyes are too pure to look on evil; you cannot tolerate wrong. Why then do you tolerate the treacherous? Why are you silent while the wicked swallow up those more righteous than themselves? (1.13) (NIV)

He wanted to understand what was happening around him. He wanted to comprehend the purposes of God in what was going on so that he could communicate them clearly to those who were looking for the way forward and wanted to know what to do.

Habakkuk probably worked at the Temple in Jerusalem as an official prophet or priest sometime around 600 BC, before the fall of the city in 587. Looking at how he wrestled with his own situation and sought to discover God's will for the future has much to teach us as we seek God's vision for ourselves and our churches.

In Habakkuk 2.1–4 (NASB) the prophet sets about his task. There are four steps that he makes that we should take note of.

1. Watch and see

I will stand on my guard post and station myself on the rampart; and I will keep watch to see what He will speak to me.

Habakkuk sees what he is doing as a 'spiritual' equivalent of the role of the city watchman. Stationed on the city walls, the watchman was charged to be attentive to what was going on outside. When he saw something that required a response it was his job to let everyone know. Habakkuk asked his questions of the Lord for his present situation. He wanted to know what God was doing and how he could work with God. So he asks questions and then watches for the Lord's response. Habakkuk's understanding of his role is that it is very much about the here and now, not some distant and far off future. What is happening now? What is God saying to us now? How does that affect where we are heading and how we look to get there? His prophetic insight is therefore not predictive of some distant future, but rather an insight into the present and how that links in to God's vision of the immediate future.

2. Write it down

Then the LORD answered me and said, 'Record the vision and inscribe it on tablets, that the one who reads it may run.'

When the Lord does respond, the first thing he tells Habakkuk to do is to write the vision down. While the Hebrew text can stand a number of interpretations at this point, the common theme is communication and action. Writing down what God is believed to have said clarifies and fixes it. This makes communication of the vision much easier, as well as the action that it requires.

It makes sense too because we easily forget and, even if we don't forget, what we remember quickly gets overlaid with other things. Having it written down gives us the opportunity to refer back to it and remind ourselves exactly of what we sensed God saying. Having it written down also makes it far easier to reflect and meditate upon. 'That the one who reads it may run!' Running straight towards what God wants because we know where we're going. Not dragging our heels behind us but with a clear sense of direction and purpose because we know how we have been led.

3. Wait patiently

For the vision is yet for the appointed time; it hastens toward the goal, and it will not fail. Though it tarries, wait for it; for it will certainly come, it will not delay.

Timing is everything. Patience, perseverance and endurance are biblical words. Our instant age expects everything to happen now and there is a danger of our expectations of God going the same way. Just because we have a vision for where God is taking us does not mean we will get there tomorrow, or even next week. The fall of Babylon that Habakkuk was looking for did not happen for another 60 years or so.

Waiting patiently, however, does not mean a time of passive inactivity until God does his stuff.

4. Work by faith

. . . but the righteous will live by his faith.

We know God and we know the direction in which he is leading us. Because we know this we can live by faith and work by faith towards that goal. Moment by moment, hour by hour, day by day, we live by faith in the light of the vision that God has given us. Thus God's vision for our future, for the future of our church, for the future of our family can be lived out in the details of our lives today. As Proverbs 29.18 rightly states, 'Where there is no vision, the people perish . . .' (KJV).

Half a dozen years ago, I was amazed to see these very principles of Watch; Write; Wait; and Work reflected in a secular leadership manual. While the spiritual dimension is absent, Warren Bennis and Burt Nanus pick up on similar themes to Habakkuk in their leadership study, *Leaders* (1985). Looking to find a way through more than 350 different definitions of leadership that had emerged from scholarly studies and empirical research during the twentieth century, they conducted their own research. They were convinced that leadership was the pivotal force behind successful organizations. Such 'transformational leadership' enables the development of vision and then mobilizes organizational change. With this in mind, they analysed the leadership style of 90 successful business executives and outstanding leaders in the public sector. They wanted to understand more adequately what was going on in those organizations that thrived.

Their conclusions were profoundly challenging. They discovered no obvious structural patterns for success, no necessary character type or personality profile on the part of the leader which guaranteed a healthy vitality in the organizations that were led. They concluded therefore that transformational leadership appears to be the marshalling of skills possessed by the majority, but only used by a few. Consequently, everyone has the potential for improving the quality of their leadership. What did emerge from their study were four major themes that appeared to be common to all. These themes demonstrate an amazing similarity to the principles outlined above from Habakkuk 2.1–4.

1 – Attention through vision

Leaders recognize the importance of vision as a bridge to the future. It provides purpose, direction and a focused agenda. However, it is not something that is imposed from above. This kind of visionary leadership is a transaction between leaders and followers. It is a sweeping backwards and forwards of ideas and energy. Bennis and Nanus discovered that it was only rarely that effective leaders were those who conceived a vision in the first place. They may have chosen it, given it form, articulated it and given it legitimacy, but its life almost invariably began somewhere else. By default, therefore, the best leaders were good askers, good listeners and good observers; they were sensitive to the past and aware of the present, while looking to visualize and anticipate what lay ahead. Their interpretation of all this information into a viable and credible vision therefore empowers and energizes others who 'buy in' to their conception of the future. These transactions between leaders and led become vital components in vision building as, by their very nature, they create unity and trust.

For the prophet it was the importance of 'Watching' to catch the vision (v. 1).

2 – Meaning through communication

Having a corporate vision is not enough. Having been agreed, it can then sit happily on a shelf and gather dust while everyone gets on with their jobs. To become a reality a corporate vision has to be effectively communicated into the very ethos and thinking of a community.

All organizations depend upon the existence of shared meanings and interpretations of reality to facilitate coordinated action. Effective leaders define and articulate these so that they cohere with the vision of the organization. 'Knowing why' is actually more fundamental to 'knowing how' in looking to communicate vision. Communicating this is not achieved through policy documents and vision statements alone, but rather by creating a new ways of looking at things. By constantly reinforcing the vision by repeating it, by identifying with it and by personifying it, effective leaders give shape and substance to the ethos and culture of their organization, an ethos and culture that embody the vision. Some have called this the 'social architecture' of an organization.

Habakkuk was told by the Lord to 'write' the vision down to effectively communicate it, ' . . . so that he who reads it may run' (v. 2).

3 – Trust through positioning

Trust is the lubrication that makes it possible for organizations to work. It implies accountability, predictability and reliability. Leaders who are trusted make themselves known and their positions clear. It also has to do with the passage of time so that consistency is established. Such trust is the glue that bonds leaders and followers together.

Positioning is the least understood part of building trust. It has to do with the set of actions necessary to implement the vision. These are identified and the leader must take them up with the epitome of clarity, constancy and reliability, thus creating 'organizational integrity'. However, these things do not happen overnight; Bennis and Nanus speak of the need for 'courageous patience', as trust can only be earned over time.

Habakkuk was told, 'The vision is yet for the appointed time . . . Though it tarries, wait for it . . . ' (v. 3).

4 – The deployment of self through positive self-regard

When the leaders were asked about what personal qualities were important in running an organization, they never mentioned charisma, time management or some other glib formula. The things they did highlight included self-knowledge, commitment, consistency and, above all, openness to learn.

'Positive self-regard' is not, therefore, some egotistical self-centredness, but rather the self-awareness of effective leaders that means that they know their strengths and weaknesses. Recognizing strengths and compensation for weaknesses is the first step in achieving positive self-regard. The second is to keep working on and developing one's talents by setting higher goals and objectives. Such leaders are 'self-evolvers'.

Such clear self-awareness means that they learn to compensate for their weaknesses, broaden the base of leadership and empower others to grow too. Their 'self-regard' is therefore counterbalanced with 'other-regard'. The environment that they establish is one that is thirsty to learn and understand and, as a consequence, sees mistakes and set backs as opportunities for learning rather than failures. These leaders therefore live and work in the light of their vision as they seek to make it a reality.

As the prophet saw, '. . . the righteous will live by his faith' (v. 4).

It seems to me that when an Old Testament prophet and well-researched, contemporary leadership 'gurus' are speaking much the same language, maybe we should sit up and take notice as we probably have something useful to learn!

Note

1. Roberts and Ross (1995); Harvey, Cottrell and Lucia (2004).

References

Bennis, Warren, and Burt Nanus (1985), *Leaders: The Strategies for Taking Charge*, New York: HarperCollins.

Harvey, Eric, David Cottrell and Al Lucia (2004), *The Leadership Secrets of Santa Claus*, Dallas: The Walk the Talk Company.

Roberts, Wess, and Bill Ross (1995), *Make It So: Leadership Lessons from Star Trek, the Next Generation*, New York: Pocket Books.

Part 6

Transforming People's Lives

36. Discover your creator contacting you

ALAN FRASER BELL AND
HEATHER LOUISE BELL

Discover Your Creator Contacting You is the title of a book, which was once described by a well-known religious publisher as: 'too unorthodox for publication'. Since then, however, it has been published and is available worldwide.[1] Our book is a work in progress – for it shows people how to experience their creator as a reality in today's life, to grasp that invisible force for which we all reach.

Carl Jung

It was Carl Jung the psychologist who said, 'One of the main functions of formalized religion is to protect people against a direct experience of God.'[2] So it's no surprise that our book was considered too unorthodox to publish, for it describes exactly how anyone can have a direct personal experience of God's presence, Jesus and the Holy Spirit. This is real, it doesn't depend upon belief or faith.

Our book details a deeply moving account of many ways to experience the unique phenomena described by Jesus in biblical texts, concerning God's presence. These are a very powerful message, available to each and every one of us, regardless of religious belief.

Free to feel

We want to share details from the book, which show how easy it is to hear God's high-pitched chord in only one ear, and the warm breeze which blows between two people in his presence. There are pinpoints of light that hover over someone who is being helped, and other sensations. No one needs to be protected, as Carl Jung said. We need to be freed from restrictions and rituals and reach out personally to our creator himself and give him the chance to touch us. He does, but many don't listen, or pause long enough to feel. Nothing is more important than this.

The time has come

It is truly time for everyone to experience God's presence before it's too late. He has already shown us how late it is by the changes to our beautiful planet. He has always been very gentle and patient over thousands of years, but how much more evidence do we need, before we begin to live in harmony with God, each other and the planet?

Surely the true purpose of all religious beliefs is to experience God's presence, and to know it is him.

Hundreds of ordinary people are experiencing his presence. They are writing and talking about what they have seen, heard and felt. Many don't know what it is, but Jesus told us over 2000 years ago, so why have we taken so long to understand? It's all there in our book, and it's very simple.

Jesus' living words

Jesus said in the biblical texts that the only way to reach the Father was through him (John 14.6). He came to Earth to show us the way and he did. He still does.

> Jesus said:
> 'I will give you . . .
> What the eye has not seen, what the ear has not heard,
> What the hand has not touched,
> And what has not arisen in the heart of man.'[3]

Here Jesus is telling us how he will contact us and make himself known to future generations, not only those of his own time. As Jesus and God are one in the Trinity, we are therefore being contacted by God.[4]

'I will give you . . . '

This saying of Jesus is a clear indication how we can all experience God's presence. Many people have seen or heard something and felt a touch, without knowing what it is. These usually occur during prayer, meditation or when in a state of distress or when thanking God or asking for his help.

I will give you what the eye has not seen.

Many people see pinpoints of light which hover near someone in need of help or when losing consciousness.

I will give you what the ear has not heard.

This is the high-pitched sound that occurs in only one ear.

I will give you what the hand has not touched.

This is the warm breeze that blows gently between the hands of two people in his presence.

I will give you what has not arisen in the heart of man.

This is the spontaneous realization that we have actually experienced God's presence. We are not alone; we did not come into existence by chance; we were all created by a superb loving intellect and wisdom, who continues to contact us today.

God and Google

For many years we have been seeking ways to communicate our message concerning Jesus' sayings to a greater audience in order that they may be experienced worldwide as a reality in today's life. The advent of Google's 'Book Search' facility enabled every page of our book to be placed on Google's web site, in full colour and clarity, so that it may be read by everyone across the world. Each page can be studied on Google, even on a laptop in the middle of a jungle.

This was the opportunity we had been seeking and we did not just add a few pages to tempt readers to buy our book – but have made every page available on Google – because to us the most important thing of all is to fulfil our 'calling' to share something so special. It belongs to no one and everyone . . .

We take so much delight in helping someone make that step beyond belief into knowing we are not alone; we were all created and didn't happen by chance. You can see, hear and feel the creator's presence.

Search now

Take a look now on Google Book Search. Every page is available to read. Follow the links below to find our book on the internet:

Call up the web address <http://books.google.co.uk>.
Then type in the title of the book, *Discover Your Creator Contacting You*.
Then click on the *<Search Books>* button.
The book title will appear with a small image alongside; click on the title and see the book appear (allow time for pages to load).
If you haven't time to read it all, start on page 117 to change your life.
Just enter the page numbers in the box above the page image and press the return key; 'How We Discovered God's Presence' will appear.

Prepare to be astonished as you experience his presence, as a high-pitched sound in only one ear, or small pinpoints of light, hovering near you, or a warm breeze or tickling sensation on your forehead and cheeks. A muscle may give a single twitch in an arm or leg.

A personal experience

You can carry out these directions at home in the tranquillity of your own space; there is no need for instruction by a charismatic personality or demonstrations in a meeting hall. It's a personal relationship with God everywhere and at all times. You don't even have to believe it, just try it, and give him a chance to touch you. This is not a test to see if he will make himself known; it's a test of yourself, to allow it to happen. But the experience is more beautiful if you do have a hint of belief. Then you will know you are not alone.

To believe or not

If you have utter disbelief, try to suspend it for a few moments to allow yourself to reach through your own barrier, because disbelief is a powerful negative force.

Your creator will change your life.

Jesus has shown us and told us something very special – beyond all religions – how to experience our creator's presence and communicate directly with Him, without rituals, procedures and religious wars. There is a great joy in knowing that God is guiding us all, with capabilities thousands of times greater than the minds of all the scientists and thinkers added together.

My Father's house

In the Gospel of St John we read that, 'In my Father's house are many mansions' (14.2). This is not a house as we know it, and the mansions are not rooms, but dimensions. All these experiences above are God's extra dimensions beyond the four in which we live.

The pinpoints of light that people see, exist in one or more of these extra dimensions and cannot be physically touched.

The high-pitched sound in only one ear is not from an external source, but is within the brain. A direct communication.

The warm breeze that blows between two people cannot be measured, it can only be felt.

Direct communication

All of these phenomena and others not detailed here are experienced by parts of the brain, which are probably not used for any purpose other than to receive communications from God. How profound to know that if we listen and observe, cast doubt aside and suspend our critical faculty for a while, we will receive information directly into our brain at a spectacular speed that passes through into consciousness when needed and completely changes our life.

In the silence you will hear

The last of our senses to fade after we slip into the next dimension (at the end of physical life) is hearing – all you have to do is listen. In this technological, multi-communication age in which we live, there is a profound eloquence knowing there will always be a signal from our creator.

I will speak to you throughout eternity. Be still, know I Am God.[5]

Enoch was asked to listen for the voice of God in all creation. God's presence through space and time.

The Trinity

We all live in a four-dimensional world, of height, length and width (spatial dimensions) and time. We all know about these, but to talk of ten dimensions becomes rather difficult, and yet quantum physicists frequently think in ten dimensions. The research at CERN[6] in the underground tunnels expects to discover new dimensions. Unimaginable sums of money have been invested in research to unlock these mysteries.

Now if we were to say that our creator made these ten dimensions, then it follows that he must reside in an eleventh or higher dimension. He cannot be in one that he has not yet created.

So if mankind understands the first three, height, length and width, and scientists are conversant with ten dimensions, it should be easier for us to think of our creator perhaps residing in the eleventh, twelfth and thirteenth, or as many as he wishes. Thus, having a dimension each, for the Father, the Son and the Holy Spirit – the Trinity.

They are all one, in the same way that our dimensions of height, length and width can describe one object, such as a simple cube, a sphere or anything else. This uses three dimensions to describe one object and is similar to the three dimensions of eleven, twelve and thirteen, describing the Trinity as one.

Many mansions

When Jesus speaks of his Father's house having many mansions, he is not talking of houses, rooms or buildings, but of many dimensions. ('In my Father's house are many mansions: if it were not so, I would have told you. I go to prepare a place for you' [John 14.2]). The Father, Son and Holy Spirit are the three dimensions which describe the Trinity as one, in the same simple way that we describe one cube with the three dimensions of height, length and width.

The most enlightening definition of the time dimension is: 'A realm or dimension in which cause and effect phenomena occur.'[7]

Resurrection

Thus Jesus would have no difficulty appearing to the Disciples in a locked room as in the Bible, because he exists in another dimension; he could then reorientate into our worldly three dimensions, having arrived inside the room and become a reality capable of being touched and asking for food and drink to demonstrate that he was not a vision.

Similarly, Jesus could leave the tomb in his unique dimension without moving the stone and again reorientate into our earthly three dimensions and appear in the fields nearby.

... came Mary Magdalene and the other Mary to see the sepulchre. And behold there was a great earthquake for the angel of the Lord descended from heaven, and came and rolled back the stone from the door, and sat upon it ... And said unto the women, Fear not ye: for I know that ye seek Jesus, which was crucified. He is not here: for he is risen, as he said. Come and see the place where the Lord lay. (Matthew 28.1–7)

The two Marys actually witnessed the stone being rolled away: and Jesus was not inside.

Turin shroud

Our creator is the cause, the effect is what he creates, and the realm is where he resides. In the mystery of the Turin Shroud the image in the material is the effect of Jesus changing from the dimensions of his physical body, into his other dimension of the Trinity. It is quite independent of physical matter and is capable of moving in and through earthly materials, perhaps as a frequency or vibration. Only Jesus, the Holy Spirit and the Father would have the ability to do this, as they would know the position and properties of every atom, and move at the speed of light, perhaps as quantum particles or photons and scorch the fibres of his shroud during the transition, thus forming the image.

Science and theology

For our creator to have made mankind and thousands of other remarkable life forms and placed them on this beautiful planet Earth, he must possess intellect and wisdom thousands of times greater than any of our quantum physicists and scientists, who have never brought anything into existence which was not already there.

If we would only have him with us in our scientific deliberations, we may begin to understand and reach beyond the confines of our four dimensions, instead of pretending that we have all evolved by pure chance. By so thinking, we limit our possibilities to those of the four dimensions of our physical world, whereas the healings we have seen clearly show other dimensions, because these healings should not be possible at all in our simple four-dimensional existence.

Living souls

Heather and I have enjoyed a scientific education and have applied these principles to our research into God's presence, so it came as an interesting comment of Carl Jung when he said: 'Learn your theories as well as you can, but put them aside when you touch the miracle of a living soul.'[8] This is what we have to do as we witness the phenomena and healings which do not belong to the dimensions in which we live.

Understanding the Trinity

The three dimensions of the Trinity are made known to mankind through the human brain and consciousness and we become aware of them.[9] As no scientific device exists for their display, we tend to ignore them, and yet our intellect and consciousness are already a very small part of our creator's presence and should be encouraged to develop, just by asking, then waiting for his communications. His ways of replying are also detailed in the book, as described by Jesus.

Many people have great difficulty understanding the Trinity as one and call it a contradiction. They also indicate other inconsistencies in the Bible and then tend to dismiss all the biblical writings; but they are not contradictions; they are only paradoxes waiting to be understood. The more we discover, the closer science and theology will draw together. There are many scientific reasons that show the messages in the Bible are the work of our creator, who brought us into physical life having 'loved us' before he made the Earth (John 17.24). Because, as Jesus said: 'We were all loved by the Father before he gave foundation to the earth.'[10]

The creation event

We could have existed before the creation event of the universe, the so-called Big Bang. We could have been in a different time dimension, because scientists tend to think of time as starting at the Big Bang. Are we all time travellers, but what dimension were we in before the creation event? Perhaps a similar one to that of Jesus, but we have become locked into the physical earthly materials of three spatial dimensions plus time, and are only released when our body turns to dust, whereas Jesus can transpose himself from one dimension to another at will – his own will.

Free will

He can be with each one of us today in any of his many dimensions. We are not alone; we have a predestined framework in which we can exert our free will and must accept responsibility for our thoughts and actions.

We all have free will, but are not able to change from one dimension to another. It is our conscious mind that exerts free will. Our creator made it so. But when someone is unconscious they are already in his care, where predestination takes over and free will is suspended. However, their creator is with them all the time, which is how we possess life and he maintains it until he finally takes it away. So free will and predestination are complementary not contradictory as many people seem to think.

Dimension suspended

When someone awakens from an unconscious state, the first words they speak are: 'Where am I?' Even if they are in the same place as before, they are aware of having been somewhere else, then suddenly know they are back. They have been in some other place (or dimension) and our creator has been looking after them and, when it's safe to do so, he re-establishes their free will so that they can care for themselves once more.

When we leave this 'mortal coil' we may return to the dimension in which we existed before God 'gave foundation to the earth.' He gave us the chance to find him with our free will, but he will not allow our pollution of the planet to spoil his purpose. He may start again to create a new living world, with less free will or none at all. This may be his purpose for reaching so many of us, to help inspired people to restore the Earth.

Virgin Mary

In the biblical writings, Mary was overshadowed by the Holy Spirit, then found to be with child. She was a virgin and had known no man. This may be equivalent to a present-day scientific process in which genetic material is fused together without fertilization by using a 'spark' of electricity, to create another living creature.

This biblical story is not contradictory to belief but is a paradox that seems to be explained by modern science. Was the overshadowing similar to the brilliant light that accompanied the birth of baby Jesus.

This was the presence of the Father, for Jesus said: 'The Father is concealed by his light.'[11]

The Book of John the Evangelist (probably dating to the sixth or seventh century) attributes these words to Jesus: 'When my Father thought to send me into the world, he sent his angel before me, by name Mary to receive me. And I when I came down entered in by the ear and came forth by the ear.'[12]

There are many references to the ear in biblical texts.

Bright light

Although Mary had been overshadowed by the Holy Spirit to initiate the formation of a pure physical body for Jesus, could it have been his spirit dimension that entered by the ear, and came forth by the ear (perhaps as a high-pitched sound)?

A bright light shone around, so that no one witnessed Jesus' birth.[13]

Was it a bright light that overshadowed Mary?

With modern quantum physics this is not as impossible as it seems, but is a way of describing something which was not understood at that time, but is beginning to have meaning today. This is surely God's presence as Jesus said that no one would see the Father, for he is concealed by his light.[14] Jesus was a physical human being, with one or more extra dimensions of the Father, and in his ministry in later life he spoke of these phenomena: 'You hear with one ear.'[15] 'I will give you what the ear has not heard, and what the eye has not seen.'[16]

Spark of life

What made the scientists think of using a spark of electricity to bring the fused cells 'into life', as this would be unknown in biblical times? What was the Greek or Hebrew word that was translated to mean 'overshadowed': was it the nearest the scholars could find to the word 'spark' or flash of light? First John states 'God is light' (1.5) and in scientific terms light has many wavelengths (frequencies, colours), carrying different energy values, and the mysterious photons.

Light is invisible unless we place something in its path, as it travels at a speed beyond which nothing else can move. God is invisible, but when we stand in his path and ask that he touch us, we are illuminated. Perhaps the phrase 'become enlightened' has a far deeper meaning than we understand.

We invite readers to explore the fascinating concepts we have touched on in these few pages and more deeply in our book. The experience of God is within reach. We are all the same distance from him.

Hundreds of people

Throughout the years we have helped hundreds of people to overcome many health problems and, interestingly, their letters show how they have also developed a tangible awareness of God. Many describe his contact through the physical and mental senses, just as Jesus foretold all those years ago. These people are actually experiencing God's presence.

We have witnessed many miracles and beneficial changes by placing our hands on someone's head or body, who was suffering, then praying (in our minds, not necessarily out loud), asking God, Jesus and the Holy Spirit for help. It is that simple, and it stems, not from belief, but from knowing. We can all see, hear and feel our creator's presence, if we allow it to happen, instead of always thinking negative thoughts which act as a barrier, demanding that God himself breaks through to us.

There is nothing we could add to our work that would make it any better, no rituals or methods. It is all God's work and he does it in his own time and in his own way. On some occasions, he would cure something other than that for which our request had been made, because, unknown to us, it was necessary for that healing to take place first.

Discovery

Soon, we realized that the healing work was only part of what was really ahead for us. Our main purpose in life from then onwards was to help everyone to experience God's presence. Our whole book should be studied to follow this journey of discovery as it details how to achieve a direct communication with God. It is beyond belief. It is knowing.

When you become aware of the high-pitched sound 'in only one ear', then ask, 'Is that you Jesus?' and the sound swells up in an unusual way: without becoming any louder, it is more intense. This makes it difficult to describe, but you will know what it is. One or more of the other sensations we have mentioned may also occur at the same time.

This must always be done in a positive way, not as a test to see what happens. This is your attempt; it is you reaching out, because you want to know him as a reality. Allow the communion to take place, by breaking through your own barrier.

He answered our prayers

Some years ago, in our time of great need, we stumbled upon these unique phenomena, which to our surprise are identical to those spoken of by Jesus in biblical texts. These bring his sayings directly into today's world, not in terms of the gloom and doom of modern-day prophets and scientists, but as an absolute confirmation of his presence here and now.

All is well with the world and our futures will be special. This is why he is reaching out to us, ever more intensely as each year passes, and why so many people are experiencing his presence in these turbulent times.

Follow this path

Speak with him, and know it is he who answers, for his reply will be only in one ear.

Meditate on God's presence to receive his messages.

Step from belief into knowing our creator without having to acquire great knowledge and skills, or by enduring deep intellectual processes.

Keep our planet as a Garden of Eden, to work with God, not against him.

Restore the gift of communication with our creator. We all had this in abundance as a newborn baby, but over the years many have lost contact.

Change the world by thought and prayer alone, but, first, you may have to change yourself, to go beyond belief into knowing the creative force who brought you into life.

The future

Heather and I are continuing our research in many areas and have a small document in preparation concerning this work that we hope to send to those who are interested, particularly extending ways of perfecting the human body and soul, as a temple to receive God's presence, for his creative purpose. We have added several more anti-cancer herbs to the already lengthy list of over 60, noted in *Discover Your Creator Contacting You*, as more natural benefits become available, with some remarkable successes, instead of the more destructive chemical and other treatments.

Jesus said: 'I come because you need me'[17]

We have included some moving extracts from letters received by us, during 30 years of research, that make fascinating reading. There are hundreds of these from the many people we have helped to discover God's presence and to overcome their illnesses. These letters describe the remarkable phenomena experienced by the writers, which are identical to those spoken of by Jesus in biblical texts. They show how he will make himself known to us all, in the years following his ministry here on earth. (Names and addresses supplied, but not published to maintain confidentiality.)

I thank you both for praying for me, they have been answered, I have heard the Healing Wavelength, very strong indeed. (Mr B. – North Wales)

I thank God most fervently, after three days she was out of bed, and after five, was going for walks. I feel at peace and full inside, instead of empty desolation and frustration. (Mrs W. – London)

I have this week experienced the high-pitched sound; I have felt the tickling twice in my face and an action in my leg muscles. (Mr R. – California, USA)

When I meditate I have the tickling on my face, I have the quiet high-pitched sound in my ear, the muscles moving in my body and a lovely warmth on top of my head. (Mrs R. – Gwynedd)

While I was reading your book, the feeling of loneliness left me and a contentment came over me, and I no longer feel alone. (Mrs B. – Derbyshire)

Many thanks for all your prayers, I now know God is with us. (Miss P. – Paris)

A few nights ago whilst meditating a light breeze crossed my face, then a few seconds later my whole body began to tremor for about 30 seconds, then last night the same happened again. (Mr N. – Liverpool)

I first experienced the Healing Wavelength over 25 years ago, when I sought help from you and Heather, and I still hear it whenever I meditate. At the time my son and I benefited tremendously from this. (Mrs C. – Manchester)

I did hear a sound in my right ear last night, quite strongly. I have derived tremendous benefit from your prayers, and have resumed reading my Bible and praying each day. (Mrs B. – W. Yorkshire)

I meditate each evening with you between 10.00 p.m. and 10.30 p.m., and I am very much aware of The Healing Wavelength. I feel a tingling sensation down one side of my neck and feel very relaxed. (Mrs M. – Leeds)

I always awaken with the musical sound in my ears, and still experience that strange and wonderful sensation that goes right through me, and I do believe that through my contact with The Healing Wavelength I have been cured of Asthma that I suffered from nearly all my life. I wish you and Heather, as always, continued success in your mission to heal the sick. (Mrs C. – Swinton)

I keep seeing different lights around the house, mostly silver and a beautiful blue and I thank God I am not so alone. (Adelaide [address not known])

I receive the high-pitched musical chord chiefly at my left side and chance to be completely deaf in that ear. I feel one does not hear it in the ordinary sense. Whenever I think of you I am aware of the high-pitched chord, and have been conscious of it most of the time I have been writing this. (Mrs B. – Leicester)

During meditation last Sunday I had a sensation of being surrounded by a shower of sparks of light, followed by a tingling inside my entire body. After meditation I felt the urge to open the family Bible for a message. Job 19:21; 'Have pity upon me O ye my friends; for the hand of God hath touched me.' The tingling sensation occurs each time I repeat these words. Thank you again. (Ms V. – Florida, USA)

I feel tremors and mild currents passing up and down my legs and sometimes cobwebs brushing on my face. (Mrs P. – Liverpool)

I am getting the Healing Wavelength a clear ringing tone above my left ear, though not my right. (Mr and Mrs F. – Birmingham)

I prayed as you directed, I feel they are being heard, I can feel a tingling right on top of my head. (Mrs H. – N. Ireland)

Thank you for letters and prayers, it's been such a miracle for me. (Miss B. – USA)

Whenever I talk to God and tell Him I am 'ready to receive Him' then I have such a warm glowing feeling in my hands . . . it is an amazing feeling and the warmth is not from heat exactly, it is a different sensation, almost like coming from inside out. My sister talks about 'being on a journey with God' as though He is teaching her lots of things, He is constantly with her. When she entered the Chapel the sound in her ear was SO strong. (Mrs G. – Hampshire)

I still receive The Healing Wavelength, it is such a comfort to know that God is near. (Mrs S. – Liverpool)

I felt such an overwhelming sense of peace that I cried. (Mrs R. – Preston)

I was blind, but now I can see all the colours and those either side, but not yet the shapes. (Miss H. – Yorkshire)

I feel no sorrow, I know no pain, I am unconcerned with all the stress around me. When I think about your garden and all this beauty, I am filled with complete peace, tranquillity and love. These are all feelings that I have never before experienced. (Miss L. – Pennsylvania, USA)

I am a Methodist minister in the field of clinical pastoral psychology. I am particularly interested in the different manifestations of God's divine power. When I read the account of the 'whistling sound' or 'high frequency vibrations', as described in the National Enquirer about your healing experiences, I was deeply moved by this. A few days before reading the article the Lord had been putting on my heart the thought that he comes in a high molecular energy fashion. After this thought came to me I read the article the following day. (Rev. P. – Oklahoma, USA)

Warm breeze

Jesus said, 'I will manifest myself' (make myself known) (John 14.21). All these people have experienced Jesus and God's presence, and he had already described how he would do this, by saying, 'You hear with one ear.'[18]

We have written about this earlier, as the high-pitched sound in only one ear. He continues to show himself in the pinpoints of light and mauve shapes, which appear when you ask for his help. And the warm breeze that blows between two people in his presence. Also the tickling sensations on the forehead and cheeks, which are identical to the experience of his disciples, when he: 'breathed on them', and they were filled with the Holy Spirit (John 20.21–2). The great step forward is from belief, hope and desire that God exists, into knowing that he really does and that he is with us all always.

Transforming energies

Carl Jung said: 'I cannot prove to you that God exists, but my work has proved empirically that the pattern of God exists in every man and that this pattern in the individual has at its disposal the greatest transforming energies of which life is capable. Find this pattern in your own individual self and life is transformed.'[19]

Notes

1. Bell and Bell, 2002.
2. See Darryl Pokea, <http://www.drpokea.com/thoughts.html>.
3. *Gospel of Thomas*, Logion 17 (cf. 1 Corinthians 2.9 (KJV)).
4. Bell and Bell, 2002, p. 129.
5. *The Gospel of the Essenes*, Book II, 'The Vision of Enoch, the Most Ancient Revelation – God Speaks to Man', trans. Edmond Bordeaux Szekely, listed in Bell and Bell, 2002; also Psalm 46.10 (KJB).
6. CERN: Council for European Nuclear Research – the world's largest particle physics laboratory.
7. Ross, 2001, p. 116.
8. Dana Ullman, <http://www.healthy.net/scr/Article.asp?Id=795>, 5th paragraph.
9. Bell and Bell, 2002, p. 196.
10. *The Gospel of the Essenes*, Book II, 'Essene Gospel of John', trans. Edmond Bordeaux Szekely, p. 86, listed in Bell and Bell, 2002; also John 17.23–4 (KJB).
11. *Gospel of Thomas*, Logion 83.
12. *Apocryphal New Testament*, 1953, p. 191; also at: Wesley Center Online <http://wesley.nnu.edu/biblical_studies/noncanon/writing/jonevan.htm>, para. 21.
13. Elliott, 1993, p. 64, para 19.
14. *Gospel of Thomas*, Logion 83.
15. Papyrus Oxyrhynchus I.1.

16. *The Gospel according to Thomas*, Logion 17; Coptic text established and translated by A. Guillaumont, H.-Ch. Puech, G. Quispel, W. Till and Yassah 'Abd al- Masih, listed in Bell and Bell, 2002; also 1 Corinthians 2.9 (KJB).

17. *Gospel of Peace of Jesus Christ by the Disciple John* (1947), p. 30, line 1; also John 14.18 (KJB).

18. Papyrus Oxyrhynchus I.1.

19. <http://www.dailycelebrations.com/jung.htm>, home page, last para.

References

Apocryphal New Testament (1953), trans. M. R. James, Oxford: Clarendon Press.

Bell, Alan Fraser, and Heather Bell (2002), *Discover Your Creator Contacting You*, Southport: Peacock Quill <www.alan-fraser-bell.com>; email: peacockquill@breathe.com.

Elliott, J. K. (1993), *The Apocryphal New Testament: A Collection of Apocryphal Christian Literature in an English Translation*, Oxford: Oxford University Press.

Gospel of Peace of Jesus Christ by the Disciple John (1947), trans. Edmond Székely and Purcell Weaver, Rochford: C. W. Daniel; Leatherhead: Bureau of Cosmotheraphy, 2nd edn.

Ross, Hugh (2001), *The Creator and the Cosmos: How the Greatest Scientific Discoveries of the Century Reveal God*, Colorado Springs: NavPress, 3rd expanded edn.

Part 7

Appendices

About the contributors

Peter Bates (*Anglican*)
Peter Bates was employed for over 30 years in the Electricity Supply Industry, for many years as a management scientist, and latterly as Customer Services Manager.

After a year on secondment to a homelessness charity, he accepted an offer of early retirement and since then has practised as a freelance consultant on ministry, church and charity matters. He has carried out extensive studies of the use of time and the setting of objectives by clergy and charity workers, dioceses and deaneries etc. He is a founder member of MODEM and has served continuously on its national Leadership Committee holding office as Membership and Finance officer.

Alan Fraser Bell
Heather Louise Bell (*Anglicans*)
A pharmaceutical chemist for 23 years and member of the Royal Pharmaceutical Society for 54 years, Alan Fraser Bell retired in 1976. Since then, as a health consultant, he and his daughter Heather, a gemmologist, have been involved in independent research covering healing through prayer and the use of natural nutrients, vitamins, minerals and herbs. Their work has featured on TV, radio, newspapers and magazines throughout the world.

Their work has primarily involved the study of ancient biblical texts and documents concerning Jesus' sayings and the relevance they still have in today's world. Alan's experience in codes and communications was useful in understanding the subtle messages of Jesus.

Similarly, communication has played an important part in Heather's writing and creative skills and vital for identifying the facts needed in her role for several years as Pre-Press Supervisor with the *Liverpool Daily Post & Echo* and, more recently, as an internet research writer.

Together they have written the book *Discover Your Creator Contacting You*, which provides an understanding of how to experience God's presence as a reality. They may be reached by email: peacockquill@breathe.com

Dr Peter Brierley (*Anglican*)
Initially a government statistician, then a Bible Society Director. Started MARC Europe in 1983 and Christian Research in 1993. He is known as the editor of the *UK Christian Handbook* (started 1972) and *Religious Trends*, the author of several books on management and leadership as well as being responsible for comprehensive church censuses in England, Wales and Scotland. He now acts as a consultant for churches and Christian agencies in vision building, interpretative research and strategic enabling, with a specific interest in strengthening leadership. He may be reached on peter@brierleyres.com

Revd Bob Callaghan (*Anglican*)
His main achievement is to have demolished the church of which he has been vicar since 1991. Rebuilt as a Healthy Living Centre, St Edmunds, Dartford, is now a flagship project in the Thames Gateway. It serves the local community as the Anglican parish church as well as a GP centre, IT training suite, community café and Sure Start Children's Centre. Prior to Dartford, Bob worked in London at St John's Hyde Park and St Paul's Winchmore Hill. He trained for the ministry at King's College, London and Lincoln Theological College. More recently he completed an MA in Community Development.

Revd Dr David Clark (*Methodist*)
He was a presbyter in the Methodist Church for many years. He served in circuits in Sheffield and Inner London before moving to become a Senior Lecturer in Community Education at Westhill College, Birmingham. During that time he set up the National Centre for Christian Communities and Networks, the Christians in Public Life Programme, and the Human City Institute. He has written widely about the Christian Community Movement, lay ministry in public life, schools as learning communities and urban renewal. In 2005 he moved out of Presbyterian ministry to become a member of the Methodist Diaconal Order.

Revd Geoff Cornell (*Methodist*)
Geoff Cornell is currently Superintendent of the West London Mission of the Methodist Church where he leads a team of four ministers and one deacon. He began his ministry in the Mid Glamorgan Mission team Ministry before serving in Stockport and Kenton in North London. His 2001 Sheffield MA resulted from the consultancy for Mission and Ministry Course at Cliff College.

Revd Professor Leslie Francis (*Anglican*)
Professor of Religions and Education within the Warwick Religions and Education Research Unit, Warwick University. He is also Canon

Theologian at Bangor Cathedral, North Wales. His research interests draw together the fields of religions education, practical and empirical theology, and the psychology of personality and individual differences. He is a Fellow of the British Psychological Society, President of the Rural Theology Association, Vice President of the International Society for Empirical Research in Theology, and a Trustee and Board Member of the International Seminar on Religious Education and Values.

Tim Harle (*Anglican*)
A business ecologist working at sustainable organizational change at the interface of business and faith. His career includes a senior role in a FTSE100 company, director of a small company and work with UK government ministers. His recent publications include contributions to *John Adair: Fundamentals of Leadership* (Palgrave Macmillan) and *Leadership: The Key Concepts* (Routledge). He is a Licensed Lay Minister (Reader) in an Anglican diocese and a Visiting Lecturer with the Bristol Business School.

Alan Harpham (*Anglican*)
A part-time Chairman of the APM Group <www.apmgroup.co.uk>, with a portfolio of other interests including being a director of major-sporty <www.majorsporty.com>, chair of the Ecumenical Board of Workplace Ministry Hertfordshire and Bedfordshire <www.work-placeministry.org.uk> and a board member of the International Centre for Spirit at Work <www.spiritatwork.org>. He has been a director of P5 – the Power of Projects and Subject Matters, Managing Director of Nichols Associates (now the Nichols Group) and a former director of the MSc in Project Management at Cranfield University's School of Management. He is a former chair of MODEM and a former Council member of the APM. He focuses on business start-ups, programme and project management and executive coaching for individuals and teams.

Revd David Hewitt (*Baptist*)
A Regional Minister with the South West Baptist Association, based in Exeter. He has previously been Assistant Minister of Upton Vale Baptist Church in Torquay, Minister of Counterslip Baptist Church in Bristol and Churches Secretary with the Evangelical Alliance and Minister of Andover Baptist Church. He is married to Katheryn and they have three children and three grandchildren. Besides the family, he lists his interests as cricket (watching and playing), books (writing and reading), music (playing and listening) and surfing (trying and failing).

Revd Shaun Lambert (*Baptist*)
He has been Senior Minister of Stanmore Baptist Church for ten years. Before entering the ministry, he worked for Lloyds Bank. He is a

regular contributor to the Baptist Times, and is particularly interested in leadership issues and the interface between psychology and theology. In developing that interest he has done a number of years training at Roehampton University in counselling and psychotherapy. In his role at Stanmore he has always worked as part of a team and believes in the importance of mentoring. He is married with two children and enjoys skiing, painting and walking and reading children's novels.

Dr Tony McCaffry (*Roman Catholic*)
He has specialized in religious education, first with children in schools, then with adults. He had studied philosophy in Ireland, theology in Canada, English and French at Southampton and for a Postgraduate Certificate in Education (PGCE) at Nottingham. He was the first lay principal of the Roman Catholic Westminster Adult Religious Education Centre and based his doctoral studies (University of Surrey 1988) on that experience. He was a Senior Lecturer in Theology, and then managed a local Council of Voluntary Service. Retired now with his wife in Surrey, he remains active in ecumenical and interfaith relations, social inclusion and striving for justice and peace.

Alistair McKay (*Mennonite*)
Serves as Director of Bridge Builders at the Mennonite Centre. He has been leading training courses in transforming church conflict since 1996 when he co-founded Bridge Builders. He also leads mediation and reconciliation courses for individuals and groups within churches and church-based organisations.

He has an MA in Conflict Transformation from Eastern Mennonite University and is now studying for a Doctorate in Ministry at Spurgeon's College. He wrote on congregational decision-making in the book *Making Peace with Conflict* (Herald Press 1999). He is always facing the challenge of integrating his teaching into his daily life.

Revd Roger Martin (*Baptist*)
Currently the Senior Minister in The Tabernacle, Stockton-on-Tees – one of the largest Baptist churches in the UK.

He was trained at Spurgeon's College and is now its Vice-Chairman, having been a Governor for a number of years. During his 40 years in ministry, he and his wife, Liz, have helped a considerable number to enter full time service in the Baptist Church and are passionate about supporting those who are serving Jesus on the front line.

For three years he was the Moderator of the Baptist Union Council and with Liz has been overseas on many occasions in places like Albania, Afghanistan and Brazil in order to take conferences and to encourage Christian workers.

They have four sons, two of whom are pastors.

About the contributors

John Nelson (*Anglican*)
An Anglican layman working as a management consultant with the Diocese of Liverpool. Formerly Head of Management Studies at the former Liverpool Polytechnic (now John Moore's University).

Edited *Management and Ministry* (1996), *Leading, Managing, Ministering* (1999), and with John Adair, *Creative Church Leadership* (2004) for MODEM and published by Canterbury Press Norwich.

Revd Brian Nicholls (*Baptist*)
Senior Pastor at South Parade Baptist Church, Headingley, Leeds, a lively evangelical church with five congregations and a further group emerging in a nearby inner city area. He has previously served as pastor of a group of churches in rural mid Derbyshire (1973–82) and in a larger multi-ethnic city church in Nottingham (1983–95). For the next ten years he was General Superintendent and then Regional Minister Team Leader in the Heart of England Baptist Association serving the Baptist churches of the West Midlands. He is Moderator of the Mission Executive of the Baptist Union of Great Britain.

Revd Dr Ben Rees (*Welsh Presbyterian*)
A native of West Wales, he has served in the full time ministry with the Presbyterian Church of Wales for 45 years: in the Cynon Valley (in which he made a sociological study of the area chapels in the valley (Wirral, 1975); and, since 1968, in the city of Liverpool in the Allerton/Wavertree, Garston and Waterloo areas.

His service has included ministry as a hospital chaplain, lecturing in higher education institutions, preaching ministry in Britain and the USA and leading 20 pilgrimages to the Holy Land. He has also been a pioneer in ecumenical work, Jewish–Christian affairs, as well as a motivator of charitable organizations, author of 48 books and pamphlets in Welsh and English. He has edited a supplement for three weekly newspapers since 2003.

Carol Richards (*Anglican*)
Graduated in philosophy and sociology from Exeter University in 1981. She has worked in urban ministry ever since, becoming a Church of England Licensed Lay Reader in 1987. She currently works at St John's Church in Stratford in the London Borough of Newham where her husband, David, is Vicar. She also works part time as the Bishop of Barking's Regeneration Adviser.

Revd Dr Vaughan Roberts (*Anglican*)
An Anglican priest who has served in a variety of churches whilst also being a hospice and university chaplain, vocations adviser and director of ordinands. As well as degrees in biblical studies and theology he has

a PhD in organizational psychology and management from Bath University. He has written and reviewed widely on the nature of ministry as well on as his other interests – including film, story and poetry.

He contributed to *Managing the Church*, edited by G. R. Evans and Martyn Percy.

Paddy Rylands (*Roman Catholic*)
An Adult Education Adviser for the Roman Catholic Diocese of Shrewsbury. Her long and wide experience makes her a much sought after training resource across England and Wales.

Len Simmonds (*Anglican*)
Spent most of his working life as a senior manager and director in newspaper publishing, but now a business and management consultant helping a wide range of organizations that want to make a change in the way that they operate.

He has a keen interest in the challenges of leading, managing and ministering in the twenty-first-century church and plays an active role in dealing with issues to do with the church in the city centre and workplace chaplaincy. He serves on numerous committees connected with his own diocese, church and village community.

Revd Roger Standing (*Baptist*)
A Baptist minister, presently tutor in Mission, Evangelism and Pastoral Ministry at Spurgeon's College in London. Having previously ministered in Liverpool, Leeds and Croydon, he was for seven years the Regional Minister/Team Leader of the Southern Counties Baptist Association where he led an association of 175 churches. An occasional contributor to *Third Way* and the *Baptist Times*, his publications include *Finding the Plot: Preaching in a narrative style, Preaching for the Unchurched in an Entertainment Culture* and *Re-emerging Church: Strategies for reaching a returning generation*.

Revd Dr Peter Stevenson (*Baptist*)
Director of Training at Spurgeon's College in London, before joining the staff in 1995 he had served for 17 years as a Baptist Minister in Bedford, Shirley (Solihull) and West Norwood in South London. He enjoys teaching various aspects of Christian doctrine and practical theology and spends a lot of time encouraging students to
preach and communicate more effectively. He oversees the MTh in Applied Theology and the Doctorate of Ministry Courses for people involved in various aspects of Christian leadership. He is the joint author with Stephen Wright of *Preaching the Atonement* (2005).

About the contributors

Revd Peter Stevenson (*United Reformed Church*)
Currently completing the Princeton (USA) Doctor of Ministry Degree in which he is looking at the way community ministry is perceived.

When ordained into the United Reformed Church in 2000 he believed his calling was to the wider community. Encouraged by the congregations at Holyhead Road, Brownshill Green and Keresley in Coventry, he has developed a close relationship with local schools, residential care homes and Jaguar Cars Limited.

He is married with two children: Adam is doing postgraduate studies in Creative Writing and Faye is studying for her A levels.

Professor Jennifer Tann (*Anglican*)
Professor of Innovation at the University of Birmingham Business School, an independent consultant and a senior associate with Caret. Author of a large number of papers on innovation and organization change, she has contributed to management videos and appeared on TV and radio.

She is now a member of the Bishop's Council, the Pastoral Group and Diocesan Synod in Gloucester. She is work consultant to two bishops and several other clergy besides being executive coach to several senior executives in the public sector and is churchwarden in the country parish in which she lives.

Major Ivor Telfer (*Salvation Army*)
Became a Salvation Army Officer in 1984 after a career in finance including merchant banking.

Married to Carol (also a Salvation Army Officer) they have three children. Periods of service in the Salvation Army have included church work in Northern Ireland, England and Canada, international development in Pakistan and in Canada, linking with the government. Media and mission work in the Manchester SA HQ followed. He was Chair of the Gold Group – an umbrella group for the churches serving the Commonwealth Games in Manchester, achieving his Master's Degree in Strategic Management during this time.

In 2006 he became Divisional Commander for the Salvation Army in West Scotland responsible for all aspects of SA work in the area.

Revd Terry Tennens (*Baptist*)
Executive Director of International Justice Mission UK, a Christian Rights organization that pursues the skills of criminal investigators and lawyers to rescue people from violent injustice in Africa, Asia and Latin America. He is also an accredited minister of the Baptist Union of Great Britain.

He was formerly Director of Building Bridges of Hope for Churches

Together in Britain and Ireland (CTBI) which developed the practice of Mission Accomplishment in order to assist local churches in God's mission. He is an Associate Minister with Fresh Expressions and part of the leadership of Work Dynamics, a workplace mission unit in Central Colchester.

Andy Williams (*Anglican*)

The Youth Worker at REVIVAL, the Youth Congregation of St John's Church in Woodbridge, Suffolk. Coming to the end of his fourth decade, he has been a full time church based youth worker for nine years and as a volunteer for a further twelve.

Having completed a BA (Hons) Degree in Applied Theology at Moorlands College, he is now with his second Anglican church and is passionate about encouraging young people to grow in their faith and for churches to engage with young people.

He is married with two young children.

Keith Williams (*Ecumenical Anglican*)

A Director of *Energise* which is a social enterprise dedicated to helping individuals and organizations reach their full potential. He specializes in coaching leaders and management teams in the voluntary sector, social enterprises and entrepreneurs.

He is on the Ecumenical Board of Workplace Ministry in Hertfordshire and Bedfordshire and is Treasurer of MODEM.

Prior to joining Energise he had 24 years consultancy experience with leading management consulting firms and was formerly a Vice President of A.T. Kearney, responsible for its European Transformation practice. He has led many change programmes in the private and public sectors.

Heather Wraight (*Baptist*)

Committed first of all to serving God and secondly to good communication. She spent 22 years making Christian radio programmes for developing countries and then turned her skills to research. As Deputy Director of Christian Research she undertook most of its qualitative research alongside editing the *UK Christian Handbook*.

Outside work her passion is to share Christ with young people, especially 11–14 year-olds who are likely to drop out of church. Recently retired, she has moved and has had to find a new welcoming church for herself!

MODEM

MODEM exists to enable churches to explore and engage with managerial and organizational issues. Its primary task is to lead and enable authentic dialogue between exponents of religious and secular leadership and management.

Formed in 1993 as a national ecumenical registered charity MODEM has become established as the 'Voice of Leadership, Management and Ministry'.

Building on the work of others

MODEM replaced the former Christian Organisation Research and Advisory Trust (CORAT). In 1991, CORAT decided to call a consultation meeting of all interested parties to review its work over the previous 20 or so years and to determine whether or not it should continue as an organization. A further meeting agreed to encourage the creation of a new network of communication for individuals and organizations relating to the managerial and organizational aspects of the work of the churches and other Christian bodies.

What's in a word

The word MODEM was originally an acronym for 'Managerial and Organisational Disciplines for the Enhancement of Ministry'. Subsequently, it has (like British Telecom's 'BT') become a term in its own right, symbolizing a two-way facilitator in which the insights move freely back and forth between the worlds of management and ministry.

Who is MODEM?

You are! MODEM is a gathering of people, the members of MODEM who are passionate to see good ministry and good management working together to build up all God's people whether in the church-place or the workplace.

Emerging soley from that gathering are the Trustees, the Patrons and the leadership committee. While most members are individual, some also represent groups and companies. There are also a number of 'emeritus' members who provide an important reference point for MODEM practice and policy.

MODEM in the marketplace

MODEM provides a forum for the exchange of experience in the practice of leadership, management and ministry in the secular world and in the Church. It has a particular focus on the development of good organizational and leadership models. The strength of its growing numbers in membership demonstrates that a significant number of practitioners want to associate themselves with MODEM's aims and objectives. We receive frequent positive acclamations about our work.

MODEM is a collaborative organization. We try to involve our members in our activities and our projects. We also set out to work in cooperation with organizations with similar interests. We are members of a forum of sister organizations which meets regularly. These include the Christian Association of Business Executives, the Industrial Christian Fellowship, the Network of Ministers in Secular Employment and the Ridley Hall Foundation.

MODEM is an Asssociate Member of Churches Together in Britain and Ireland and works closely in partnership with it as the Voice of Leadership, Management and Ministry.

MODEM publications

MODEM has produced three bestsellers to date, published by Canterbury Press. These have received much attention and have been well reviewed. Two of them have had to be reprinted to meet demand, especially in the USA.

Management and Ministry (1996) tackles the issue of churches needing to manage their resources effectively and efficiently.

Leading, Managing, Ministering (1999) explores the wider issues of managing in ministry as well as ministering in management and of both in leading organizations, sacred and secular.

Creative Church Leadership (2004) focuses on creative church leadership which raises questions that are crucial for the Christian Church today as it faces challenges within its own ranks, from other faiths and from a world in need of spiritual wisdom and direction. A team of eminent writers and practitioners in the fields of leadership, management and ministry reflect on issues that are crucial to the future of the Church.

MODEM also responds to the critical managerial and organizational issues affecting the mainstream denominations of the Church. Papers are available from MODEM in response to the Turnbull Report on the Church of England's organizational structure and the Hurd Report on the See of Canterbury. The latest paper is an exploration of a Christian understanding of leadership.

MODEM books and other publication have provided the focus for gatherings across the UK through a series of book launches, seminars and conferences. The MODEM newsletter, *MODEM Matters*, and the magazine, *Spirit in Work*, keep members well informed of MODEM activities.

MODEM – research and development

As part of an overall commitment to research, MODEM produced the report, *Hope of the Manager*, which examines energizing for leadership. The leadership committee attend a bi-annual residential conference which has focused on important and topical areas of Christian leadership and have resulted in the publication of papers in this area.

Modern MODEM

> MODEM has carried the torch for the importance of considering issues of leadership and management in relation to those of ministry. (Sir Philip Mawer, Parliamentary Commissioner for Standards, Patron of MODEM)

MODEM Matters and *Spirit in Work* are now produced in electronic format, available as a direct email or via the MODEM web site. The web site <www.modem.uk.com> is now fully operational and gives easy access to all MODEM papers and activities.

Contact MODEM

To find out more about MODEM, its work and its membership, visit the web site <www.modem.uk.com> or contact the MODEM National Secretary, John Nelson, on 01704 873973.

Patrons

MODEM National Leadership Committee

Emeritus

Premier Corporate Member

Premier Group Member

Churches Together in Britain and Ireland (CTBI) (MODEM is an Associate Member of CTBI)

Individual members

MODEM has attracted approaching 300 individual members – clergy and lay from Church and business

Thinking about Christian leadership

A short MODEM paper which brings together the leadership displayed by Jesus, some of the present-day thinking about leadership of Professor John Adair, and the key principles of the Christian Association of Business Executives (CABE)

MODEM is a national and ecumenical Christian network which seeks to initiate authentic dialogue between exponents of leadership, organization, spirituality and ministry in order to aid the development of better disciples, communities, society and the world.

One of the short-term objectives of the MODEM Leadership Committee is to invite the Churches to renew their commitment to the leadership of people by encouraging and facilitating 'Thinking about Christian Leadership', based on the life and teaching of Jesus that will be of help to people both in the respective Churches and to Christians serving in other organizations. Every organization today has to take account of change. Change calls for leadership. Therefore, at the present time, of considerable change, MODEM hopes that this paper will be found helpful to both leaders in the Churches and to leaders in the business community.

Setting the scene

In his book *The Leadership of Jesus and Its Legacy Today*[1] Professor John Adair, Britain's first Professor of Leadership and a renowned authority on the subject, drew attention to the fact that Jesus had a genius for leadership. It is therefore reasonable for Christians to believe that the example of leadership set by Jesus ought to be better known to Christians and to be practised more widely. It is also interesting to note that many experienced leaders, both past and present, regard the Bible as 'the greatest book on leadership ever written'. As well as including the story of Jesus it also tells of people before Him who, putting their faith in God, allowed God to lead them; and of people who, after Jesus' life and Resurrection, sought the help of God the Holy

Spirit to guide them in the way ahead. Furthermore, Christianity has a rich heritage of wisdom, and effective leadership requires wisdom! As the Bible says: 'The beginning of wisdom is the most sincere desire for instruction, and concern for instruction is love of her' (of wisdom) (Wisdom 6.17) (KJB).

The early roots of leadership – the Ancient Greeks, Judaism, the Jews and the Romans

Well before the birth of Christ the first thoughts about leadership in the Western world were being expressed in Ancient Greece by philosophers such as Socrates and Xenophon, Plato and Aristotle. Their ideas had a profound influence throughout the known world. Ancient Greece was to become the cradle of Western civilization and it is interesting to note that much of Plato's thinking was carried forward through the Neoplatonists; for example, the question of the immortality of the soul. Subsequently, much later, under Thomas Aquinas, some aspects of Aristotle's philosophy were also incorporated into Christian theology, basically, the idea that, although revelation was primary, logical argument based on observed facts from the natural world had its own sphere of authority.

Meanwhile, probably for around 2000 years, a great depth of learning and wisdom had been accumulated by Judaism (as recorded in the Old Testament). This vast fund of knowledge had a great influence on all aspects of Hebrew life, ethics and law. Indeed, it shaped the basis of Israelite culture and society, the society into which Jesus was born and in which he grew up. The ancient Hebrew legacy concerning the remarkable exploits of Moses and his encounter with the voice of God on Mount Horeb is of fundamental importance to Judaism, greatly influencing over the centuries Jewish life, as it still does today. This legacy also suggests that some early appreciation of both leadership and management, particularly some understanding about basic logistics, must have existed in some form or other at the time of Moses. A series of long hot journeys mostly on foot into the dry, dusty, waterless Sinai Desert over a period of 40 years involving many thousands of men, women and children together with all their belongings was not something to be undertaken lightly! It was a feat that must have required considerable practical logistical ability. This early appreciation of the art of leadership was passed on to Joshua, the Judges, David and Solomon, and the accumulated fund of knowledge and experience has impacted for centuries on the development of leadership. It was the seed bed out of which the Christian Church, the New Israel, grew.

Later, from about 753 BC, Rome gradually grew in size and influence so that by about AD 117 the vast Roman Empire had become the dominant power around the Mediterranean, in parts of Europe, the British Isles and the Holy Land. The authorities in Rome, responsible for governing and administering this vast far-flung empire, appreciated the importance of leadership. They expected those in authority under Rome to demonstrate timely practical leadership. In particular, they emphasized the great importance of leaders thinking ahead so that they developed foresight which would help them to have a clear vision about future tasks. They were then expected to share that vision with those they led. The Romans expected their leaders to be totally committed to the task in hand and to expect a similar commitment from their own subordinate leaders. Thereafter, Rome required its leaders to identify clearly and precisely what had to be done and to delegate accordingly. These thoughts on leadership and no doubt many others were probably well known in the Holy Land during Christ's early life. Almost certainly they were known to the Roman procurators.

An early example of the moral leadership of Jesus was shown while he was still a young man in Judea. He was led by the Spirit into the desert where he fasted for 40 days and nights and was tempted by the devil many times. Finally, Jesus said: 'Away from me, Satan! For it is written: "Worship the Lord your God, and serve him only"' (Matthew 4.10) (NIV). Serving the will of God was the mission of Christ's ministry and it was His remarkable leadership that led to the formation of Christendom.

Leadership has a strong moral dimension. When a leader is seen to ignore morality, trust in that particular leader is often reduced or lost. Like faith, leadership is a personal matter but it requires a degree of personal effort, a view that was expressed by Field Marshal Viscount Slim, the leader of the 14th Army in Burma during WW2 when he once said:

There is no one who, with a little thought, could not improve his or her ability as a leader.

The governing philosophy

The greatest commandment to love,[2] as expressed in ancient Greek by the word *agape* meaning 'duty or a commitment of devotion', is the embodiment of the life and teachings of Jesus. It is at the heart of the Christian Faith and consequently Christian leadership. The first two commandments (Mark 12.29–31) to 'love the Lord your God with all your heart and with all your soul and with all your mind and with all your strength' and to 'love your neighbour as yourself' (NIV) emphasize the importance of love, and they require Christians to put self-interest last. Therefore any act, especially by a leader, which detracts from the duty of devotion to those he or she leads contradicts Christianity. Accordingly, moral courage, and sometimes physical courage, humility and wisdom are all important qualities of a leader. Jesus set aside personal ambition, willing to take a road, if needs be, that led to a cross. From time to time in any walk of life, adversity will prevail and sometimes the going can get tough. Mistakes are made, human weaknesses show forth. Leaders must try to anticipate such events and be prepared to respond to difficulties with courage, humility and wisdom. Just as Jesus drew attention to the importance of the two Commandments so a leader must draw attention to the importance of the Aim. Without a clear, concise Aim any team will soon splinter.

Definition of Christian leadership

Christian leaders, remembering the teachings of Jesus, have a duty of devotion to their people. Accordingly, they inspire and give confidence so that the task, no matter how daunting, is achieved. Hence the old and hallowed motto of the Royal Military Academy, Sandhurst, 'Serve to Lead'. To lead effectively and gain respect and trust, leaders need to be discreet servants of those they lead, displaying leadership and an awareness of the importance of management. Leaders who set such an example soon form impressive teams. Jesus was the leader of just such a team. He showed throughout his ministry that he was the servant of his team. He was not above carrying out the humblest of tasks, such as washing his disciples' feet at the Last Supper. Humility and selflessness are natural qualities of a leader.

Vision and strategy

As already mentioned, the Romans had emphasized the importance of vision but its supreme importance had already been recognized centuries beforehand in the Holy Land. The book of Proverbs (29.18) states: 'Where there is no vision, the people perish: but he that keepeth the law happy is he' (KJB). Foresight, the ability always to think ahead, is a discipline required by everyone but it is an absolutely essential discipline of leadership, particularly if leaders are to honour what Jesus referred to as the two most important commandments

417

(Mark 12.29). It means thinking ahead about any problem or proposal and considering likely implications, thereby becoming fully prepared. Jesus' parable about the Good Samaritan tells how two people thought that the risks of being neighbourly were too great! (Luke 10.25–37). To achieve success at a higher or wider level, each team leader needs to ensure that his or her vision not only inspires the team but also meets the expectations of those above, as defined in their strategy. Therefore, it is particularly important that leaders ensure that their proposed vision conforms to the relevant strategy. This principle of harmonization is firmly based on loyalty, the first quality of any Christian. The fostering of unity in any organization is dependent upon leaders, at every level, conforming to the overall needs of higher strategy. The transcendence of Jesus' vision may have brought a unique quality of leadership available to no one else. 'Ye are the light of the world. A city that is set on an hill cannot be hid' (Matthew 5.14) (KJB).

Planning and teamwork

Success in any task, great or small, depends upon turning the strategy into a PLAN which, with foresight, takes full account of likely advantages and disadvantages. It needs to be well prepared, kept simple in chronological sequence with each phase delegated to a particular person who has a small team to help. Leaders must then with humour, encouragement and tact, build a cohesive team, keeping in balance the needs of the **Task** to be done, the needs of the **Team** and the needs of the **Individual** (TTI). The more team members are actively involved, the more successful the team is likely to be. Jesus was a genius of leadership. A major part of his life was spent inspiring and giving confidence to His disciples. They were an outstanding team. The example of teamwork that Jesus gave stands today, as it has for over 2000 years, as the ultimate example of teamwork. He delegated to his team and, following the Resurrection, the disciples, less Judas, went on to complete the Great Commission from which Christianity has grown (Matthew 28.16–20).

The relationship of leadership to management

Leadership is about people

It is an art in which some well-proven principles are very important, but the manner in which those principles are actually applied by a leader will depend entirely upon that leader. Every individual is unique (including every leader) – so every leader will lead in his or her own particular manner. However, every leader must take care to respect the principles of leadership that were learnt from Jesus. Therefore, there is no such thing as a 'Leadership Style' because every leader already has his or her own personal style. Everyone is born as a unique individual, so the way they lead in later life is also unique to them. Leadership, like Faith, is a very personal matter but there is nobody who, with a little personal effort, could not greatly improve their powers of leadership, nor should it ever be forgotten that the position of a leader can often be lonely.

Management is about material things

It is a science concerned with the efficient, effective and economic use of material resources in conjunction with the work of people. There are formulas that must be followed and measurements that must be made. However, management and leadership are inseparable because a problem concerning a material resource facing a team invariably results in an adverse effect on that team. It requires the team leader and the manager concerned to work together to find a solution. Jesus indicated as much when he spoke of the owner of a vineyard, his foreman and the labourers (Matthew 20.1) and the importance of good stewardship of resources (Luke 16.1–13).

The core principles of leadership displayed by Jesus

Throughout his ministry Jesus demonstrated his genius as a leader and the impact of his leadership is still felt over some 2000 years later. Jesus displayed four core principles which are evident in the Gospels and these same principles have been incorporated into numerous leadership models. Although advances in technology have radically changed, and still continue to change the world, these principles remain as important today as they were in biblical times.

The ability to communicate

Jesus was an absolute master of the ability to communicate. His ministry focused on teaching, preaching and healing. All three of these undertakings are concerned with timely communications. On the Sabbath he taught in synagogues and during the week he preached to larger crowds in the open air, using parables to portray and clarify his messages. The fame of his powers of healing spread all over Judea and Samaria and attracted large crowds. When he saw such crowds, he communicated verbally with them. On one such occasion, he delivered what has come to be called 'The Sermon on the Mount'/'The Sermon on the Plain' (Matt 5—7; Luke 6.17–49). It defined the moral and ethical standards expected of all Christians but was of such a high moral standard that it was realized that, without the help of God, man alone cannot cope or hope to attain such standards. Jesus chose this moment to pass this important but poignant message of humility and sincerity to humanity. Leaders must constantly listen, keep things simple and ask themselves, 'Have I made myself clear? Does the team understand all that they should?' Or, as modern people might say, 'It is not what we say, but what people hear that counts'. Jesus brought alive the vision of the Kingdom of God to His disciples.

Knowledge

'*The fear of the Lord is the beginning of knowledge*' *(Proverbs 1.7).* Those famous words taken from the Wisdom writings highlight the fundamental principle that a wise way to live is to develop a relationship of reverence for and submission to God. Jesus understood this from an early age. St Luke tells us that, as a young boy, Jesus took the opportunity to listen and to ask questions of the teachers in the Temple (Luke 2.41–52). Later, after His Baptism, He took some time out – 40 days in the wilderness – to reflect on God's purpose for him and his life. Thereafter, filled with the Spirit and knowledge of God, he was able to announce that the Kingdom of God is at hand. For a Christian leader Jesus' example is of great importance because it requires the leader to think about or reflect upon a particular issue by considering God's purpose as revealed in the teachings from scripture before making a final decision. Therefore the study of scripture is important to a Christian leader: 'The words I say to you are not just my own. Rather, it is the Father, living in me, who is doing his work' (John 14.10) (NIV). Likewise, it is widely acknowledged in life that authority goes with the one who knows and reflects in order that they lead wisely and with authority. Accordingly, in every profession, authority stems from relevant professional knowledge. Hence the wisdom of the motto: 'Knowledge dispels fear'.

If a leader incorporates into his or her life some of the wisdom learnt from Jesus, he or she is unlikely to fail. It means acquiring a fund of knowledge on Christianity as well as professional expertise. Much of that knowledge is often enhanced through a leader's preliminary consultation with a superior or with an appropriate expert; an experienced mentor, a wise counsellor, can be an invaluable help to a leader. Wherever and whenever possible, a leader should involve his or her team. Trust in their leader is strengthened by such involvement and by frequent and clear delegation of leadership responsibilities. Perhaps the most valuable component of knowledge is common sense – it is not always that common!

Care of people

To all Christians, especially leaders, people matter most. 'Recognition is the oxygen of the soul.' People are more important than anything else in life. Accordingly, they should be treated at all times with courtesy and compassion and be treated as one would wish to be treated oneself. Of supreme importance is the actual state of individual and collective morale. Therefore, leaders must constantly be assessing the morale of their team and its members. Napoleon, who was a remarkable leader, considered that morale was three times more important than any physical or material benefit. Morale is the greatest single factor affecting the performance of any team! Accordingly, individuals should not be put into jobs for which they have not been trained or prepared and in which they will probably not be adequately supported. It is a leader's job to think ahead, select the best person available (or cause selection to take place) and then to arrange the necessary training. This process can often identify talents, potential talents which a leader will take care to develop by using suitable opportunities. Jesus Himself gathered various groups of people around Him, initially a group of 12 people, later a group of 72 (Luke 10.10), giving them tasks to do and caring for them as they served and learned. Whenever possible, Christian leaders delegate and thereby foster trust and a team approach to work, but they must never delegate ultimate responsibility. Whenever anything goes wrong, especially on a delegated matter, leaders must always shoulder the full consequences. Mishaps often happen in life, things do not always go well, but respect and affection for a leader are soon lost if he or she ducks out.

Christian leaders have an acute awareness of the special significance of 'Loyalty'. To them it is not an old fashioned virtue nor a misunderstood one – my leader right or wrong – but loyalty first and foremost to God and his Kingdom. It is an essential element of Christianity. By virtue of the second Commandment, Christian leaders have a special responsibility for the care of other people, especially those placed in their care. Speaking about people, Jesus said, 'Are not two sparrows sold for a penny? Yet not one of them will fall to the ground apart from the will of your Father. And even the very hairs of your head are all numbered. So don't be afraid; you are worth more than many sparrows' (Matthew 10.29–31) (NIV).

Ability to inspire: Jesus, the greatest role model

The inspiration that Jesus gave as the founder of Christianity makes him a truly unique and magnificent role model for all Christians. His inspiration was such that the disciples followed him throughout his life and after the Resurrection. No doubt in a state of considerable shock, 11 disciples went to a place in the mountains near Galilee where Jesus delegated to them enormous responsibilities for which some of them were to lose their lives. Jesus said, 'Therefore go and make disciples of all nations . . . teaching them to obey everything I have commanded you' (Matthew 28.19–20) (NIV). He was a master of inspiring people: 'This, then, is how you should pray' (Matthew 6.9) (NIV). The fact that the Lord's Prayer has been said for so long as he wished, is a tribute to his remarkable ability to inspire. It makes other efforts by man to inspire pale into insignificance. There are numerous examples in the Gospels of Jesus giving thanks. The importance of a leader pausing to reflect and to express thanks to those concerned is a key part of inspiring leadership. *Please, thank you* and occasionally *well done* are some of the most important words in any language because people appreciate recognition when it is due. Leaders know that 'recognition is the oxygen of the soul'. Leaders always show a positive outlook – the glass is half full, not half empty. Achieving the task in hand or the target to be met is what matters and leaders appreciate fully that their own enthusiasm, body language and inspiration are critically important – especially when the going gets tough.

The characteristics of a Christian Leader

Moral and physical courage

Courage is rightly esteemed to be the first of human qualities because it is the quality which guarantees all others. It is not a chance gift of nature like an aptitude for games or the ability to make a cold choice between two alternatives. It is a mental state whose strength comes from Christian Faith and other material intellectual sources. There are two types of courage. First, that which urges an individual to risk injury or death in the face of danger – that is physical courage. Second, a different type of courage based on a reasoning attitude that causes an individual to stake his or her career, personal happiness or indeed their whole future on what he or she judges to be right – that is moral courage. Every human being is born with a certain amount of physical courage but if that inbuilt reserve becomes expended then the individual concerned will break down. Those situations in life that call for physical courage can be made a little more familiar by realistic preliminary training but no such preparation can be made to impart true moral courage; a quality that is deeply rooted in the Christian Faith, it places concern for another individual or for a group of people above all personal interests. Hence, moral courage tends to be a rarer virtue than physical courage but both are all about will power. Little remains certain in this life. Events occur far beyond the control of even governments but leaders must be able to ride out the resultant storms and find a positive response. They must be at ease with uncertainty by maintaining a positive and realistic outlook.

Integrity

A leader, especially a Christian leader, has to be totally trusted and be worthy of that trust if he or she is to lead people. Complete honesty and total integrity are most precious qualities – once lost they are seldom recovered. Usually the trust of other people is lost for ever. One of the greatest attributes of integrity – especially for any Christian – is loyalty. It is a sacred trust involving loyalties upwards to the boss, to one's colleagues and to one's own team and its members. At each level, the leader expresses the same view. Moral courage and integrity are closely related qualities. Sir Ernest Shackleton (1874–1922),[3] a former officer of the Royal Navy and the leader of the British Trans-Antarctic Expedition 1914–16, has been widely acknowledged as one of the greatest leaders. His example of remarkable selfless leadership in the face of acute danger and terrible weather conditions rescued and saved the lives of the 27 men who had been stranded with him for almost two years on an Antarctic ice floe.

Awareness of change

The world is undergoing massive changes. In every conceivable field, as never before in history, anyone who aspires to be a leader has to appreciate that success in the future will demand an even greater emphasis on foresight and creativity. A sense of vision is needed that enables leaders to anticipate what might happen in the future and what the outcomes might be for their own organization and then to think about the possible consequences and options. This is not something that can be done overnight. It is an ongoing function of a leader's daily life. They must frequently question their team members 'What do you think?' Leaders create change; at times of change people look for leaders. It must never be forgotten that Jesus brought into the world in the Holy Land the greatest change of all times.

Taking the team with you

Leadership is about taking people with you by encouraging them to go in the best possible direction. It means being a facilitator and not a dictator. It is a similar role to that of a conductor in an orchestra. He or she does not play an instrument but, with the leader of the orchestra, the conductor inspires and gives confidence to either individual players or to sections within the orchestra, so that the musical score is confidently brought alive to the total satisfaction of the audience. In particular, it means developing a rapport with the team which requires taking time to listen and to reflect privately upon the views expressed – often there is considerable value in those views.

Obtaining the best from people

The late President Eisenhower once said that leadership 'was the art of getting someone else to do something you want done because he or she wants to do it'. Leadership involves inspiring a team and receiving back extraordinary results from ordinary people because they enjoy it and have confidence in what they are doing. They are totally committed. This can only be done when the relationship between individual team members and their leader is based on absolute trust. To build that trust a leader has to appreciate that every team member is unique, each with their own personality, strengths and weaknesses, but everyone has two sides to their nature; on one side – rational thinking, on the other – emotion. Leadership is about appealing to those deeply seated human desires by giving inspiration and fostering confidence.

Emotional know how (sometimes known as emotional intelligence)

There are some most unpleasant adverse situations in life that can cause grave personal distress or acute collective anxiety, possibly even panic. Such situations can have a serious effect on morale. Recent research has shown that these situations usually involve Fear, Anger, Revulsion, Sorrow or Sadness (FARS). Leaders need to be aware of these dangers. Sorrow occurs naturally from time to time but the Christian Faith provides great comfort. Bad anger, which has been described as 'The anaesthetic of the mind', is the antithesis of love and is best avoided; whereas righteous anger, when confronted by evil or incompetence causing unnecessary suffering, is to be encouraged.

The reverse side of love (in the *agape* sense) is to hate evil. A good leader can be tough and demanding, even formidable, especially when having to deal with thoughtless or dangerous incompetence. Christian leaders when justifiably angry do not, however, lose their temper or self-control, instead in a calm, controlled and collected manner they are seen to take steps to resolve the problem. Love and compassion are deeply seated in a Christian leader's nature.

Tolerance

Prejudice is sadly inherent in the basic nature of humanity. It has been the cause of many past troubles, even wars, and today it has become the catalyst that creates the level of hatred that has brought about international terrorism. Leaders need to be aware of its awful dangers and to foster views that encourage tolerance and mutual regard for people of different cultures, ethnic backgrounds, races or Faiths. Jesus spoke about tolerance in the Beatitudes. 'Blessed are the peacemakers, for they will be called sons of God'. (Matthew 5.1–12) (NIV).

Conclusion

Christian leaders carry a great responsibility to ensure that the manner in which they lead their people makes life fun, truly mean-ingful and fulfilling so that the task, whatever it may be, is achieved on time, to budget and to a standard that totally satisfies everyone concerned. Despite all the tribulations of life, a leader has constantly to be alert to the needs of the team both individually and collectively. The challenges of leadership are considerable. The love of God, good health and other material aspects of life bring happiness, success, joy and mirth to people and their families (and to your own family).

Pressures are therefore placed upon those chosen to be leaders. However, Christians have the enormous strength afforded by their faith in God's loving purpose, but that profound strength must be carefully related to the more humble problems which will inevitably face any leader. That requires them to take time to think – to reflect. Those brief periods of reflection give Christian leaders an opportunity to seek guidance, 'Ask and it will be given to you; seek and you will find' (Matthew 7.7) (NIV). Having taken time to think, to consider deeply the various views of their team members, and having sought guidance, leaders actually become much more powerful. Their influence is greatly enhanced because their proposed course of action is based on wisdom. He or she becomes a disciple of Jesus.

The wisdom that is rooted in the 'fear of the Lord'
Is the hallmark and strength of every Christian Leader

What kind of leader are you?
What do you aspire to be?

Notes

This Occasional Paper is based on an original written by Major General (Ret) Peter Chiswell, member of MODEM's Leadership Committee.

1. Adair, 2001.
2. Frequently this word is confused in English today with the Ancient Greek word also meaning love – *phileo* – which also *means* expressing friendly affection.
3. Morrell and Capparell, 2002.

References

Adair, John (2001), *The Leadership of Jesus and Its Legacy Today*, Norwich: Canterbury Press.
Morrell, Margaret, and Stephanie Capparell (2002), *Shackleton's Way*, London: Nicholas Brealey.

Leadership formation and development in the Christian Church

Introduction

The Church is increasingly recognizing the importance of leadership and effective team working.

This brief discussion paper outlines a leadership development programme for students at theological college, for those recently ordained, for those ordained some years ago and for ministers in senior appointments. It is hoped that this paper is equally relevant and helpful for leaders and all who support them in all Christian denominations.

Our aim is to bring together key trainers and educators from the denominations to begin a process of integrating the learning and formation opportunities which are on offer. This could prevent competition, identify gaps in provision and begin to establish a continuing ministerial education highway. Our work might become a resource for the new Regional Training Partnerships which are being developed across the country.

We will ensure that each learning and development programme is

1 written in the context of Christian theology and ministry;
2 forms part of an ongoing programme of reflection and learning; and
3 covers what a leader needs to be (character and calling) as well what h/she should do (skills).

The programme is structured around the key transition points in ministry i.e.

A Undergoing theological training
B Entry into public ministry
C Minister in charge
D The next transition

E   Senior appointment
F   Planning for retirement

In section G there are some stand alone 1 – 2 day programmes

A Undergoing theological training

A 1 *Foundational theological training*

Leadership can be woven into most of the subjects covered in the theological colleges. Topics that might be covered include:

- Christian roots of leadership and how they still influence today's leaders
- Relevance and importance of leadership to ministry
- The differences between leaders in the churches and leaders in business
- Understanding the context in which leadership takes place
- The importance of character as well as calling, gifts and skills
- Levels of leadership – personal, team, area, overall, community
  Functions of a leader – planning, briefing etc.
- Essence of servant leadership, collaborative leadership and community building
- Leadership and change and transformation

B Entry into public ministry, for example, curate or probationer minister

Introduction: Concept of a threshold, of lay person to ordained. Shaping the participant's expectation of the culture; continuous learning; discernment, and from hereon, in using a consultant or mentor, peer support, self-managed learning.

B1 *Personal leadership programme (360° feedback plus 3-day workshop)*

Primarily, covering the attitudes and skills of personal effectiveness. Topics might include:

- adapting continuous learning to match preferred learning styles and multiple learning intelligences
- the learning cycle and learning journals

- shifting mental perceptions
- creative thinking and problem-solving techniques
- self-limiting beliefs
- balance
- proactivity
- generating choices
- meditation
- introduction to EQ
- managing own energy level
- sense of uniqueness
- clarifying what is important
- preparing a personal vision
- using time effectively
- setting goals; planning the week
- dealing with time stealers
- personal action planning

B2 Developing effective working relationships (2 days) – for all individuals and intact teams

This workshop focuses on issues which participants bring along. Subjects might include:

- Building rapport, trust and credibility
- What motivates me and other people
- Contextual listening
- Seeing situations from multiple points of view and generating options
- Mirroring other people's preferences in the way they think, communicate and make decisions (possibly Myers Briggs Personality Types and their relevance)
- Win-win thinking and outcome thinking
- Persuading and influencing
- The roles that suit me best
- Handling conflict
- Tips on building up networks
- Celebrating diversity
- Personal action planning
- Sustaining the learning

C Appointment as a minister (a challenging transition)

Introduction: Moving to the next team-working position. Now the person in charge. The team leader. An opportunity to reconnect with one's own personal vision.

C1 Being the new leader (2 days)

- Discerning, perceiving, communicating
- Finding your feet
- Understanding the parish as a family system
- The importance of discussing the purpose of the local ministry and the benefits of a shared mission, vision and values
- Clarifying roles
- Leading and enabling others including volunteers
- Getting support, for example, coaching and mentoring
- Bringing more than one parish together
- Leading change and transformation
- Giving and receiving feedback
- Handling difficult situations and complexity
- Representing the local church beyond the parish and relating well to the wider Church and with other faith leaders

C2 Team leading (2 days) – for team leaders

The programme is built around participants' learning objectives. It includes exercises in team leading. Topics likely to be included are:

- Types of teams and groups
- What a team leader needs to be and do
- The functions of a team leader
- Team charter (mission, vision etc.)
- Team roles
- Stages of team development
- Situational leadership
- Team mapping
- Practical problem solving on, for example, managing expectations

C3 Communicating effectively (2 days) – intact ministry teams

- Effective communication at its best
- Current reality and the things I/we need to improve
- Intention, behaviour and impact
- Win-win-win thinking

- Creating synergy
- Contextual listening
- Giving and receiving feedback
- Communicating to a range of audiences
- Consulting and influencing
- Chairing meetings effectively
- Managing good communication channels
- Developing, managing and using an effective network of contacts.

C4 Coaching and mentoring (2 days) – for incumbents, ministers in charge, other team leaders and external coaches

- Definition and benefits of coaching
- Why a coaching system is being introduced
- The coaching model we will use
- Appreciating the context and roles of the person being coached
- Types of questions
- Giving feedback
- Contextual listening
- Practice sessions
- Personal coaching styles
- How people see the world – facts and interpretations
- Other models, for example, situational leadership, the learning cycle
- Use of cards, objects, movement
- Ethical guidelines; coaching *v.* counselling
- Administrative matters and ongoing training and support.

C5 Valuing diversity (2 days) – for all individuals and intact teams

- Defining diversity and what it means in local ministry
- Exploring differences of attention, learning preferences and work focus, in yourself and others
- Identifying the consequences and implications of this diversity in teams and for your team
- Exploring diversity of basic drivers, assumptions and blind spots
- Identifying a vision of valuing diversity and your own level of skill
- Working to improve relationships within the team
- Identifying cultural differences which can influence effective team working
- Identifying ways of working to make more effective use of the diversity within the team.

D The next transition

Introduction: may be to a different context, to a more complex role, renegotiating where you are, moving to a different type of ministry

D1 *Personal transition at a time of change (1 day) – for any individual going through major change*

- Change (external) and transformation (within)
- Key models and processes
- Personal and group exercises
- Tools to facilitate problem solving
- Strategies for handling future changes

D2 *Leading and managing change in the Church (1 day introductory) – also suitable for senior ministers*

Ample time is given for reflection and discussion. Topics will also include:

- Change and transformation at the personal level
- Key models, for example, four states of 'being'; the change curve
- Ecclesiology – building the Church and engaging with the community
- Creating the need and the desire to change
- A process for leading and managing change in the local church
- Case studies, including turning round a declining church, leading two or more parishes

E Senior appointment

E1 *Area leadership (2 days) – for senior clergy [also suitable for ministers who lead large congregations]*

- The functions of an area/strategic leader
- Discerning and deciding the journey; creating a shared mission, vision, values and plan
- Aligning the capabilities, structure and communication channels with the plan
- Developing and maintaining a culture conducive to building trust, learning and personal accountability
- Creating a talent-valued culture, succession planning
- Communicating effectively within and outside the church
- Building alliances, partnerships and effective networks

- Supervision; coaching colleagues and being coached
- Developing strategies for decline, growth and risk

E2   Building and sustaining effective partnerships and alliances with other churches/organizations (2 days) – for senior ministers [also suitable for ministers who lead large congregations or who are involved in new forms of Church]

Facilitator inputs, personal work and working in small groups covering:

- Rationale for alliances and partnering arrangements
- Effective mindsets for partnering
- The need for shared objectives
- Choosing balanced success measures
- The role of the sponsor
- Legal considerations
- Key interpersonal skills
- Creating an influence plan to effect change
- Managing changing expectations
- Exchanging insights with the partner
- Evaluating progress
- Strategies for exiting an alliance

F   Planning for retirement (Age 59 onwards)

Small group discussions dealing with topics the participants want to discuss. These might include:

- Strategies for keeping fresh and keeping the vision alive – for oneself and for the local church
- Preparing for loss of role and other adjustments
- Considering options on retirement including, for example, 'permission to officiate'

G   Stand alone 1/2–2-day workshops and/or self managed learning aids

These could include:

- Building and maintaining a talent-valued culture (2 days)
- Building personal networking capability (2 days)

- Facilitation skills (2–3 days)
- Using time and energy effectively (1 day)
- Effective motivation and delegation (1 day)
- Effective presentations/proposals (1 day)
- Effective meetings
- Handling difficult situations
- Communicate well
- Optimize your decision making
- Influence positively
- Creating and sustaining an action-learning set
- Counselling skills programme
- Disability equality training
- Recruitment and selection skills
- Assertiveness
- Effective learning and memory skills
- Emotional intelligence
- Capitalizing on using the Internet
- How stories and metaphors facilitate learning
- Decision-making and problem solving
- Working with volunteers
- The supportive spouse
- Gender issues

With financial support a wide range of learning options could be made available including:

- Learning by phone
- One to one coaching
- Action learning sets
- E-courses
- CDs
- Web based audios of live classes
- Special interest groups

This paper is based on an initial draft by Richard Fox, a member of MODEM's Leadership Committee. Richard is a partner in The Learning Corporation LLP, Guildford. He has worked with over 200 ministers on leadership, change, working well together and coaching.

Several senior ministers have contributed to Richard's draft as have other training providers to the churches and also members of MODEM's Leadership Committee.

April 2007